RESEARCH FOR THE HELPING PROFESSIONS

RESEARCH

FOR THE

HELPING PROFESSIONS

WILLIAM K. WILKINSON

Western Health Board, Galway, Ireland

KEITH McNEIL

New Mexico State University

BROOKS/COLE PUBLISHING COMPANY

I(T)P™ An International Thomson Publishing Company

Pacific Grove • Albany • Bonn • Boston • Cincinnati • Detroit • London • Madrid • Melbourne
Mexico City • New York • Paris • San Francisco • Singapore • Tokyo • Toronto • Washington

 A CLAIREMONT BOOK

Sponsoring Editor: *Claire Verduin*
Editorial Associate: *Patricia Vienneau*
Production Editor: *Tessa A. McGlasson*
Manuscript Editor: *Mary P. O'Briant*
Permissions Editor: *Linda Rill*
Art Editor: *Kathy Joneson*
Interior Illustration: *Kathy Joneson*

Design Coordinator: *E. Kelly Shoemaker*
Interior and Cover Design: *Cloyce Wall*
Marketing: *Nancy Kernal*
Advertising: *Jean Thompson*
Typesetting: *Kachina Typesetting, Inc.*
Cover Printing: *Color Dot Graphics, Inc.*
Printing and Binding: *Quebecor/Fairfield*

For more information, contact:

BROOKS/COLE PUBLISHING COMPANY
511 Forest Lodge Road
Pacific Grove, CA 93950
USA

International Thomson Publishing—Europe
Berkshire House 168-173
High Holborn
London WC1V 7AA
England

Thomas Nelson Australia
102 Dodds Street
South Melbourne, 3205
Victoria, Australia

Nelson Canada
1120 Birchmount Road
Scarborough, Ontario
Canada M1K 5G4

International Thomson Editores
Campos Eliseos 385, Piso 7
Col. Polanco
11560 México D. F. México

International Thomson Publishing GmbH
Königswinterer Strasse 418
53227 Bonn
Germany

International Thomson Publishing—Asia
221 Henderson Road
#05-10 Henderson Building
Singapore 0315

International Thomson Publishing—Japan
Hirakawacho Kyowa Building, 3F
2-2-1 Hirakawacho
Chiyoda-ku, Tokyo 102
Japan

Printed in the United States of America.

10   9   8   7   6   5   4   3   2   1

Library of Congress Cataloging-in-Publication Data
Wilkinson, William K., [date]
    Research for the helping professions / William K. Wilkinson, Keith McNeil.
        p.   cm.
    Includes bibliographical references and index.
    ISBN 0-534-34003-2
    1. Human services—Research.   I. McNeil, Keith, [date].
    II. Title.
    HV11.W575 1995
    361.3'072—dc20   95–22697
                                                     CIP

Credits continue on page 440.

CONTENTS

PREFACE

THIS TEXT IS INTENDED for graduate students in the helping professions, especially students seeking advanced degrees in counseling, social work, nursing, family and community services, education, and other related disciplines. The text is primarily descriptive and rudimentary; we assume that readers have little or no prior background in research design, methodology, or statistics.

We have found that students in predominantly applied programs often place greatest priority on acquiring applied competencies so they will be able to function effectively in future employment settings. However, in addition to learning applied skills, many graduate training programs require that students take a course in research design and methodology. In this context, the research class serves two related functions: (1) to help future practitioners become informed consumers of research literature and (2) to prepare students to conduct a research project.

As for the first function, most helping professionals are repeatedly exposed to research that bears on their theory and practice. Helping students begin to comprehend and critically analyze existing research is part of the purpose of this textbook. We hope that by understanding the research process, readers will be better able to evaluate and judge the adequacy of previous research as well as the implications and applications of research investigations to their own practice. Being familiar with current research is an ethical necessity for all helping professionals; equally important is learning to be a critical consumer of research results.

Second, a research class provides students with enough knowledge to carry out a research project and to do so competently and efficiently. For instance, some graduate programs require a thesis at the master's degree level. Almost all doctoral programs require a dissertation, which is an extended, more in-depth investigation than a thesis. The information in this text will provide readers with the knowledge needed to conduct both. But our greatest hope is that we will stimulate readers' imagination with regard to research so that some may even conduct research studies when not required to do so.

We wrote this text because we believe that students do not always see the relevance of research to their profession and that professors usually do not relate research concepts to applicable helping professions issues. Further, research texts too often emphasize research concepts in a vacuum, that is, without sufficient context or application to practical settings. This text was designed to help students and instructors overcome these difficulties.

We will make this text more applicable, relevant, and meaningful in the following ways. First, we intend to link research concepts to scenarios that are familiar to those who work in the helping professions. These "case vignettes" are designed to thematize the research concepts. As one example, in Chapter 3 a mental health worker wonders which of two psychotherapeutic approaches would be most effective with bulimic clients. Building on this hypothetical research situation, we show how the worker might go about finding an answer. We illustrate the necessary research concepts to answer the question from a scientific perspective. Again, our goal in using case illustrations is to promote relevance, importance, and the applicability of the tools of scientific investigation to practice.

Second, we have written simply. We have included no long, technical discussions; citations to literature outside the helping professions are few. Unfortunately, much writing about research tends to focus too much on research concepts per se rather than stressing the use of these methods as vehicles for promoting understanding of professional theory and practice. We have made a concerted effort to engage readers' interest in research by using clear, straightforward language.

Third, in selecting from a vast array of possible research terms to include in a textbook like this, we chose the concepts most relevant to helping professionals. For example, in discussing helping professions research, we stress issues such as locating and recruiting participants for studies and making sure studies are valid, as well as concerns about cultural considerations. We also provide practical tips, such as how to conduct research ethically, how to select good tests, and how to develop a realistic timeline. We also offer advice about writing and disseminating research results.

Fourth, we present this material using examples from research topics of relevance and of potential interest to prospective helping professionals. For example, we chose topics related to counseling formats, the mental health of graduate counselors in training, AIDS, career development, sex education programs, bedtime routines for hospitalized children, and many more. We hope the result of our effort will be that readers will understand the concepts presented and find them stimulating and relevant.

Finally, we included two journal articles (Appendix E) as a reference for both the instructor and student. These articles are intended to be used concurrently with the text. We hope that instructors and students will systematically incorporate the information into classroom instruction by using the articles as examples of particular research concepts. In Appendix F, we provide a Research Evaluation Form on which readers can analyze journal articles in terms of the major research concepts presented in the text.

We would like to thank the many students who provided comments on the earlier drafts of the manuscript and Margie McIlvoy for the background information for the Maria vignettes. Also, we especially want to thank Ruth Herrera for authoring Chapter 7, and the following reviewers: Steve Backels, Pennsylvania State University—Harrisburg; Stephen S. Feit, Idaho State University; Amy Hittner, San Francisco State University; Diane McDermott, University of Kansas; Spencer Niles, University of Virginia; and Norman Stewart, Michigan State University.

William K. Wilkinson
Keith McNeil

1

INTRODUCTION TO HUMAN SERVICE RESEARCH

MARIA GONZALEZ has just completed her first semester of a master's degree program in general counseling. As she became better acquainted with other students in the counseling program during the semester, she found that some of her peers were intent on completing a master's thesis, although there were no formal requirements to do so. Apparently, some students believed that by finishing a thesis they would enhance their chances for acceptance into doctoral programs. Other students were simply interested in collecting data about a topic of interest.

As she became aware of her classmates' intentions, Maria asked some of these students how they identified topics to research, what those topics were, and how demanding thesis research would be. Responses to her questions were varied. For example, one student indicated that he and a professor shared an interest in stress management, an area in which the student was planning to conduct research for his thesis. Another student had completed an undergraduate research paper about biofeedback and planned to pursue this subject for her thesis. Yet another student had not decided on a topic, although she was interested in perceptions of pain, cultural differences, and hypnosis.

None of the students knew about the exact demands of thesis research, but all were under the impression that completing a thesis was difficult. For example, these prospective researchers believed that much library research and reading was required if they were to develop meaningful research questions. In addition, thesis students were aware that data would need to be analyzed statistically and that a written thesis report must be completed.

As she learned more about the thesis, Maria began to doubt that she would undertake this type of research project. While she has always recognized some potential advantages of completing a thesis, she also realizes there are practical limitations in doing so. For example, balancing work, school, and family demands might become even more difficult. Further, Maria's intent in earning the master's degree in counseling is not to do research but to learn skills and techniques associated with the profession of mental health counseling. Thus, she is more interested in courses in which professors teach practical competencies like individual and group counseling techniques and ways to identify difficulties in life-span development. In contrast, she perceives research as an activity associated with people she considers to be academic—doctoral students, professors, and those employed in research institutions.

Although she is skeptical about doing a thesis, Maria understands the need for scientists to collect and analyze data and to publish their results. Indeed, Maria recognizes her own need to read and understand current research findings. In this respect, she looks forward to completing her required research course next semester. She knows that learning about research principles will help her understand the latest research results.

In the chapters to follow, we will update Maria's progress through her program. Specifically, we will note the role that research plays in her academic and career development.

I f you are considering conducting a research project, either as a thesis, dissertation, or on your own volition, this vignette may sound familiar. Perhaps you have wondered how to identify a research topic or how demanding research would be. Do you know exactly what stages are involved in empirical research? Perhaps you ask more fundamental questions like, Why is a research course necessary? or What is the relevance of research to practicing professionals? In our experience, these are the types of questions prospective researchers do ask. In subsequent chapters, we will follow Maria Gonzalez as she attempts to find answers to these and similar questions.

Since we emphasize research as it pertains to the helping professions, it is important to define a helping professional. In general, a helping professional is any individual with special skills and knowledge related to improving the human condition (Combs, Avila, & Purkey, 1978). Sometimes, the helper's intent is to rehabilitate individuals with a medical or psychological illness. For example, a clinical psychologist might help a depressed client become productive again, or the helping professional may seek to optimize human functioning by preventing unhealthy events from occurring—as a social worker might do at a well-baby clinic. In still other situations, the helping professional may intervene to help individuals resolve common problems. A family therapist might help family members learn to communicate with each other more effectively, for example.

The names of helping professions are many, as are the environments in which helping professionals carry out their responsibilities. Some common titles given to those in the helping professions are *mental health counselor, guidance counselor, college student personnel worker, school counselor, psychologist, psychiatrist, family therapist, clinical social worker, community social worker, hospital social worker, school social worker, physician, nurse, regular classroom teacher, special educator,* and *school psychologist.* The contexts in which helping professionals carry out their duties are equally varied. *Mental health agencies, hospitals, residential treatment centers, public schools, private practice,* and *state and federal agencies* are just a few examples.

In this text we draw research examples from a variety of fields in the helping professions, concentrating generally on *psychology, education, social work,* and *nursing.* We now turn our attention to basic terminology and to the underlying assumptions regarding research in the helping professions. Then we will consider the relevance and meaning of research as it affects the helping professional.

Research and Science: Conceptual and Philosophical Foundations

The terms *research* and *science* are used frequently, but what do they actually mean? In broadest terms, **research** means getting more information. **Empirical research** refers to the data-based, systematic study of some natural phenomenon, such as an aspect of human behavior. When doing empirical research, the investigator engages in a series of time-intensive activities like developing research hypotheses, obtaining research samples, selecting measuring devices, and collecting and analyzing data. Empirical research is an activity implied by the philosophical term **scientific method**—a method presuming a logical, observational, and cautious approach in the pursuit of knowledge.

Although they are less common, **nonempirical studies** can be conducted. The researcher does not gather new data but reads previous studies for the purpose of developing an innovative position. The researcher might integrate different theories or summarize previous research in order to distill logical or methodological issues in need of further study. Nonempirical research results in position papers or literature reviews.

While research is best characterized as a process, science is a product—the knowledge that develops from research. The term scientific knowledge implies that the knowledge derived is based on systematic, structured, and careful observation, precisely the type of observation that characterizes empirical research. In Figure 1-1, we illustrate the relationship between empirical research and scientific knowledge.

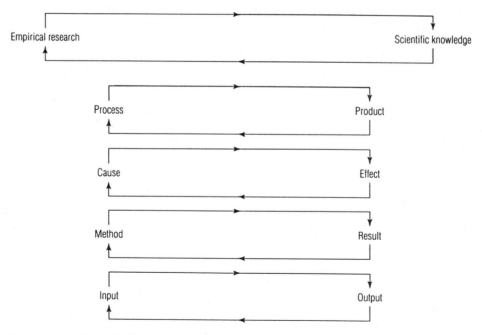

FIGURE 1-1   The relationship between empirical research and scientific knowledge.

The solid arrow shows that empirical research is a prerequisite for scientific knowledge; all the terms on the left are logical antecedents to their companions on the right. As one example of the linear relationship between empirical research and scientific knowledge, consider the case of cigarette smoking. A great quantity of empirical research exists concerning the relationship between cigarette smoking and cancer. It is now considered a scientific fact that cigarette smoking is dangerous to a person's health and can contribute to lung cancer. In other words, this scientific knowledge about smoking is a product—a type of knowledge based on the process of empirical investigation.

However, Figure 1-1 also shows that empirical research and scientific knowledge are reciprocally related. That is, as knowledge develops from research, that knowledge base can be used to guide future empirical study. This reciprocity is true of all the terms matched in Figure 1-1. Continuing with the cigarette smoking example, as each piece of empirical research becomes available, investigators use existing results to plan original studies.

How many pieces of empirical research are required before a scientific fact is established? Does each empirical study yield one scientific fact? These are difficult philosophical questions with no clear answers. However, one approach to addressing issues like these is to examine an actual research topic like cigarette smoking and lung cancer and answer the following question: If a single empirical research study addressed the relationship between smoking and lung cancer and found a positive link, would you take that finding to be scientific knowledge?

While you may be tempted to conclude that this single study establishes a relationship between cigarette smoking and lung cancer, it is doubtful that one study yields true scientific knowledge. There is doubt for two reasons. First, since knowledge implies certainty (Capaldi, 1969), repeated empirical studies must be conducted if any degree of certainty is to be developed. Thus, if the single study of cigarette smoking and lung cancer were replicated 100 times and all the results yielded similar positive relationships, the link between smoking and lung cancer would be established as a scientific fact.

Second, we noted that the scientific method is a cautious, self-critical approach to knowledge. Therefore, in the spirit of critical analysis, few would take as scientific knowledge the results of one empirical study. Rather, most investigators look for trends in accumulated data; if these trends are clear and consistent, certainty develops.

THE DYNAMIC RELATIONSHIP BETWEEN EMPIRICAL RESEARCH AND SCIENTIFIC KNOWLEDGE

So far, we have kept our discussion of empirical research and scientific knowledge as simple as possible. However, the relationship between empirical research and scientific knowledge is complex. To help disentangle this relationship, we provide Figure 1-2, a fictional knowledge structure for the research topic *psychotherapy outcomes*.

To understand this knowledge structure, note that the three terms to the left of the structure represent different knowledge types: *context, operation,* and *population.* We believe these knowledge types are fundamental to all research topics, not just the one given in Figure 1-2.

Context refers to the setting in which the study was conducted. Some examples shown in Figure 1-2 include the location of the study, such as the client's home or mental health clinic, and therapists' qualities, such as level of training, gender, or level of mental health. Since all research contains contextual elements, knowledge about these elements is an essential knowledge type.

The second level of knowledge refers to operations—the specific procedures used in the study. The type of treatment and measures of treatment outcome, such as the results of projective tests, are examples. Since the aim of research is to measure and quantify a phenomenon of interest, investigators must define all procedures in the data collection process.

Finally, knowledge about populations pertains to the characteristics of a sample—level of client disturbance, diagnosis, gender, geographic region, and so forth. In all empirical studies, a sample from some type of population will be used, making this information critical to any research endeavor.

Note that the boxes representing the different knowledge types differ in width. These differing widths represent a hypothetical amount of existing research about that topic. The larger boxes represent more information; smaller boxes represent less. For example, with regard to knowledge of populations, relatively little is known about social validity, for example, about client belief in the validity of psychotherapy. Comparatively more is known about client diagnosis and therapist training.

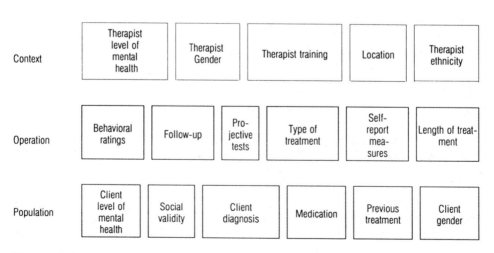

FIGURE 1-2   A possible knowledge base for the topic *psychotherapy outcome.*

While the knowledge structure in Figure 1-2 appears to be static, it only represents the current status of information about the topic *psychotherapy outcomes*. An actual knowledge structure for this or any other topic would change constantly, thus making the structure dynamic. The most dynamic aspect of the knowledge structure is the nature of topics within each knowledge type. For example, the topic *therapist level of training* could be empirically examined in seemingly infinite ways. A researcher might ask: What instructional methods are used to train therapists? How long should training last? Under what conditions should training take place? How is degree of skill assessed? Should other skills be assessed? As empirical research accumulates regarding these topics, the broader topic of *therapist training* expands.

Besides accommodating knowledge growth within a single topic, researchers can address unexplored issues creatively to form new boxes. A researcher might, for example, develop a context area examining therapists' reasons for participation. Also, topics can be combined uniquely within and across knowledge levels.

To illustrate the last point, consider a study by Antonuccio, Lewinsohn, and Steinmetz (1982); their general topic was psychotherapy outcome. Specifically, these researchers were interested in how therapist characteristics may affect client outcome. To address this issue, they devised a study to decide (1) whether psychotherapists with equal amounts of training and experience provide a cognitive-behavioral treatment for depression differently, even when working with similar clients and (2) whether any therapist differences that do emerge would affect client outcome.

The answer to the first question was yes. Despite their similarities in experience and training, the therapists differed on several variables like clarity, specificity of feedback, warmth, session length, and group cohesiveness. In other words, each of the therapists applied the cognitive-behavioral treatment in a unique way.

As for the second question, the data suggested that despite therapists' differences, clients' depression abated significantly as reflected in posttest and follow-up measures no matter which therapist they were assigned. In other words, although the group leaders differed on several factors in the administration of the groups, their clients improved significantly despite the idiosyncratic ways the treatment was applied.

Let us examine the results of the Antonuccio, Lewinsohn, and Steinmetz (1982) study as they relate to the knowledge structure in Figure 1-2. First, one of the most noticeable features of the study was that it creatively combined different topics across knowledge types. The investigators attempted to control differences across all knowledge domains: (1) level of training (all therapists were said to be trained equally before the study), (2) type of treatment (only cognitive-behavioral treatments were examined), and (3) client diagnosis (only clients with depression were included). Again, this illustrates how researchers can creatively combine boxes across levels to devise original research. In Figure 1-3, the boxes combined are linked with arrows.

The researchers expand several topics, namely *therapist level of training, type of treatment,* and *client diagnosis.* Thus, the width of these boxes expands to

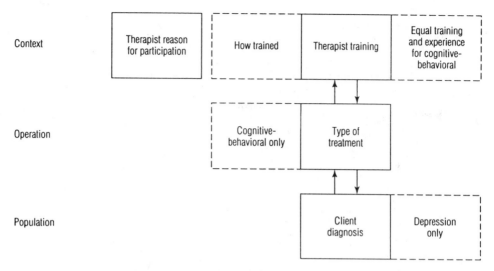

Context	Therapist reason for participation	How trained	Therapist training	Equal training and experience for cognitive-behavioral

| Operation | | Cognitive-behavioral only | Type of treatment | |

| Population | | | Client diagnosis | Depression only |

FIGURE 1-3   Accommodation and potential future growth of knowledge base for the Antonuccio, Lewinsohn, and Steinmetz study (1982).

account for their data, as illustrated in Figure 1-3. A future researcher might read the Antonuccio, Lewinsohn, and Steinmetz (1982) study and expand a particular topic or propose an entirely new topic. Someone may wish to identify variables that could account for the data. In the former case, a new subtopic related to therapist training might be how therapists were trained. For example, different instructional approaches may yield no therapist differences in treatment provision. In the latter case, perhaps a new context variable—therapist reason for participation — explains the Antonuccio, Lewinsohn, and Steinmetz results. Therapists who are paid to participate might reveal different treatment techniques from the ones revealed by therapists who participate for learning. These potential future topics also are illustrated in Figure 1-3.

One final question about the dynamic nature of scientific knowledge must be raised. How can scientific knowledge be certain if it is dynamic? The key lies in the statement we made earlier that all research fits into more than one box. Thus, while all researchers plan original studies, isolated data in a study can be used to corroborate other results. For example, the Antonuccio, Lewinsohn, and Steinmetz (1982) data showed positive outcomes as measured by client's self-report using the Beck Depression Inventory (BDI). Researchers can use this bit of information to support other, similar positive outcomes using the BDI. Thus, a degree of certainty develops—therapy outcomes tend to be positive when employing the BDI.

Role of Theory

Another vital concept in research is theory. We frequently encounter the term *theory*—Freud's theory, theories of pain, theories of intelligence, and so on. But

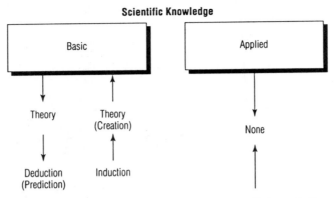

FIGURE 1-4   The role of theory in the two types of scientific knowledge.

what is a theory? In the helping professions, a **theory** is a coherent set of propositions that explain and predict human behavior. The set of propositions may pertain to a clearly defined phenomenon like forgetting words in the middle of a list. Theoretical propositions also may pertain to more vague concepts like mental illness.

In Figure 1-4, we schematize the terms we will discuss next. The figure shows that theory plays a prominent role in **basic research** in which investigators focus on theory as the primary context for developing an empirical research study. Typically, basic researchers either use existing theory to guide their research methods and predictions or use their findings to derive new theories. In the first case, a theory already exists and the researcher creates predictions that logically follow from the theory. This is called the **deductive** use of theory, as illustrated in Figure 1-4. Deduction operates downward from theory to prediction, from the general to the particular.

A classic example of the deductive use of theory in science was the tremendous amount of research generated by Clark Hull's learning theory in the middle part of the 20th century. Hull (1943) developed an elaborate learning theory that allowed the prediction of specific events given certain conditions. For example, the intensity of an organism's response to a stimulus was said to be directly related to the organism's drive strength, which in turn was presumably based on the time of last reinforcement. Accordingly, a deductively derived prediction from Hull's theory is that response intensity will be stronger as the interval since the last reinforcement becomes longer. Indeed, many such deductions were tested using Hull's theory.

In contrast, Figure 1-4 also reveals the **inductive** use of theory in which data are analyzed and a theory built (upward) that links and ultimately explains the data on which it was constructed. For example, assume that a patient is not complying with a schedule for taking medicine. The patient's nurse decides to develop a contract with the patient; both then know exactly what medicines will be taken daily and the consequences for the patient of either complying (extra recreational time) or not complying (loss of privileges). After implementing the contract, the nurse finds that the patient regularly complies. The nurse tries a similar contract with several other patients who do not comply with prescribed drug regimens and finds that the contract works in each case. To explain the effectiveness of the contract procedure, the nurse develops a theory of "behavioral self-empowerment." She reasons that patients will increase drug compliance when they have an active say in developing rules and consequences for their behavior. In this example, the nurse induced a theory from these separate cases in an effort to unify and explain why these results occurred.

When engaging in **applied research,** there is no emphasis on theory, explanation, or prediction. Instead, applied researchers solve practical problems. They find ways to improve organizational policies, treat migraine headaches more effectively, or organize social work teams. An example of an applied research scenario would be when a physically handicapped student wants to convince university administrators of the importance of providing more wheelchair ramps to university buildings. The student develops a survey and asks other physically disabled peers to rate the university on handicapped students' access to buildings, restrooms, eating facilities, and parking spaces. The survey results clearly show that physically disabled students are not satisfied with their access to university buildings, and this information is then presented to the administration.

The researcher's goal in this example was to find out whether students were in fact dissatisfied; if so, these data would be presented to appropriate administrators. The investigative purpose was not pertinent to basic research because the student was interested neither in developing a theory that explains why students were dissatisfied nor in predicting future dissatisfaction. To make the research more basic in nature, the researcher might determine how physically disabled students adjust to their handicap and what factors in their background might explain their different adaptational strategies.

Stages of Empirical Research

It is helpful to conceive of the empirical process as a series of ordered stages; these are given in Figure 1-5.

STAGE 1—SELECTING A TOPIC TO RESEARCH.   The importance of this initial stage is easy to overlook. While the fundamental precursor to conducting research is having something to investigate, newcomers to research should understand the importance of careful topic selection, since the investigator will be "married" to a chosen subject for quite some time. Further, the specificity of the topic has critical implications for the amount of library research required, an issue to be explored in Chapter 2.

What exactly is a **research topic**? It is the unique domain of knowledge that the researcher wants to investigate. The list of available research topics is enormous and can be found in major research information sources such as *Psychological Abstracts*. A few examples of topics possibly relevant to human service re-

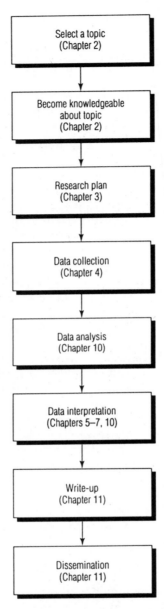

FIGURE 1-5   The relationships among the stages of empirical research.

searchers are: causes of disorders; the prevention, assessment, diagnosis, and treatment of disorders; agency policies, learning styles, discipline problems, teaching methods, program evaluation, child-rearing methods, stress management, chronic illness, parenting styles, parent-child interactions, and children's social skill development.

Researchers do not pull topics magically out of thin air. There are systematic ways to identify topics to investigate, and these will be discussed further in Chapter 2. It is a myth that research topics are difficult to find; in fact, just the opposite is true. If most people kept a tally of the frequency of interesting topics they encounter each day, the number would be surprisingly high. While everything that is interesting does not become the subject of research, it is precisely these interests that can lead to further investigation.

STAGE 2 — BECOMING KNOWLEDGEABLE ABOUT A TOPIC.   One of the most time-consuming and pervasive aspects of the research process is becoming knowledgeable about the research topic. This involves extensive library work and a substantial amount of reading and critical analysis. Many prospective researchers get bogged down at this point because library work is time-consuming and its rewards are not immediately clear. Needed materials may be hard to find; then when they are obtained, the researcher must read the articles, books, book chapters, dissertations, and technical reports thoroughly. Ways to gather and analyze information about a research topic of interest will be detailed in Chapter 2.

The first two stages are necessary but not sufficient for empirical research to commence. In other words, a person may be curious about a topic and want to learn more about it but never plan to do empirical research on it. In essence, the purpose of the initial two stages determines what they are leading to. For example, if a person wants to do a research study, topic identification and increased knowledge about it are used to form an empirical research plan (stage 3).

On the other hand, a person may become knowledgeable about a topic but have no intention of completing empirical research. For example, a nurse might become knowledgeable about the effectiveness of contingency contracts with patients who are noncompliant with medicine prescriptions. This can be accomplished without doing a research study. More knowledgeable sources, like the resident physicians, might be consulted, or the local library might contain several resources on the topic. Again, only when a person intends to use the outcomes of stages 1 and 2 to develop a research plan has the process of empirical research actually begun.

STAGE 3 — FORMULATING THE RESEARCH PLAN.   As already mentioned, the third stage in the research process is the development of a research plan. If stage 2 was completed properly, prior research serves as a starting point for developing the research plan. The research plan includes the final research question to be explored, specific hypotheses, independent and dependent variables, population samples, sampling procedures, and a thorough methodological plan for answering the research question. The development of the research plan signifies the intention of the researcher to engage in empirical study.

The research plan is the foundation of the research study. It serves as a kind of blueprint, specifying exactly what a study is about and how the researcher will go about answering the research question. At this stage, needed materials such as questionnaires, videotapes, and other equipment must be gathered.

Further, important practical decisions must be made, such as how subjects will be sampled and where the research will be conducted. The research plan is discussed generally in Chapter 3 and more specifically in the context of various research types in Chapters 8 and 9.

STAGE 4 — DATA COLLECTION. The research plan serves as the organizer for the researcher's observations in data collection. This stage includes the implementation of the research, such as conducting counseling groups, observing teachers, requiring subjects to read vignettes and answer questions, or interviewing subjects. It also includes overseeing and proctoring the completion of forms such as questionnaires, tests, interviews, or whatever else the researcher chooses as a source of data. This can take several months and in some studies several years. Specific instruments that may be of use in the data collection process are the subject of Chapter 4.

STAGE 5 — DATA ANALYSIS. At this point, the researcher has collected data and is ready to perform appropriate statistical tests to determine how the data bear upon the research question. This stage is heavily dependent on statistical and computer applications, understanding of data entry procedures, and the ability to execute various statistical programs to analyze the data. If the researcher does not have statistical and computer skills, it is highly advisable that an expert be in charge of this stage so that the data can be adequately and accurately analyzed. Data analysis is the subject of Chapter 10.

STAGE 6 — DATA INTERPRETATION. This stage is probably the most enjoyable; this is when the researcher is ready to interpret the results of data analysis. What were the results? How do they answer the initial research question? Why were those results obtained? This is where scientific imagination and knowledge of the topic are critical; they enable a researcher to make sense of the derived data. Drawing conclusions from data is highlighted in Chapters 5, 6, and 7.

STAGE 7—WRITING UP THE RESEARCH REPORT. One of the most laborious stages in doing empirical research is developing the written report of research results. Usually, the written report includes an introduction, a method section, results, and discussion, as well as references and tables or figures. The structure and content of the written research report will be discussed in Chapter 11. However, one point needs underscoring here. Most prospective researchers do not realize how difficult it is to write professional research articles. The writing process is the most intellectually taxing part of research. Researchers must transfer concepts and schemes to written prose and make this prose understandable, meaningful, and salient in terms of all aspects of the research conducted. The researcher, now turned reporter, must address such issues as the importance of the research question, the adequacy and novelty of the design employed to answer the question, and the bearing of the results on the question posed. Writing takes a considerable amount of reading and editing to be done properly. In fact, it would not be unreasonable to allow several months to produce a quality document. The written research report is discussed in Chapter

11, both in terms of content and the organizational formats typically adopted by research writers.

STAGE 8 — SUBMISSION OF WRITTEN REPORT FOR DISSEMINATION.   Although this stage is optional, once the written report is completed the researcher(s) may submit the work to a journal for professional dissemination. The process of editorial review and feedback and the final editorial decision is another time-consuming process. Sometimes, research reports are flatly rejected, which means the researcher must consider rethinking and rewriting the report and perhaps submitting the article to another journal. Editors may request that a researcher resubmit the article with further clarification and explanation. It is not unreasonable to allow at least 6 months to receive editorial feedback. In Chapter 11, we describe the dissemination process in more detail.

You can see by now the difficulty and time-consuming nature of research. This is why individuals who complete a research study must demonstrate qualities of tenacity, motivation, and commitment to the empirical method. Without these traits, it would be difficult to imagine anyone completing the process. Even when individuals are required to complete a research study as part of their degree requirements, the completion of the research piece is not always a given. This is why you sometimes encounter the term ABD—All But Dissertation. Some doctoral students have difficulty balancing the rigors of research with course work, vocations, and their personal life. When you look at all the stages of research, you can appreciate why this phenomenon occurs and better recognize the achievement of those who do complete the entire process successfully.

One of the major goals of our book is to help the novice researcher successfully complete all the stages of empirical research, from asking the initial research question to disseminating the results of a study for professional publication. Although this process is extremely demanding and difficult, when completed it is a tremendous accomplishment and one that brings great personal satisfaction.

RESEARCH AS ONE PATH TO KNOWLEDGE

Earlier it was noted that data-based research is referred to as empirical research. However, the empirical method is just one path to knowledge. There are other ways to explain why we know something. Maybe you know a person, or know how to counsel angry parents, or know the best referral agency for battered women. If someone wanted you to justify your knowledge, what would you say? You might justify your certainty using any of the following paths to knowledge.

One path to knowledge is **expert opinion,** typically from those in positions of social prestige such as lawyers, doctors, and professors. For example, if you are complaining of a tight feeling in your chest, you might consult Dr. X, a cardiologist. If Dr. X diagnoses you with angina, then you might tell someone, "I know I have angina because Dr. X told me so." Please note that no reference is made to how experts justify their knowledge, only that the lay person can take expert opinion at face value.

A second path to knowledge is **tradition,** which is accepting prior practices as knowledge. A good example of this is when parents follow their own parents' advice in rearing children. When your mother tells you that it is about time for her granddaughter to be potty trained because she potty trained you at this age, you might concur and accept this statement as knowledge. Again, we are not questioning the knowledge through tradition. Rather, we are indicating that tradition can be used to justify statements of certainty.

A third way of knowing is **intuition,** or extrasensory knowledge. In some problem-solving situations, an individual might resort to intuition. A person who is lost in a forest, for example, may state that the way out is by route X. If that person were pressed to justify why route X is right, he or she might respond, "I just know it." Thus, intuition is personal knowledge that is very difficult to articulate or analyze. Personal knowledge simply exists.

Reasoning and the use of logic define a fourth path to knowledge. Perhaps the easiest way to illustrate this way of acquiring knowledge is by using syllogistic logic, a reasoning strategy. Pretend you are a practicum student and you want to know the best way to counsel Mrs. Sue, an Asian American. You ask your supervisor about this during your next meeting, and she states that directive counseling is the best counseling format for Asian Americans. She might justify this by using syllogistic logic:

Mrs. Sue is Asian.
Asians report liking directive counseling styles the most.
Mrs. Sue should be counseled using a directive approach.

The fifth and final way of knowing is through experience. Experience can take two forms. One form is **anecdotal** in that we perceive or observe something without controlled, systematic methods. A social service professional may state, "Compared to the rest of the agencies I have interacted with, I know that agency A is the best shelter for battered women." The social worker's statement of knowledge is anecdotal because it is based on unsystematic, uncontrolled observations. Yet, anecdotal experience may still lead to the conclusion that we know something. As you will see in Chapter 8, anecdotal experience underlies the case study approach.

When we structure our experiences so they are based on carefully controlled, systematic, and objective observation, we adopt an **empirical approach** to knowing. For example, a social worker could spend time observing different agencies and rate these agencies on several variables previously identified as characteristic of effective operating procedure for battered women. Data could then be analyzed to see which agency is operating most effectively with respect to these criteria. It is the empirical approach to experience that underlies most of the material in this text, because the empirical method of knowing is the basic philosophical approach of the vast majority of research.

With respect to ways of knowing, four points need underscoring. First, while each path to knowledge is unique, many people combine different knowledge perspectives in concluding that they know something. In fact, the empirical method, while primarily objective, also requires reasoning. Obviously, humans must interpret and analyze the controlled observations they make.

Second, while all methods of knowing have merit, among researchers there is a tacit acceptance of the empirical method as the most powerful road to knowledge. As Neale and Liebert (1986) state, "The purpose of research in science is to bring a higher level of confidence and certainty to our understanding than is possible by belief, faith, or reason alone" (p. 9). Thus, as a researcher you implicitly make a commitment to the empirical approach and to all the concepts that underlie this approach: precision, hypothesis testing, reliability, operational definitions, control groups, manipulation of variables, statistical analysis, and so on. If you do not believe firmly in the power of the empirical perspective, you might question whether or not you should attempt an investigation.

Third, the power of the empirical approach is sometimes found by comparing it to other knowledge paths, mainly intuition and tradition. For example, many professional practices are driven by intuition, but when such practices are submitted to empirical scrutiny, they often are not supported. In education, a classic case in point was the way teachers used to deal with individual differences. In the late 1960s, the traditionally accepted practice was to group children by ability, usually into one of three ability levels: high, middle, or low. Typically, grouping was based on grades or scores on ability tests. The educators reasoned that students at each level would progress better because instruction and work assignments could be tailored to students' skill levels.

When empirical research accumulated, it was found that ability grouping did not lead to equal progress; rather, the highest groups prospered, the middle groups stayed average, and the low groups got worse (Hallinan & Sorensen, 1983). Ability groups, as they were once constructed, led to more academic inequality than equality. The effect of these findings was that researchers began to devise alternate grouping methods such as mixed ability groups, cooperative learning groups, and peer tutoring approaches. Indeed, if they were subjected to empirical standards, many current professional behaviors might not stand up to objective scrutiny.

Finally, a cautionary note is in order. None of the ways of knowing yield absolute knowledge. All ways of knowing have difficulties. Experts can be wrong, intuition and common sense can be misleading, tradition can be a course of transgenerational misinformation, logic can disagree with experience, and experience can be based on biased perceptions. Indeed, even empirical observation can be faulty, as you will see in the chapters in which we discuss threats to internal and external validity. Yet, as you also will learn, most faults with the empirical method can be corrected. When they are not, such weaknesses must be stated in the final research paper as limitations to the research investigation.

In summary, we hope that, above all else, you adopt a critical attitude with respect to knowledge. No matter how you prefer to acquire it, we hope you concur that any knowledge claim must be evaluated cautiously and skeptically. Although in this text we promote the merits of the empirical way of knowing, we will do so with caution and a critical attitude. Research is a highly complex process, and whether or not we can claim to know something based on a single study is a question that is open to many considerations. We will present some of these considerations in this book in the hope that you can better evaluate existing research critically, as well as design your research in a way that will strengthen the conclusions you draw and the validity of the knowledge thus derived.

SPECIAL ISSUES IN HUMAN-SUBJECT RESEARCH

Conducting research with human subjects differs from investigations in other scientific fields such as biology, agriculture, or chemistry. With its focus on human behavior, helping profession research is prone to four noteworthy concerns.

Ethical Treatment

One major concern in human subjects research is that human subjects be treated ethically. **Ethics** are moral principles, which in research pertain to treating subjects fairly and responsibly throughout the research process. The American Psychological Association (1992) has published a set of ethical guidelines to help researchers ensure that (1) subjects are informed about the research they will participate in; (2) subjects have the freedom to participate and withdraw at any time without penalty; and (3) there are procedures for ensuring confidentiality of subject data. The current version of the American Psychological Association (APA) ethical principles related to research is given in Appendix A. All prospective researchers should have a complete understanding of the APA's ethical principles before conducting research with human subjects. We will discuss some of these principles in more detail in Chapter 3.

Cause and Effect

A second concern that is pertinent to human subjects research is the quest for **cause and effect** outcomes. That is, in many research studies the goal is to be able to state that only the variables manipulated (the independent variables) caused the observed effect on some outcome measures (the dependent variables). When researchers want to make cause and effect statements, they take great care to manipulate the experimental conditions so that only the independent variables of interest are free to vary. The other variables that might affect the outcome are said to be controlled, that is, removed as factors that affect subject performance on the dependent measure. Yet, with human subjects, how much control can researchers exert across all the myriad factors that may pertain to study outcomes? Most of the time very little control is possible.

To illustrate the issue, let us refer to an example from the literature. Daley, Bloom, Deffenbacher, and Stewart (1983) wanted to determine the relative effectiveness of different types of Anxiety Management Training (AMT) in reducing self-reported anxiety among college students as compared with a control group. Two AMT groups were constructed. One was small-group AMT that consisted of two groups of approximately 11 subjects per group; the other was large-group AMT in which AMT was administered to 27 subjects at once. These groups were compared to a no-treatment control group. The administration of AMT was purportedly the same across the different groups. Also, the subjects participating were comparable in level of self-reported anxiety so that the groups did not contain subjects with either more or less severe degrees of anxiety. The dependent measures were posttest and 7-week self-reports of anxiety and personality adjustment. The results showed that small-group AMT was more effective in lowering self-reported anxiety at posttest and 7-week tests when compared to large-group AMT or a no-treatment control group.

Note that the researchers tried to ensure that the only factors free to vary were the size of the AMT group and whether subjects received or did not receive the AMT treatment. Everything else that might affect the dependent measures of anxiety and psychological adjustment was potentially eliminated by securing the equivalence of groups before intervention and purporting that AMT was administered similarly in small- and large-group formats. As a result, the researchers concluded that small-group AMT caused the significant reduction in anxiety.

But can this kind of cause and effect conclusion be made? In the Daley et al. (1983) study, were there any other factors that might explain why subjects in the small-group AMT improved more than subjects in the other groups did? For example, it was noted that the senior author conducted the groups in collaboration with an advanced doctoral student. Were these researchers equally skilled in delivery of AMT? How many groups, or sessions within groups, did each of the different leaders conduct? Could the researchers' prior expectations have influenced the outcomes? Perhaps the researchers had some initial expectation that small-group AMT would be more effective, and this initial belief subtly influenced the outcome. Perhaps they conducted the small AMT groups with more warmth and genuineness than the large groups.

The point is that even when investigators go to great lengths to ensure that the independent variable and no other variable caused the observed effects on the dependent variable, cause and effect statements can never be made with absolute confidence in social science research. However, as you will see in Chapter 5, researchers can increase their confidence in stating cause and effect relationships. For example, in the Daley et al. (1983) study, subjects were randomly assigned to groups. The process of random assignment is the single most important factor in ruling out additional subject variables that could influence the dependent variable.

Individual Differences

Individual differences—the fact that each human being differs from the next—raises a third issue in human subjects research. The problem arises in that human subjects research typically focuses on groups rather than individuals. That is, research usually is **nomothetic** in that groups form the primary unit of analysis.

Thus, instead of studying individuals, nomothetic researchers concentrate on the aggregate unit—the average of the group, not just one person.

For example, a research study on the effects of Rogerian counseling on clients' self-esteem could be designed. One group of 25 subjects could receive 15 weeks of Rogerian counseling, while another group of 25 subjects would not receive any type of counseling but would simply be placed on a wait-list. Both groups could then be tested on a self-esteem measure at the beginning and end of the 15-week period. Imagine that this study was conducted and that the results showed significant group differences such that the group receiving Rogerian counseling had higher self-esteem than the group receiving no counseling.

Note that the focus of the study is nomothetic in that documenting group differences in self-esteem is the primary objective. However, individual subjects within the groups may vary from pretest to posttest in a way that is contrary to the predicted direction. Perhaps one or two subjects in the Rogerian group had lower self-esteem at posttest time, while several subjects in the no-counseling group may have shown higher self-esteem at the conclusion of the 15-week period. Of course, if many subjects had followed this contrary course, the results would show no differences between groups in posttest levels of self-esteem. However, the point is that the groups could still differ significantly while one or two subjects deviate from the predicted outcome.

The isolated cases make many people uncomfortable with a total reliance on nomothetic research methods. We cannot say that Rogerian counseling increases self-esteem for all subjects. Instead, what we can say is that Rogerian counseling has a positive effect on self-esteem for most people, although there may be a few exceptions.

In an attempt to move away from the reliance on group methods in research and accommodate individual differences, some researchers adopt an **idiographic** approach. Idiographic methods focus on single cases and the documentation of interventions on a case-by-case basis. For example, if an adult presents with severe public speaking anxiety, a mental health counselor might decide to treat this person using guided imagery and relaxation. The counselor may ask the person to visualize a sequence of steps before and during the delivery of a speech and then teach relaxation techniques to reduce the anxiety associated with each step in public speaking.

The counselor could collect data on this treatment using empirical methods. For example, at the beginning of treatment the counselor could ask the client to visualize an upcoming speaking engagement and then have the subject complete a self-report inventory of anxiety. A similar method could be used several times during treatment. If the results show a reduction in speech anxiety as intervention progresses, this would indicate that the counselor intervened effectively for this subject.

The most obvious difficulty with the idiographic approach is that the generalization of research results is limited to single cases. Whether this intervention would work for any other individual is an empirical question needing verification. That is, using an idiographic approach means that treatment effectiveness must be validated on a case-by-case basis. On the other hand, when groups are studied, generalization to other cases becomes more valid as a function of the size of the group sampled. The topic of generalization of research results will be examined in detail in Chapter 6.

Behavior in Context

A fourth issue with human subjects research is that human behavior is to some extent a function of environmental context. Subjects in a contrived, artificial, experimental setting may behave differently than they would if placed in a more natural context. When research requires participation in laboratory settings, the obvious question is whether the results can be generalized to more natural settings such as classrooms, offices, and therapy rooms. Again, the question can only be answered through further collection of data in various environments to determine whether the results obtained in one setting are generalizable to others.

RELEVANCE OF RESEARCH TO HUMAN SERVICE PROFESSIONALS

We have discussed some preliminary terminology and processes that are the foundation for research in the helping professions. But what about the practical meaningfulness of research? How is research relevant to the helping professional?

If you recall the vignette, Maria revealed the personal significance she attached to research. While she recognized the need to read the latest research findings, she felt that the conduct of research was more for academic people, and is of less importance for the practitioner-oriented student. Actually, her position regarding the significance of research may be more favorable than that of many others; many helping professionals see little of relevance in any aspect of research. In fact, they sometimes resent having to participate in a research course (Winfrey, 1984).

There are several reasons for negative attitudes. One difficulty is that some helping professionals (like Maria) see themselves primarily as practitioners (Watkins, Campbell, & McGregor, 1989). Their primary goal is to obtain needed practical skills through hands-on experiences like practicing counseling techniques. On the other hand, research skills and investigative experiences associated with an academic role are seen as far less important by many undergraduate and graduate students. That many helping professionals identify with a practitioner role rather than an academic role suggests that they will attach little importance to the research process, either as a consumer or conductor of research.

In the vignette, Maria raised a practical concern about her ability to conduct research. She believed that even if she saw herself as an academic type of person, she would not be likely to do a thesis because the added demands of research would further reduce her time for family commitments. She may be right. It would be misleading not to mention the rigors of research. We have found that prospective researchers do not grasp the painstaking, time-consuming, even expensive nature of research. As we noted earlier, there are many stages involved in conducting research. Using the library—finding materials, ordering information, copying—is extremely laborious when done properly. In addition, when data are collected, there is the demanding task of data entry and analysis, which may require a significant amount of computer time. As if that were not enough, the generation of the research report still must be completed.

If helping professionals see little of relevance to them in research or doubt that they can include the rigors of conducting research in an already busy schedule, how can these impediments be overcome to encourage the conduct of research? In the sections that follow, we directly address the first issue. We show why research is relevant to practitioners and why it should not be perceived as the exclusive domain of the academic and scholarly professions. These sections describe the scientist-practitioner model and accountability. A final section describes the potential professional benefits to be derived from completing a research investigation. We hope that by listing the benefits of research potential conductors of research will see it as a more significant activity.

The second issue—the demands of conducting research—is real and cannot be avoided. Thus, the capacity to complete a research study must be honestly evaluated by each prospective researcher. If such introspection results in considerable doubt about completing an empirical study, the study should not be begun.

Scientist-Practitioner Model

Proponents of research in the helping professions stress the importance of research to both theory and practice and the need for feedback among these three domains. The feedback loop between theory, research, and practice (Barlow, Hayes, & Nelson, 1984) is referred to as the **scientist-practitioner model** and is presented in Figure 1-6. Those advocating a scientist-practitioner model believe that all three areas are interdependent.

The model can be illustrated as follows. Imagine that a mental health counselor practices from a rational-emotive theory. One of the methods used in this approach is to confront and challenge individuals who hold irrational beliefs.

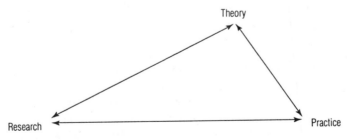

FIGURE 1-6   The relationships among theory, research, and practice.

For example, if a client says, "Nobody likes me," the counselor might challenge this statement with, "That cannot be true. I like you, and I bet if you think about it, you can think of other people who like you too." Thus, a counselor subscribing to this theory will be likely to use this confrontational technique in practice. Research fits into the picture because research can answer the question, Does confronting and challenging irrational beliefs make beliefs more rational? Without an answer to this question, the practice remains empirically unjustified. If a research study finds that the practice does make beliefs more rational, that is evidence that the technique is effective. Just as important is the fact that the rational-emotive theory gains credence from such a finding. If research results showed that this practice was not effective and that clients' beliefs were no more rational after confrontation, the practice of confrontation would not be advisable. Further, rational-emotive theory would need modification to account for this finding. Clearly, adopting a scientist-practitioner view means acknowledging that research plays a critical role in the helping professions.

Although the scientist-practitioner perspective seems ideal, there is debate about its meaningfulness. For example, in counseling, several noteworthy theorists—among them Perls (1971) and Adler (1927)—believed that research was not a valid mechanism for confirming theory. Because this attitude has been espoused by several leading authorities in helping professions, it is no wonder that some people see little usefulness in research for the helping professional.

To sum up our discussion, consider this human relationship analogy. One can be "married" to the scientific approach in the sense of spending much time conducting research. Such marriages are usually reserved for those in research or academic positions. Further, one can "date" science by completing a thesis or dissertation and then by being a consistent consumer of the latest empirical findings after graduation. However, even those who do not see much meaning in empirical research may "flirt" with it. This is especially true if you consider that the theories and techniques developed for helping professions are based on empirical research. Here, the flirter implicitly accepts the empirical research on which his or her practice is based, even if he or she dislikes the scientific method.

Finally, consider how difficult it is to be completely "divorced" from the scientific perspective. No theory is completely devoid of a research base, even if a theory's creator discourages empirical research. The only way to conceive of a complete divorce is to suppose that a theory's adherent remains ignorant of the empirical research regarding the theory. A good example of such a divorce may have been when devout followers of Perls used highly emotional psychotherapeutic techniques with clients in the late 1960s. As we noted, Perls did not believe that research was an appropriate means to validate his theory. Thus, it is possible that Perls and his devout followers never consulted the empirical literature but relied on the expert opinion of Perls himself and, perhaps, anecdotal experience as the foundations of knowledge.

The danger in complete divorces is that empirical research can contradict both expert opinion and experience. Such was the case with the techniques of

Perls. As empirical data accumulated, researchers found that certain Gestalt techniques that Perls favored, when used with certain clients, can do more harm than good.

Accountability

Accountability refers to the evidence of competent practice. Accountability is an attempt to ensure quality control among helping professionals and thus increase public confidence in the helping professions. In most agencies, there are ways to evaluate whether individuals are performing responsibly and ably such as supervisor ratings, client feedback, or peer evaluations. As you might have gathered, evaluations of practice are frequently based on some type of empirical evidence. For example, counselors may be rated on their interactions with clients. We recommend that you, as a prospective helping professional, understand the principles and assumptions underlying empirical methods. This will allow you to be a knowledgeable participant in creating feasible, reliable, and valid evaluation methods for your own professional practice and the practices of others.

Professional Benefits

Research may be personally relevent to the helping professional because of the benefits derived from completing an investigation. In the stages of empirical research, we mentioned an optional final stage of dissemination for publication. Publication is clearly commendable and noteworthy; it results in obvious gains such as greater professional prestige and increased employment security. The freedom to select from a wider range of job opportunities could be another benefit. Further, recall in the vignette that some students were completing a thesis because they felt it would increase their chances of being accepted into doctoral programs. Graduate admissions committees do consider publication and professional dissemination of research to be an important accomplishment (Goldberg, 1977; Purdy, Reinher, & Schwartz, 1989). Thus, all other factors being equal — experience, letters of recommendation, grade point average—the applicant who publishes a research paper may have an advantage.

In some cases, if the research is of high quality it can be submitted for a special type of institutional, local, regional, or even national award. For example, some colleges offer an award for the most outstanding dissertation. Many such opportunities are available; you may simply need to know where to locate research awards.

Even if a paper is submitted for professional publication, it can still be submitted to a professional organization for presentation at a national, regional, or local conference. In fact, most researchers do both. They submit their work for publication in journals and also present the research at a suitable conference.

Finally, newcomers to research need to understand that research costs may be covered by an agency interested in the piece of research. Such agencies can provide **grants**, the external money—funds from outside sources—needed to conduct the research.

CONCLUDING COMMENTS

In this introductory chapter, we discussed basic questions that beginning researchers may have about research. By demystifying research, we hope we showed you how to begin assessing whether or not research fits within your own unique circumstances.

For example, as we previously discussed, most helping professionals have some type of relationship with research, either as a maker or consumer. Both relationships are important and require a basic understanding of the general research principles that we will discuss throughout this text. If you want to do research, knowing how to (1) find and read literature in your field, (2) develop a research plan, (3) observe and measure behavior, (4) make appropriate conclusions from data, (5) design different types of research, (6) engage in statistical analyses, and (7) write and disseminate research are all vital.

However, being an able consumer of research requires similar knowledge. After all, how can a person understand the meaning of a single piece of research without knowing something about the way the literature was reviewed, the adequacy of the research plan, the way behavior was observed, the appropriateness of the design, the validity of the statistical analysis, the restrictions to conclusions as they relate to internal and external validity, and multicultural differences?

In sum, research is a vital activity, not only as it affects practice but perhaps more importantly as it stimulates critical thinking. Empirical research, rooted in the scientific method, is an inherently cautious approach to building knowledge. It requires careful observation, precise definitions of variables and samples, and statistical analyses. Although empirical research is not infallible, it does contain many checks and balances. In the remainder of this text, we hope to make these procedural safeguards clear to you.

EXERCISES

1. Select an article of your choice. After reading the article, construct a knowledge structure, using Figure 1-2 as a guide.
2. Using the eight stages of empirical research, discuss the topic of alcoholism in the Navajo Nation. Illustrate, in general, the steps you would take to complete each of the eight stages.
3. Consider a job you hold, or have held. How is research relevant in this context?
4. Read the article by Daley et al. (1983) in Appendix E. After reading the article, answer the following questions:
   a. Is the article primarily basic or applied research? Why or why not?
   b. What do you think were the motives of the researchers in conducting this study?
   c. How might the results of the study relate to your scientific or clinical practice interests?
5. If you are considering doing a thesis, list some of your interests (social, professional, academic, recreational, and so forth). Identify potential research topics you would like to investigate in these areas.

2

INFORMATION GATHERING AND ANALYSIS: BECOMING KNOWLEDGEABLE ABOUT AN AREA OF RESEARCH

MARIA GONZALEZ is now beginning the second year of graduate study in her counseling program. As part of her fall course work, she enrolled in a counseling practicum conducted at the University Counseling Center. Now several weeks into her practicum, she is counseling women with a binge-and-purge eating disorder known as *bulimia*. She finds herself becoming increasingly interested in this disorder, especially its treatment. In fact, she sees possible merit in undertaking a research project concerning bulimia.

Maria finds herself less intimidated by the prospect of conducting a research study than she did a year ago. Perhaps part of her new attitude about research is a function of having completed her required research course the previous spring, a course in which she read research papers. During this process, she came to realize that understanding research is as important as practical, technique-oriented skills. In addition, she is becoming increasingly intrigued by the professional growth and benefits that accrue to individuals who do research. She is even entertaining the notion of doing doctoral study and sees the thesis as a helpful and requisite experience.

Before making a final decision regarding whether she will do a research study to complete the master's program, she consults several faculty members in the department as well as faculty in the departments of social work and nursing, since she feels that these departments might be relevant to her study. Maria also confers with her Ph.D.-level practicum supervisor, who is familiar with literature concerning bulimia. Having discussed her ideas with these professionals, Maria is now convinced that she can complete a thesis in a year—the time she has remaining before graduation.

As a result of her discussions and her further reflection about bulimia, Maria is interested in determining the most effective treatment for clients exhibiting bulimia. Specifically, Maria wonders which therapeutic approach—client-centered, cognitive-behavioral, or psychodynamic—is the most effective in reducing maladaptive behaviors associated with bulimia. However, she feels uneasy with this research question; she guesses that this idea has already been investigated or that her topic is either too broad, too narrow, or perhaps even irrelevant. She wonders how to proceed further.

I n this chapter, we focus on the first stages of research—identifying a topic to research and becoming knowledgeable about it. Note that toward the end of the vignette, Maria completed the first stage of empirical research when she identified a topic to research. She now questions whether her chosen topic and the question she formulated regarding it are appropriate. Her concern is part of the natural process leading to stage 2—becoming knowledgeable about the topic. Maria must now figure out the extent to which her research idea has been investigated, the types of modifications she might need to make in her initial research question, and how to obtain and evaluate the information currently available regarding the treatment of bulimia.

Note that the term *knowledgeable* is relative. How knowledgeable and how expert must a researcher be? Many factors determine a researcher's depth of knowledge; some are directly related to the researcher's characteristics, such as aptitude and motivation. The amount of knowledge a researcher has is also influenced by the difficulty of the subject being studied, the time available to do the research, and the purpose for which the researcher conducts the study.

These factors aside, the process of learning about a research topic is one of the most difficult of investigative activities. Not only does the researcher have to locate and read a great quantity of research literature, the investigator must also identify a problem in that literature. In other words, the researcher does not read simply to understand but to critique other investigations with the intent of identifying an inherent weakness in them. While the specific types of weaknesses depend entirely on the type of subject matter examined, general problem categories can include theoretical predictions not yet tested, methodological weaknesses, and alternate conclusions. To be able to detect a problem with previous research, a premium is put on the researcher's intellectual skills, particularly abstract reasoning, critical thinking, creativity, and imagination.

The difficulty of this stage of research is compounded by the sheer amount of reading required. To grasp this fact, let us return to Maria's research topic and assume that she located the following relevant documents: 2 books, 8 chapters, 3 conference papers, 10 journal articles, 3 unpublished reports (manuals for parents and technical reports), and 5 dissertations. To put her reading task in perspective, assume that reading assignments in graduate classes are one or two textbooks and perhaps several journal articles. Unpublished documents and dissertations can approximate book length. By way of comparison, Maria will read the equivalent of 10 books and enough chapters to make up another book. Add in the other documents and you can see that if Maria could disengage from all her other academic responsibilities, she probably could spend an entire semester just reading full-time. Further, as we noted earlier, becoming knowledgeable about a research area requires more than just superficial scanning of information. Critical review adds to the total time required to complete this stage. Mix in the practical constraints on researchers, such as finite time lines for the completion of research, and you can see how demanding this phase of research can be.

While stage 2 is demanding, there are ways to increase efficiency and improve time-management while becoming knowledgeable about a topic. In this chapter, we discuss these methods, dividing the process of becoming knowledgeable into two parts: *obtaining information* and *analyzing information*. In the section about gathering information, we will discuss using the library; a library can be an ally or an enemy. Subsequently, we provide hints about general library usage. Of course, since each library is unique, it is best to discuss library research in the human service professions with your institution's reference librarian.

The second phase — information analysis — entails a critical reading of all the procured information. Tips to help you with this process will be described in this section. However, before detailing either of these stages in knowledge development, let us return to stage 1 and examine how research topics are identified.

IDENTIFYING A TOPIC TO RESEARCH

Why did Maria change her attitude about research from that of a doubting skeptic to believer? Maria's research class may have helped reduce her fears about research. The ultimate answer, though, may be that she found a topic of sufficient personal interest to stimulate her scientific curiosity. For Maria, working in the counseling center with a particular population led to her increasing interest in bulimia and its treatment.

Indeed, the most important reason to do research is high interest, so it makes sense to pick a topic of great personal interest. What is the source of a researcher's interest? Sometimes, interest is driven simply by the need to know more, perhaps to resolve contradictory information, or to treat the subject in a new, creative way. In essence, personal interest can stem from intellectual curiosity.

In other instances, motivation stems from the researcher's personal involvement with a subject. For example, a woman with epilepsy may want to know the effects of neuroleptics such as Tegratol on various cognitive tasks. Perhaps this beginning researcher has heard that neuroleptics impair specific cognitive functions and is worried that her job performance will be adversely affected by neuroleptic medication. Here, the researcher's personal experience with the topic would be the primary reason for engaging in research.

Occasionally, researchers begin the research process with minimal personal interest in any one topic. As the research process continues and the investigator becomes more knowledgeable about a specific aspect of the subject, interest heightens. For instance, as the prospective epilepsy researcher learns more about the topic, she may read that the neuroleptic medication she is taking can affect cognitive processing. This potential relationship is very intriguing to her, and as she continues to investigate, her personal interest increases even more.

If you are interested in doing research but presently cannot think of anything that stimulates your scientific interest, we provide the following tips. First, you may find it useful to keep a note pad handy for jotting down ideas of interest. You will be amazed at the number of ideas that will surface in just a single day.

A second way to identify a research topic is to recall a class, lecture, workshop, or other activity that piqued your curiosity. If you can, relocate reading material related to a particular past event like a class textbook, lecture hand-outs, or a workshop manual. As you being to read, your interest may continue to develop with further study.

Third, even without an initial topic, you can start reading current periodicals with the aim of locating a topic. For instance, if you want to complete a master's degree in social work, reading some of the latest periodicals in social work will probably provide some promising leads regarding subjects to study empirically. The faculty adviser of the first author of this text directed him to several current periodicals. After reading one article, the adviser was consulted and a topic was identified. The types of periodicals in which prospective researchers may find research topics will be discussed later in this chapter.

A final way to identify a research topic is to consult with knowledgeable individuals. Sometimes it is helpful to contact relevant community resource people such as business leaders, mental health professionals, or hospital staff members. University professors can provide promising leads; discussing topics with fellow students may also be useful.

In contrast to identifying a single topic, in some cases you might have several topics to choose from. In this situation, rank order the topics and pursue the one of most interest to you. If it is difficult to select between equally interesting subjects, it is again helpful to confer with knowledgeable sources. These individuals can direct you to important issues surrounding particular topics, and such leadership may be helpful as you begin selecting from several attractive topics.

Topics can be stated vaguely — epilepsy may be a topic — or more specifically—the relationship between neuroleptics and cognitive processing may be a topic. The specificity of the topic has important implications for the beginning researcher because the more global and vague the initial topic, the more time is required to break the subject matter into manageable research parts. The investigator must research the broader topic simply to find a specific topic for study. This narrowing process can be very time-consuming and frustrating.

Thus, identifying precise topics early can prevent the frustration and wasted time associated with narrowing a broad topic into manageable parts. But how can the beginner move from general to more specific topics? Again, consulting with knowledgeable experts can prove very helpful. Experts can guide the newcomer to specific parts of a subject in need of further study. Thus, it was wise of Maria to consult with various knowledgeable sources before going to the library.

Second, it may be useful to pose an initial research question about the subject matter. By asking an initial question, the researcher is forced to think more specifically about the topic. For example, when the researcher interested in epilepsy tries to determine what she wants to know about this topic, she might ask, "What are the side-effects of neuroleptic medications?" Note the increased specificity that results when an initial question about the topic is posed.

To develop an initial question about your topic, determine what, specifically, you would like to know about it. After you do this, devise several possible ques-

Topic 1: Child-rearing practices	
What is the most effective discipline technique for temper tantrums?	Can a child be toilet-trained in one day?

Topic 2: Client-social worker interactions	
What is the effect of ethnic matching on social worker-client interactions?	What social worker personality factors predict effective interactions with clients?

Topic 3: Cross-cultural counseling	
What techniques facilitate counseling with minorities?	Do cultural groups differ in beliefs about the validity of counseling?

FIGURE 2-1   Sample research topics and associated research questions.

tions, making sure your sentences are in question form. Any common interrogative can be used such as what, when, how, who, where, and why. In Figure 2-1, we give examples of research topics and several questions about each topic.

One matter we have overlooked is the problem of knowing the degree of specificity possible in a topic. When beginning library research, you can get a general idea of the number of research studies that use a particular topic in the research abstract. As we will discuss shortly, thousands of these abstracts are stored in large information bases that are readily retrievable through computer technology. If you find that the term epilepsy occurs 100 times, this topic is probably far too general and some narrowing of the subject matter will be required. On the other hand, if you search for the terms neuroleptics and cognitive processing and retrieve 10 records, your topic has ideal specificity. That is, these 10 records could be retrieved, reviewed, and any further citations in these papers pursued. Later, when we return to the specificity of Maria's initial question, you will see exactly how many references to the treatment of bulimia were found in one database.

With a topic identified, the researcher can begin learning more about it. Again, this process entails two phases: gathering information then analyzing it. We next discuss these phases.

INFORMATION GATHERING: USING THE LIBRARY

Using the library to obtain relevant literature on a topic can be done efficiently, especially if the library patron knows the facility. Further, with increasingly sophisticated computer technology, information can be reviewed quickly and comprehensively. Almost every university has certain information sources that greatly simplify the process of doing a literature review. In the sections that follow, we first discuss central sources; later we will show how to search these sources using the computer. Last, we note other potentially helpful sources and provide a concluding comment about gathering information.

Central Sources

Central sources are those databases that store thousands of references and brief abstracts to journal articles, books, dissertations, and other manuscripts. Because these sources include complete references, the user will know where to go to obtain the complete document, should it be required. While most libraries have several central sources, we describe five that are particularly relevant to human service professionals: Educational Resources Information Center (ERIC), *Psychological Abstracts* (PA), *Sociological Abstracts* (SA), Medline (MED), and *Dissertation Abstracts International* (DAI). Since these central sources are all accessible through computers, we will later provide a strategy for improving the accuracy of a computer search. We conclude our coverage of information gathering by noting ways to use other potential sources: locating books, book chapters, and review journals, and contacting authors.

EDUCATIONAL RESOURCES INFORMATION CENTER. The **Educational Resources Information Center** (ERIC) is a national information system that collects and stores information pertaining to education. It operates through 16 major clearinghouses and 5 adjunct clearinghouses, each established to place educational literature within a specific area. For instance, the ERIC clearinghouse in Reston, Virginia is designed to collect, store, and enter in the ERIC database all the material regarding handicapped and gifted children. On the other hand, the University of Michigan has an ERIC clearinghouse responsible for all the literature on counseling and personnel services. All ERIC clearinghouses prepare references to educational literature for storage and access within a centralized ERIC database, which is then purchased by libraries for patron use. Since approximately 1,500 new journal articles are entered every month, ERIC is an invaluable source of information for educators, counselors, mental health specialists, social workers, and other behavioral specialists. We strongly recommend that all literature reviews include the ERIC database.

The literature contained in the ERIC database and in other central sources can be searched manually or by computer. A manual search would involve an examination of the two paper indices associated with ERIC: *Current Index to Journals in Education* (CIJE), which contains references to articles in relevant journals, and *Resources in Education* (RIE), consisting of references to material not published in journals such as unpublished reports, papers presented at conferences, and books. Since these indices are published so frequently and contain such a large amount of information, a manual search of ERIC is tedious.

In contrast to a manual search, a computer search of ERIC can be accomplished in two ways, either by requesting that the reference librarian do the search online, or by the researcher searching using ERIC CD-ROM. We will discuss both of these methods further when we discuss how to do a computer search.

PSYCHOLOGICAL ABSTRACTS.   As the name implies, *Psychological Abstracts* (PA) provides brief descriptions of journal articles taken from roughly 1,300 journals in psychology and education. Paper volumes of PA are produced monthly by the American Psychological Association, and each issue contains abstracts of articles as well as an author and subject index. The PA volumes occupy a large area of any library, since they go back as far as 1927. Although PA consists primarily of journal articles, other documents like technical reports, books, and dissertations also can be retrieved in PA. In fact, beginning in 1987, books and chapters in edited books have been systematically entered in the PA database. Since PA is so comprehensive and relevant to those in the human service professions, it must be consulted when doing a literature review.

As with ERIC, the PA database can be searched manually or via computer. The researcher can search PA using CD-ROM if the library has SilverPlatter's PSYCHLIT. If the researcher does a computer search, the strategy discussed next also will apply to PA. The only difference is that PA has its own thesaurus called the *Thesaurus of Psychological Index Terms*. Fortunately, this and most other thesauruses use standard codes, making the computer search of any database fairly standardized.

SOCIOLOGICAL ABSTRACTS.   *Sociological Abstracts* (SA) centers on a variety of social topics such as group interaction, the family and social welfare, studies in violence and power, women's studies, and social development. It is published by Sociological Abstracts, Incorporated five times a year and indexes about 3,300 documents between updates. As with ERIC and PA, SA indexes mostly journal articles, although conference papers are also contained in the SA database. Some books are also abstracted, but these are best searched elsewhere. Again, a computer search can be done by the researcher using CD-ROM if the library has SilverPlatter's CD-ROM SOCIOFILE. Also, SA has its own thesaurus called the *Thesaurus of Sociological Indexing Terms*.

SA is an invaluable source for any human service researcher because it provides research topics that have a social perspective. For example, when Maria retrieves document abstracts related to the treatment of bulimia, she might find that papers focus more on family interventions such as altering family social patterns that contribute to bulimic behaviors. Because of its unique social perspective, the SA database can prove useful in a literature search.

MEDLINE.   **Medline** is a comprehensive central source for biomedical research and is an extremely valuable database for researchers interested in primarily medical, physiological, and physical health topics. Medline has three separate indices: *Index Medicus, Index to Dental Literature,* and *International Nursing Index.* The Medline database consists mainly of journal articles, including those published in over 3,000 national and international journals. Chapters and monographs are retrievable but only for a 5-year period—1976–1981. As with all the previous databases, Medline can be searched using CD-ROM, the title of which is MEDLINE. The Medline thesaurus is the *Medical Subject Headings*, a reference that contains the vocabulary relevant to medical topics.

DISSERTATION ABSTRACTS INTERNATIONAL. A comprehensive literature review should include a search of doctoral dissertations, since doctoral research is a large and potentially relevant source of information to any proposed study. *Dissertation Abstracts International* (DAI) is the best source for dissertation information. It is published monthly by University Microfilms International (UMI) and contains the abstracts of dissertations submitted by almost 500 universities in the United States and Canada. UMI publishes dissertation abstracts monthly, and each issue contains an author and subject index of dissertations. Yearly cumulative indices are also published by UMI.

A manual search of DAI could be performed, although the time involved would be exorbitant. Like the other centralized databases, DAI should be computer searched. For example, a reference librarian can search a database called Dissertation Abstracts Online, which has abstracts of almost every American (and some British) dissertations published since 1980. Incredibly, Dissertation Abstracts Online collects about 3,500 new dissertations per month. Although this online service does not contain abstracts before 1980, you can retrieve full citations dating back to the creation of DAI in 1949 and then obtain the abstract from a printed DAI volume in the library holdings. There is also a CD-ROM disc available from UMI, called DISSERTATION ABSTRACTS ONDISC.

What is slightly trickier with dissertations is obtaining the complete dissertation when the abstract is not sufficient. For example, you might need to know more about the procedures used, how the treatments were defined, and characteristics of subjects. In these cases, the complete dissertation can be obtained in one of two ways. The least expensive way is to request that the dissertation be loaned to you from the university library where it is located. Unfortunately, not all universities loan dissertations, so this option is sometimes unavailable. Your reference librarian can determine which libraries loan dissertations. If you cannot get the dissertation on loan, you may decide to purchase a copy of it from UMI. A summary of the key elements of the five major central sources just noted is presented in Table 2-1.

Computer Search

Note that all the central sources can be searched manually by perusing bound volumes that contain the same information that is in the computer database. For example, a comprehensive manual search of Medline would include scanning each of its three bound indices, volumes that are printed every month. For ERIC, the monthly editions of CIJ and RIJE would need review. When you consider, for example, a 5-year review period multiplied by the number of months and number of relevant indices, you can see that manual searches are time-consuming and tedious. Therefore, a computer search is recommended, since the user can quickly scan information stored in large databases. All the central sources previously mentioned can be computer searched either by (1) preparing a list of searchable terms and having a library technician access an

TABLE 2-1 Summary of central sources.

Type of Information	Documents Retrieved	Scope of Information	Search Options	Thesaurus
Education	Primarily journals; also books, unpublisheed papers, and conference papers	1,500 journals updated monthly	Manual and computer (ERIC CD-Rom)	ERIC descriptors
Psychology Education	Primarily journals; also unpublished papers, books, book chapters, and dissertations	1,300 journals updated monthly	Manual and computer (PSYCHLIT)	Psychological index items
Social Topics Society	Primarily journals; also conference papers	3,300 documents approximately five annual updates	Manual and computer (SOCIOFILE)	Sociological indexing terms
Biomedical Physiological	Primarily journals; chapters and monographs available from 1976–1981	Over 250,000 records added annually	Manual and computer (MEDLINE)	Medical subject headings
Various topics in helping professions	Dissertations only	3,500 dissertations per month	Manual and computer (DISSERTATION ABSTRACTS ONDISC)	

online system like the DIALOG system or (2) using a computer terminal if your library has the database on ERIC CD-ROM.

The **DIALOG Information Retrieval Service** is an information company that contains about 300 major databases, including all five of the central sources noted earlier. In addition, DIALOG contains databases for fields such as chemistry, engineering, business, and many others. Using DIALOG, the researcher typically provides the reference technician with a formal search strategy, dates to be searched, and the databases of interest. One main advantage of DIALOG is that it is updated weekly so that even the most current information is retrievable. Also, using DIALOG, the reference librarian can search several databases simultaneously. Unfortunately, DIALOG entails some cost; prices vary depending on library policy. Another concern is that the searcher does not use the computer terminal to make search decisions because a library technician is responsible for DIALOG access.

As we have noted previously, the other method requires the investigator to conduct the search from a computer terminal using a compact disc (CD). These disks are developed by information and technology companies like SilverPlatter, an organization established in 1983 specifically for information retrieval using CD technology. SilverPlatter produces the PSYCHLIT, SOCIOFILE, and ERIC CD-ROMs.

Whether the investigator uses CD-ROM or lets the library technician do the search, all computer searches must be planned before being conducted. If they are not planned or if planning is poor, the researcher will not be taking full advantage of computer technology but will be using an unreliable, hit-or-miss method. If done properly, a computer search will yield profitable results.

Here are some steps to follow in conducting a successful computer search. In providing these suggestions, we illustrate the search strategy with actual results obtained from an ERIC computer search conducted by Maria Gonzalez. The search was conducted using ERIC CD-ROM.

STATE TOPIC BRIEFLY. When conducting a computer search, begin by stating your topic in one or two sentences. For example, Maria's initial research question was, Which therapeutic approach — client-centered, cognitive-behavioral, or psychodynamic — is the most effective in reducing maladaptive behaviors associated with bulimia? This question could be used verbatim as her brief description of the topic.

BREAK TOPIC INTO KEY IDEAS. Most research topics are composed of two or three meaningful parts. For example, neuroleptics and cognitive processing clearly involve two related parts that are given directly in the topic. As Maria reviews her question, she is likely to note that it forms an interrelated set of three ideas. One idea is the type of disorder—bulimia. Another key component is treatment type — client-centered, behavioral-cognitive, and psychodynamic. Finally, treatment effectiveness could be considered a third key element.

SELECT SYNONYMS FOR KEY IDEAS. To determine what terms are related to your key ideas, first think of your words for each of the ideas. For example, Maria may think of anorexia nervosa as similar to bulimia because both are eating disorders. When you consider the second idea, you may think of counseling and therapy as relevant terms. Write each term under the component idea.

Second, after developing your search terms, you should use a thesaurus to confirm your list as well as to identify additional terms relevant to a particular database. In ERIC, the thesaurus is called the *Thesaurus of ERIC Descriptors*. When Maria goes to the ERIC thesaurus and looks up the term bulimia, she will find the information given in Table 2-2. A brief review of Table 2-2 reveals the following. First, the date the term bulimia was added to the ERIC thesaurus is noted to the far right of the term. Bulimia was added as of April, 1986. Second, the number of times the term bulimia was used in the ERIC database (called a posting note) either as a title, as a key term or descriptor, or in the article abstract is stated for both indices. Thus, for CIJE the term was used 39 times, while for RIE it was cited 19 times. (GC is a unique three-digit group code that can be used in a search but rarely is.) Third, SN is a scope note that provides a definition of the term. Note that bulimia is used for (UF) bulimarexia. That is, ERIC catalogs bulimarexia as bulimia.

Of most importance are the categories BT, RT, and in some cases, NT. BT refers to a *broader term* than the one being used, which for bulimia is diseases. In each case, the searcher must decide whether the broader term should be included in the search. In Maria's case, it seems needless to include the word diseases in her search, since diseases is a term that would yield hundreds of citations, only a few of which may be germane to her topic.

RT is a *related term,* and the table reveals six related terms for bulimia. Again, a decision has to be made regarding which of the related terms should be included in a search. Maria may decide that only anorexia nervosa is related closely enough to bulimia to be included and that all the other terms are too general to be useful in a search.

NT is a *narrower term,* and although bulimia is fairly narrow, other indexed terms may not be as specific, which will require another decision by the searcher. For example, while Maria may feel comfortable with how she will search ERIC regarding bulimia, she still must include terms relevant to each of three different counseling approaches and their effectiveness. She could use a broad term like counseling in her search, or she could leave out counseling and choose any or all of the 13 narrower terms related to counseling such as adult counseling, family counseling, and individual counseling.

DECIDE ON BOOLEAN OPERATORS.   The fourth and final planning step is to determine what connecting words, called *Boolean connectors,* you will use to link some or all of the component ideas of your research topic. In Figure 2-2, we show how the AND and OR connectors work.

The *AND connector* narrows a search by retrieving only those records containing at least one term from each idea. For example, if Maria wanted to, she could limit her search by using AND to connect the synonyms that represent her three ideas—bulimia with counseling/therapy with results/outcomes. In

TABLE 2-2   ERIC Thesaurus information for the term BULIMIA.

BULIMIA				Apr. 1986.
CIJE: 39		RIE: 19	GC: 210	
SN	Disorder characterized by recurrent binge eating, usually followed by self-induced purging—attended by depressed moods and self-deprecating thoughts			
UF	Bulimarexia			
BT	Diseases			
RT	Anorexia Nervosa			
	Body Weight			
	Eating Habits			
	Emotional Disturbance			
	Nutrition			
	Physical Health			

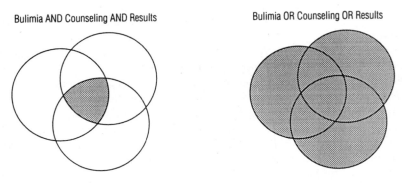

Bulimia AND Counseling AND Results　　　Bulimia OR Counseling OR Results

FIGURE 2-2　The effects of Boolean connectors during a computer search.

this fashion, Maria is limiting her search by requesting that only records containing a term from each idea be retrieved. In Maria's case, Figure 2-3 shows how the AND connector focuses the search; the shaded area indicates relevant information.

The *OR connector* broadens a search by retrieving all records containing at least one of the search terms entered. In Maria's case, she could retrieve far more citations if she requested bulimia OR counseling, since she also would get all the records associated with counseling in general, not just counseling with bulimic clients. In essence, OR is used between synonymous terms within an idea grouping, while AND is used to connect separate idea units. In Table 2-3, we provide a summary sheet for Maria's computer search, a summary that includes the unique uses of the Boolean operators AND and OR.

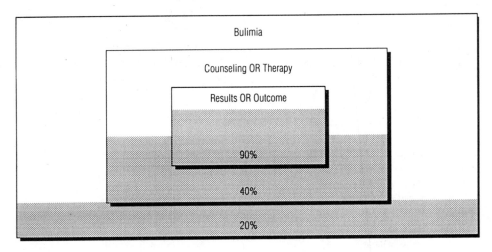

FIGURE 2-3　Related topics and proportional citations for Maria's study.

TABLE 2-3   A completed search strategy form for
Maria Gonzalez.

Step 1.   Describe topic briefly

Which therapeutic approach—client-centered, cognitive-
behavioral, or psychodynamic—is most effective in reducing the
maladaptive behaviors associated with bulimia?

Step 2.   Break topic into key ideas

Idea 1	Idea 2	Idea 3
bulimia	therapy	effectiveness

Step 3.   Select synonyms for key ideas

Idea 1	Idea 2	Idea 3
bulimia	therapy	effectiveness
anorexia	counseling	results
	psychiatry	evaluation
	behavior	outcome
	modification	outcomes

Step 4.   Decide on boolean descriptors

Idea 1	Idea 2		Idea 3
bulimia	therapy		effectiveness
OR	OR		OR
anorexia	counseling		results
	OR		OR
	psychiatry	AND	evaluation
	OR		OR
	behavior		outcome
	modification		OR
			outcomes

In Table 2-4, we give the results of Maria's search. Maria had requested that the computer find each of the terms in her search strategy individually (lines 1, 2, 4–8 and 10–14) and in combination (lines 3, 9, 15, and 16). Also note that the first three lines relate to the first component in her research topic—bulimia. Lines 4–9 relate to the second component—treatment approaches—while lines 10–15 focus on the third component—treatment effectiveness. The number of records shows how often the term appeared in the ERIC database.

The key line in the search is the final one that uses the Boolean operator AND. Note that Maria limited her search by requesting that ERIC search only those records that contained a term for each of the three component ideas in her research topic. This resulted in 31 records located, far fewer records than in any of the previous lines. Maria can now review cited documents and decide which of the 31 citations she will retrieve. Note that 31 can be taken as the degree of specificity in Maria's topic, a number that is large but not unmanageable.

TABLE 2-4 ERIC CD-ROM output using search strategy in Table 2-3.

SilverPlatter 1.6		ERIC (1/83–3/90) ESC = Commands F1 = Help
No.	**Records**	**Request**
#1	149	Bulimia
#2	117	Anorexia
#3	194	Bulimia or anorexia
#4	8656	Counseling
#5	2765	Therapy
#6	18581	Behavior
#7	2152	Modification
#8	294	Psychiatry
#9	11690	Counseling or therapy or behavior modification or psychiatry
#10	31386	Results
#11	20775	Effectiveness
#12	37757	Evaluation
#13	1785	Outcome
#14	7248	Outcomes
#15	76257	Results or effectiveness or evaluation or outcome or outcomes
#16	31	#3 and #9 and #15

In Table 2-5, we provide an example of a citation that includes full bibliographic information and an article abstract. Note that the article is extremely relevant to Maria, since two different treatment approaches—cognitive-behavioral and nondirective—are compared to see which is more effective with bulimic clients.

When the search is completed and relevant citations are obtained, the documents must be retrieved from library holdings. If a desired document is a journal article, the researcher should consult the library's periodicals list to see if the library has the specific journal and volume needed. If it does, the periodicals list will show a call number indicating where the journal can be found in the library. Although it is possible to read an article and make notes without photocopying it, we recommend that all papers deemed relevant be copied so that a permanent file can be kept, thus enabling quick and easy reference to any particular document. If the library does not have the journal or a particular volume of it, then **interlibrary loan** must be used to request the journal from another library. Interlibrary loan is an arrangement between participating institutions, usually defined by geographic location, to help patrons in different libraries retrieve the information they need by pooling resources. So, if the library at your institution does not have what you need, a form is typically

TABLE 2-5   An example citation of an article from the ERIC database.

SilverPlatter 1.6   **ERIC (1/83–3/90)**

AN: EJ317920
AU: Kirkley.-Betty-G.:And-Others
TI: Comparison of Two Group Treatments for Bulimia
PY: 1985
JN: Journal of Consulting and Clinical Psychology: v53(1), 43–48 Feb 1985
AV: UMI
AB: Examined the relative efficacy of two group treatments for Bulimia patients (N = 28). The cognitive-behavioral group was instructed to make changes in eating and vomiting behavior, whereas the nondirective group was given no instructions. The cognitive-behavioral treatment tended to have fewer dropouts and yielded significantly greater decreases in binging and vomiting.

completed directing library personnel at the nearest library to locate and copy the information requested. Interlibrary loan is usually successful, but it can take several weeks to retrieve information. You should request documents through interlibrary loan early in the review process.

Other Sources

Besides central sources, there are other methods for getting information that we suggest can be used with central sources. These other sources should rarely be used alone because the risk of missing pertinent documents is quite high. These alternate methods are reading books, book chapters, and review articles, as well as contacting authors directly.

BOOKS AND BOOK CHAPTERS.   The value of books and book chapters must be emphasized since a recent textbook or chapter in a book usually contains extensive bibliographies. These bibliographies are helpful in tracking down pertinent information. The most common method for obtaining books and book chapters is through the *library card catalog*. The catalog can be searched manually or by computer if your library has computerized the card catalog. Typically, library card catalogs organize information by author, subject, and title. Each citation contains a complete bibliographic reference as well as call numbers to help you locate the book in the library. Almost every library card catalog is indexed according to the *Library of Congress Subject Headings*, a four-volume document that operates like a thesaurus for the card catalog.

A more recent source in which to search books and book chapters is **PsycBOOKS**, which is published annually by the American Psychological Association. Started in 1987, this annual index includes a cumulative author and subject index and four separate subject volumes: (1) Experimental Psychology—Basic and Applied, (2) Developmental, Personality, and Applied, (3) Professional Psychology—Disorders and Treatment, and (4) Educational and Health Psychology. For single-author books, *PsycBOOKS* contains a complete bibliographical citation, table of contents, and short statement about book content. For edited volumes, *PsycBOOKS* includes a list of chapters, authors of chapters, and statements about the content of chapters and is thus a convenient source for obtaining hard-to-locate books and book chapters.

REVIEW JOURNALS.   A direct and quick way to see what information is available on a topic is to scan a current **review journal.** Editors of review journals are interested in papers that contain extensive literature reviews. Typically, the authors of review papers summarize past findings, attempting to shed light on theoretical issues or methodological weaknesses and provide recommendations for future research. Recent review articles can be found either in the library's current periodical holdings or in a bound journal issue that has been recently shelved. Sometimes, review journals contain a paper relevant to your topic, which means you can locate articles, conference papers, dissertations, books, and book chapters cited in the review author's bibliography. The following is a brief list of review journals in the areas of psychology, education, social work, and nursing:

PSYCHOLOGY:
American Psychologist
Psychological Bulletin
Annual Review of Psychology

EDUCATION:
Review of Educational Research

SOCIAL WORK:
Social Service Review

NURSING:
School Health Review
Health Care Management Review

However, be aware that authors of review articles do not cite all the relevant literature, since writers may not be aware of papers in journals that are not well known. Further, some review writers may deem that a particular piece of research is not of sufficient quality to be included in the review. Also, if the review article was published one or more years ago, you will not have the most recent information, which can be a glaring problem in a literature review. This is why we suggest that you read review articles in conjunction with the use of central sources.

AUTHOR CONTACT.   As the name implies, *author contact* refers to communicating directly with knowledgeable researchers. Sometimes, when students attend a professional conference, they have the opportunity to meet and gather information from researchers already familiar with the topic. Or, while learning more about a research topic, the beginning researcher may call or write those authors who have researched the topic of interest. Authors include their addresses on published documents; this is one way of finding out where to contact them. Also, many professional organizations have membership directories. Ask your reference librarian about which professional associations provide current author affiliations and addresses.

In conjunction with central sources, direct contact with authors can provide yet another valuable source of information on a research topic. Unfortunately, most prospective researchers are intimidated by the idea of contacting well-known investigators. If this fear can be overcome, the benefits are potentially great. One benefit is that these authors are familiar with an area of research and can cite many relevant documents from memory or at least provide several key citations—perhaps even a written bibliography. Another advantage of directly contacting authors is their awareness of the most recent work in a field—work that may not yet be published but is in progress. A citation or two of work in progress may be very valuable to you because it may impress those who evaluate your literature review, such as journal editors or members of thesis committees.

Another advantage of author contact is that experts may know about obscure bibliographic sources or other professional groups in which you can be networked to others. In fact, by contacting several researchers in the area of epistemological thinking, one of the authors of this text became aware of a bibliography of articles about the literature on epistemological thinking as well as an international group devoted entirely to this topic. Had these contacts not been made, this information would have been missed altogether.

Factors Influencing Information Gathering

There are three factors to consider in conducting a literature review: (1) the degree of overlap among sources, (2) the purpose for conducting a literature review, and (3) the need for strategic, systematic use of computer technology.

INFORMATION OVERLAP. What kind of overlap can you expect if you use every central source as well as the additional sources mentioned above? To be sure, each database will contain some redundant information. The exact amount of overlap depends in part on such variables as the thoroughness of the search and the number of databases included. In our experience, a rough estimate of the percentage of overlap between ERIC and PA is about 40%. Add SA, and the duplication across all three sources would be slightly lower. *DAI* conceivably could not overlap at all with ERIC, PA, or SA if you request that no dissertations be cited when you search these other databases. Clearly, some information will be redundant. But, if you exclude a database because of potential overlap, you run the risk of missing the unique citations available only through that particular information source.

PURPOSE FOR CONDUCTING THE LITERATURE REVIEW.   Perhaps the single most important consideration in gathering information is the reason for gathering it, since this reason will influence the expected adequacy of the review. For example, if a literature review is for an undergraduate or graduate term paper and the professor states that at least 10 to 20 references should be cited, you can search the literature in a way that will yield the desired number of references. Perhaps you could scan one central source and a review article. Here, a premium search is not expected.

If your literature review is for a master's thesis, your search plan will need to be more thorough. In this case, you should search at least two major databases and employ alternate retrieval strategies as well. For dissertations and review articles intended for publication, the search strategy will need to be maximal in scope, requiring a search of all relevant central databases as well as other sources. The point is that the purpose of your review determines how thorough it should be. When you review for class assignments or job duties, less effort is usually needed. For other purposes, such as for theses, dissertations, and published articles the review should be much more comprehensive.

COMPUTER TECHNOLOGY.   Finally, the wave of the future in information storage and retrieval will continue to be computer technology. CD-ROM technology is growing rapidly, as are computer work stations in libraries for patron use. As Mason and Bramble (1989) note, this is both a blessing and a bane. The blessing is that computerized databases allow for quick and efficient scanning and for putting thousands of documents at your fingertips. The bane is that using computer technology requires careful, systematic planning. If researchers fail to do the necessary planning, it is conceivable that a large percentage of pertinent research can be missed entirely. If this problem goes uncorrected, the literature review will be poorly conducted, which will be glaringly obvious to those familiar with the topic. The moral of this story is obvious: plan ahead and be strategic in the use of computer technology.

Criteria for Evaluating the Adequacy of Information Gathered

There are several yardsticks by which to judge the adequacy of information retrieval: the number, variety, currency, and spread of references. As a consumer of research, you can use these criteria to evaluate the adequacy of literature reviewed in the studies you read. Or, if you plan to do research, it may be useful to keep these guidelines in mind during your information search.

NUMBER OF REFERENCES.   The number of citations is important but unfortunately it is impossible to provide a set rule about how many citations is enough; every topic has a different amount of previous study. However, even when research on a topic is original or even pioneering, previous, related research exists. If you recall the knowledge structure in Figure 1-2, you will know that a researcher cannot build a completely separate knowledge structure that is disconnected from any other existing information. For example, consider acquired immune deficiency syndrome (AIDS), a phenomenon that gained worldwide attention in the early 1980s. When researchers first began studying AIDS, were there any relevant references? Even if there were no references to AIDS, what about research pertaining to the immune system? What about references having to do with viral strains that affect the immune system? What about general references to viruses? Even though AIDS itself was a new phenomenon, several areas of potential relevance were available to the first researchers.

In sum, while a set number of references cannot be stated, the researcher must cite previous study in areas of closest proximity to the exact topic. As the areas become increasingly removed from the specific focus of the study, citations to more detached areas can be eliminated.

VARIETY OF REFERENCES.   Another consideration in judging the quality of information gathered is the range of information sources included. For example, high-quality reviews include many types of documents: journal articles, books, book chapters, dissertations, manuals, papers presented at meetings, and even unpublished papers. Besides the range of sources, the range within a particular source, especially journal articles, is important. For example, high-quality reviews include references to papers in many different journals, whereas reviews of lesser quality consider only research published in one or two prestigious journals or journals only related to the field most closely aligned to the research. For example, in counseling, only counseling journals would be included. In the former case, researchers may argue that only one or two journals were reviewed because only investigations of the highest standard are published in those journals. While such a case may be made, it is dangerous to assume that good research does not exist in the less prestigious journals. Therefore, we suggest that reviewers cite references from a variety of journals.

CURRENCY OF REFERENCES.   The year of publication of some citations should be close to the publication year of the study. For example, research published in 1993 should include references to research published in 1992 and 1991, perhaps even in 1993. Glaring gaps in information are noted when, for example, a 1993 publication contains no references later than 1988. Readers may wonder what has happened in the last five years.

SPREAD OF REFERENCES.   The expression *spread of citations* refers to (1) citing studies throughout the paper as opposed to just one or two sections and (2) avoiding a predominance of citations from one or two authors. A writer usually includes references in the introduction and discussion, but it is also useful to cite studies related to (1) methodological considerations such as subject and instrument selection and (2) results, especially why particular data analyses were conducted. For a reviewer to do a truly noteworthy job in gathering information, references should be included throughout the manuscript.

Information Analysis: The Researcher as Consumer

Again, becoming knowledgeable about a topic requires the related activities of obtaining, then using available information about the topic. After locating all relevant citations in the library, it would be ideal if the researcher could then walk through the library with a shopping cart, get the needed documents, and then leave within an hour or two. If this were the case, the steps of acquiring information and then analyzing it would be clearly distinct. Unfortunately, since retrieving relevant information can take several months, the researcher will have to start reading papers before all relevant sources are acquired and the two processes will overlap.

In the sections that follow, we provide tips to help you, a prospective researcher, become an informed consumer of topic-related research. Specifically, we divide this section into three parts, beginning with the often overlooked detail of organizing the information you obtain. We then provide tips for reading and analyzing documents and finish with hints for summarizing what you have read.

Document Storage

As you collect information, it is important to organize materials so they are easily accessible. Document storage is best done by developing a centralized storage system. One way to store information is to place material in clearly labeled hanging folders; labels should identify the type of information contained within. For example, Maria could route papers to one of three folders, depending on the emphasis given to her three key ideas—bulimia, treatment approaches, and treatment effectiveness. Another useful storage method is to three-hole punch papers and file them in large, three-ring binders. This is an especially neat, organized, and effective way of keeping papers together. Although document storage may seem of trivial importance, as you accumulate information, you will frequently need to refer to it. The neater and more topically organized your storage system, the easier it will be for you to find materials, which will save time and reduce frustration.

Document Reading

Careful document reading is essential because the formulation of the research plan depends completely on how well you understand previous literature; your depth of understanding is revealed in the *research problem* you detect. That is, as noted earlier, your goal is to find an unresolved problem in previous research, asking general questions like What haven't researchers done yet? or What could researchers do better? or How could this theory be applied in a unique way?

Regarding the research problem, several points should be mentioned. First, how does the research problem fit with identifying a research topic and generating an initial question about it? The first two components—finding a topic and posing a related question—are more rapidly occurring events than finding a research problem. After becoming more knowledgeable, you must examine how other researchers have explored a topic or question, reading with an eye to discovering a problem in need of further exploration. Thus, compared to topic identification and generation of an initial question, finding a research problem is a much more formidable task that requires more time and intellectual effort.

Second, identifying a good research problem depends on two types of knowledge: knowledge of research principles and knowledge of a topic. *Knowledge of general research principles* is understanding measurement, research design, internal and external validity, types of research, and statistical techniques. The more you know about these general research principles and procedures, the easier it is to detect a research problem. For example, if you understand research design, you might detect design flaws in previous literature. Design would then become the research problem. Your research plan can improve on previous design, but such a plan is determined by how much you know about the general principles of research design.

The second type of knowledge is *topic-specific* knowledge. For example, if you were interested in the effectiveness of shelters for battered women and had worked for a shelter agency or read about shelters and the clients they served, your understanding of previous literature and subsequently, skill in identifying a research problem, would be better than without such a background.

As you might guess, finding a problem is easiest when the reader has both knowledge of general research principles and topic-specific knowledge. You may be reading this text to become more knowledegable about the former. Also, after selecting a research topic, stage 2 in empirical research requires you to become something of a topical expert. As you develop knowledge in both domains, you will find it easier to detect problems with previous research—problems that may become the focus of your empirical research.

Finally, because you are not reading previous literature simply to understand it but rather to improve it somehow, you must read differently than you would ordinarily. For example, when reading textbooks, your goal is usually to understand the points presented. However, when reading previous literature, you must not only understand what you read but try to critique, extend, and improve upon it. Because this type of reading is more intensive, we provide reading tips in Table 2-6.

Document Summary

After reading each piece of information, you should do a document summary— that is, condense its contents. You should write or type your summaries on separate pieces of paper (5 × 8 index cards are also useful) and keep those pages with the documents. The organization and content of your summary will de-

TABLE 2-6 Tips for finding problems when reading research.

Idea	Suggestions
Read actively	1. Stop frequently and ask questions. What can you predict?
	2. Look for inconsistencies in arguments.
	3. Extend authors' points (new samples, measurements).
Integrate general research knowledge	1. Classify type of research. (In Chapters 8 and 9, we describe many common types of research.) Identify disadvantages and recommendations for improvement.
	2. Classify research design (Chapters 3 and 5). Note potential weaknesses and ways to improve.
	3. Identify threats to internal and external validity (Chapters 5 and 6); identify multicultural beliefs (Chapter 7).
	4. Identify strengths and weaknesses of the measuring format (Chapter 4).
	5. Verify that proper statistical techniques are used (Chapter 10).
Integrate topic	1. Note your experiences relative to the topic; what would you predict given your experience?
	2. Use your developing knowledge of the topic to integrate one piece of research with the next (e.g., how do articles A and B differ? Do these differences suggest a problem?).
Use creative processes	1. Throughout your reading, let your imagination prevail. Rest frequently, pause, and ask what if. . . .
	2. After completing several research papers, synthesize and unify. What are some common denominators (e.g., use of theory, methods, results).

pend in part on the type of document summarized. If it is a journal article, dissertation, or conference paper that reports original research (not simply reviews other data), the suggested outline and content of the summary provided in Table 2-7 will suffice. If the document is a book, book chapter, review article, or conference paper that reviews but does not present original research, then the summary outline and content will need some adjustment. For example, with a chapter or a review paper, you might organize your summary according to the author's outline and include several pertinent sentences within each section. For a book, your summary might outline specific chapters and include a few comments about their contents.

No matter what type of document is being summarized, the entire summary should fit on one double-spaced page or one 5 × 8 index card. Each summary should contain a full bibliographical citation and not just detail what was in the document. It should also include your personal analysis and critique of the paper.

Why bother with a summary when the document abstract seemingly does the same thing? The author's summary is based on his or her perspective, not yours. Thus, when you summarize an article you are forced to read and analyze it carefully, looking at the research from your viewpoint. Most importantly, since

TABLE 2-7   Organization and content for summarizing journal articles on 5 X 8 index cards.

Full citation: Author(s), year, title, journal, volume, pages

Introduction (Roughly two sentences containing some or all of the following):
   Research question
   Hypotheses
   Why the questions/hypotheses are being investigated

Methods (Roughly two sentences containing some or both of the following):
   Subjects
   Procedures

Results (Roughly two sentences containing the following):
   Findings in relation to hypotheses

Discussion (Roughly two sentences containing some or both of the following):
   Implications
   Limitations

Comments or analysis (Roughly two sentences containing some or all of the following):
   Opinion about article
   Strengths and weaknesses
   Relevance . . . how article fits with your research plans

---

the summaries are handy abstracts written in your words, synthesis across documents may be easier.

LITERATURE REVIEWS

The literature review is a unique research step because it has two partially overlapping purposes. For example, recall that in Chapter 1 we mentioned empirical and nonempirical research and noted that one reason for using reviewed literature is to support the conduct of empirical studies. In these instances, the literature serves as a springboard from which the researcher develops a unique research question. Prior information can serve as support for both the question posed and the methods used to answer the question. As support for a data-based study, the literature review gives foundation for the remaining investigative stages discussed in Chapter 1.

The second use for a literature review is as an end in itself—as a type of nonempirical research. In other words, literature reviews can be written with publication—not more empirical research—as the desired goal. When an author writes with an eye toward publication, the stages of empirical research beyond stage 2 are unnecessary. Indeed, there are many published research articles in which the investigator did not observe a single subject or conduct a single statistical analysis. In these articles, the researcher's goal is to summarize and critique previous research in order to guide future study.

We now focus on this second purpose of literature reviews, treating this type of review as a specific and unique type of research. In the sections that follow, we discuss common elements of literature reviews and provide sample literature reviews from the fields of counseling and nursing.

Common Features

All literature reviews share common features. First, they all rely on bits of information—published articles, paper presentations, technical reports, dissertations, chapters, and books—as the raw materials from which the review is constructed. This puts an absolute premium on the adequacy of the literature search; the reviewer must carefully and comprehensively gather information.

The other similarities of review papers pertain to organization and content. Literature review papers typically begin with an introduction to the topic, and while the content of each review introduction may vary, the review writer must (1) define and describe the theories, variables, or methods used and (2) delineate the questions that will be posed of the research reviewed.

The second and usually longest component of review papers is the presentation of past research. Formats for this presentation vary, depending on the topic reviewed and the questions posed. Sometimes, research can be presented in chronological order—in summary fashion, almost like a string of abstracts. The advantage of this format is its brevity, allowing the reader to go from study to study without interruption. The disadvantage is that presenting abstract after abstract makes it difficult for the reader to figure out how each study answers the initial question developed by the reviewer.

Another format for presenting previous research is to organize the introduction around specific theories and methodologies and then present the literature within each perspective. This format is appropriate when such review questions are posed as, Which theory or methodology is more valid? or What can be learned from a comparison or contrast of position X with position Y?

Finally, writers typically finish the literature review with a conclusion section that addresses personal insights gained from the review and suggestions for further research. In this section, the reviewer must interpret past research; the outcomes of interpretations can be (1) a synthesis of prior research to develop new perspectives for theory development and study, (2) judgments about the relative merits of different theories and methodologies, (3) limitations of past research, or (4) proposals for future investigation.

To help you understand literature reviews better, we summarize two review papers. The first pertains to mental health counseling, the second to nursing.

Illustration from the Literature—Mental Health Counseling

Sharkin (1989) reviewed the literature on how counselor trainees respond to client anger. In the introduction, he notes the importance of eliciting client emotions like anger but shows that counselors in training paradoxically discourage and avoid client expressions of anger. He poses the following questions of the literature: How does the counselor trainee learn to respond to client anger?

and Is the skill of responding to client anger learned with counseling experience, or should it be formally addressed in training programs?

Sharkin's review of past research is organized into three sections; each section contains chronologically ordered studies. The first section reviewed is the nature of counselor trainee responses to anger. Studies reveal that counselors in training find client expressions of anger threatening, anxiety-provoking, and something to be avoided. The second section pertains to counselor response to client anger as a function of experience. The reviewed research shows mixed results; some studies find that experienced counselors are more comfortable with client expressions of anger, and others show the opposite effect. The final section deals with specific training procedures for helping counselor trainees handle client anger. The results from these studies suggest that specific training techniques can be used to improve trainee response to client anger.

The review paper concludes with a section outlining implications for future research. The main recommendations are to (1) systematically incorporate teaching procedures espoused by Sharkin into graduate training programs to help counselor trainees respond more effectively to client anger and (2) develop and validate new teaching procedures through further empirical research.

Illustration from the Literature—Nursing

Kedas, Lux, and Amodeo (1989) reviewed the literature regarding life-cycle changes in sleep patterns. Although not explicitly stated, it appears that the reviewers' intent was to present empirical research relating aging to sleep variables. The implications of this literature review would be relevant to (1) determining the accuracy of previous models of aging and sleep patterns (Kupfer & Reynolds, 1983), (2) delineating methodological and conceptual issues in sleep research with elderly populations, and (3) outlining practical implications for nursing professionals.

As for previous models, the reviewers note that previous literature both supports and disconfirms the Kupfer and Reynolds (1983) model of aging and sleep patterns. For example, Kupfer and Reynolds propose that total sleep time (TST) decreases with age, but the available data show that TST may increase with age, be unrelated to age, or decrease with age, as Kupfer and Reynolds assert.

According to the writers, inconsistent results may be due to several methodological issues, namely how sleep is measured, how long sleep is recorded, the type of subjects studied, and measurement concerns like subjective versus objective sleep data. For instance, from a measurement perspective, there is an inconsistent relationship between subjects' self-report about sleeping behavior and mechanical measures like electroencephalogram (EEG) recordings.

Further, the reviewers identified two conceptual concerns: maturation versus pathology and sleep need versus ability to sleep. In the former, the question is whether changes in sleep patterns for elderly subjects are part of normal maturation or reflect increased psychological and physiological dysfunction. (For example, elderly individuals have insomnia more often and increased brain stem activity). A second unresolved matter is whether elderly people have less need for sleep or have less ability to sleep as well as younger subjects.

Finally, regarding practical implications, the authors believe that although many nursing professionals inform elderly individuals about the negative changes in sleep naturally occurring with increased age, such information ignores the available literature. Thus, nurses are encouraged to read the literature and cautiously consider how previous data relate to their patients' particular sleep practices.

Advantages and Disadvantages

Literature reviews, as just shown, are publishable works. The researcher has two options: conduct the review first, then do a subsequent empirical study based on the review. Thus, the literature review increases the number of publication alternatives. The reviewer could also consider publication without conducting original empirical research. After completing the review, analyzing the literature, and writing the review paper, the author may be in a position to publish the manuscript. Thus, compared to original empirical research, literature reviews may be published with less time and effort.

Perhaps the greatest advantage of doing the literature review is the potential for the review author to direct attention to salient issues in the profession. This is precisely what Sharkin (1989) and Kedas, Lux, and Amodeo (1989) did. In essence, review authors can shape and direct future research in their profession.

Perhaps the single greatest disadvantage in literature reviews is the susceptibility of reviews to an author's particular *interpretive bias*. The reasons behind such biases are many, including personal values, commitment to a particular theoretical or methodological view, wanting to discount the work of research deemed inadequate, or being asked by an editor to adopt a certain perspective to promote debate and further discussion. When bias operates in literature reviews, the writer uses a particular perspective to filter the available research and select primarily the bits of information that support that perspective.

Let us illustrate the point using the chapter vignette. Maria, a novice researcher, had to complete 60 hours of master's level training before being eligible to begin an internship. During her training, she was exposed to several counseling theories and associated techniques. Based on her academic courses and applied experience, she now believes that her interpersonal style is most closely related to client-centered counseling theory. While she does not oppose other counseling theories, she feels that the principles of client-centered counseling are the most effective of all the various views of counseling practice.

Let us suppose that Maria was intent on writing and publishing a nonempirical review of the literature regarding treatment effectiveness for bulimia. Given her theoretical perspective, it is possible that her already ingrained client-centered counseling theory may bias her review. For example, she may be less interested in obtaining all the behavioral intervention papers, or she may read these articles quickly and with less comprehension because she does not see much merit in the behavioral perspective. Thus, the accuracy and comprehensiveness of her review would ultimately reflect the influence of her personal bias.

In addition to the problem of interpretive bias, writing a high-quality review paper is inherently difficult. Consider the degree of abstract thinking required. The author must synthesize previous literature and then (1) identify a single problem with multiple parts or separate problems, (2) show why these problems are significant, and, perhaps most difficult, (3) propose a change that would ameliorate current problems. The researcher must be aware of, and fully understand, previous literature if such synthesis is to occur.

Recommendations for Writing High-Quality Literature Reviews

The review writer must be explicit in describing both how information was located and how it was interpreted. Regarding the former, the literature review writer should show exactly how and where the literature was gathered. This is essential, as is apparent when you recall that literature reviews are derived from bits of information. Therefore, the writer should explicitly state how and where these pieces of information were gathered. By doing so, the reader can evaluate the adequacy of the search. This is why many review writers indicate which sources were searched and include details about the search strategy.

In terms of how the information is interpreted, it is doubtful that a researcher can be completely nonbiased. Values, commitments to theoretical perspectives, and experience result in our developing specific perspectives—perspectives that subtly influence how we gather, read, and interpret information. At the least, whenever personal biases influence the quality of the review, the writer is obliged to inform the reader that such biases are operating, why they are operating, and how these biases will affect the paper.

CONCLUDING COMMENTS

What has Maria learned from her literature review? Recall that Maria's initial research question was, Which treatment— client-centered, cognitive-behavioral, or psychodynamic—is the most effective with bulimic clients? She started with a general research question, then conducted her literature review to see what information was available on this subject. As she read and summarized the relevant documents, her understanding of how bulimia is treated increased, and she came to the following conclusions.

First, Maria now recognizes that her initial question was not a relevant one. She notes that researchers no longer adopt traditional client-centered or psychodynamic approaches because without modifications, these treatments have been found to be inappropriate and ineffective with bulimic clients. Instead, recent researchers have been more interested in combining techniques associated with traditional psychotherapies as well as other experiential and educational group counseling approaches specifically designed for bulimic clients. Based on her analysis of the literature, Maria distills two major treatment approaches for bulimic clients.

One set of counseling techniques Maria has labeled multifaceted; this treatment combines experiential counseling techniques such as anger control, assertiveness, coping, body image, and self-expectations. In this context, bulimic clients are encouraged to explore feelings, self-perceptions, and the role of others in shaping their bulimic behaviors.

Maria has identified another frequently employed treatment strategy as educational in nature, since it involves teaching group members about diet, medication, nutrition, physical health, appropriate eating behavior, and exercise. In contrast to the multifaceted approach, the educational strategy is entirely didactic and informational; personal explorations are not encouraged.

Of most importance, Maria has identified a research problem. Researchers have yet to examine the relative effectiveness of these two group interventions in reducing the inappropriate behaviors associated with bulimia. Since no previous study has compared the relative efficacy of multifaceted and educational interventions, she modifies her research idea to compare the effectiveness of these two treatment approaches in reducing the destructive behaviors associated with bulimia.

Now that Maria has identified a missing fact, she must consider how to translate the problem into an original research study. That is, she must transfer the problem into an empirical research plan. We discuss this plan in the next chapter.

EXERCISES

1. Identify a topic to research. Consider your motives for conducting your research and honestly assess how these motives will facilitate or hinder your scientific pursuit.
2. Given the question, "How effective is Beck's Cognitive Theory in helping Chinese clients with depression?", develop a search plan following the four steps in conducting a computer search.
3. Compare and contrast data and non-data based research in terms of the eight stages of empirical research discussed in Chapter 1. What are the advantages and disadvantages of non-data based research?
4. After reading the paper by White and Franzoni (1990) in Appendix E, evaluate the following:
   a. Number of references.
   b. Variety of references.
   c. Currency of references.
   d. Spread of references.
   e. Does the literature reviewed clearly support the hypothesis given? Why or why not?

5. If you are planning on doing a thesis, carry out the following activities:
   a. Identify a research area. In reviewing your topic, is it broadly or narrowly stated? If broadly stated, make it more narrow. If narrowly stated, make it broader.
   b. Engage in some hands-on learning at your university library:
       I. Select a topic and make a list of all relevant information sources that might be useful.
      II. Use your selected topic, find five articles in both ERIC and PSYCHLIT and print out the abstracts.
     III. Go to the *Dissertation Abstracts International* (DAI) and find three abstracts related to your subject. Evaluate their usefulness.
      IV. Explore ERIC, PA, SA, Interlibrary loan, and DAI to find 10 topic-specific sources of information regarding a topic of your choice.
       V. Do a document summary of the literature you have found in the above literature review. Follow instructions in Table 2-7.
      VI. Summarize an assigned journal article using the outline suggested in Table 2-7. Compare your summary with the author's abstract and note similarities and differences.
     VII. Pick a sample psychological research term and, before consulting the *Thesaurus of Psychological Terms*, give two examples each of broader terms, narrower terms, and related terms. Determine how accurate your examples were by consulting the *Thesaurus of Psychological Terms*.

3

GETTING STARTED: DEVELOPING THE RESEARCH PLAN

MARIA REALIZES she must develop a research plan showing how she will investigate the problem she identified in her literature review. First, she begins by formulating a final research question: "Which approach—multifaceted or educational—is more effective in treating bulimic women? Second, she develops hypotheses about her research question. One hypothesis is that bulimic university women who receive 3 months of weekly, multifaceted group counseling will show fewer incidents of binging and purging than bulimic women who receive 3 months of weekly, educational group counseling.

Third, while Maria thinks this would be the outcome of a study comparing the two approaches, she considers various threats to the validity of this conclusion. Some potential concerns might be that (1) her expectations may influence the results and (2) if subjects are aware that two groups exist, they might react in a way that would change the results. For example, educational-group subjects may try to outdo multifaceted-group subjects because they correctly believe that their group is expected to show less improvement. Fourth, assuming that her data are reasonably valid, Maria considers their generalizability. To whom can she apply the data? Under what conditions can it be applied, and what research procedures should be used? Fifth, Maria is aware that the different cultural perspectives of her participants may influence the data. For example, members of a particular culture may respond negatively to multifaceted groups if they are less comfortable expressing their feelings openly.

Sixth, Maria considers some ethical concerns; she determines how she will ensure that all subjects are treated humanely; she plans to see that they are properly informed and sufficiently debriefed. Seventh, Maria begins planning how she will measure subjects' responses by identifying the constructs of interest as *bulimia* and *treatment*. She defines each operationally: (1) bulimia will be defined as a total score on some test that measures related symptoms of bulimia; and (2) treatment will consist of two conditions—one educational and the other multifaceted. Treatment is further operationally defined by the specific techniques associated with each group. For instance, educational-group participants will receive relevant information about diet, nutrition, and appropriate eating habits; the multifaceted members will be encouraged to express their feelings about self and others.

Maria decides to run treatment groups for 3 months, and after all participants have completed either the educational or multifaceted treatment program, she will posttest all subjects. Eighth, Maria turns to practical constraints such as setting up a time line for completing proposed research activities and determining the costs to be incurred during the investigation. After completing time and cost analyses, she is confident that she can complete her study in a timely fashion and that she can afford the expenses associated with her study. Finally, Maria's choice of a statistical technique is the *t*-test for the difference between two gains.

C onsider an analogy between research and home construction. In home construction, builders map out a blueprint detailing how a home will be constructed. The plan represents substantial thought and preparation by the designer and as a result is extremely detailed, including all the specifics about where materials should go, the order of construction steps, and possibly, the reasons the designer developed the plan in a certain way—why a window is here or a door is there. The purpose of the plan is to describe exactly how the house will be built and the order in which the stages of construction will proceed.

Similarly, a **research plan** is the blueprint that guides the researcher in answering the question posed. Once the researcher recognizes that a question exists, he or she can begin determining how the question will be addressed. Development of the plan is a unique part of the investigative process in which the researcher relies on intellectual powers of reasoning, logic, creativity, and imagination. A well thought out research plan is critical if the research is to be of good quality.

The elements to consider in developing the final research plan are given in Figure 3-1. First, note that the research question is interrelated with all the other plan elements. Figure 3-1 shows that a researcher can start with a research question and use the question as a lead in determining hypotheses, design, and all subsequent plan elements related to design. Researchers can deduce (downward arrows) the entire research plan from the question. On the other hand, the research question frequently needs modification as a result of the planning considerations. For example, after considering the multicultural element, Maria could modify her question by expanding it to include both the general effectiveness of one treatment as opposed to another and the effectiveness of treatment according to ethnicity. Note that the research question would be altered to reflect this modification and that this type of modification is done inductively—from specific parts of the plan to the more general question.

Second, Figure 3-1 shows that a researcher's topic knowledge is intimately related to the research question. It follows that a thorough understanding of previous research is a prerequisite to the development of a sound research plan.

DEVELOPING A RESEARCH QUESTION

A **research question** shows the overall focus of a research study by revealing the general topic under investigation. Essentially, research questions are restatements of the research problem in question form. Consider Maria's final research question: Which approach—multifaceted or educational—is most effective in treating bulimic women? Although data addressing this question have important implications, the problem is that researchers have yet to compare these two treatments.

In developing a research question, four factors must be considered. First, it is assumed that every research question is to some extent a novel one. Certainly, the researcher is looking for new problems to solve when reading existing literature. When it comes time to formulate the research plan, the researcher should be secure in the feeling that the question is unique. Even when researchers make a concerted effort to duplicate a previous research procedure, the research question itself changes. The new question is, Can the results of study X be replicated? As noted in Chapter 1, this is why knowledge structures for research topics are dynamic.

Second, research questions must be researchable; that is, they must be objective, testable, and verifiable. For example, could the question, Do ghosts exist? be researched? How would one go about it? Because there actually is no method for answering this question, it cannot be researched. If the question were changed to, Do a majority of people in Anywhere, U.S. believe in ghosts?, then it could be researched. A single question about whether people of a given community believe in ghosts could be mailed to a representative sample of the community and the data tabulated to answer the question.

Another unresearchable question would be, What is the best way to rear children? This question is unresearchable since what is best is a value judgment that cannot be empirically verified. One should ask, best in what way? On the other hand, the question, Do children with permissive parents develop greater self-esteem than children with authoritarian parents? could be researched. The revised question has empirical referents—namely, children's self-esteem and permissive and authoritarian parenting styles, all of which could be objectively defined and studied. When you generate a research question, ask yourself, Can the question be researched? Does it imply a method for answering it that is

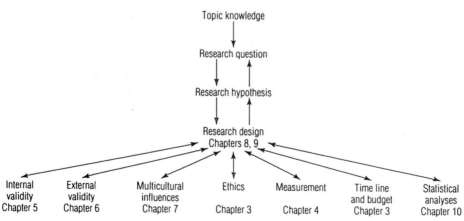

FIGURE 3-1 Components of the research plan.

objective, testable, and verifiable? If the answer is yes, your research question satisfies these criteria. If your question does not suggest a way to find an answer, it needs further refinement.

Third, the feasibility of the research question is important. Feasibility refers to practical issues such as the amount of time and money needed to answer the question. Consider this research question: Does early school prevention program X change high school students' drug and alcohol use when compared with students who do not receive prevention program X? This is a researchable question, but is it feasible? The method for answering it would involve following two groups of preschoolers, one participating in the prevention program and one not receiving the program, through high school. It would take roughly 14 years before all the data were collected. While this may very well be an interesting and worthwhile research question, it is clearly not very feasible for a student. The answer to the feasibility issue ultimately depends on the anticipated timeline for completion of the research study (which we discuss later in this chapter) and the resources available, such as equipment, rooms in which to meet research subjects, and the amount of time the researcher has free daily to devote to the research study. When developing your research question, pause to consider whether or not you can answer it within the context of your setting, your purpose, and the time you have available to devote to research.

Finally, the research question must be significant, either from a basic or applied science perspective. A straightforward test with which to determine the significance of a research question is the "so what?" test. In other words, ask yourself—now that you know a preliminary answer to the research question—so what? Consider the following question: How do people chew gum? Assume that the results show that people use different chewing motions—up and down or side to side or both. What is the theoretical or practical significance of these results? It is difficult to see the significance of the study for theory, and knowing that people use different chewing motions seems of little use to anyone, even to dentists. The sheer triviality of the topic would raise questions about its significance.

DEVELOPING RESEARCH HYPOTHESES

A hypothesis is a declarative statement about problem solution and predicted outcomes. It modifies the general research question by making it clear what solution will be used to answer the question and the expected outcomes of the solution. Recall Maria's final research question: Which approach—multifaceted or educational—is most effective in treating bulimic women? A hypothesis about this question could be: Bulimic university women who receive 3 months of weekly, multifaceted-group counseling will show less binging and purging than women who receive 3 months of weekly, educational-group counseling.

We next describe three basic types of hypotheses. First, whenever a researcher has reason to believe that the expected outcomes of a study can be stated precisely and that one group should fare better than another group, the hypothesis should be stated to reflect this prediction. This is called a **directional hypothesis;** the researcher predicts the direction of the outcome—either Group A will be higher than Group B or Group B will be higher than Group A. Recall Maria's hypothesis—bulimic university women who receive 3 months of weekly, multifaceted-group counseling will show *less* binging and purging than women who receive 3 months of weekly, educational-group counseling. Since her hypothesis predicts that the multifaceted group will have fewer incidents of binging and purging than the educational group, it is a directional hypothesis.

How can a researcher predict an outcome before a study begins? Or, in Maria's case, why does she believe that multifaceted-group counseling will reduce bulimic behaviors more than the educational treatment? Predicting outcomes is really an educated guessing game. Clues can be found in the literature, in personal experiences, and in the experiences of others. Some element of guessing is involved because a proposed study has never been conducted, so the results are not certain. Consider Maria's study. If the multifaceted approach had already been compared with the educational approach using the same methodology, her research question would already have a partial answer. She would need to change her research question to focus on another clue provided in the literature such as length of counseling, individual vs. group counseling, or the duration or severity of the bulimic condition.

Second, if researchers feel less confident about predicting the direction of an outcome, a **nondirectional hypothesis** can be stated. A nondirectional hypothesis states that the groups will differ but does not state exactly how. In Maria's case, a nondirectional hypothesis would be: Bulimic university women who receive 3 months of weekly, multifaceted-group counseling will show *different* rates of binging and purging than women who receive 3 months of weekly, educational-group counseling. Note that the only difference between this nondirectional hypothesis and the directional one is that the word "different" (no direction) is substituted for "lower."

It is critical to understand that if a researcher states a nondirectional hypothesis and a difference emerges, the researcher can only conclude that the groups differed. The researcher cannot conclude direction after the fact. Thus, a researcher's conclusions are severely restricted when nondirectional hypotheses are employed. Because of this, we strongly encourage using directional hypotheses.

Finally, both directional and nondirectional research hypotheses can be contrasted with what is called the statistical or **null hypothesis**—a hypothesis that states that there is no relationship or difference between experimental conditions and that whatever differences might be observed are so small as to be due to chance. The null hypothesis is a statistical concept that we will discuss in more detail in Chapter 10. In Maria's case, the null hypothesis would be: Bulimic university women who receive 3 months of either weekly, multifaceted- or educational-group counseling will not show different rates of binging and purging.

Comparing and Contrasting Research Questions and Hypotheses

Research questions and hypotheses differ on two dimensions. One is a grammatical difference—research questions end in question marks, while hypotheses are declarative statements. The other difference is that research questions are general, while hypotheses are more specific. For example, when posing a research question, the variables are referred to loosely. A treatment may be described as generic; outcome may be described in general terms. On the other hand, a hypothesis contains more specific information about the variables. Treatment format—whether individual or group—or length of treatment may be specified. Also, general terms like "outcome" would be more specifically defined in a hypothesis. In this case, outcome might be defined as "number of self-reported incidents of binging and purging."

To illustrate the difference between a research question and a hypothesis, we provide Figure 3-2, which shows a topic presented earlier in Table 2-1. The topic was child-rearing, and one of the initial research questions posed was, What is the most effective discipline technique for temper tantrums? In Figure 3-2, we expand this question to include several possible hypotheses about it. Each hypothesis is a more specific form of the general question it represents. Thus, instead of mentioning discipline in general, specific discipline techniques are given such as planned ignoring, response cost, punishment, and differential reinforcement of other behavior. Further, "temper tantrums" becomes a measurable phenomenon, since the hypotheses contain expressions like, "parent report of frequency of temper tantrums."

Locating Research Questions and Hypotheses in Research Articles

As we noted in Figure 3-1, formulating the research question and the experimental hypotheses are the first stages in making the research plan. After completing these two steps, the researcher has already achieved a significant amount of direction and focus. Given the importance of the research question and the hypotheses, we believe that researchers should include the research question and associated hypotheses in the research report. We find that the clearest research reports are the ones that masterfully weave past literature with the investigator's question and hypotheses. Unfortunately, research questions are rarely stated in research articles, and while hypotheses are given more often, we think they should always be included in the written report. There seems to be a tacit and questionable assumption that readers can infer the research question and its associated hypothesis without seeing them in print. Further, some writers so

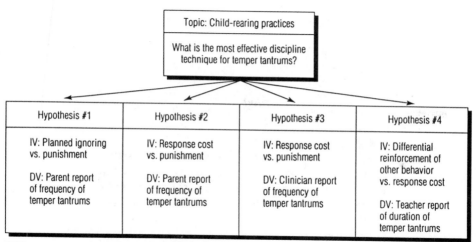

NOTE: IV = independent variable; DV = dependent variable.

FIGURE 3-2   Going from research question to research hypotheses.

emphasize the previous literature that little space is given to how the literature led to the proposed research question or to hypotheses about it. Thus, often the reader is left to infer either the research question, the hypotheses, or both.

If you are reading a research report in which either the research question or the hypotheses are not explicitly given, we offer the following tips to increase your successful creation of these missing elements. First, sometimes research questions and hypotheses are disguised as purposes for which the study was conducted. For example, if Maria says that the purpose of her study is to determine the relative efficacy of multifaceted and educational treatments in reducing bulimic behavior, the reader can simply turn this purpose into a question.

Second, while it seems most logical to state the research question and hypotheses early in the paper, perhaps in an introduction section, this is not always done. We recommend scanning the entire paper first to see whether the writer may have stated the research question or hypotheses in later sections of the paper, possibly in a method section, results section, or even in the discussion. In our experience, the best way to infer the hypotheses is to look in the results section because each bit of analyzed data implies a research hypothesis. As you come to understand statistics and as you read more research reports, making these inferences will become increasingly easy.

MARIA REVISITED

Let us now examine Maria's research question in terms of (1) the four factors related to research questions and (2) how her research question and hypothesis differ in terms of specificity. First, is Maria's question novel, researchable, feasible, and significant? As for novelty, since Maria found that no previous investigators had compared the relative effectiveness of the two bulimia treatments, her question is original.

Is her question researchable? Yes, it is. Note how a method is implied (but not directly stated) for answering the question in the way it is worded. The implication is that Maria will form two counseling groups; one will receive a multifaceted treatment; the other will receive educational treatment. After group intervention, some measure of bulimic eating behavior such as self-reported incidents of binging and purging could be obtained to compare the effectiveness of each group in altering bulimic eating habits. With a good research question, the methods for answering it are easily inferred even when they are not directly stated.

Is her question feasible? Yes, it is feasible because she already counsels bulimic subjects. She could use the counseling center to conduct the two treatment groups. Further, subjects could be expected to improve in the period of a semester. The amount of money needed would be minimal, perhaps limited to the copying costs for some paper materials such as interview sheets, self-report questionnaires, and consent forms.

Finally, is her question significant? Maria's results have great practical implications because knowing the most effective treatment would be important to all clinicians who see bulimic clients.

What about the specificity difference in Maria's research question and hypothesis? Her hypothesis is stated specifically so that it can be tested. Bulimic participants will receive 3 months of either multifaceted- or educational-group counseling and the effect of each treatment can be compared by examining participants' self-reported incidents of binging and purging. This method was never directly given in her research question. In addition, her hypothesis specifies an expected outcome: multifaceted counseling is predicted to be more effective than educational counseling. No such outcome is predicted in her research question.

RESEARCH DESIGN

Research design refers to the procedures the researcher uses to address a research question and its associated hypotheses. We refer to research design as the label given to general research procedures like correlational, experimental, survey, and so on. In fact, it is common to hear of correlational design or quasi-experimental design because these terms refer to the general methods used to examine research questions and hypotheses. While we introduce some aspects of research design in this chapter, in Chapters 7, 8, and 9 we will specifically cover seven general research designs: case study, correlational, survey, developmental, ex post facto, quasi-experimental, and experimental.

Again, once the researcher has a research question and related hypotheses, much of the research design is delimited. In fact, as noted earlier, if the research question is properly stated an implicit research procedure follows logically. For example, given Maria's research question, design considerations narrow considerably, leaving her the logical choice of using two groups to determine the effectiveness of these groups on an outcome related to bulimia. In addition, if the researcher were interested in asking a question like What is the relationship between variables X and Y?, the logical research design to use would be correlational because a correlational procedure is required by this type of research question (as we discuss in detail in Chapter 8).

As Figure 3-1 reveals, research design is a multidimensional concept consisting of seven general topics. It is useful to consider the material in subsequent chapters when planning a research study. Further, knowledge of research design will help researchers uncover meaningful research problems when reading existing literature.

In this chapter, we introduce research design concepts. When an entire chapter is to be devoted to a particular design element—as internal validity is the subject of Chapter 5—we only define the term in this chapter, reserving extended discussion for later.

VALIDITY: INTERNAL AND EXTERNAL

A fundamental goal for all researchers is to get valid results. Researchers want to conclude that the results were due to factors under investigation and to no other factors. This is referred to as *internal validity*. For instance, Maria wants to conclude that it was her treatment, and no other factor, that created the change in bulimic behavior. Can she conclude this with any degree of confidence? The answer to this question, in part, depends on how well Maria controls for other influences like subject perceptions, her own biases, adequacy of her measurement system, and many other factors. Because internal validity is such a fundamental research concept, Chapter 5 is entirely devoted to considerations regarding this type of validity.

Whereas internal validity concerns the degree to which the variables under investigation explain the results, *external validity* pertains to the degree to which the results are generalizable. One basic type of external validity is **population validity**—the degree to which results generalize to the researcher's population of interest or to the consumer's population of interest. For example, Maria may wish to generalize her results to all bulimic college women in the world. Can she make this generalization? How confident can we be that her results are generalizable to all bulimic women in the world? Similarly, the reader of research must consider how applicable the results are to his or her population. For example, assume that a consumer is interested in the treatment of eating disorders in college students and reviews Maria's research outcomes. Can the consumer apply this outcome to eating disorders other than bulimia, possibly to anorexia? Can the reader apply the results to another sample of bulimic college students in another geographic region or to a sample of women of a different ethnicity or socioeconomic status?

In the sections that follow, we briefly introduce concepts central to population validity. We will more thoroughly explore population validity in Chapter 6.

Population

Usually, we think of a **population** as an entire set of people or objects. For example, in common parlance, the population of AnyCity, U.S. defines all the people living in AnyCity. Populations can be construed broadly as the population of all women with bulimia in the world or more conservatively as the population of bulimic women in the college in which Maria conducts her research.

Sample

A **sample** is a subset of people or objects selected from a population—a segment of the population but not the entire population. If we observe 100 people from AnyCity, these 100 individuals define a sample from the AnyCity population. A key word in the definition of sample is *selection* since samples are selected from populations.

Sampling Techniques

There are three general sampling techniques. One is a **simple random sample,** which requires that (1) every member of the population has an equal chance of being selected for inclusion in the sample and (2) the selection of any member of the population does not preclude the selection of any other population member. An example of simple random sampling would be if a researcher defines 200 hyperactive fourth- through sixth-grade boys in School District X as the population and the first 50 randomly drawn names (drawn from a hat) as the sample. A simple random sample is illustrated in Figure 3-3.

Another sampling technique is **stratified random sampling,** a procedure requiring the researcher to divide the population into categories and then use simple random sampling to select subjects from within these categories. This type of sample is commonly used in tests of intelligence, achievement, and personality because the goal in developing a norm-referenced test is to select test standardization subjects according to the same categories (ethnicity, sex, income level) and percentages within categories as they occur in the population. For

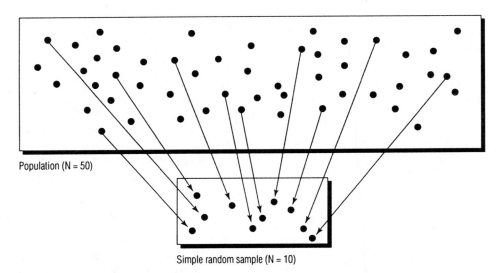

Population (N = 50)

Simple random sample (N = 10)

FIGURE 3-3   Simple random sample.

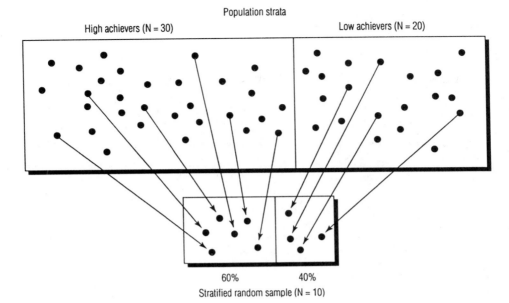

Population strata

High achievers (N = 30)   Low achievers (N = 20)

60%   40%
Stratified random sample (N = 10)

FIGURE 3-4   Stratified random sample.

example, if the population is 2% Asian, the researcher would select a sample that is also 2% Asian. A random sample stratifying achievement in a population of hyperactive children is given in Figure 3-4. Note that the final sample will consist of 60% high achievers and 40% low achievers.

Perhaps the most common type of sample in helping professions research is the **convenience sample**. As the name implies, a convenience sample is a sample nearest at hand, specifically those subjects who happen to be most available for research participation. Convenience samples do not require the researcher to select subjects systematically from the population as do the other two techniques. Examples of convenience samples are (1) an outpatient group of hyperactive children, (2) a group of high school students seen by Counselor X, and (3) students in Professor Z's psychology class. A convenience sample is illustrated in Figure 3-5. Note that only the population elements nearest at hand are selected.

Random Assignment

Random assignment is not a sampling procedure per se but a method for assigning each member of a selected sample to a certain group or treatment. Once the final sample is obtained, the researcher uses a random selection technique to place subjects in at least two different groups. For example, after selecting the final sample of 50 hyperactive children, these children could be randomly assigned to one of two treatment groups—Ritalin alone or behavior

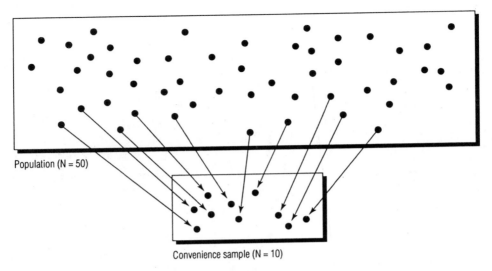

Population (N = 50)

Convenience sample (N = 10)

FIGURE 3-5   Convenience sample.

modification alone. As will be clear later, random assignment is the essence of experimental research. In Figure 3-6, we depict random assignment to groups from a randomly selected sample.

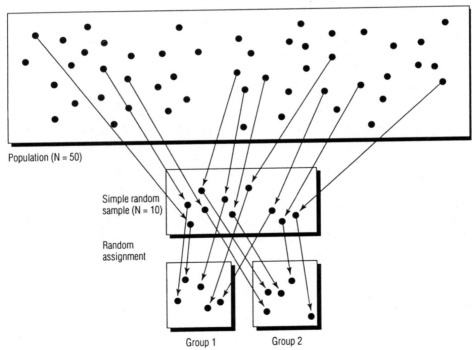

Population (N = 50)

Simple random sample (N = 10)

Random assignment

Group 1   Group 2

FIGURE 3-6   Groups randomly assigned from a random sample.

In Chapter 6, population validity, as well as other forms of external validity, will be discussed in detail. We will also return to Maria's research to see how she applied population validity concepts.

MULTICULTURAL INFLUENCES

Individuals do not participate in research as blank slates with no prior conceptions about scientific investigation. More likely, individuals have unique perceptions about the relevance and meaning of empirical study (Wilkinson & Migotsky, 1994). The cultural background of research participants probably plays a key role in shaping perceptions about scientific research. Given the increasingly multicultural context in which researchers now conduct investigation, it may prove beneficial to consider how culture affects the research process. The role of cultural diversity as it pertains to investigation is the focus of Chapter 7. Briefly though, researchers should analyze how cultural differences affect their research, especially (1) the degree to which culture interacts with the variables of interest and (2) the generalization of results in light of the specific cultural influences of the investigator, subjects, and setting. If researchers take a proactive stance regarding the relevance and possible inclusion of multicultural factors, then the meaningfulness of research results will be greatly increased.

ETHICS IN RESEARCH

Ethics are generally considered to be the moral obligation of professionals to ply their trades appropriately, competently, and with respect for the consumers they serve. Similarly, in research, human subjects must be treated with dignity, fairness, and respect.

Why are ethics considered to be a separate element in the research plan? The moral obligation of researchers to prevent unethical treatment of human participants requires that ethical issues be carefully considered before an investigation is begun. The outcomes of a researcher's deliberations regarding ethics may affect the research design. For example, in treatment outcome studies, researchers may decide to compare a new treatment with no treatment. Is it fair to withhold a new treatment from those who need it? Should the new treatment be compared to an existing treatment? In the case of discipline techniques for temper tantrums, is it ethical for parents to use corporal punishment? As you can see, decisions about ethical issues can greatly influence the research design.

Next, we discuss ethical principles germane to human subjects research; our discussion is based on the ethical principles developed by the American Psychological Association (APA). Note that ethical codes are developed within specific helping professions, so researchers should consult relevant specialty area ethics. For example, medical researchers should subscribe to American Medical Association research ethics. We chose the APA ethical guidelines because (1) these research ethics are pertinent to a wide range of helping professionals and (2) APA research ethics are thorough and well explicated. In Appendix A, we provide the latest APA guidelines for human subjects research (1992). Initially, we address research roles, then, using Appendix A as a guide, we focus on the fundamental research ethics of responsibility (6.07), informed consent (6.11), debriefing (6.18), and institutional approval (6.09).

OVERSEEING ETHICS: WHO IS RESPONSIBLE?

Before discussing specific research ethics, a general concern is, Who is primarily accountable for ensuring that ethical codes are followed? Responsibility for ethics is based on clear definitions of research roles and the associated responsibilities of each party for ensuring that ethical standards are met.

Research Roles

The following roles have been suggested (APA, 1982). The first is that of **principal investigator** (PI)—the person who conceives of, designs, and plans the research study. Where there is one PI and that person carries out all phases of research without assistance, responsibility for the ethical treatment of subjects lies solely with this individual. If there is more than one PI, the ethical treatment of subjects is the shared responsibility of all.

Another role is that of **research assistant,** the individual (or individuals) who help the PI with such activities as subject recruitment, data collection, and data analysis. Research assistants are just as responsible for the ethical treatment of subjects as the PI, but the PI must ensure that research assistants are knowledgeable about ethical codes and must supervise assistants to ensure that ethical standards are followed.

Finally, the **research supervisor** is typically an experienced researcher or academic trainer who advises students or employees in independent research. An example would be academic faculty in graduate training programs who supervise students in the completion of a master's thesis or a doctoral dissertation. Again, the responsibility of meeting ethical research standards is shared by both student and supervisor. However, unlike research assistants, graduate students fulfilling research requirements are usually knowledgeable about ethical procedures and have been trained to conduct independent research. Therefore, the relationship between supervisor and student is one of mutual respect, and the APA guidelines make it clear that if the student has difficulty with an ethical aspect of research, the supervisor must respect the student's opinion.

Besides research roles, researchers usually have other professional functions such as professor, mental health practitioner, or administrator. Researchers may interact with human subjects both as a researcher and in some other professional capacity, which creates the possibility of *dual relationships.*

The problem with dual relationships is that research subjects may feel obligated to participate in order to gain credibility with researchers in some other professional interaction. Thus, participants may feel coerced. Their voluntary involvement is in fact violated. A case in point is a professor who requires students to participate in his or her research as part of student evaluation. Students may not want to participate, but they know their grades will be in jeopardy if they do not.

While all dual relationships should be avoided, if this is not possible, the researcher must minimize the degree to which subjects' participation is involuntary. For example, voluntary involvement would be increased if students could participate in research other than with their own professors. Also, professors could allow students to select an assignment other than research as part of academic evaluation.

Risks in Research

Every ethical code regarding research is designed to ensure that participants are treated humanely. Indeed, one of the researcher's primary objectives is to consider the ethicality of the proposed study, paying primary attention to subject risks. Such risks may be physical, involving pain, exposure to loud noises, or electric shock; or risks can be psychological, as when anxiety or stress are induced or when subjects unexpectedly experience psychological distress.

Whenever potential risks to participants are identified, the researcher is obligated to seek ethical advice and consider alternate research methods that would yield similar results but reduce any harm to subjects. If no such alternate methods are available and the research is deemed of significant scientific worth, the researcher further reduces risk factors by (1) ensuring that subjects are fully aware of the risks, (2) recognizing that their participation is voluntary, (3) eliminating certain subject groups—for example, not including children in a learning study using electric shock—and (4) taking necessary safety precautions such as ensuring that equipment is in good working condition.

Further, there may be instances in which risk is not expected initially, but the possibility exists that participants may react negatively to research treatments. For example, a therapy condition that increases subject discomfort or provides potentially self-damaging information—a subject might reveal significant depression on a personality inventory—could jeopardize a participant's well-being. Such negative reactions and information must be carefully monitored by the researcher, and when signs of discomfort emerge, it is the researcher's duty to remove these consequences. For example, the researcher could remove the participant from the aversive treatment. Additionally, ethical dilemmas can arise when researchers employ control groups.

Control Groups

Some researchers in the helping professions use a **control group** in which participants agree to have treatment withheld in order to compare the effects of newly developed interventions with a no-intervention baseline. The ethical issue is that control-group participants must delay receiving potentially beneficial treatments. Because the delay in receiving treatment may increase subject discomfort, the ethical concern is for protecting the welfare of the control-group participants. Note that the key word is *potentially* beneficial. Without data, whether or not treatment is beneficial remains an unanswered question and answering the question is the point of the proposed research project. Logically, however, it must be assumed that the new treatment will prove to be effective, otherwise the use of control groups would not be an ethical concern.

One way to reduce risk to control-group subjects is to compare the treatment with already existing treatment(s) of known effectiveness. That is, researchers should try to eliminate the need for a no-treatment control group, but this solution is only applicable when such a treatment exists. For example, in Maria's research, assume that previous results indicate that the educational approach reduces bulimic symptoms better than earlier treatments. However, she recognizes that the multifaceted approach is emerging as a viable competitor to the educational approach. Therefore, her decision to compare the two treatments avoids the ethical issue because all subjects are presumed to be receiving effective treatments.

When such alternate interventions do not exist, the researcher cannot immediately prevent possible negative side-effects for subjects in the control group. However, if the treatment under consideration does prove to be effective, the researcher is obliged to see that control-group subjects have access to the treatment when the research concludes. When this strategy is used, subjects are said to be in a **wait-list control group**—participants who do not receive treatment but who will have immediate access to treatment once the results are known.

Informed Consent

Informed consent is an explicit agreement between subject and researcher specifying the responsibilities of each. There are two key issues with respect to informed consent. The first is the question of when consent is needed. When research is minimal in risk, it is permissible to omit consent. For example, a minimal-risk study would be when a researcher is interested in the effects of advance stop lines and warnings on drivers' stopping behavior. This researcher can hardly leave an observation post, run out into the street, ask subjects to sign a consent form, and then have the driver put the car in reverse to see what happens at the stop sign the second time the driver approaches it. This study contains a minimal risk—in fact it may lower the risk of accidents—and consent would not be needed. Although determining when consent is needed is not always so easy, several guidelines can be found in an article by Davison and Stuart (1975).

The second matter concerns explicitness. This is a complex concern, mainly because it requires the researcher to find a balance between subject awareness of study objectives and the degree of **concealment** or **deception** required. Concealment involves omitting key features of the study, such as methodological manipulations, while deception is misinforming participants about the purpose of the study. Some argue that concealment and deception are necessary if researchers are to obtain valid data. Some researchers contend that when participants are truthfully informed of study goals, their suggestibility and desire to perform in socially desirable ways will vitiate obtained data.

Other investigators believe that subjects should receive complete and accurate information about study objectives and that concealment and deception are contrary to the meaning of informed consent. Because the balance between informed consent and concealment and deception is so troublesome, APA guidelines enumerate specific points (6.15 and 6.18) that researchers should consider in making this decision.

Informed consent can be viewed as a general ethical principle with many sub-parts, specifically (1) requirements and expected benefits, (2) voluntary nature of participation, and (3) confidentiality of data. We discuss each of these issues next.

REQUIREMENTS AND EXPECTED BENEFITS.   Informed consent typically includes statements about what the researcher expects from participants and what the researcher's obligations are. With respect to the former, researchers need to inform subjects about what they will do during the study and how long participation will take. As for the latter, the researcher's commitments are discussed, such as answering participants' questions during or after the study.

In addition, the expected benefits of the study are clarified. Expected benefits are many but can be roughly divided into external benefits such as extra credit points or money or internal benefits such as personal knowledge or recognizing one's contribution to the advancement of science.

VOLUNTARY NATURE OF PARTICIPATION.   One guarantee typically included in informed consent is that subjects' participation in research is **voluntary.** That is, subjects are informed that they have the freedom to participate or to withdraw their participation whenever they want to without penalty.

Unfortunately, the voluntary nature of research usually competes with some type of external inducement (see principle 6.14). The famous introductory psychology class subject pool is a great example, because these subjects most likely participate for extra credit or as a required part of the course. Their participation can hardly be called voluntary. The same is true in many other instances, but it is especially troublesome when subjects feel that not participating would jeopardize their position, perhaps even adversely affect a professor's opinion or an employer's perception. Thus, it is incumbent upon researchers·to stress the voluntary nature of research participation and ensure that the consent agreement is very explicit about subjects' choices regarding participation.

CONFIDENTIALITY.   Finally, consent forms must address the issue of **confidentiality,** which refers to subjects' right to privacy and includes subject anonymity and disclosure of information. A consent form should be explicit about confidentiality. A researcher can ensure confidentiality by (1) using identification codes and not subjects' names in scoring protocols, (2) not disclosing information to a third party without the prior consent of the participant, and (3) not using any names in subsequent research reports. Limitations to confidentiality might include legal restrictions. For example, research data might be requested by the court. The discovery of potentially damaging information during the research study, such as a subject showing signs of suicidal ideation, would also limit confidentiality.

Debriefing

While informed consent is the initial agreement between subject and researcher, **debriefing** is the concluding information provided to subjects. Typically, when subjects are debriefed, misconceptions that may have developed during participation are clarified. Considerations regarding debriefing include (1) how it will be given, individually or in groups, and (2) the precise wording of debriefing. How much about the research plan—the research question, the hypotheses, the sample—should be revealed? Also, researchers using concealment or deception should give a clear rationale for doing so.

Institutional Review Boards

All the ethical issues we have discussed are initially addressed by the researcher, either alone or in consultation with other professionals. As a further check on the ethical acceptability of proposed research, most institutions have review boards that are composed of individuals familiar with institutional policies, legal mandates, and ethical principles. Researchers typically submit to this board a brief description of the study as well as ethical issues, along with assurances that the welfare of subjects will be safeguarded. In minimal-risk research, ethical issues are diminished, and it is likely that the review board will accept the proposed study. However, as risk increases, the board may request further information of the researcher before the study will be approved. The review board may reject the proposed research, requiring that the researcher reconsider study purposes, methodological alternatives, or ethical safeguards.

MARIA REVISITED

Maria assumes the position of principal investigator because she developed the research question and the methods for addressing it. She will oversee data collection and data analysis, and she will write the final report. However, Maria also recognizes that her academic adviser will act as her research supervisor; when she is unsure about an ethical issue, she will consult her supervisor.

She also prevents any dual relationships by enlisting only participants who are not now her clients. This way, subjects will not be both her client and her subject. However, clients who choose not to participate in her study are informed of the option to (1) pursue individual counseling with Maria but not as a research subject or (2) see another counselor. Maria's consent form is provided as Form 3-1.

Maria discusses participant responsibilities, including the number of meetings, period of involvement, and length of each meeting. She also notes that subjects will complete several inventories. Expected benefits are addressed in the beginning of the second paragraph, where Maria indicates the purpose of the groups—to improve understanding about self and behavior. She states that participation is voluntary and that subjects can withdraw at any time during the research should they so desire.

Maria is fortunate in that all her subjects will be receiving treatment, either a new, unproven technique or a standard procedure already used by the counseling facility. Thus, she is not

FORM 3-1   An example consent form for Maria's research study.

The purpose of the proposed research is to study the relative effectiveness of different treatments for bulimic women. If you decide to participate, you will be expected to attend 12 weekly 1-hour appointments to be scheduled during the evening hours at the University Counseling Center. The meetings will be held with other bulimic women; the exact size of each group will be no less than 5 and no more than 7 participants. Participation also involves the completion of several brief inventories about your background and about your eating habits. All groups will be conducted by me, Maria Gonzalez, a master's degree student completing a 1-year internship at the Counseling Center. Although I am the primary researcher in this study, my research is being supervised by Dr. Smith, my faculty adviser in the counseling department.

The purpose of the groups is to help women better understand bulimia and themselves. During group meetings, some participants may experience uncomfortable reactions like negative feelings about self or others. Although these feelings are expected, if negative responses continue and the format of the groups is not to your liking, you are under no pressure to continue. In fact, your participation in this study is entirely your choice, and you may discontinue your involvement at any time during the course of the research. Please note that if negative feelings do develop, you are encouraged to share them during the group meetings and to recognize that such adverse reactions may be a sign of a healthy attempt to cope with your feelings.

Also note that all questionnaire data will be kept confidential during data scoring and analysis, and in any subsequent reports, by using no names. Instead, subject identification codes and only group—not individual—data will be used. No disclosure to third parties such as parents or employers will be made without your prior consent to do so. During meetings, I will keep random and informal notes in order to monitor individual responses, improve my skills, and monitor group effectiveness. These notes will be kept in a file accessible only to me and will not be discussed with any other professional unless I think that a particular individual is not benefiting from the group. In these cases, I may seek professional consultation in order to determine whether an alternative program may be more effective.

Please take time to consider the above statements. If you have any questions about the material, you are encouraged to seek additional clarification from me at this point.

If *you want* to participate, please sign your name on the line below:

Name: _____   Date _____

If *you do not want* to participate, please sign your name on the line below:

Name: _____   Date: _____

Thank you for considering my research study.

Sincerely,

Maria Gonzalez, B. A.
Intern Counselor
555-5555

withholding treatment from subjects. While she hopes that all subjects will benefit from participation, she includes a clause about possible adverse reactions.

Confidentiality is the focus of the third paragraph, and Maria states that no names will be used on instruments or in reports generated from the data. She also identifies one limitation to confidentiality, which is seeking professional consultation should she believe that a client is either not responding or is reacting adversely to the group. This is a good example of intent to treat subjects responsibly, since she recognizes that not all participants will benefit from the group; in such cases, she is obligated to help the client find a more appropriate therapy.

As part of standardized research protocol, Maria develops a debriefing form, the content of which is given in Form 3-2. In this document, Maria provides participants with more specific information about her research, such as the methods used—including information about the two treatment groups. Maria tells participants that upon hearing the description of both groups, they may choose to enroll in a group other than the one to which they were assigned originally. Also in her debriefing form, Maria informs interested subjects about how they can obtain their individual results.

FORM 3-2   An example debriefing form for Maria's research study.

The study you just completed was specifically intended to examine the relative effectiveness of two different approaches to the treatment of bulimia. Of the 50 subjects participating, 25 met in education-treatment groups, the other 25 in multifaceted-treatment groups. In education groups, the leader was more direct and informative, providing group members facts about the causes and treatment of bulimia, along with pertinent national and community resources. The education program has been the most consistently used to date, and research shows it to be effective in reducing some of the inappropriate eating behaviors associated with bulimia.

However, a more recent trend is the development of a multifaceted approach. As the name implies, multifaceted means that many theories of human behavior are simultaneously applied. In essence, the leader in the multifaceted groups is nondirective, seeking to listen and clarify subjects' feelings about self and others. Since no research to date has compared the two approaches in relative effectiveness, this was the expressed intent of this study. To make this determination, the amount of group reduction inappropriate eating behaviors, as determined by the inventories you completed, will be compared. A statistical analysis will be performed to see if there are any differences between the two treatment groups. This analysis will be completed in 3 weeks, and after that time, you can contact me at the number provided on this form to find out either the group results or to make an appointment with me about your individual results. In the meantime, if you desire an alternative program, would like to continue your program, or need additional help, please contact me. If you desire, I can put your name on the client schedule at the Counseling Center or direct you to the appropriate agency.

I sincerely appreciate your participation in this study, and I enjoyed meeting and getting to know each of you.

Sincerely,

Maria Gonzalez, B. A.
Intern Counselor
555-5555

Since Maria is performing research in a university setting, she must get institutional approval from the university review board. So, she completes an institutional review board research form, describing briefly her study, potential risks, expected benefits, and assurances of confidentiality. The board reviews her proposal, and approves her research.

MEASUREMENT IN RESEARCH

Another integral part of research design is **measurement**. In general, measurement defines how numbers are assigned to subjects. For example, Maria might assign number 1 to subjects in the multifaceted treatment and number 2 to educational participants. Then, when determining the level of bulimia, Maria might have subjects complete a test of bulimia in which numbers on the test serve to quantify the severity of bulimia for each subject.

We introduce measurement concepts in Figure 3-7. In Figure 3-8, we illustrate measurement concepts with actual examples. Our remaining discussion of measurement will focus on these two figures.

Constructs

Constructs are hypothetical terms designed to classify and give meaning to human behavior. Constructs are hypothetical because they are abstractions inferred from behavior. For example, the construct "anxiety" is an abstract generalization of a cluster of phenomena. We could say that Joe is anxious because (1) we see him cry, worry, and tremble; (2) he scores high on self-report tests of anxiety, or (3) Joe's physiological measures, like his heart rate, are elevated. There are thousands of constructs in research on the helping professions such as anxiety, intelligence, achievement, motivation, self-concept, health beliefs, and empowerment, just to name a few.

You probably use constructs all the time in everyday language. For example, you might tell a friend about your lack of self-esteem, your spatial intelligence,

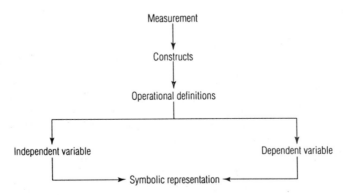

FIGURE 3-7   Concepts associated with measurement.

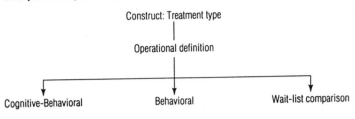

Example 1: Independent variable

Construct: Treatment type

|

Operational definition

|

Cognitive-Behavioral   Behavioral   Wait-list comparison

Example 2: Dependent variable

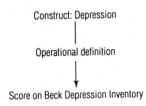

Construct: Depression

|

Operational definition

|

Score on Beck Depression Inventory

FIGURE 3-8   Examples of relationships among constructs, operational definitions, and variables.

or your interpersonal warmth. While these general terms give meaning to large clusters of behaviors, they are not behaviors per se. Your friend might ask, "What do you mean you don't have any self-esteem." If you reply, "I don't initiate conversations with people I work with because I feel bad about myself," then the abstract entity of "self-esteem" becomes more tangible, observable, and measurable.

At the highest level of abstraction and generality, all researchers study constructs. In fact, constructs are so global that they act like general research topics. For example, Maria is interested in the construct "bulimia," a term defining one of her general areas of interest. Nonetheless, constructs are the starting point for increased precision and specificity.

Operational Definitions

Operational definitions are the specific methods used to quantify and measure constructs. Since measurement refers to the assignment of numbers to subjects, when a construct is operationalized it exists in at least two states—or at least two different numbers can be assigned to subjects based on the construct. Essentially, operational definitions turn a construct into a variable, since a **variable** is any phenomenon that can exist in at least two different states. For example, in a school consisting of boys and girls, gender is a variable because it varies, that is, it exists in two different levels in this school group. In a college classroom, grade point average (GPA) is a variable if students have differing GPAs, say 2.5, 2.6, 3.0, and 3.5. In Maria's study, treatment type—multifaceted vs. educational—is another variable because treatment exists in two states—multifaceted and educational. The opposite of a variable is a **constant**—a characteristic that does not vary in a group. For example, gender would not be a variable in an all boy or all girl school because all subjects would be of the same gender. In many research studies, variables are classified as either independent or dependent variables. These categories are discussed next.

INDEPENDENT VARIABLES.   **Independent variables** are any characteristics, events, or situations that are presumed to affect another variable. If researchers classify variables as independent, these variables must be operationally defined. For example, in studies using different treatments, the format of each treatment must be described in terms of whether treatment is administered individually or in groups, the length of sessions, and total number of sessions. Even more important is to describe the techniques used in each session. For example, if the treatment involves teaching subjects new skills, specific teaching techniques should be clearly delineated. These could include lecture, programmed instruction, practice until reaching a learning criteria, use of positive reinforcement and shaping, modeling, or using positive and negative examples. Finally, the goals and intent of the entire treatment and (sometimes) the objectives at the end of each session should be clearly specified.

Variations in the independent variables are referred to as **independent variable levels**. These levels are not classified as separate variables per se but delineate the categories defining the variable. For example, in Figure 3-8 the independent variable—treatment type—exists in three levels: cognitive-behavioral, behavioral, and a wait-list control group.

Researchers study different types of independent variables. One distinction is manipulated vs. nonmanipulated independent variables. When the researcher creates different levels of the independent variable, it becomes a **manipulated variable**. The researcher's goal is to draw cause-and-effect conclusions like, If independent variable then dependent variable. In Figure 3-8, the researcher's goal is to conclude, *If* participants receive the treatments of cognitive-behavioral, behavioral, or no-treatment, *then* different levels of depression.

On the other hand, sometimes it is impossible for the researcher to manipulate an independent variable, even though this variable is believed to be related to a dependent variable. If the independent variable cannot be manipulated, the research is labeled nonexperimental. An example of a commonly encountered, nonmanipulated independent variable is gender, since subjects come to a research study already possessing gender and one of its two levels. However, the investigator may believe that gender is related to differences in spatial skills. The key word is *related* because without direct manipulation of the independent variable, researchers cannot make cause-and-effect conclusions. For example, gender per se may not cause differences in spatial skills but rather any of several variables associated with gender may be the cause—parent encouragement, modeling, or amount of exposure to toys designed to improve spatial ability.

DEPENDENT VARIABLES.   The **dependent variable** is the variable presumably affected by an independent variable. When operationally defining the dependent variable, researchers may assign numbers to subjects by recording their responses on standardized tests, questionnaires, or frequencies of behaviors. In Figure 3-8, the dependent variable, depression, is operationally defined by the Beck Depression Inventory, a self-report questionnaire in which respondents receive a total score indicating the severity of depression.

Symbolic Representation of Variables

When concluding measurement planning, it is helpful to represent variables symbolically, as suggested in Figure 3-7. In Table 3-1, we provide four different representations of variables. In designs 1, 3, and 4, the X refers to some event (treatment, experimental group) that the researcher is interested in; that is the

TABLE 3-1   Symbolic representation of variables.

Design 1:   One group, posttest only:

	Treatment	Posttest
Group 1	X	0

Design 2:   Correlational design:

	Variable X	Variable Y
Subject 1	—	—
Subject 2	—	—
.		
.		
.		
Subject N	—	—

Design 3:   Pretest-posttest, two intact groups:

	Pretest	Treatment	Posttest
Group 1	01	X1	02
Group 2	01	X2	02

Design 4:   Two randomly assigned groups, posttest only:

	Random assignment	Treatment	Posttest
Group 1	R	X1	01
Group 2	R	X2	01

independent variable. The dependent variable, O, is the outcome of X. So for example, in design 1, subjects get X and then are measured on O. In design 3, two groups of subjects are first measured (pretested) on some dependent variable (O), then one group receives treatment one X1; the other group receives treatment two X2; each group is subsequently posttested. In design 4, two groups of subjects are used, and each group is randomly assigned to two different treatments: X1 or X2. Both groups are posttested (O). In design 2, each subject is measured on two variables: X and Y. Usually, in design 2 neither X nor Y is referred to as an independent or dependent variable.

Each of the four designs represents one of the major types of research we will discuss in later chapters. For example, when only one subject is used, design 1 approximates the descriptive case study—a single subject gets some treatment and then is measured on O. Design 2 represents correlational research because the outcome of this research will provide an index of the relationship between X and Y. Design 3, because of its manipulated independent variable (X1 vs. X2) but lack of random assignment, is known as a quasi-experimental research. Finally, design 4, which includes both random assignment and a manipulated independent variable, represents a true experiment.

As you might guess, the number of ways Xs and Os can be represented is seemingly infinite. At this point, you should attempt to diagram your proposed research in terms of Xs and Os. Do not be too concerned if this proves to be difficult. We will return to diagramming several different research designs in later chapters. Perhaps most importantly, in Chapter 5, we note the relevance of research design to internal validity. In fact, the most important implication of research design is its relationship to the control of extraneous variables that may threaten the internal validity of research results.

MARIA REVISITED

How will Maria approach measurement in her study? Assume that Maria defines her independent variable as treatment type, which has two levels—multifaceted and educational. She operationally defines each treatment approach as follows. The multifaceted group sessions emphasize (1) reflecting client communications, (2) keeping content focused on the here and now, (3) encouraging client exploration of feelings regarding body-image, anger, and self-expectations, (4) role-playing of alternate behaviors, (5) goal-setting, and (6) summarizing group content. For the educational approach, Maria defines this treatment as teaching and informational in nature and as pertaining to topics such as diet, nutrition, physical health, appropriate eating behavior, and exercise.

She operationally defines her dependent variable—binging and purging—as scores on the BULIT-R, a self-report test regarding bulimic behavior.

Finally, Maria represents her design as a true experiment:

R   X1   O
R   X2   O

Her design starts with random assignment to the two treatment groups. Her treatments are represented as X1 (educational) and X2 (multifaceted). Her diagram concludes with a posttest.

Projected Time Line and Budget

Research essentially reduces to two practical matters—time and money. Most experienced researchers would prefer to have an endless supply of both, but real-world demands dictate that both entities need careful consideration if the research is to be completed on time and in a cost-effective manner. Unfortunately, in our experience novice researchers frequently overlook this planning step; they fail to develop a realistic time line as well as a realistic budget.

In research, a **time line** graphically displays the expected dates on which the various research stages will be completed. Because time is such a precious commodity, researchers can use time lines to assess the feasibility of completing a study in a given period of time. Such a framework can also provide clear parameters for factors such as how many subjects can participate, how much time will be allotted for participant recruitment, and how much time will be given to writing the research report. Another important function of a time line is the impetus it provides the researcher to complete activities in the time provided. Without such structure, we find that many prospective researchers get sidetracked by other duties and fail to complete their projects.

An excellent example of a time line is provided by Gay (1987). In Table 3-2, we adopt this time line for Maria's research study. Note that this time line graphically illustrates when each stage of research will be started and completed, as well as showing when several overlapping activities will occur. This latter feature helps researchers isolate particularly busy research stages, thereby allowing them to adjust other responsibilities accordingly.

Finances must also be planned. In research, a budget enumerates all research expenses. Researchers should consider potential opportunities for either internal or external funding for research costs. **Internal funding** is the financial support given the researcher by the researcher's employing agency. So for example, if a hospital reserves funds for research by staff, a hospital staff member could

TABLE 3-2 Proposed time line for Maria's research study.

Activity	June	July	Aug.	Sep.	Oct.	Nov.	Dec.	Jan.	Feb.
Review literature	*******************								
Finish plan		************							
Prepare materials			****						
Recruit subjects			*******						
Implement treatment				************************					
Posttest subjects							**		
Analyze data							*************		
Write report				***					

NOTE: This thesis will take approximately 8 months to complete. Some master's theses will take longer.

develop a research proposal and an associated budget and request hospital funding. Such funding could take many forms, such as direct costs for recruitment, travel, and instruments. One of the most important supports would be for release time in which the hospital would allot so many hours per day to the staff member's research and would continue to pay the researcher's regular salary. **External funding** refers to financial support given the researcher by outside funding agencies. Funding agencies usually focus on content areas, such as

> Counseling and Psychology: National Institute of Mental Health (NIMH);
> Social Work: Administration for Children and Families (ACF);
> Medical Nursing: National Institute of General Medical Science (NIGMS); and
> Education: Fund for the Improvement of Post Secondary Education (FIPSE).

There are countless external funding agencies offering support at the national, state, and local levels. Since most new researchers are unaware of the types of financial support available, obtaining more information about funding sources is a good idea. Such information is usually available from university research support centers or from any professional person who is aware of funding sources.

MARIA REVISITED

Maria's budget might look like the one in Table 3-3. It would be typical of the expenses incurred for a master's thesis or dissertation. Of course, there is great variation, depending on how much of the cost the researcher's employing agency is willing to pay. In any case, a well-planned budget will save delays and problems in funding that might arise without a detailed cost analysis.

TABLE 3-3   Budget for Maria's research project.

Item/Activity	Expense
Library reproduction (predicted)	$ 25.00
Interlibrary loan charges (predicted)	$ 5.00
Dissertation purchase (predicted)	$ 40.00
Note-taking supplies (known)	$ 10.00
Agency copy costs (known, e.g., consent and debriefing forms, progress notes)	$ 15.00
Materials for the BULIT-R:	
1. Manual	
2. 50 forms A and B	
3. 50 answer sheets forms A and B	
4. Computer scoring software	
(known)	$100.00
TOTAL COST	**$195.00**

STATISTICAL ANALYSIS

One of the most important planning steps in completing the research design is considering how data will be analyzed statistically. Ultimately, statistical techniques determine what kinds of conclusions can be drawn, a fact that relates directly to how the research question will be answered. Indeed, determining how to analyze data statistically may be the most direct way for the planner to determine how well the research design answers the question and its associated hypotheses. In Chapter 10, we will elaborate on statistical methods, with emphasis on how these methods answer specific research hypotheses.

CONCLUDING COMMENTS

You can now see that a significant amount of thought and careful deliberation is required to develop a research plan. A researcher must first obtain the relevant literature and then formulate a research plan that shows (1) understanding of the literature, (2) analysis of the literature as it relates to the current proposal, and (3) a basic understanding of the research principles underlying the plan. In this chapter, we introduced research concepts that define the plan; in the remaining chapters, we hope to deepen your understanding of plan elements.

Once the research plan is acceptable to the principal investigator or research supervisor, the next step is to put the plan into action by conducting the study; that is, beginning data collection. Clearly then, the completion of the research plan represents a major turning point in the conduct of an empirical research study. The role of the research plan as it relates to implementation is shown in Figure 3-9.

In the next chapter, we elaborate on the process of data collection; Chapter 10 focuses on statistical analysis. Finally, in Chapter 11 we will discuss research report writing and publication.

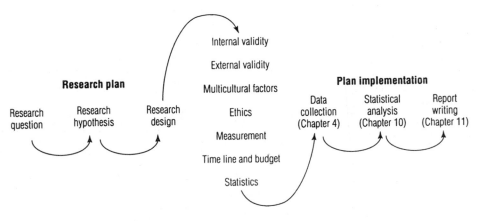

FIGURE 3-9 Research plan and its implementation.

EXERCISES

1. Consider the following research question: "What is the best way to teach graduate students about research?" What is wrong with this research question and how might you restate it?

2. In designing an experiment to determine whether treatment A is more effective than treatment B in improving the quality of life, describe how you might operationally define *quality of life*.

3. With your research topic in mind, evaluate external validity with regard to the population you wish to generalize your results to. What exactly is this population? Can you generalize to this population? Why or why not?

4. Using the Daley study in Appendix E, do the following:
   a. Identify a research question.
   b. State two different hypotheses, one a null hypothesis, the other directional.
   c. Evaluate whether your hypotheses account for all the data presented in the Table.
   d. Determine whether the sample was convenient or randomly selected and defend your answer.
   e. Assess whether the subjects were randomly assigned to groups.
   f. State clearly the independent and dependent variables.
   g. Using the X and O format, identify the research design.

5. If you are contemplating a thesis, examine the following ethical and practical issues:
   a. *Ethical:* What are the primary ethical concerns in your research area? Will you be conducting this study by yourself, or with the assistance of a research supervisor? Do you intend to publish the study, and if so, who will be first author? Will you be in a position of having dual relationships with subjects? How will you proceed with informed consent and debriefing? How will you protect confidentiality?
   b. *Practical:* Develop a time line and budget in accordance with Tables 3-2 and 3-3.

4

PLANNING DATA COLLECTION: METHODS FOR COLLECTING DATA

NOW THAT MARIA has settled on her general research question, she can begin to think of how to define bulimia operationally. This operational definition will include who will provide the data and in what form the data will be obtained. In her review of the literature, Maria has been introduced to many ways of operationalizing the construct of bulimia. What are some issues that she must consider before she makes the decision that is best for her?

A research question can be operationalized in many different ways. In this chapter, we discuss the various possibilities for collecting information and discuss the major concerns in selecting a specific measure: reliability, validity, and usability. Our central theme here is that there are many different ways to answer a research question, and the way chosen rests on many considerations.

QUESTIONS ABOUT DATA COLLECTION

Before beginning to search for an instrument to measure the construct(s) mentioned in his or her research question, a researcher must consider several questions. Nine of these questions follow.

Why Observe Human Beings?

Research in the helping professions naturally will focus on human beings, the organizations they form or use, and their reactions to the services they receive.

Since human beings are complex, they require intensive and careful study, often with multiple observations. These observations can take place over a period of time or can be obtained during one time period, depending upon the research question posed.

Who Decides What Information Is Needed?

A consistent thread in this text is that the researcher's research question and research hypothesis will dictate the researcher's actions. Thus, there can be no one right way to collect data; rather, a multitude of options are available. Which option is best is dictated by the research question and by the researcher's creativity and resources, as well as by the cooperation of those from whom the data will be collected. Ultimately, decisions about how the data will be collected are shared with the research community in the research report. If decisions are deemed wrong or more likely, less than desirable, then other researchers can investigate those concerns. Therefore, it is crucial to document procedures and to provide a rationale for why certain decisions were made.

A person's reasons for doing a piece of research also affect what information is needed. For instance, a master's level student probably would not have access to enough money to study the intelligence of large numbers of subjects. A smaller sample would have to suffice. Similarly, a master's degree student probably would not have enough time to replicate a study in successive semesters. One semester would have to suffice. Nor would a master's level student have the expertise to administer an instrument that requires training in its interpretation. A simpler and possibly less valid instrument would have to suffice. Even in the above situations, however, the master's research project would still have value in that other members of the research community may have additional resources that would allow them to build on the master's research and obtain a more defensible answer to the research question.

Who Can Provide the Information?

Too often, beginning researchers think the research question can be answered solely with information provided by the subjects. Even though the subjects may be the most direct source, other information can be obtained from subjects' parents, siblings, significant others, trained observers, friends, and sometimes even enemies. The researcher can even gather data through systematic observation.

Research can often be improved by obtaining information from various sources rather than relying solely on one source. Any one source may not be totally accurate or may not have enough information to provide a complete picture. Researchers refer to the use of multiple sources as **triangulation,** a surveyor's term meaning that more than one reference is needed to determine a fixation point. Often, more than two reference points are required, particularly if the sightings are not accurate or if they are on distant objects, such as when stars are used as fixation points by ocean navigators. In the helping professions, triangulation means using results from several sources to obtain a more accurate conclusion. Such conclusions are usually more defensible than those based on single sources. Therefore, whatever concerns the research community may have about any one of the sources can be ameliorated by information from the other sources.

While obtaining information from various sources may require extra work, the benefit of doing so usually far outweighs the added costs; other researchers are often willing to provide requested information. If that information is accurate, it should be included.

How Can the Information Best Be Obtained?

Just as there are many sources of information, there are many methods of data collection, and there is usually not a single answer to the question. The researcher's goal is to be confident in a conclusion, and obtaining information from various methods will help in reaching that goal. Triangulation can involve both multiple sources of information and multiple methods of data collection. The various methods of data collection will be discussed in the following pages.

Returning to Maria's research as an example: Maria wants to reduce the occurrence of bulimic behavior in her clients. Who could provide her with information on bulimic behavior? Information could be provided by any number of sources: subjects' significant others, parents, trained observers, the researcher herself, and the subjects in her study. Cost, quality, and the feasibility of getting the information will vary from source to source. For instance, neither trained observers nor Maria would probably have as much direct access to the bulimic women's lives as would their significant others. On the other hand, bulimia is a behavior that is often denied by significant others, especially family members. The subject herself is in the best position to report on her condition if she can be trusted to do so.

How each subject would provide information also varies from study to study. Maria may prefer to use a standardized instrument; another researcher, trained in administering personality tests, might argue for a particular personality measure. Another researcher might argue for an in-depth interview or for having subjects keep a journal of their eating behavior. Again, there is no right or wrong method—each has its own advantages and disadvantages.

In summary, once the research question has been specified, the researcher needs to operationalize the construct of interest by selecting a measurement of that construct. All constructs must have operational definitions of the independent variables, the dependent variables, as well as any variables identified in correlational questions.

There are several ways to categorize measures: (1) standardized or nonstandardized, (2) structured or nonstructured, and (3) cognitive or noncognitive. We next discuss the issues surrounding these categories.

Should a Test Be Standardized or Nonstandardized?

A **standardized test** is one that has been administered and scored in a standard way. Standardized tests usually are normed, that is, they are administered to a large group of people (the norming sample) who are selected because they represent some population. If standardized test administration practices were used in the norming sample and if the norming sample represents the stated population, then the scores provide interpretive value. Some common norming variables are (1) region of the country, (2) gender, (3) socioeconomic status, (4) race and ethnicity, and (5) the nature of the problem. There should either be specific norms for the groups representing these variables or enough subjects included in the norms like the ones under consideration that valid inferences can be made.

Examples of standardized measures include achievement tests, intelligence tests, aptitude tests, and perceptual motor tests. Behavioral rating measures can be standardized and normed if they are administered and scored in a systematic fashion with a large representative sample of a particular population. Examples of each of these tests will be provided later.

A **nonstandardized measure** is one that does not meet the criteria for standardized tests. There is no norming group; administration is not standardized, and scoring is not done in a standardized fashion. If a measure has not been administered in a consistent way to a representative sample of subjects from a target population, there is no way to interpret the results with respect to that population. All that can be known is a general description of how a person responded. Examples of nonstandardized tests are most questionnaires, interviews, record reviews, behavioral observations, and case studies, which are discussed in detail in later sections. Each of the above measures could be standardized, and we will present standardized behavioral ratings later in the chapter.

When a researcher wants to compare results or subjects to a target population, a standardized test should be used. If the research question can be answered without making such comparisons, nonstandardized measures could be used. Nonstandardized measures also are used when no adequate standardized measure exists, which forces the researcher either to use an existing nonstandardized measure or to develop one.

A third instance when nonstandardized measures would be called for is when a population is being investigated that is different from the population that the standardized measure was standardized on. For instance, if Maria found a measure of bulimia that had been standardized on older women in Mexico, could she compare younger women in the United States to that population? Differences in culture, age, and language would call the use of the existing instrument into question. This is an obvious example, but researchers often force an existing instrument to fit a situation it was not designed for. When a researcher must develop a measure, the recommendations listed at the end of this chapter should be followed.

Should a Test Be Structured or Nonstructured?

Another way to categorize measures is by whether they are structured or non-structured. **Structured tests** provide the same stimulus to each subject and the same set of possible responses; they are scored by a set procedure for each subject. **Unstructured measures,** on the other hand, allow both subject and observer to make changes during the process. Examples of unstructured measures include naturalistic observations and unstructured interviews.

Structured measures direct the observer to a prespecified set of behaviors on which every subject will be measured. Unstructured measures can provide a richer description of an individual subject's behavior, but the usefulness of these measures depends on the verbal ability of the subject and the creativity of the observer. Drawbacks include the inability to compare across subjects and the inability to compare across researchers. If the subject does not want to go into detail or if the observer is not a keen and penetrating observer, then additional and richer descriptions will not be obtained. Since different sets of questions are probed for each subject, the researcher will not have the same information on each subject. Unstructured measures thus have some of the shortcomings of nonstandardized tests in that there is no basis for comparing a particular subject's unique response with any other responses.

The choice, then, is between unique and penetrating information from unstructured measures or consistent and prespecified information from structured measures. For example, a researcher investigating why high school students drop out of school could interview subjects who are considered to be at-risk for dropping out of school. A structured interview might include the question, Have you ever thought about dropping out of school? If the answer is yes, the researcher could follow up with, Did you discuss this thought with a school counselor? In an unstructured interview, the interviewer might ask, What did you do when pondering dropping out of school? and then probe more deeply with an unspecified follow-up question. Because the follow-up question is unspecified, the subjects' answers cannot be aggregated, but they may in fact relate more closely to what each subject did.

While this discussion has presented structured and unstructured as opposite terms, they are really two ends of a continuum. Tests fall somewhere on that continuum; usually they are neither purely structured nor purely unstructured but a combination of the two—semistructured.

Should a Standardized Test Be Cognitive or Noncognitive?

Cognitive tests measure the knowledge, learning, and skill level of a subject, while **noncognitive tests** measure attributes other than knowledge, such as preferences, beliefs, and attitudes. Figure 4-1 shows how cognitive tests can be divided into achievement (tests of school learning), ability (capabilities), and aptitude (specific abilities), with the aptitude category further divided into intelligence, specialized, and neuropsychological.

While cognitive tests all measure what the person being tested can do, noncognitive tests measure what the person likes to do. These tests are broadly classified as, for example, general personality, psychopathology, career interests—or some other specialized construct. Each helping profession field focuses on one of these areas. For instance, most mental health providers and researchers focus on measures of general personality; most vocational counselors focus on career interest batteries; most social workers focus on specialized measures such

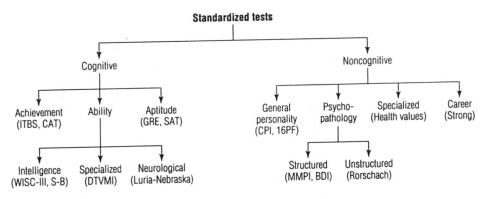

NOTE: ITBS = Iowa Test of Basic Skills; CAT = California Achievement Test; GRE = Graduate Record Examination; CPI = California Psychological Inventory; 16PF = 16 Personality Factor Questionnaire; MMPI = Minnesota Multiphasic Personality Inventory; BDI = Beck Depression Inventory; WISC-III = Wechsler Intelligence Scale for Children, 3rd ed.; S-B = Stanford-Binet, 4th ed.; DTVMI = Developmental Test of Visual Motor Integration.

FIGURE 4-1   Classification of standardized tests.

as drug and suicide measures; and most educational diagnosticians focus on achievement and intelligence measures.

Where Can I Get the Information I Need?

Most researchers limit their data gathering to obtaining new information directly from sources, but there are two other ways to obtain data. One is to rely on existing records—data that have been collected for another purpose. Another way is to collect data indirectly, that is, in an unobtrusive manner without the subject realizing it.

EXISTING RECORDS.   **Existing records** are sources of data that have already been collected for reasons other than the researcher's reasons. The advantage of such information is that it is readily available, but unfortunately, such data have usually not been collected on all the subjects needed, and the conditions under which the data were collected may have been less than desirable. A researcher should always consider the possibility of including existing records as one piece of information in the triangulation process, however. Federally funded research is made available to other researchers and may provide the exact data needed. There are over 100,000 databases available (Inter-university Consortium for Political and Social Research, 1991).

For example, Maria might be interested in obtaining information from her subjects' records—prior attempts at treatment, previous weight history, attendance at extracurricular activities in high school and college, or prior academic performance. Some of these records would be less accessible than others; some would be inaccessible without the subject's written permission.

UNOBTRUSIVE MEASURES.   **Unobtrusive measures** are those obtained when subjects are unaware that they are being measured. Such data can be collected during the study routinely, or they can be collected in a fabricated setting. Sometimes this requires deception. While ethical considerations often restrict the obtaining of data unobtrusively, researchers should consider this method as an option because, as will become clear in Chapter 5, subjects often do not respond honestly. Some subjects try to help the researcher, while others try to counter the research effort. If subjects do not know they are being measured, they cannot do either one. Unobtrusive measures run the gamut from already existing data, to data obtained by researchers in hiding, to data obtained in a contrived way. This last type is the most unusual and has resulted in much creativity.

For example, researchers have measured the wear on carpet in front of various museum paintings to determine which is the most popular painting. Confederates have been used to make subjects believe that electrical shock is being administered. Letters addressed to the two major political parties in the United States have been strewn on city streets and political party support inferred from the proportion returned. The key to using unobtrusive measures is inference. Most unobtrusive measures require making more inferences than do measures that directly measure subjects' responses. But the additional effort it takes to make inferences may be worth making. The researcher can avoid the effects of role-playing.

Consider Maria's research. She could obtain unobtrusive measures of bulimia by hiding in the women's bathroom to see how often each subject purges; but this procedure would not work for subjects who live in other dorms. Also, she could not monitor the entire day's behavior—only behavior at the dorm. A passive procedure would be to analyze each subject's garbage. Discarded food wrappings could indicate binge episodes. Since most subjects have roommates, there would have to be some allowance for contributions by those roommates—again indicating the difficulty of making inferences with some unobtrusive measures.

Another possibility would be for Maria to place binge food in the lobby of the residence and observe how much disappears. If the amount taken seems to be within the normal range, Maria can assume no binging has occurred. If an inordinate amount disappears, she can infer that the bulimic subject took the food and binged. However, this inference might be incorrect because (1) the subject's roommate might have binged, (2) the food might have been given to other friends, (3) a pet might have been the beneficiary of the food, or (4) the food might have been thrown away. In spite of the problems, however, we think unobtrusive measures deserve consideration.

COLLECTING NEW DATA.   Usually, a researcher will choose to collect his or her data. Since the research question drives the research hypothesis, useful data on the specified population will not be likely to exist, and the researcher must do the collecting. Instruments that already exist can be used, however, or instruments specific to the situation can be developed. We treat instrument development, an intricate process, at the end of this chapter.

Where Can I Get Information About Tests?

There are several valuable collections of test reviews that a researcher should investigate first. These collections provide cross references; describe the purposes of the tests; describe tests' reliability, validity, and usability; and give test administration requirements. Information about ordering tests is also included; often there are critical reviews of the tests. The first six references at the end of this chapter are a good place to start locating information. Depending on the researcher's success with these, the remaining sources may or may not provide additional information. All the references are well-indexed and can lead the researcher quickly to various tests.

STANDARDIZED MEASURES

The most available and widely used tests are standardized tests, which are reviewed periodically in the *Mental Measurements Yearbook* series. The *Tenth Mental Measurements Yearbook* (Conoley & Kramer, 1989) contains reviews of tests' measurement properties (reliability, validity, and usability) and summaries of current research. The classification index from this most recent yearbook illustrates the broad range of tests that are available. There are more than 100 tests on vocations, 72 personality tests, and 22 specialized tests on speech and hearing alone.

Standardized measures have undergone extensive development, tryout, revision, and subsequent administration to a large norming sample. Consequently, standardized tests yield scores that show a subject's position relative to the norming sample. Given that the subject is like the norming sample (or more correctly, that there were sufficient subjects like that subject in the norming sample), then the subject's test score can be usefully interpreted.

Figure 4-1 introduced our classification of the standardized tests to be discussed in the following sections. Note that the major distinction is between cognitive and noncognitive tests. Within the cognitive branch are achievement, ability, and aptitude; in the noncognitive branch are general personality, psychopathology, specialized measures, and career. Each of these categories is discussed in detail in the following sections.

Cognitive Measures

Cognitive tests measure how much a person knows. The content of the various cognitive tests is sometimes similar, with the primary distinction being the purpose of the test, as indicated in Table 4-1. If the purpose of a test is to measure past learning, an achievement test is called for. If the purpose is to measure present learning capabilities, an ability test is in order. If the purpose is to predict future learning capabilities, an aptitude test would be used. Each of these tests is discussed in detail in the following sections.

TABLE 4-1   Relationships among achievement, ability, and aptitude tests.

	Achievement	Ability	Aptitude
Time	Past	Present	Future
Purpose	Assess past learning	Assess present capability	Assess future learning

ACHIEVEMENT MEASURES.   Tests that provide a measure of the subject's general educational development and amount of school-related learning are classified as **achievement tests**. Such tests can provide insight into strong and weak areas through comparison to the subject's peers by using normed scores such as percentiles, grade equivalents, or NCEs (Normal Curve Equivalents—see Chapter 10). Achievement tests usually provide scores on various subtests, which provide some diagnostic information about academic strengths or weaknesses. Additional diagnostic testing is usually called for, as the achievement test only provides general tendencies. Some more widely used achievement tests are the California Achievement Test (CAT), Metropolitan Achievement Test (MAT), Iowa Test of Basic Skills (ITBS), and the Stanford Achievement Test (SAT). Although these four tests are all standardized, and all purportedly measure the same constructs, they measure those constructs in different ways. When selecting this or any other kind of measuring instrument, a researcher must decide whether or not using it will answer the research question.

Table 4-2 shows the names of subtests and the number of items they contain for four commonly used tests that measure reading by second graders. (We have deliberately used out-of-date tests so as not to appear supportive or critical of any one test.) The subtest names provided by the test publishers suggest that there are some unique characteristics in the four tests, though they all presumably measure the construct of reading. While inspection of the instructional objectives and the actual items might lead to finding a match between some subtests and other subtests or combinations thereof, the fact remains that the MAT78 had six subtests, while the other three tests had only about half as many. Clearly, potential users must identify the subtests they need and choose a standardized test accordingly.

Within any one test, a subtest may use a unique measure. For instance, on the MAT78, the Auditory Discrimination subtest has four skill areas. Two are measured by four items each (initial single consonant and initial consonant blend), and the other two (final single consonant and final consonant blend) are measured by eight items each. Also, the subtests measure specific areas of reading, as these are defined by the developers of the test; each is composed of even more specific areas, which can be thought of as reading skills or instructional objectives, depending on the perspective.

ABILITY MEASURES.   Standardized tests of ability can be classified into one of three categories: (1) **intelligence tests** measure general cognitive functioning;

TABLE 4-2 Number of items on reading subtest of four commonly used reading tests.

Subtest name	MAT78	SAT73	ITBS78	CAT77
Auditory discrimination	26			
Sight vocabulary	30		30	15
Phoneme-graphene consonants	27			
Word part clues	24			
Vocabulary in context	24			
Reading comprehension	55			20
Word meaning		45		
Explicit and implicit meaning		42		
Word study skills		60		
Listening			32	
Word analysis			49	
Reading			66	
Structural analysis				11
Phonic analysis				25

(2) **specialized abilities tests** measure specific cognitive functioning; and (3) **neurological measures** attempt to identify brain-behavior relationships.

Intelligence tests can be administered in either a group setting or an individual setting. The advantages and disadvantages of both are depicted in Table 4-3. In a clinical setting, an individually administered IQ test would probably be preferred, although in a clinical research situation a researcher might choose to administer a group IQ test to all subjects simultaneously.

The Wechsler Intelligence Scale for Children—third edition (WISC-III) is the latest revision of the original WISC (Wechsler, 1949). The WISC-III contains subtests in two major areas: verbal and performance. The verbal area consists of tests for information, arithmetic, vocabulary, comprehension, finding similarities, and digit span (the number of digits that can be immediately recalled from a random list of digits). The performance area consists of picture completion, picture arrangement, block design, object assembly, coding, symbol search, and mazes.

Most intelligence measures employ primarily nonculturally relevant items but also use some culturally relevant content. Such tests have been criticized for being biased against examinees who are less aware of the dominant culture. Culture-fair tests have been developed to avoid this problem. Such tests rely on numbers or shapes, as shown in Figure 4-2.

Specialized abilities tests measure any one of many specific skills. For example, one specialized abilities test focuses specifically on eye-hand coordination and is used for estimating readiness for learning, particularly for early schooling.

TABLE 4-3   Comparison of group and individual IQ tests.

Group IQ tests:

   Are typically used in schools or industry.

   Require limited responses (usually multiple-choice).

   Are easier to administer.

   Can be administered to many examinees at one time.

Individual IQ tests:

   Are typically used in clinical settings.

   Usually contain items that increase in difficulty. Therefore, items that are judged to be too
      difficult do not have to be administered.

   Take more time to administer, score, and interpret.

   Allow the examinee's test-taking attitude to be inferred by examiner.

The Developmental Test of Visual-Motor Integration (Beery, 1982) requires the examinee to copy 24 shapes similar to those in Figure 4-3.

Neurological tests are typically administered to individuals who are performing below expectations. These tests attempt to assess whether the performance is related to brain or nerve damage rather than to the manifest cause—low ability or lack of nurturing for the brain. Although tests can be used to facilitate such a diagnosis, precise diagnosis is often difficult. For example, Anastasi (1988) points out potential problems in making the correct diagnosis, including (1) brain injury may produce a variety of behavioral changes; (2) symptoms of brain damage vary, depending on the age, intellectual development, and edu-

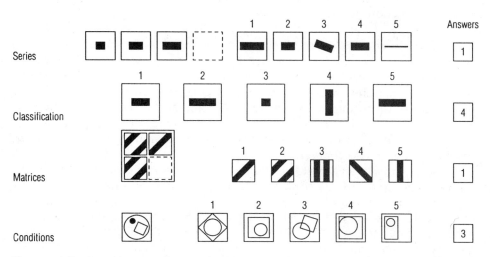

FIGURE 4-2   Sample items from the Culture-Fair Intelligence Test, Scale 2, Form A. Copyright © 1949, 1960. Institute for Personality and Ability Testing. Reproduced by permission.

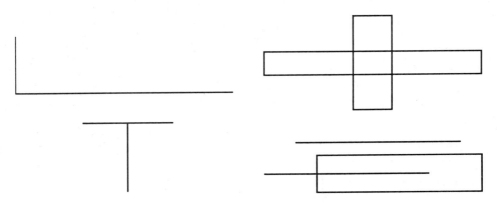

NOTE: Examinees are shown one shape and are asked to reproduce that shape.

FIGURE 4-3   Items similar to those on the Developmental Test of Visual-Motor Integration.

cational level of the individual; (3) symptoms are affected by the level of the damage; and (4) behavior may be an indirect result of brain damage.

The Luria-Nebraska Neuropsychological Battery (Golden, 1987) is one example of a test that can be used to screen for brain damage. The battery contains 11 subtests that measure such functions as visual acuity, tactile sensitivity, and the ability to perceive rhythm. Scale scores for each subtest range from 0 to 2; a 0 suggests normal functioning, and a 2 suggests possible brain injury. The STROOP Neuropsychological Screening Test (Trenerry, Crosson, DeBoe, & Leber, 1989) is another test measuring neurological functioning. The examinee reads a list of colors (red, blue, and so on) that are written in a different color of ink. The word red might be written in blue ink, for example. See Table 4-4 for an explanation of the test.

APTITUDE MEASURES.   While the previous categories of tests measure the general level of past or present cognitive functioning, **aptitude tests** measure specific educational or perceptual skills. A helping professional can use such information to help the examinee make educational or occupational decisions about the future. Once the examinee and the helping professional are aware of the level of these skills, a more appropriate decision can be made. The purpose of a test like this is to predict future success. (The concept of predictive validity will be discussed later in this chapter.)

One example of an aptitude test is the Differential Aptitude Test (DAT). The test is designed to provide educational and vocational information to students in grades 8–12. Items such as the ones in Table 4-5 show relative capabilities in five specific job-related areas (clerical speed and accuracy, mechanical reasoning, space relations, spelling, and language usage) and three general intellectual areas (verbal reasoning, numerical ability, and abstract reasoning).

A test that was specifically designed for vocational counseling is the General Aptitude Test Battery (GATB). The test is designed to be administered to high school seniors and adults looking for employment. An examinee's profile of 9

TABLE 4-4   Items similar to those on the
STROOP Neuropsychological Screening
Test.

purple	(in brown ink)
brown	(in black ink)
orange	(in purple ink)
black	(in orange ink)
brown	(in purple ink)
orange	(in black ink)
black	(in brown ink)
purple	(in orange ink)

NOTE: Examinees are presented one list and are asked to read the word.
Then the examinees are presented the other list and asked to read the
color.

scores can be compared to the profile of 36 different occupational patterns. The
idea is that the better the fit between the examinee's profile and that of a
particular occupation, the more successful (and possibly happier) the examinee
would be in that occupation.

Noncognitive Measures

When a researcher wants to measure something other than knowledge or skill
level, noncognitive measures should be considered. Noncognitive measures
differ in three major ways from cognitive measures. First, noncognitive tests
usually measure a typical performance, while achievement tests measure maximum performance. Second, the score a person receives on a noncognitive test
can often be easily faked, or at least it is susceptible to response bias. Third,

TABLE 4-5   Items similar to those on the General Aptitude Test
Battery.

1. Which two words have the same meaning?
    (a) old   (b) sad   (c) unhappy   (d) young
2. A woman works 8 hours a day, 5 days a week. She earns $8.50 an hour. How much does she
    earn per week?
    (a) $68.00   (b) $42.50   (c) $360.00   (d) $340.00   (e) $34.00
3. Which pair of names is the same?
    (a) B. J. Williams   B. I. Williams
    (b) Wilkinson & McNeil   McNeil & Wilkinson
    (c) Educational Testing Service   Educational Testing Service

noncognitive constructs tend to fluctuate over time or from one situation to another. Noncognitive measures are discussed in the following broad categories: general personality, psychopathology, specialized, and career interests.

MEASURES OF GENERAL PERSONALITY. The focus of general personality tests is on healthy populations, whereas the psychopathology tests focus on personality flaws that may be diagnosable as psychological disorders.

The California Psychological Inventory (Gough, 1957) and the Sixteen Personality Factor Questionnaire (16PF) (Cattell, 1949; Cattell, Eber, & Tatsuoka, 1970) are two widely used personality instruments. Both instruments (1) require examinees to respond on paper to many questions about themselves, (2) include several questions for each subsequent score, (3) include adjustments for response bias such as lying or faking goodness, and (4) provide a profile of the examinee's personality. Structured tests do not allow probing into areas that might seem especially important in a particular case. The assumption with these instruments is that the entire range of the examinee's personality is being adequately assessed. Table 4-6 contains the 16 Personality Factors measured by the 16PF.

PSYCHOPATHOLOGY. Tests that can identify psychological disorders are referred to as tests of psychopathology. These tests can either be structured or unstructured. Structured tests must be administered in a specific fashion and have detailed scoring and interpretation guides; unstructured tests provide ambiguous stimuli to the examinee and have less precise scoring requirements.

Pathological personality can be measured by such structured instruments as the Beck Depression Inventory (BDI) and the Minnesota Multiphasic Personality Inventory (MMPI) (Hathaway & McKinley, 1943). The latter test has recently been renormed on a broader target population and is available as the MMPI-2. Figure 4-4 contains a profile sheet from the MMPI-2, with a typical profile of a bulimic client. Notice that comparisons can be made with the norming sample (T-score of 50), as well as with established clinical groups such as bulimics who often have been observed to have elevated T-scores on scales 2, 4, 6, and 8 of the MMPI.

Personality can also be measured using projective tests, the assumption being that these tests can elicit particularly meaningful inner feelings. While the stimuli for projective tests are often ambiguous, the scoring of the tests can be objective; administration and scoring often require extended training. Since they have no right answers, such tests are less susceptible to faking and to other response biases.

The classic example of a projective test is the Rorschach Inkblot Test (Exner, 1974; Goldfried, Stricker, & Weiner, 1971; Rorschach, 1921). The present authors' attempt at an inkblot is shown in Figure 4-5. Two additional projective measures of psychopathology are the Holtzman Inkblot Test (Holtzman, Thorpe, Swartz, & Herron, 1961) and the Thematic Apperception Test (Murray, 1943). A less structured projective test is one in which the examinee is given the beginning of a sentence and asked to complete it, as is done in the Rotter Incomplete Sentence Blank (Rotter & Rafferty, 1950). Several examples of incomplete sentences are shown in Table 4-7.

TABLE 4-6   A profile sheet for the 16PF.

Factor	Low Sten score description (1–3)	High Sten score description (8–10)
A	Cool, reserved, impersonal, formal, aloof	Warm, outgoing, kindly, easygoing, participating, likes people
B	Concrete-thinking Lower scholastic mental ability	Abstract-thinking, bright Higher scholastic mental ability
C	Affected by feelings, emotionally less stable, easily annoyed	Emotionally stable, mature, faces reality, calm
E	Submissive, humble, mild, easily led, accommodating	Dominant, assertive, aggressive, stubborn, competitive, bossy
F	Sober, restrained, prudent, taciturn, serious	Enthusiastic, spontaneous, heedless, expressive, cheerful
G	Expedient, disregards rules, self-indulgent	Conscientious, conforming, moralistic, staid, rule-bound
H	Shy, threat-sensitive, timid, hesitant, intimidated	Bold, venturesome, uninhibited, can take stress
I	Tough-minded, self-reliant, no-nonsense, rough, realistic	Tender-minded, sensitive, overprotected, intuitive, refined
L	Trusting, accepting conditions, easy to get on with	Suspicious, hard to fool, distrustful, skeptical
M	Practical, concerned with down-to-earth issues, steady	Imaginative, absent-minded, absorbed in thought, impractical
N	Forthright, unpretentious, open, genuine, artless	Polished, socially aware, diplomatic, calculating
O	Self-assured, secure, feels free of guilt, untroubled, self-satisfied	Apprehensive, self-blaming, guilt-prone, insecure, worrying
Q_1	Conservative, respecting traditional ideas	Experimenting, liberal, critical, open to change
Q_2	Group-oriented, a joiner and sound follower, listens to others Group adherence	Self-sufficient, resourceful, prefers own decisions Self-sufficiency
Q_3	Undisciplined self-conflict, lax, careless of social rules Low integration	Following self-image, socially precise, compulsive High self-concept control
Q_4	Relaxed, tranquil, composed, has low drive, unfrustrated	Tense, frustrated, overwrought, has high drive

NOTE: A *Sten* (short for Standardized Ten) scale divides the normal distribution into 10 parts. 50% of the distribution falls above or below a Sten of 5.5 (the scale mean). Low Sten values (1–3) represent the lowest 16% of the distribution, whereas high Sten values (8–10) represent the highest 16% of the distribution. From the Administrator's Manual for the 16 Personality Factor Questionnaire, Copyright © 1972, 1979, 1986 by the Institute for Personality and Ability Testing, Inc. Reproduced by permission.

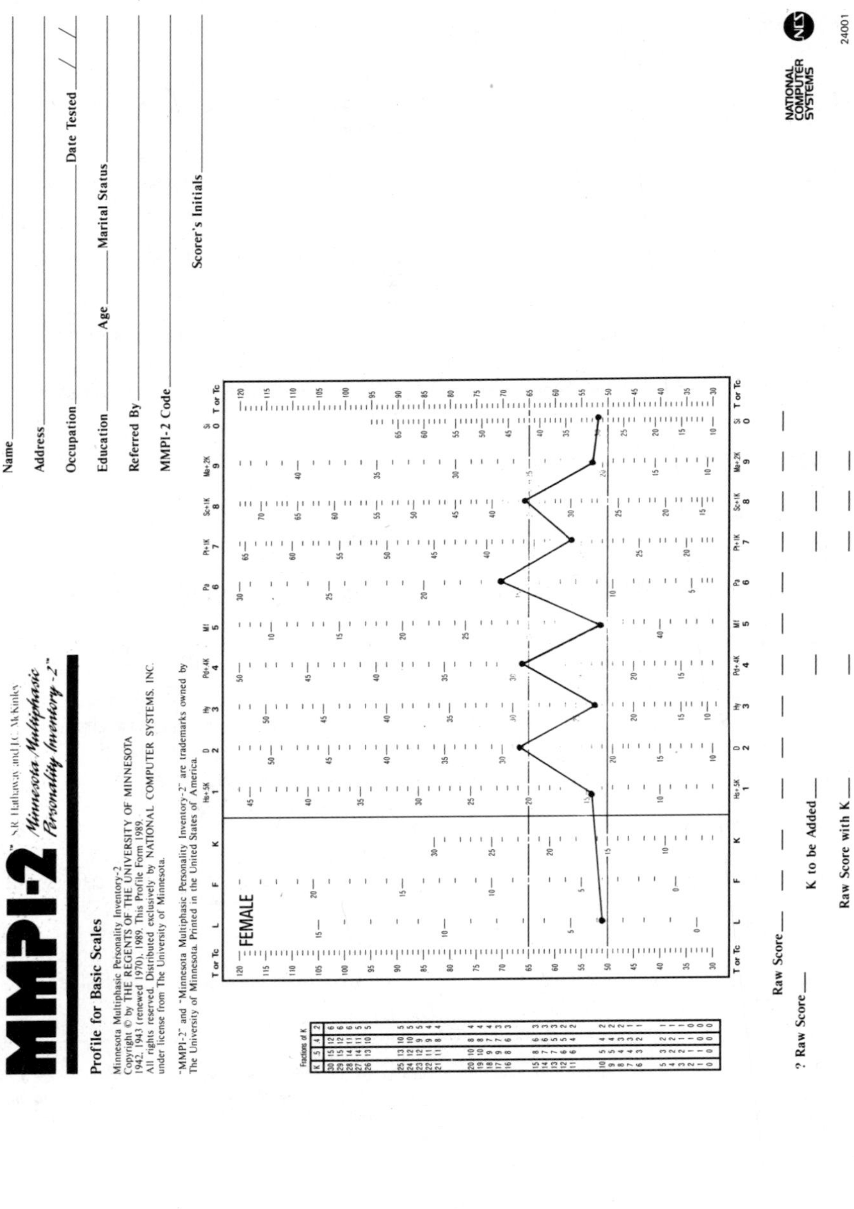

MMPI-2 ™ SR Hathaway and J.C. McKinley
Minnesota Multiphasic
Personality Inventory -2 ™

Profile for Basic Scales

Minnesota Multiphasic Personality Inventory-2
Copyright © by THE REGENTS OF THE UNIVERSITY OF MINNESOTA
1942, 1943 (renewed 1970), 1989. This Profile Form 1989.
All rights reserved. Distributed exclusively by NATIONAL COMPUTER SYSTEMS, INC.
under license from The University of Minnesota.

"MMPI-2" and "Minnesota Multiphasic Personality Inventory-2" are trademarks owned by
The University of Minnesota. Printed in the United States of America.

Name_____
Address_____
Occupation_____ Date Tested __/__/__
Education_____ Age_____ Marital Status_____
Referred By_____
MMPI-2 Code_____

Scorer's Initials_____

FEMALE

Raw Score _____
? Raw Score _____   K to be Added _____
                        Raw Score with K _____

NATIONAL
COMPUTER
SYSTEMS

24001

FIGURE 4-4 MMPI-2 profile of "Jane Doe." (Note that scales 4, 6, and 8 are elevated, a typical profile for a bulimic woman.)

FIGURE 4-5   Example of an inkblot.

SPECIALIZED MEASURES.   Often, a researcher's question requires a more specific measure than the ones discussed above. When this is the case, library research can reveal whether or not a good instrument already exists. (See the end of this chapter for some widely used resources.) The best place to start is with *The Tenth Mental Measurements Yearbook* (Conoley & Kramer, 1989). Then, the researcher should investigate those sources that appear to be most relevant to the field and to the content area being assessed. These resources should be exhausted before a researcher even considers constructing an instrument. Seldom can a researcher develop an instrument that approaches the reliability and validity of those already existing.

CAREER INTEREST INVENTORIES.   Interests are feelings and beliefs about an activity; **career interest inventories** measure likes and dislikes of various occupations and activities. Examples of widely used career interest inventories are the Kuder Occupational Interest Survey (Kuder, 1979) and the Strong Interest Inventory (Harmon, Hansen, Borgen, & Hammer, 1994). The purpose of these measures

TABLE 4-7   Three examples of incomplete sentences.

1. When I was young, I _____

_____

2. I am often sick when _____

_____

3. My friends think _____

_____

is to provide information useful in advising students about vocations and about their future education.

Figure 4-6 contains feedback from one of the most widely used career inventories—the Strong Interest Inventory (Harmon, Hansen, Borgen, & Hammer, 1994). The standardization sample consisted of people who had worked in their occupations for at least 3 years and who indicated a high level of satisfaction. The feedback indicates activities and vocations that are similar, moderately similar, and very dissimilar to the interests and preferences of the test-taker.

Behavioral Checklists

Behavioral checklists systematize and quantify a subject's behavior. While many different kinds of behavior could occur, the behavioral checklist only records behavior in which the researcher has interest. In addition, either a frequency count (of the number of times that behavior occurs) or a rating of the intensity of the behavior is included. One other advantage of a behavioral checklist is that one can be developed to meet the specific needs of the researcher.

However, if there are no previous data on this behavioral checklist, there is no context within which to make conclusions. For example, if 45% of the subjects exhibit a certain behavior, is that more than should be expected? There is no comparison information on which to base a conclusion. There are two ways to get around this problem. The first is to obtain information on two or more occasions so that comparisons can be made, not to a particular population but between times with the same subjects. Progress could thus be determined from the beginning of treatment to the end or to 6 months after the end of treatment.

The second way to avoid this problem is to use a standardized behavioral checklist with norms on a population that is similar to the researcher's. This means the behavioral checklist must contain the behaviors in which the researcher is interested. Many researchers base their research hypotheses on available standardized instruments instead of on the phenomenon they want to study.

Many standardized behavioral checklists have been developed, such as the Conners Rating Scale (Conners, 1985). Items similar to those on the Conners appear in Table 4-8.

TABLE 4-8 Items similar to those on the Conners Rating Scale.

For each of the following items, rate how much the child has been bothered by this problem during the past month; (a) not at all, (b) just a little, (c) pretty much, or (d) very much

1. Cannot focus for more than 10 minutes.

2. Has problem learning.

3. Behavior changes quickly.

STRONG INTEREST INVENTORY

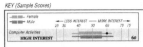

GENERAL OCCUPATIONAL THEMES

BASIC INTEREST SCALES

KEY (Sample Scores)

The phrase printed below the scale name compares your interests to those of people of your own gender. The upper bar shows the range of scores for a group of women from many occupations; the lower bar, the range of scores for a group of men. The number in the right-hand column, represented by the dot, is your score compared to both men and women.

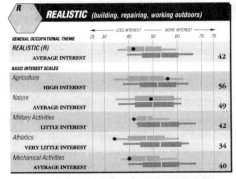

REALISTIC (building, repairing, working outdoors)

GENERAL OCCUPATIONAL THEME	
REALISTIC (R)	
AVERAGE INTEREST	42
BASIC INTEREST SCALES	
Agriculture	
HIGH INTEREST	56
Nature	
AVERAGE INTEREST	49
Military Activities	
LITTLE INTEREST	42
Athletics	
VERY LITTLE INTEREST	34
Mechanical Activities	
AVERAGE INTEREST	40

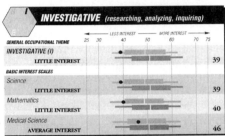

INVESTIGATIVE (researching, analyzing, inquiring)

GENERAL OCCUPATIONAL THEME	
INVESTIGATIVE (I)	
LITTLE INTEREST	39
BASIC INTEREST SCALES	
Science	
LITTLE INTEREST	39
Mathematics	
LITTLE INTEREST	40
Medical Science	
AVERAGE INTEREST	46

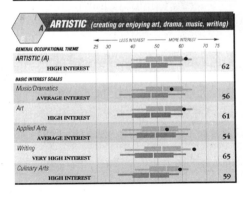

ARTISTIC (creating or enjoying art, drama, music, writing)

GENERAL OCCUPATIONAL THEME	
ARTISTIC (A)	
HIGH INTEREST	62
BASIC INTEREST SCALES	
Music/Dramatics	
AVERAGE INTEREST	56
Art	
HIGH INTEREST	61
Applied Arts	
AVERAGE INTEREST	54
Writing	
VERY HIGH INTEREST	65
Culinary Arts	
HIGH INTEREST	59

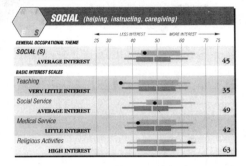

SOCIAL (helping, instructing, caregiving)

GENERAL OCCUPATIONAL THEME	
SOCIAL (S)	
AVERAGE INTEREST	45
BASIC INTEREST SCALES	
Teaching	
VERY LITTLE INTEREST	35
Social Service	
AVERAGE INTEREST	49
Medical Service	
LITTLE INTEREST	42
Religious Activities	
HIGH INTEREST	63

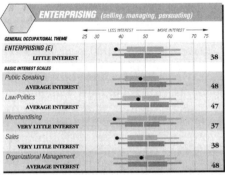

ENTERPRISING (selling, managing, persuading)

GENERAL OCCUPATIONAL THEME	
ENTERPRISING (E)	
LITTLE INTEREST	38
BASIC INTEREST SCALES	
Public Speaking	
AVERAGE INTEREST	48
Law/Politics	
AVERAGE INTEREST	47
Merchandising	
VERY LITTLE INTEREST	37
Sales	
VERY LITTLE INTEREST	38
Organizational Management	
AVERAGE INTEREST	48

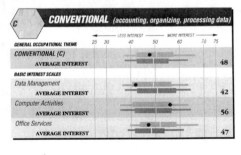

CONVENTIONAL (accounting, organizing, processing data)

GENERAL OCCUPATIONAL THEME	
CONVENTIONAL (C)	
AVERAGE INTEREST	48
BASIC INTEREST SCALES	
Data Management	
AVERAGE INTEREST	42
Computer Activities	
AVERAGE INTEREST	56
Office Services	
AVERAGE INTEREST	47

CPP CONSULTING PSYCHOLOGISTS PRESS, INC. • 3803 E. Bayshore Road, Palo Alto, CA 94303

FIGURE 4-6   Typical feedback from the SII.

Nonstandardized Data Collection Methods

In the previous sections, we discussed various standardized ways to obtain information. As we noted, however, a researcher may determine that these instruments are inadequate to test the research question. In that case, the researcher may turn to a nonstandardized measure—one that is not administered or scored the same way from person to person and lacks norms for score interpretation.

We place the nonstandardized measures in Figure 4-7 into three categories, depending on how the data are collected. If the subject reports the information, we call this *subject self-report*. Questionnaires and surveys are prime examples of self-report data. If the researcher observes the subject in some way, we call this *other-report*. The researcher could observe the subjects, or the researcher could rely on significant others or trained observers such as trained research assistants. Interviews are in another category of nonstandardized tests in which the researcher interacts with the subject.

Questionnaires and Surveys

Research questions often lead a researcher into areas that existing instruments do not address. If the information needed to answer the question can be obtained from subjects without being in their presence, the researcher uses a **questionnaire** or **survey**. Of course, the researcher could administer the questionnaire personally to increase response rate and to answer unforeseen questions. Such an instrument does not vary in administration from subject to subject and usually taps noncognitive beliefs or behavior.

Another reason for using these tools is that they can preserve anonymity. Researchers usually believe they can get more accurate information on attitudes and opinions when subjects answer anonymously. People tend to hide negative feelings and unpopular (politically incorrect) opinions unless their anonymity keeps them safe enough to be honest and open. As we discussed in the previous chapter, the ethics of research on human subjects require that participants be guaranteed confidentiality.

Questionnaires or surveys will either be administered by mail, telephone, or in person to a large group, usually with some time limits. Since the researcher does not have the luxury of explaining the instrument in detail, it must be carefully developed. The developer must anticipate any possible confusion as well as all possible responses. Survey research is discussed in detail in Chapter 8.

Behavioral Observations

Behavioral observations are recordings of behavior made by an observer. The real-time behavior is in some way captured, often by scripting the event or by audiotaping or videotaping it. The researcher may not state what specific behavior is being sought. Only a broad term may be used such as "discipline problems." Therefore, behavioral observations are probably the weakest kind of measurement; they require much inference by the researcher, and they yield data that could be contaminated by the researcher's expectations. We will dis-

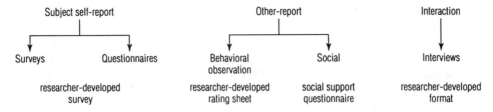

FIGURE 4-7   Categorization of standardized data collection procedures.

cuss this problem in more detail in Chapter 5. Whenever possible, a researcher should include additional data that go beyond what can be obtained from an unstructured behavioral observation. On the other hand, if a specific behavior has been clearly identified, behavioral observations can be a valuable tool.

Sociometric Methods

Researchers use **sociometric methods** to obtain information about the interaction or lack thereof in social relationships. Sociometric methods may obtain information from subjects themselves or from others in the subject's social circle—their class, housing unit, or therapy group. Information can be obtained either on real, desired, or fantasized relationships, although it has been found that the more realistic the situation, the more valid the information obtained.

The Social Support Questionnaire (SSQ) (Sarason, Levine, Bashhnan, & Sarason, 1983) is a self-report measure of social support. The questionnaire has 27 items, each with 2 parts. Subjects must indicate (1) the people who can be counted on for support in given situations and (2) the overall satisfaction with these supports. Table 4-9 contains items similar to those found on sociometric measures.

Interviews

Interviews, whether conducted by the researcher or a trained interviewer, can provide in-depth information from different information providers. Interviews can be totally structured, that is, follow a prescribed list of questions, and interviews can be standardized on a large sample from a target population. This allows for comparisons with that population. If a researcher needs some flexibility, an unstructured interview can be conducted. Such an interview would have a general purpose in mind, would be individually conducted, and would change from person to person, depending on the responses elicited. The advantage of a structured interview is that it provides comparable data from all those interviewed.

The unstructured interview, on the other hand, allows the interviewer to probe interesting avenues that are identified during the interview. While such questioning may provide a deeper understanding of each individual, it usually does not provide data that are comparable across subjects. In addition, unstructured interviews are susceptible to the interviewer's expectations.

TABLE 4-9   Sample items measuring social competence.

Related to peers:
    Does the child cooperate with peers by initiating activities?

Related to the teacher:
    Does the child follow the teacher's directions?

Related to when the child is alone:
    Does the child express anger through physical means?

Researchers frequently use a **semistructured interview,** a combination of the structured and unstructured interview, that capitalizes on the unique benefits of each. The semistructured interview provides summary data on all subjects and amplified data for some subjects. A final benefit of the semistructured interview is that an avenue can be explored for all subjects that may not have been anticipated when the interview was designed.

A study on recidivism by Barton and Butts (1990) used the structured interview format to evaluate three in-home supervision programs. The researchers wanted to supplement court records on offenses by juvenile delinquents with the delinquent's own self-report of delinquent behaviors. The subjects were asked if they engaged in any of 26 different behaviors. These 26 behaviors were later grouped into 4 categories: (1) drug and alcohol offenses, (2) property offenses, (3) violent offenses, and (4) minor offenses.

MARIA REVISITED

While conducting her library research, Maria discovers the many ways she could measure bulimia. She realizes that self-reported binging and purging would require the least amount of inference but that respondents could easily fake or fail to remember exact information. She could observe the behavior herself, but that would be costly and possibly difficult. Maria knows that observing people continuously might very well change their behavior or at least cause them to become very secretive in their binging and purging.

Maria knows that the diagnostic interview conducted at the beginning of counseling contains criteria for the determination of bulimia. For example, her interview requires questioning each subject about symptoms related to a variety of psychological disorders. These disorders and symptoms are listed in the *Diagnostic and Statistical Manual of Mental Disorders,* third edition and revised (DSM-III-R) (APA, 1987). By interviewing participants in this way, she can determine their degree of bulimia as well as assess other coexisting psychological conditions. [Researchers should keep abreast of updates. When Maria conducted her study, the DSM-III-R was the most current version. An update of the DSM-III-R now exists—the DSM-IV (APA, 1994)]. Regarding the specific assessment of bulimia, paper and pencil self-report measures have been the usual means for assessing bulimic behavior. Maria found that four such tests have been used extensively. Garner and Garfinkel (1979) developed the Eating Attitude Test, and Garner, Olmstead, and Polivy (1983) developed the Eating Disorders Inventory. The BULIT was developed by Smith and Thelen (1984) and is based on the criteria specified in the DSM-III (APA, 1980). Since the DSM-III was revised and the diagnostic criteria for bulimia became more stringent, the BULIT was also revised (Thelen, Farmer, Wonderlich, & Smith, 1990) and now goes by the acronym of BULIT-R. So, Maria chose the BULIT-R as the operational measure of her dependent variable—bulimic behavior.

CONCERNS RELATED TO SELECTING AND DEVELOPING A TEST

Three major concerns are related to selecting and developing a test: reliability, validity, and usability. **Reliability** is the degree of consistency of scores over repeated testing, while **validity** is the degree to which the test measures what it purports to measure. Validity is the more important criteria of a test, subsuming the concept of reliability. **Usability** refers to the practical considerations in using the test—considerations like time, cost, and the availability of qualified test administrators. These concerns are intertwined and they sometimes depend on how the tests are implemented. That is, a test does not have an inherent degree of reliability, validity, or usability but these characteristics differ, depending on the application of the test. Some tests have been used over a long time period as measures of a particular construct. But if the population, setting, or methods change, the reliability and validity would have to be reestablished.

Figure 4-8 contains a visual analogue for reliability and validity. Imagine that a researcher has developed different procedures for throwing darts. The goal is to hit the bullseye. Procedure A is very inconsistent. The darts do not land in any one place, and therefore we would say that procedure A is not reliable. Neither is it valid. A test with low reliability cannot have a high degree of validity. Procedure B results in darts landing in the upper right corner of the target. Therefore, procedure B is somewhat consistent but is not on target. While the reliability of procedure B is better than that of procedure A, we would not be satisfied with using procedure B because none of the darts are on target. Procedure B has a high degree of reliability, but since the procedure is consistently off target, it is not valid. Procedure C results in all darts hitting the middle of the bullseye, so we would say that procedure C is both reliable (consistent) and valid (consistently on the bullseye). Procedure C is the one we really want to use, as the darts are not only consistent but they are all on the bullseye as well.

Reliability and most validity measures are numerically indexed with a correlation coefficient. (The reader should refer to Chapter 10 if not already familiar with the concept.) Correlational values range from –1.00 to +1.00; the two extremes show a high degree of relationship; values close to .00 show little relationship. Validity coefficients are usually given as the correlation between a test and another measure; reliability coefficients correlate a test with another version of the same test. While the researcher wants to obtain tests with perfect reliability and validity indices of +1.00, reliability indices are commonly in the .80 to .90 range. Usually, the more effort put into the development of a test, the

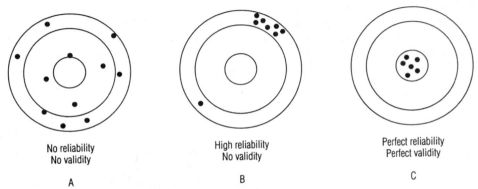

No reliability	High reliability	Perfect reliability
No validity	No validity	Perfect validity
A	B	C

NOTE: The bullseye represents the construct that is to be measured; each dot represents repeated measures of one individual.

FIGURE 4-8   Reliability and validity schematically represented.

higher its validity. Usually, the less inference required, the higher the validity. Although validity is the more important concern, validity is limited by reliability and is therefore substantially lower.

Reliability

Reliability refers to the degree to which the results of testing are attributable to systematic sources of variance (Committee, 1985). There will usually be some nonsystematic sources of variance in any test. The degree to which there is only systematic variance is called the *magnitude of the reliability coefficient*, which is based on observed test scores. The nonsystematic sources of variance are indexed by the standard error of measurement. The higher the reliability coefficient, the lower the standard error of measurement.

Any score on a test can be conceptualized as a person's true score plus error:

observed test score = true score + error

The less error there is in a testing situation, the closer the observed test score approximates the true score.

A major concern is when a source of error has a large, systematic impact on the observed scores. Examples of systematic error would be (1) several test questions being leaked to students before the exam, (2) a scale being reset from 0 pounds to 4 pounds, and (3) the scoring key being incorrect for one of the test items. Such a systematic error cannot be detected by the various reliability approaches we will discuss. It is up to the researcher to avoid systematic errors through careful design and careful implementation of the study.

The major sources of error can be placed into four categories. First, the length of the test is an important factor. If too few items are included, the construct may not be adequately assessed since each item usually only approximates the construct. If too many items are included, the respondents may become fatigued or irritated. A balance should be sought, but what that balance is cannot be clearly delineated.

Second, if the examinees are similar to one another, it will be difficult for any test to distinguish between them. The more heterogeneous the examinees are on the tests, the more reliable the test is, but if tests are to be useful, they must discriminate. This is hard for some new researchers to face. For example, if everyone gets 100 on a test—third graders, doctoral students, psychotics—what do the test scores reveal? Most researchers in the helping professions would like to see their subjects do well, but if all subjects always do well—both before and after treatment—then their doing well cannot be attributed to treatment. Subjects would have to do poorly before treatment if the desired inference that treatment caused them to do better is to be made.

The item difficulty of the test is a third factor affecting reliability. This factor relies on the same logic as above. If the items are too difficult or too easy, the test will not differentiate between examinees. Consider a test with all easy items—so easy that all examinees obtain a perfect score before treatment. How can treatment make their scores any higher? More importantly, are all the examinees really at the same level of the construct? All we know is that because the test is an easy one all examinees perform minimally on the construct. The optimal difficulty level for differentiating between examinees is .50—half of the examinees get each item correct.

The fourth factor affecting the reliability of the test is the number of alternatives available to the examinee. The fewer the number of alternatives in each item, the lower is the reliability. That is why true-false tests, in general, are less reliable than multiple-choice tests. Table 4-10 shows the major ways to obtain a reliability index. Which one is chosen depends on the use of the test and the major sources of random error in the testing situation.

Test-retest reliability is the correlation between two successive administrations of the same test and should be used when the construct being measured can be assumed to be stable over that period. Other measures of reliability would be desirable if the construct being measured is expected to change over time, as with rapidly developing children or people with degenerating brain disorders.

Alternate forms reliability is obtained from the correlation between two successively administered forms of the same test. If the test has a high degree of alternate forms reliability, the researcher can assume that the same construct is being measured by both forms. Several factors could lower this reliability measure, including fatigue, practice, different administrators, different test administration instructions, and different content on the two forms.

Internal consistency reliability is the consistency of the test as determined from one test administration. This approach avoids all the factors of potential unreliability related to alternate forms reliability by creating two forms from

TABLE 4-10 Ways to obtain reliability.

Method	What the Method Measures	Content	Time Interval	How Obtain
Test-retest	Stability in relative standing of examinees	Identical	Varies	Give same instrument twice (test-retest correlation)
Coefficient of equivalence	Relationship between two parallel forms	Different	None	Give two forms—correlate
Internal consistency	Homogeneity of items	Different	None	Divide instrument into
				(a) two halves— split-half
				(b) KR-20: all possible halves with dichotomous items
				(c) Cronbach alpha: all possible halves with polychoto- mous items
Interrater reliability	Consistency of rating	Identical	None	Correlate observers' scores

NOTE: Another way to obtain coefficient of equivalence is to give two forms at different times—thus varying the time interval as well as the content.

one. Two forms can be created by comparing the first half to the second half, by comparing performance on the odd items to performance on the even items, or by getting the average of all possible combinations. The often-used procedures, Kuder-Richardson 20 (Kuder & Richardson, 1937) and Cronbach's alpha (Cronbach, 1984), calculate internal consitency based on all possible combinations. While internal consistency reliability reduces or eliminates many sources of error, the coefficient can be deflated when items differ in format, difficulty, or in the construct being measured.

Interrater reliability is required when the measure is not scored objectively but is scored subjectively. The goal here is to provide evidence that the same score would be awarded by two independent judges. The process requires that a sample of the responses of a subset of examinees be scored by two judges. Those scores are then correlated and if there are differences in how the two judges view their scoring responsibilities, interrater reliability will be lowered. Extensive training is often required if respectable interrater reliability is to be obtained. (See the single-subject study provided in Chapter 9.)

Since there are many factors that can lead to error in an examinee's score perhaps a positive approach should be considered. What can a researcher do to decrease the error and therefore increase reliability? Table 4-11 contains seven tips for increasing reliability.

The first four suggestions relate to how the test is constructed. Increasing the length of the test and including items of medium difficulty have already been discussed. Eliminating ambiguous items makes sense because each item then measures one and only one construct. If the test measures more than one construct, its reliability (and validity) will be curtailed.

The last three suggestions in Table 4-11 deal with test administration practices. Following standard testing conditions will mean that the data obtained are comparable to those of the norming sample. If testing conditions differ drastically from those specified in the test manual, something other than what the test manual stipulates has probably been measured. Likewise, the test-takers should be motivated to take the test but not overly motivated. For example, students who are asked to take a test that will not count toward their grade will not be as motivated, and therefore will not do as well, as those who are told that the test will count as 50% of their grade. Finally, accurate scoring of tests is related to obtaining a reliable indicator. Random errors, as well as systematic errors, will reduce the interpretive value of the test.

Validity

As discussed in *Standards for Educational and Psychological Testing* (Committee, 1985), validity "refers to the appropriateness of inferences from test scores . . . (a) What can be inferred about what is being measured by the test?, and (b) What can be inferred about other behavior?" Validity is the degree to which the test measures the construct it purports to measure. Validity is thus a higher-order construct, subsuming reliability.

For instance, a ruler with its first 3 inches removed will provide the same

TABLE 4-11   Tips for increasing reliability.

1. Increase the length of the test.

2. Make sure the test measures only one construct.

3. Include items that are of medium difficulty.

4. Eliminate ambiguous items to reduce guessing and frustration.

5. Follow standard testing conditions.

6. Make sure that examinees are motivated to provide accurate information.

7. Score tests accurately.

score on successive measurements and is thus highly reliable, but each measurement will overestimate by 3 inches the length of any object; thus it lacks validity. An intact ruler measuring how tall people are would produce highly reliable readings, as well as valid readings for measuring the construct of height, but those height readings would not be a valid measure of intelligence or anxiety.

The validity of a measure is always inferred instead of being measured directly. In addition, validity must be reassessed for every application. For instance, a test that measures attitudes toward AIDS in college students may not be readable by third-graders and thus could not be a valid measure of third-graders' attitudes toward AIDS. In summary, the validity of a test is a matter of degree and pertains to the intended use of the test. It is not inherent in the test itself.

Face validity is a form of validity that is not recognized in the *Technical Standards*, although the concept is still appropriate. The test must appear to the test administrator, as well as to the subject, to be a reasonable way to measure the construct. Otherwise, neither will approach the testing situation with a serious intent. If a researcher wants to camouflage the purpose of a test, however, the concept of face validity does not apply. Since assuming face validity requires making a judgment call, there is no way to index the concept, and even if face validity is determined to be important, the following types of validity are always going to be more important.

Content validity is the extent to which the behaviors being measured are judged to represent the construct. These judgments are made by experts and are based on their expertise. As such, content validity is a broad term that has little to do with the empirical relationships defined by the measures.

Predictive validity is the extent to which a test correlates with some future behavior. The test and the future behavior can be measures of the same construct

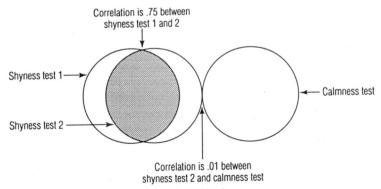

FIGURE 4-9   An illustration of construct validity.

or of different constructs. An example of the same construct would be the predictive validity of high school academic success with college success. An example of different constructs would be the predictive validity of high school motivation with college academic success. When there is a time lag in the data collection, the researcher is concerned with predictive validity.

Construct validity tells us how well the test measures the construct it purports to measure. Such a determination cannot be made in a single study but requires an extended investigation of how the test relates to other measures of the same or different constructs.

For instance, construct validity can be quantified using the correlation coefficient, as illustrated in Figure 4-9. In the figure, Shyness Test 2 is being construct validated in two ways. First, Shyness Test 2 is correlated with another existing test of shyness, Test 1. Since the correlation is .75, there is evidence Shyness Test 2 measures what it purports to. The other evidence of validation is found in the relationship between Shyness Test 2 and the Calmness Test. Since these constructs are different, a close-to-zero correlation would be expected. Since the obtained correlation is .01, this data also supports the construct validity of Shyness Test 2. The logic is that tests of dissimilar constructs should not be related—precisely the outcome in the example.

Usability

Reliability and validity are technical aspects of the test, while usability is an administrative aspect. Test usability includes administration, interpretation, reporting, and the costs associated with each. For instance, if knowing how to administer the test requires training, either a trained test administrator must be found or the researcher must undergo the training. Many tests cannot be scored by hand, resulting in additional costs and possibly delays in obtaining the scores. Reliability and validity often rely on standardized test administration and test scoring procedures, and therefore these standardized procedures must be adhered to if that test is to be used. If the costs are judged to be too high, an alternate test must be chosen.

Conclusions About Concerns

One particular data collection method will not always be the best for a given research question. Table 4-12 summarizes the advantages and disadvantages of the various methods. These comments must be related to and integrated with the specific research hypotheses tested.

Increasingly, the notion of usability is becoming the umbrella over all ideas about testing. Included in the construct now is how the test will be used for a particular situation. Each test user should consider the decisions that will be made with that test. Let us assume that test A is being considered for special education placement. First, does special education placement seem to be an

TABLE 4-12 Advantages and disadvantages of data collection methods.

STANDARDIZED MEASURES

ADVANTAGES
1. Administration is standard.
2. References to norm group are provided.
3. Individual scores are provided.
4. Using them takes less time than researcher-developed instruments.
5. Results can be compared to other research results using the same instrument.

DISADVANTAGES
1. Construct of choice may not be measured.
2. Norms may not be applicable.

BEHAVIORAL CHECKLISTS

ADVANTAGES
1. Behavior can be specified to meet research needs.
2. Behavior can be precisely defined.
3. Information can be obtained over a time period long enough to meet needs of researcher.

DISADVANTAGES
1. Raters may have different definitions of behavior.
2. Raters may see behavior differently.
3. Raters may drift over time in their ratings.
4. Raters may affect the situation they are observing.

SELF-REPORT MEASURES

ADVANTAGES
1. Inner feelings can be elicited.
2. Forced-choice items can minimize social desirability.

DISADVANTAGES
1. Respondents may not tell the truth.
2. Respondents may not be objective or may not remember.

EXISTING RECORDS

ADVANTAGE
1. Cost is low since data already exist.

DISADVANTAGES
1. Researcher is limited to existing measures.
2. Cause and effect difficult to ascertain.
3. Data may be missing.

INTERVIEWS

ADVANTAGES
1. Personal contact facilitates responding.
2. Return rate is high.
3. Respondents can clarify questions.
4. Interviewers can probe for specific or deeper meanings.
5. Respondents' reaction to questions can be reviewed.

DISADVANTAGES
1. Substantial time required to obtain data.
2. Respondents may figure out researcher's purposes.

QUESTIONNAIRES AND SURVEYS

ADVANTAGES
1. Data recording is objective.
2. Data recording is easy and relatively quick.
3. Anonymity is easy to accomplish.
4. Method is adaptable to most research situations.

DISADVANTAGES
1. There is no opportunity to communicate beyond listed alternatives.
2. People may not know, but guess.
3. Construction of instrument may take time.

appropriate idea for this age child? Second, can test A discriminate between those who are higher on the construct and those who are lower? Third, will those who are diagnosed for special placement really benefit from such placement? Will those who are not placed in special education benefit from that decision? This last question cannot be answered by test developers but must be answered by those intending to use the test. An extensive evaluation of both the regular educational program and the special education program would have to be conducted (Shepard, 1993).

TABLE 4-13   Four item formats.

1. Open-ended: What do you think about the services provided?
2. Dichotomous: Are you satisfied with the services provided?   Yes ___   No___
3. Forced-choice: Are you more satisfied with the services provided by unit A? ___
   or by those provided by unit B? ___
4. Scaled-choice: The services provided by unit A are better now than two years ago.

Strongly Disagree	Disagree	Neutral	Agree	Strongly Agree
_____	_____	_____	_____	_____

DESIGNING MEASURING INSTRUMENTS

If none of the available instruments meets the needs of the researcher, the researcher is confronted with either having to alter the research question or to accomplish the difficult task of developing a measuring instrument. The usability of specially designed instruments may override the difficulty of establishing reliability and validity. Surveys, questionnaires, and interviews are the most likely instruments that a researcher will develop. To help the researcher do so, we next discuss various item formats. We conclude this chapter with some general recommendations for instrument development.

Item Format

One primary concern when designing an instrument is the item format. For instance, a client's attitude toward a helping professional could be assessed in the four different ways depicted in Table 4-13.

OPEN-ENDED.   Open-ended questions allow respondents to indicate the detail they choose to include. Although detailed information is often difficult. The fact that the data are subjective means that two people may not agree on the interpretation because there is no common reference point. The difficulty of sumarization is further exacerbated because it is often difficult to fathom why respondents said what they did. Are the responses negative because the respondents are negative people? Or are the negative responses a result of an isolated situation? Summarization of open-ended questions is often a high-inference activity.

DICHOTOMOUS-CHOICE.   Questions that divide the universe of possible answers into two categories (usually true-false or yes-no) are referred to as **dichotomous-choice.** Since many different answers are forced to take on the same value (of either yes or no), summary of that data is easy. Two researchers, while agreeing

TABLE 4-14   Examples of forced-choice items.

1. Choose either A or B:

  A. When in a social setting, I like to talk about myself.

  B. I like to set goals for myself and then work toward them.

2. Choose either A or B:

  A. I get real upset when I fail at anything.

  B. I get anxious when making presentations.

NOTE: A subject is forced to choose either alternative A or alternative B in each of the two questions.
   In question 1, both A and B focus on "myself." The first indicates a more social orientation, while alternative B indicates an orientation toward achievement.
   In question 2, both A and B indicate negative feelings, but A indicates negative feelings toward achievement, while B indicates negative feelings toward social setting.

that 65% is definitely more than the majority, indicating wide-spread support for the issue. The other may conclude that 65% is substantially less than unanimous, indicating disagreement on the issue. Both interpretations can be defended. The consumer of research should question the supporting reasons for a number. That is, a number should not take on importance just because it is a number; it should identify a particular magnitude of some behavior.

FORCED-CHOICE.   **Forced-choice response** items force a respondent into choosing between two or more options. The best application is when the options can be viewed as equally positive options or equally negative options, as illustrated in Table 4-14. The forced-choice procedure is particularly appropriate when respondents might try to give **socially desirable responses**—ones they think they should be giving. If the options are equally socially desirable, the respondent must respond on some basis other than social desirability. The researcher, with forced-choice response items, can minimize the influence of social desirability as a response set.

SCALED-CHOICE.   Scaled-choice, or Likert-type items contain more than two points; usually five points are used. Although respondents tend to answer favorably, the scaled-choice item can be used to compare various samples or to compare different items within one sample.

CONCLUSIONS ABOUT ITEM FORM: GENERAL RECOMMENDATIONS

You can now see that each procedure has its advantages and disadvantages and that each is clearly valuable for certain kinds of questions and constraints. Also, a questionnaire need not contain items of only one type but may contain items of several types, depending on the kind of information you desire.

Table 4-15 contains our seven tips for instrument development. There are many other concerns (see Borg & Gall, 1989, Chapter 11), but if these seven tips are followed, you will have a good start on developing a reliable, valid, and usable instrument.

No matter whether data are being obtained individually, in a large group, through the mail, or over the telephone, the researcher should always attempt to establish rapport. First, respondents can be asked to provide demographic information—age, gender, place of residence, and so forth. A researcher should only request information that will be used in the hypotheses or in the description of the sample, however. The less information required of the subjects, the less likely they are to get bored and therefore to provide invalid data.

Responses always should be scored so that a high score indicates more of the construct. This does not mean that respondents should be aware of the scoring; it does mean that when the information is reported, a high score will mean more of the construct.

Since it is human behavior to try to look good, a researcher must minimize socially desirable responses. Careful instrument development usually can obscure what a desired response is. If that is not possible, reversing the wording of every other item will require the respondent to read each item clearly. Of course, a forced-choice format can reduce the incidence of socially desirable responses.

Concealing the purpose of an instrument measuring alcohol abuse, for example, can be accomplished by not titling it "Alcohol Addiction Survey." Instead, the instrument could be entitled, "Social Activity Scale," or "SA Scale," or "SAS." Nor would the items ask the respondents directly if they were alcoholics. Each item should measure some aspect of alcohol addiction or some correlate with it. Such indirect procedures should be used when it seems likely that respondents will not provide the truth if questioned directly. Additional filler items irrelevant to the purposes of the research can also help mask the real purpose of the instrument. If the above procedures do not suffice, there are procedures by which a researcher can (1) estimate the

TABLE 4-15   Tips for instrument development.

1. Elicit demographic information first to build rapport.

2. Score the test so that high scores represent high amount of the construct.

3. Try to eliminate or avoid socially desirable responses.

4. Intersperse positive and negative statements.

5. Conceal the purpose of the instrument.

6. Practice administering the instrument.

7. Practice taking the instrument.

degree of socially desirable responses by including a social desirability index, (2) obtain a social desirability score for each respondent, and (3) correlate the social desirability index with scores on the test. A low, nonsignificant correlation would indicate that the test scores were not contaminated with social desirability.

A researcher should always practice administering any instrument. If the instrument is normed, the normed scores assume the test will be given in a fashion consistent with the norming procedure. Time limits, order of subtests, norming dates, and allowable answers to questions must be clearly understood and followed by the test administrator. When researchers use instruments that they develop themselves or modify for a particular research purpose, careful test administration practices are still in order. Test responses should always be in response to the test, not the test administrator.

Finally, the researcher should always take the test. The researcher should put herself or himself in the place of the test-taker. Only then will certain questions about the test or problems with test administration become evident.

Developing a test is difficult, enormously time consuming, and fraught with difficulties. A thorough review of the available tests should always be conducted first. We include in Form 4-1 an example of a test selection worksheet for norm-referenced achievement tests as an example of the kinds of information to look for. Modifications in this form would be necessary if certain information is not essential to a particular research effort or if domains other than achievement are to be measured. Even when a researcher decides to develop a test, such a form should be used.

MARIA CHOOSES A DEPENDENT VARIABLE

Maria's research question does not specify the operational measure that will be used to test the effectiveness of the two treatments. In her literature review, she read about the value and widespread use of four self-report measures of bulimic behavior. She decided against using the Eating Disorders Inventory and the Eating Attitude Test because both were developed before the redefining of bulimic behavior in the DSM-III-R. Since the DSM-III-R is the basis for many psychological diagnoses, she felt that these two measures were tapping an outmoded construct. Maria decided to use her initial clinical interview to screen subjects for eating-related disorders; subsequently, she selected the BULIT-R to provide a more thorough assessment of behavior.

The BULIT-R is a 5-point, Likert-type scale in which the bulimic response is indicated with a score of 5. Since 28 of the 36 questions are scored for bulimia, scores range from a low of 28 to a high of 140. Previous researchers have used scores of 104 and above to indicate bulimia, and thus Maria decides to do likewise.

Fortunately for Maria, the BULIT-R has acceptable reliability and validity. Thelen et al. (1990) reported a test-retest reliability correlation of .87. Predictive validity results were reported by these same authors ranging from .64 to .89. The BULIT-R has evidenced construct validity coefficients

FORM 4-1   Test selection worksheet.

(1) PROGRAM TREATMENT: _____   RATER: _____

(2) TEST NAME: _____   DATE: _____

(3) TEST LEVEL: _____   GRADE: _____

(4) TEST FORM: _____

_____

(5) SUBTEST NAME: _____

_____

(6) CONTENT VALIDITY:	❏ Acceptable	❏ Questionable
	❏ Unacceptable	❏ Comment/sheet attached
(7) RELIABILITY	❏ Split half _____	❏ 20 _____
(8) ❏ SUB5TEST	❏ Test/retest _____	❏ KR 21 _____
❏ WHOLE TEST	❏ Coefficient Alone_____	❏ Alternative/ Equivalent _____
		❏ Form _____
(9) NORMING	❏ Other (specify)_____	
(10)	❏ Districts like mineincluded	❏ No districts like mine included

(11) EMPIRICAL NORMING DATE(s)   Fall __/__/__   Midyear __/__/__   Spring __/__/__

(12) FUNCTIONAL TESTING: ❏ Available   ❏ Not Available

In-level norms reported for out-of-level testing?   ❏ No   ❏ Yes   ❏ Do not know

If available, what is the name of the expanded score scale? _____

_____

(13) TEST SCORES:
❏ Raw scores   ❏ Stanines
❏ Grade equivalents   ❏ Percentile
❏ Standard scores   ❏ NCEs
❏ Other (specify): _____
❏ Other (specify): _____

(14) ADMINISTRATION:

(a) Type: ❏ Large group   ❏ Small group   ❏ Individual

(b) Timed test: ❏ No   ❏ Yes

(c) Appropriate timing: ❏ No   ❏ Yes

(d) Multiple level facilitation: ❏ No   ❏ Yes   ❏ Not Applicable

(e) Practice test: ❏ No   ❏ Yes

(f) Test requirements: ❏ Regular classroom
❏ Special testing area
❏ Special testing apparatus

(g) General instructions: ❏ None   ❏ Limited   ❏ Extensive

FORM 4-1   *(Continued)*

    (h) Specific Instructions: ❑ Clear, specific and readable
                                     ❑ Clear, but general and not easily read
                                     ❑ Vague, or not present

    (i)   Special Training: ❑ None
                                       ❑ Little: teacher can administer
                                     ❑ Vague, or not present

(15) SERVICES PROVIDED:

    (a) Scoring: ❑ Local scoring   ❑ Publisher scoring
                        ❑ Other scoring services

    (b) Answer documents: ❑ Consumable booklet
                               ❑ Machine readable ❑ Self-scoring

    (c) Special norms: ❑ No   ❑ Yes
    (d) Special reports: ❑ No   ❑ Yes
    (e) Matched scores: ❑ No   ❑ Yes
    (f)   Item analysis: ❑ No   ❑ Yes
    (g) Consultant services: ❑ No   ❑ Yes
    (h) Other (specify)   ❑ No   ❑ Yes
    (i)   Comments:_____

_____

_____

(16) COSTS:

    (a) Test booklets: _____ per _____ booklet(s)
    (b) Answer documents: _____ per _____ answer sheet(s)
    (c) Special materials: _____
    (d) Machine scoring costs: _____ per _____ student(s)
    (e) Test manuals: (Name) _____ No.:____ (cost) ____
                          (Name) _____ No.:____ (cost) ____
                          (Name) _____ No.:____ (cost) ____

    (f)   Staff time: _____
    (g) Special reports: (Type) _____ (oost) _____
                          (Type) _____ (cost) _____
    (h) Special Norms: (Type) _____ (costs) _____
    (i)   Other (specify) _____

_____

(17) EXPERT REVIEW: ❑ Favorable ❑ Unclear ❑ Mixed ❑ Unfavorable

    PROBLEMS: _____

_____

_____

_____

_____

_____

ranging from .74 to .93. Thus Maria's research hypothesis now is, The multifaceted approach will result in lower BULIT-R scores after treatment than will the educational approach.

SOURCES FOR TESTS

Berdie, D. R., & Anderson, J. F. (1974). Questionnaires: Design and use. Metuchen, NJ: Scarecrow Press.
> Includes information on how to design and administer a questionnaire.

Chun, K. T., Cobb, S., & French, J. R. P., Jr. (1974). Measures for psychological assessment: A guide to 3000 original sources and their application. Ann Arbor, MI: Institute for Social Research, University of Michigan.

Committee to Develop Standards for Educational and Psychological Testing (1985). Standards for educational and psychological testing. Washington, DC: American Psychological Association.
> Contains the standards that test developers and test users should follow.

Conoley, J. C., & Kramer, J. J. (1989). The tenth mental measurements yearbook. The Buros Institute of Mental Measurement, The University of Nebraska-Lincoln: University of Nebraska Press.
> Provides comprehensive reviews focusing on reliability, validity, and usability of many tests. The tenth edition focuses on tests that were new or revised after 1985. In keeping with technological advances, this edition is also available as an on-line computer service: Mental Measurement Database.

Goldman, B. A., & Osbourne, W. (1985). Unpublished mental measurements (Vol 4). New York: Human Sciences Press, Inc.
> Summarizes the research relevant to unpublished measures, as do the previous three references.

Keyser, D. J., & Sweetland, R. C. (Eds.). (1985) Test critiques (Vol 1). Kansas City, MO: Test Corporation of America.
> Provides reviews on different topical areas. Some critiques focus on specific tests as in Mental Measurements Yearbooks, while other critiques cover broad areas.

Mitchell, J. V. (1983). Tests in print III: An index to tests, test reviews, and the literature on specific tests. The Buros Institute of Mental Measurement, The University of Nebraska-Lincoln: University of Nebraska Press.
> References most of the tests printed in English. Besides basic information, it provides references to journal articles that either document the development of the test or use the test.

Research and Education Association (1981). Handbook of psychiatric rating scales. New York: Research and Education Association.
> Gives a general description and background for each rating scale, describes the type of patients for whom the scale might be used, the sources of items used in testing, and the psychometric properties of the scale.

Robinson, J. P., Shaver, P. R., & Wrightsman, L. S. (1991). *Measures of personality and social psychological attitudes*. New York: Academic Press.
Provides evaluations of the measures, as well as sample items in some cases.

Semeomoff, B. (1976). *Projective techniques*. New York: Wiley.
A good overview of various projective tests to help in making the preliminary choice.

Straus, M. A. (1978). *Family measurement techniques: Abstracts of published instruments, 1935-1974*. Minneapolis, MN: University of Minnesota Press.
Abstracts of over 800 measures relevant to the family.

Survey Research Center (1976). *Interviewer's manual*. Ann Arbor, MI: Institute for Social Research, University of Michigan.
Provides many examples on all aspects of conducting interviews.

Sweetland, R. C., & Keyser, D. J. (Eds.). (1983). *Tests: A comprehensive reference for assessment in psychology, education, and business*. Kansas City, MO: Test Corporation of America.
Format similar to *Mental Measurements Yearbooks*, containing information on over 3,500 tests.

The ETS Test Collection. Educational Testing Service has over 200 *Test Collection Bibliographies* that describe instruments and their appropriate uses. In addition, the *ETS Test Collection Catalog* includes these five volumes: *Achievement Tests and Measurement Devices, Vocational Tests and Measurement Devices, Tests for Special Populations, Cognitive Aptitude and Intelligence Tests*, and *Attitude Tests*.

Finally, testing companies provide information about new tests as well as revised tests in their catalogs. While not as systematic a resource as those listed above, these catalogs can provide information not always available in the other sources.

EXERCISES

1. Devise a behavioral checklist to observe and record the behavior of children interacting on a playground.

2. Construct a test of at least five multiple-choice questions to measure the achievement of the content of this chapter. How would you obtain a measure of the validity of this test?

3. Locate the *Mental Measurement Yearbook* in your library and find a subject area that interests you. Identify three tests you might utilize in this subject area. How would you go about obtaining a copy of these tests?

4. With respect to the two articles in Appendix E, identify the measurement

procedures used. In what other ways could the constructs have been measured?

5. For those planning on doing a thesis, develop a plan for assessing the reliability and validity of the dependent measures.

5

INTERNAL VALIDITY

MARIA'S GOAL is to increase the likelihood that her treatment, and nothing but her treatment, will change participants' BULIT-R scores. She wants to be confident in her conclusion that her treatment causes participants' bulimic behavior to improve. In planning her research, Maria learns about three ways she can improve the strength of her cause and effect conclusions.

First, she decides to make her experimental treatments as different as possible. In the first treatment session, she will inform the multifaceted participants that they will be discussing family relationships, interpersonal styles, body image, and self-esteem. In contrast, she will tell educational participants that educational groups are designed to be informational and that they will be discussing facts about physiology, diet, and proper exercise and nutrition. Further, Maria will employ different counseling techniques in the two treatment approaches. For the multifaceted groups, Maria will assume a nondirective position throughout, beginning the process of establishing rapport by reflecting client comments, showing empathy, and clarifying the meaning of client statements. As the multifaceted group continues, Maria will be a facilitator of group process by asking members to consider what their roles in the group are and how these roles generalize outside the group. She will ask members to confront each other when they perceive contradictory information and reinforce participants when they gain new insights. In the educational group, Maria will be consistently authoritative, acting as an informational resource in discussing and answering questions about medical and nutritional causes and treatments pertaining to bulimia.

Second, Maria considers how errors might affect her study—errors such as inconsistency in running the groups or errors in the instruments she uses. She will make a concerted effort to use the best available measuring instrument and further, to run the groups consistently in the manner they were intended.

Finally, Maria determines the type of systematic influences, other than her independent variable, that may affect her conclusions. Such influences are many. For example, Maria may be biased, without being aware of it, and may conduct the groups in a way that will achieve her desired results. Subjects in the educational group could become bored and drop out of the study; or some intervening event, such as the death of a popular female star to an eating disorder, may alter the results in an unintended way. When confounding factors can be identified, Maria will try either to control for them or assess their effects after her study is completed.

R ecall that in Chapter 3 we said the purpose of the research plan is to enable the researcher to answer the research question. Ultimately, the research question is answered only if (1) the variables in nonexperimental research are accurately related, or (2) the independent variable in experimental research has a causal effect on the dependent variable. The veracity of either of these conclusions hinges on a single consideration—**internal validity**—that is, the degree to which the researcher has ensured that the conclusions stated follow from the variables studied and no other research factors. The more competing conclusions a researcher rules out, the more a study is said to have internal validity. Factors other than the variables studied that also may explain study outcomes are called **threats to internal validity**. Later, we discuss two general types of threats to a study's internal validity—**error** factors and **extraneous variables** (also known as **confounding** variables).

One way you can understand internal validity is by becoming acquainted with a principle called MAXMINCON. In the remainder of this chapter, we will discuss the principle's basic tenets.

MAXMINCON AND INTERNAL VALIDITY

According to Kerrlinger's (1986) **MAX-MIN-CON principle**, internal validity is increased when researchers (1) maximize the effects of the independent variable on the dependent variable, (2) minimize error factors, and (3) control extraneous variables. An illustration of perfect MAXMINCON is depicted in Figure 5-1. While the example in Figure 5-1 is impossible to duplicate in reality—there is never complete removal of error or control of extraneous variables—we exaggerate MAXMINCON to illustrate a perfect, internally valid study. In this ideal situation, the results of the dependent variable would be due only to the effects of the independent variable and no other factor. In other words, the results obtained in Figure 5-1 imply no error and complete control of extraneous variables. Clearly, while researchers can never achieve this ideal, every investigator's goal is to approximate Figure 5-1.

To make the MAXMINCON principle clearer, we organized the remainder of this chapter around specific MAXMINCON tenets, beginning with a discussion of how to maximize the effects of the independent variable.

Maximizing the Effects of the Independent Variable

Kerlinger (1986) advises researchers to design the independent variable so that its levels are as different as possible. Consider Maria's study. She has one independent variable—treatment type—with two levels—multifaceted or educational. To maximize differences, Maria must design the treatments so that their structure and content are as different as possible. For example, the educational group should be directive and informational; the multifaceted approach should be more nondirective and self-exploratory. Maria must consistently emphasize these differences throughout each treatment program in order to increase the likelihood that the dependent variable will change as a function of changes in the levels of the independent variable.

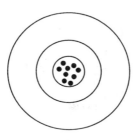

NOTE: Each dot represents a subject; the center of
the bullseye represents validity, whereas outer circles
represent complete invalidity.

FIGURE 5-1   Perfect MAXMINCON.

Problems occur when different treatment regimes become similar during treatment. For example, if Maria conducts both treatment approaches, she might find herself implementing educational techniques in the multifaceted group or vice versa. When this happens, the two treatment approaches are no longer in opposition as originally intended and thus, detecting differences between the two groups on the dependent variable measure is less likely. Methods for combatting this problem will be discussed later, specifically with reference to procedural error and instrumentation effects.

Two caveats about maximizing the effect of the independent variable are in order. First, maximizing the effect of the independent variable is possible only in experimental or quasi-experimental research because researchers in these studies manipulate the independent variable and thus can influence how the variable is designed. In nonexperimental research, the notion of maximizing the effect of the independent variable does not apply. While nonexperimental researchers do not have this benefit, the four nonexperimental strategies to be discussed in Chapter 8 are still valid. Nonexperimental researchers must simply ensure internal validity by focusing on the other two aspects of MAXMIN-CON—minimizing error variables and controlling extraneous variables. Suggestions for improving the internal validity of all types of research will be described in Chapters 8 and 9.

Second, in studies of treatment efficacy, it can be difficult to truly maximize an independent variable because participants receive an already existing treatment. However, we believe that the concept of maximizing the independent variable still applies, as long as the researcher separates groups along the dimension of most interest. For example, if the center where Maria works required all bulimic women to get basic education regarding bulimia, then Maria could not assign subjects to two completely distinct groups—that is, maximize the difference between treatment groups. Instead, she would be comparing educational treatment with education and multifaceted treatment, and her two treatment groups would no longer be completely different. However, her treatment groups would be completely different with respect to the one component she is most interested in—multifaceted treatment.

Further, even when researchers can create completely different groups, the research goal may be to minimize differences except with respect to one critical feature. For example, a researcher could create two treatment groups related to anxiety management and have each group receive identical training vis-à-vis the philosophy, goals, and techniques used by the trainer. The groups may differ only in size. Again, the experimental variable is still maximized in terms of the crucial experimental manipulation.

MINIMIZING ERROR

Error refers to any event, characteristic, or situation that is unsystematic and that fluctuates randomly. The key word in labeling a research event as a source of error is that error is always random and it changes subjects' response patterns in unique ways. For instance, if a researcher were to treat each subject differently and use a completely unreliable test, a pattern of results shown in Figure 5-2 would emerge. There is no way of knowing an individual's outcome, that is, where the next dot will be placed.

Clearly, error must be minimized, because it clouds the meaning of research outcomes, but error can only be minimized, not eliminated. There is inherent error in all research. In Chapter 10, we will show that error can be quantified statistically and that the greater the error, the less likely the researcher is to obtain statistical significance. A discussion of three general sources of error in research follows.

Subject Error

Subject error is due to unpredictable changes in subjects' physical or mental states during research participation. Specifically, subjects may become more or less attentive, fatigued, bored, anxious, drowsy, or interested during research. Such unpredictable alterations in subjects are expected; they are inevitable and, to some extent, unavoidable because error is random. One subject might become

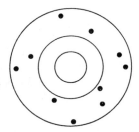

NOTE: Each dot represents a subject; the center of the bullseye represents validity, whereas outer circles represent complete invalidity.

FIGURE 5-2   Complete error, no extraneous variables.

more fatigued, the other more interested; another may be somewhere in between. Subjects' physical and mental states will vary during research, no matter what the researcher wishes.

While subject error is inevitable, when this type of error becomes more systematic, it is referred to as *maturation*—the directional changes in subjects' physical or mental states during research participation. For example, all subjects may become increasingly bored while filling out a questionnaire that takes 3 hours to complete. Later, when we discuss maturation, we give several recommendations for minimizing this type of directional subject error.

Procedural Error

We define **procedural error** as the random, unpredictable fluctuations occurring during the administration of the independent variable. Procedural error is especially salient when the independent variable is manipulated and is administered over a long period, as will be true in Maria's study. For example, as we noted earlier, Maria would commit a procedural error if she interspersed aspects of both multifaceted and educational treatment procedures in a random, unpredictable manner.

Measurement Error

Another type of error in research is **measurement error,** the error inherent in instruments used to obtain subjects' scores on the dependent variable. Examples of sources of measurement error are (1) a rater of behavior who is inconsistent in observation and data recording skill, (2) an interviewer whose skill in test administration fluctuates throughout the course of a study, (3) scorer fatigue, which may result from grading many essays every day, and (4) unpredictable changes in scorer leniency and strictness regarding interpretation of scoring rules. In Chapter 4, we noted that this error is usually quantified as the standard error of measurement.

Recommendations for Reducing Error

In Table 5-1, we review the definitions of the different types of error and provide a summary of recommendations for reducing error. The single most common way to reduce procedural and measurement error is by piloting the research procedures. **Pilot research** means test running research procedures to ensure that the variables are administered consistently. Upon completion of the pilot test, researchers should have a clearly articulated and standardized set of procedures so that anyone interested in replicating the study could do so.

Pilot research is helpful in three ways. First, by practicing administering the variables, the researcher develops a standardized procedural sequence. Second, experts can observe the researcher implementing the independent variable. Again, consider the problem Maria may face if she mixes treatment procedures in the two groups. To avoid doing this, she might have one or two experts in these types of treatments of bulimia observe her pilot one group of five subjects

TABLE 5-1 Definitions and recommendations for reducing error.

Type of Error	Definition
Subject error	Random fluctuations in a subject's physical or mental state
Procedural error	Random and inconsistent administration of independent variable
Measurement error	Random and inconsistent administration of dependent variable

Recommendations

1. Pilot research::
   a. develop standardized procedure
   b. obtain expert observations
   c. obtain subject feedback
2. Periodic observation during research

for each treatment. The expert observers could then assess the degree to which Maria adheres to the spirit of each treatment philosophy for the duration of the pilot groups. If she administers the interventions consistently and properly in the pilot, it is likely she will be consistent in her administration of treatments for the course of her study.

Finally, it may also be helpful to elicit subject feedback during pilot research. For example, after completing one educational and one multifaceted session, Maria could explain to pilot subjects the essential differences in these two treatments, then solicit their opinions about how she performed with respect to these differences and how she might improve in the future.

In the absence of such pilot research, Maria would be well-advised to have some of her groups periodically observed by experts during the course of her study. This process can help her determine whether or not she has committed a procedural error.

Measurement errors also can be minimized by piloting the tests, interviews, and other observational procedures; errors in dependent measures can be minimized the same way—with practice, expert observation, and subject feedback. Expert observation is particularly useful when the researcher is using an existing standardized measure. During pilot training, the researcher can learn administration and scoring skills from an individual who is knowledgeable about the test being used. In addition, when the researcher is developing a new instrument, pilot research is useful in obtaining preliminary psychometric qualities of the test such as reliability.

For example, take the case of a researcher who wants to develop an interview measure to determine physicians' attitudes about their graduate training preparation. Because the interview procedure is newly developed, its administration and scoring will be untested. Without piloting the interview, the researcher will be likely to administer the interview in an inconsistent manner during the study. By piloting it, the researcher can eliminate measurement error by developing a systematic, standardized interview procedure for all subjects. Further, the accuracy of scoring procedures can be determined by calculating the interrater reliability of interview protocols (see Chapter 4). Subject feedback may also prove useful. The researcher can ask the pilot subjects how well the procedure appeared to measure attitudes about medical school training.

TYPES OF EXTRANEOUS VARIABLES

As error becomes more systematic and directional in nature, it is referred to as an extraneous variable. In other words, error per se does not have the same directional biasing effect as do extraneous variables. Error factors will underestimate the relationship between variables for one subject, overestimate the relationship for another subject, and so on. To the contrary, it is assumed that extraneous variables have a similar directional effect on all subjects.

Consider this example. If Maria's participants are exposed to an event other than her experimental treatment and she finds out later that all subjects' scores were 15 points too low because of the event—a famous figure dies of bulimia and all subjects become more bulimic—then the scores are systematically biased. Here, the event would systematically and directionally bias the study results, and the event would be considered an extraneous variable. Such an outcome would result in the dot pattern shown in Figure 5-3.

Earlier, we noted that extraneous variables share a common theme—each systematically biases the results of a study. The term systematically means that each subject's standing on the dependent measure is directionally affected by some extraneous factor, and it is assumed that this effect is the same for all subjects. Thus, it is incumbent on researchers to identify extraneous variables that may be relevant to the proposed investigation and to do whatever possible to control for them.

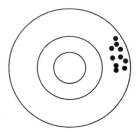

NOTE: Each dot represents a subject; the center of the bullseye represents validity, whereas outer circles represent complete invalidity.

FIGURE 5-3   Complete extraneous; no error.

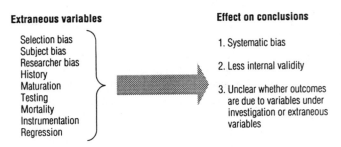

Extraneous variables	Effect on conclusions
Selection bias Subject bias Researcher bias History Maturation Testing Mortality Instrumentation Regression	1. Systematic bias 2. Less internal validity 3. Unclear whether outcomes are due to variables under investigation or extraneous variables

FIGURE 5-4   Effects of extraneous variables on research conclusions.

To organize our discussion of extraneous variables, we first define the threat such a variable can pose and then give an example. A list of nine extraneous variables and their general effects on research conclusions is presented in Figure 5-4. Definitions and examples of each of these extraneous variables will be presented shortly.

Next, we address the factors determining the relevance of each extraneous variable. The general factors influencing the prominence of extraneous variables are research design—correlational, quasi-experimental, or experimental—and research methods—procedure, sample, and context. The purpose of this section is to help novice researchers decide when a particular extraneous variable may be significant.

Finally, we show how extraneous variables can be controlled to prevent the threat or assessed to determine the seriousness of an extraneous variable after a study is concluded.

To encompass the entire discussion, we provide Form 5-1, which is a blank worksheet used for relating an extraneous variable to a researcher's own study or to published research. The worksheet includes the three general concepts just noted: name and definition of threat, relevance of threat, and methods for controlling and assessing the identified extraneous variable. We next provide definitions and examples of nine extraneous variables.

Selection Bias

In studies comparing different groups, it is possible for the groups to differ on a variable known to influence the dependent variable. This is referred to as **selection bias**. The key to determining the relevance of selection bias is noting how the researcher formed the groups receiving the different levels of the independent variable. That is, the process by which groups are selected may itself create a systematic group difference on the dependent variable.

For example, suppose that Maria should decide to select 25 bulimic women from a local hospital to receive the educational treatment and 25 university women to receive the multifaceted treatment. The problem is that the hospital and university groups may already differ on the dependent measure—bulimic episodes. For instance, if university subjects are more bulimic than hospital

FORM 5-1   A worksheet for relating extraneous variables to research.

1. Extraneous variable:

   A. Name _____

   B. Definition: _____

      _____

      _____

      Is this extraneous variable relevant _____

   A. Research type and relation to threat: _____

      _____

      _____

   B. Research method

      I.   Sample—relation to threat: _____

           _____

           _____

      II. Procedure—relation to threat: _____

           _____

           _____

      III. Context—relation to threat: _____

           _____

           _____

3. Method to control or assess extraneous variable

   A. Control method: _____

      _____

   B. Assessment _____

      I.   How was extraneous variable assessed?: _____

           _____

           _____

      II. Outcome: _____

           _____

           _____

participants, Maria would have created two unequal groups with respect to her dependent variable when she assigned subjects to groups. The educational group would probably have had more bulimic episodes simply because these subjects had more severe bulimia than the multifaceted group initially. Maria could make no meaningful conclusions with groups constituted in this way.

In certain types of research, the researcher forms groups based on an already existing quality of the subject—gender, grade level, personality type, socioeconomic status, level of self-concept, and so on. When subjects enter the study already possessing a particular level of the independent variable, the researcher can use this subject condition to form groups. In this type of study, known as **ex post facto** research, the researcher wants to conclude that, for example, different levels of self-concept (low and high) are related to intelligence (lower self-concept and less intelligence). The difficulty with this type of research is that selection bias is created artificially. Subjects with different levels of self-concept are likely to differ on several other qualities related to intelligence such as the quality of their family environment. Thus, conclusions derived when using this type of research are limited because of selection bias.

To underscore this point, consider the controversy regarding bias in intelligence test scores. Assume that a researcher forms three ethnic groups—Anglo-American, Hispanic American, and African American—and scores for each of these groups are obtained on a test of intelligence. In this case, the researcher is presumably interested in the relationship between ethnicity (independent variable) and intelligence (dependent variable). If differences are obtained, can the researcher conclude that ethnicity caused the differences in intelligence test scores? No, because the method of forming groups was inherently biased. While the relationship between ethnicity and intelligence is intriguing, the only conclusion that can be drawn from this type of research is that ethnicity and intelligence scores are related. The cause of this relationship is unknown, since any of several differences related to ethnicity—income level or exposure to the dominant culture's knowledge, beliefs, environment, and values—may be the root of the difference. In Table 5-2, we illustrate the problem of selection bias using the aforementioned study.

Subject Bias

In general, **subject bias** refers to participants' attitudes that systematically slant investigative results in a particular direction. For example, it is well-known that simply as a function of being observed, subjects perform better. This phenomenon is called the **Hawthorne effect**. Specific types of participation bias arise as subjects interact with the research environment. **Demand characteristics** are those cues in the research context that participants use to figure out the true purpose of an investigation. Invariably, subjects will read something into the context of a study, either from the title of the study, the nonverbal behavior of the researcher, or the behavior of other subjects.

As one example of a demand characteristic leading to subject bias, assume that Maria's consent form shows the title of her study as, "A Comparison of

TABLE 5-2 Selection bias in a hypothetical study of ethnicity and intelligence.

Formation of groups	Groups	Extraneous variables introduced by method of forming groups	Outcome variable	Effect on conclusions
Subject's ethnic origin used to form groups	African American Anglo-American Hispanic American	Income Acculturation Environmental quality Family functioning	Intelligence test scores	Unclear whether differences between groups are due to ethnicity, excraneous variables related to ethnicity, or both

Multifaceted and Educational Therapy in the Treatment of Bulimia." Upon reading the title alone, subjects might correctly assume that the multifaceted treatment is hypothesized to be more effective than the educational approach. The titles of the two groups may also help subjects determine which treatment they are receiving. Accordingly, subjects in the educational group may be less inclined to work hard, while subjects in the multifaceted group may be inspired to work especially hard. Thus, subject bias may account for the study outcomes. The way Maria can avoid the problem is to call her study something like "Understanding Eating Disorders" or "Improving Your Eating Habits."

Researcher Bias

Just as subject attitudes introduce potentially confounding variables, so too do researcher attitudes. Indeed, considering that demand characteristics are formed through environmental cues, who is in a better position to provide these cues than the researcher? The subtle feedback researchers give subjects about their expected behavior is called **researcher bias**. At issue is whether a researcher's preconceived notions about study outcomes may influence the results directionally.

The ways in which researchers bias study outcomes are many and can be classified generally as intentional or unintentional. Intentional biases are the most troubling because in these instances, researchers purposefully influence research outcomes by helping subjects act in ways that confirm the research hypothesis. Such cues may be nonverbal (smiling, shifting body position) or verbal (changing voice inflection). More flagrant would be a researcher who falsifies data. A famous example is that of the data on identical twins collected by Sir Cyril Burt—data he allegedly altered to show that intelligence is to a great extent inherited (Lefrancois, 1987).

With unintentional biases, the researcher is unaware of cuing subjects differentially. To illustrate an unintentional bias, consider Maria's study again. If Maria has reason to believe that members of the multifaceted group will improve more than the educational group (her research hypothesis), she may unintentionally introduce a difference between groups that was not in her original design. For example, she might verbally reinforce statements from multifaceted members about their improved eating habits, while ignoring similar statements in the educational group. Because Maria did not originally construct the two programs to differ in leader reinforcement of statements about eating habits, and since this difference may have profound effects on her dependent measure, the initially posited relationship between variables is no longer clear.

History

Every researcher's nightmare is when an unexpected event affects subjects during their research participation. When such an event occurs and when the event may explain changes in the dependent variable, **history** becomes an extraneous variable. The effects of history are problematic only when a preponderance of subjects are exposed to the unexpected event and the event has a uniformly positive or negative biasing effect. In Table 5-3, we illustrate how history might affect Maria's study, assuming that she assigns 25 hospital participants to the educational treatment group and 25 university participants to the multifaceted treatment group.

Consider another example of history. A school psychologist develops a cognitive enrichment program to speed cognitive development in children ages 3 to 5 years. The researcher pretests 20 children using problem-solving tasks and determines that all children are in the preoperational stage of cognitive development. The children are then exposed to an enrichment program in which multicolored blocks and sticks and teacher modeling of problem-solving are used for 10 weeks. Children are then tested again. What if, just after the beginning of the enrichment program, a well-known toy manufacturer begins to market a new thinking game for preschoolers, a toy that is nationally touted? Assume that parents of 15 of the 20 preschool children buy this toy. If gains on the posttest are found, the researcher would not know whether these gains were due to the enrichment program or the new toy. Here, most participants were exposed to a historical event that is presumed to be uniformly positive.

Maturation

Maturation refers to the process that systematically change subjects over the period of the research study but are unrelated to the variables under study.

TABLE 5-3   Hypothetical effects of history in Maria's research study.

Groups	Treatment	Historical event	Outcome	Effects on conclusion
Hospital	Educational	New hospital policy implemented during educational treatment: bulimic women who remain in therapy will receive a small stipend.	BULIT-R	Outcome for hospital subjects reflects both educational treatment and historical event. BULIT-R outcomes should be more favorable.
University	Multifaceted	No historical event	BULIT-R	Outcome for university subjects reflects multifaceted treatment only. BULIT-R outcomes not enhanced by historical event.

Specifically, during a research study the physical state of subjects can change, such as their alertness or boredom, and so can psychological factors like motivation, attraction, and anxiety.

Within the context of research, maturation refers to the change in a subject's physical or psychological state from the moment a research study starts to the time it concludes. Such changes are not random fluctuations but a systematic increase or decrease in functioning. The systematic nature of the changes is the one quality separating maturation from subject error. For example, maturation would be a factor if most subjects started the study feeling alert, then became more and more drowsy until the study ended. This is a systematic change and is thus covered by the definition of maturation. In Table 5-4, we illustrate the process of maturation in a study in which subjects spend 2 hours completing a questionnaire.

Consider another example in which maturation would present a risk to the researcher. A speech pathologist designs a study to lower the age at which infants say their first words. Subjects are 8 months old and are not yet speaking their first words, which are defined as clearly articulated words, for example, "dad," not "da." In one group, the pediatrician provides talking exercises, such as manipulating the mouth, slowly modeling syllables, and echoing any sounds the infant produces. In the control group, the pediatrician provides regular check-ups but no additional assistance. During the study, the pediatrician asks the parents to keep a record of the exact age when their infant first speaks and how many words the infant says. After 4 months, the pediatrician concludes the study and collects parental records.

If the data show that the children receiving talking exercises utter their first word earlier then the control group and use more words, can the investigator conclude that these differences are due to the treatment? Not necessarily. As will be clear later, if infants were randomly assigned to groups, the effect of maturation would probably be controlled. However, because infants in both groups mature in speech over the course of the study, the true effect of the treatment may be masked. That is, since both groups mature, the control group will improve, too. In essence, whatever treatment effect occurs, it will be the result of treatment and maturation rather than just maturation. Unfortunately, this is a consequence of using participants who change quickly with regard to the dependent variable of interest.

TABLE 5-4   Effects of maturation in completion of a two-hour questionnaire.

First 30 minutes	Second 30 minutes	Third 30 minutes	Fourth 30 minutes	Effects on conclusions
Accurate responses; subjects alert and interested	Fairly accurate responses; subjects still alert and interested but waning slightly	Less accurate; subjects losing interest and becoming bored	Completely inaccurate responses; subjects bored and uninterested	Scores on questionnaire do not reflect what questionnaire intended to measure; maturation systematically biases meaning of scores

Testing

The logic of **testing effects** is that the initial measurement of subjects may alter the quality being measured. Therefore, subsequent measurements may not be due to the independent variable but rather to the effect of the first test. Testing effects are most problematic when researchers measure a single group before and after intervention. In this design, there is no way to disentangle the treatment effect and the effect of the pretest. For example, testing effects would be a concern for the school psychologist interested in the cognitive enrichment program because it could be that pretest practice improve subjects' thinking skills. Thus, any changes noted on the posttest measure may simply reflect the effects of the pretest and not the independent variable.

In theory, true testing effects change subsequent measurements, even if the independent variable has never exerted an effect. That is, the initial test can act like a treatment and alter subject status on subsequent dependent measures. This would be true even without introducing a treatment variable. For example, subjects participating in a weight-control study might be asked to weigh themselves before the study. Some participants might find their initial weight so aversive that their motivation to lose weight is greatly heightened. These participants may visit specialists, request surgical procedures to have fatty deposits removed, and so on. Despite whether or not a weight-control program was ever given to these subjects, the pretest prompted subjects to treat themselves. Subsequent change in their weight does not pertain to the independent variable but to the systematic change in subjects' motivation as a function of the pretest. In Table 5-5, we depict this testing effect.

Mortality

Mortality refers to the loss of research subjects during the study. Subjects may depart the research study for many reasons—boredom, illness, relocation, rescheduling, or because participation in the study did not meet their expectations. For example, consider students' ratings of professors' courses. If these ratings are obtained toward the end of the semester, as is usually the case, those students who were doing poorly in the class or who related poorly to the instructor or the material may decide to drop out of the course. Thus, ratings will be spuri-

TABLE 5-5   Hypothetical example of testing in a weight-control study.

Pretest	Testing effect	Treatment	Posttest	Effect on conclusions
Subjects' weight	Some subjects find initial weight so disturbing that they seek help over and above treatment.	Weight-control training	Subjects' weight	Unclear whether results are due to treatment effectiveness, increased subject motivation to lose weight based on pretest alone, or both

ously positive because those students most likely to give the lowest ratings of the course have dropped out. Again, note the systematic effect of mortality.

A related term is **differential attrition**, which applies when the researcher forms at least two experimental groups. Differential attrition can occur when subjects in one group drop out simply because of the treatment they receive, while subjects in other treatments do not drop out in similar proportion. This creates a problem similar to mortality. Those subjects who respond most unfavorably to the treatment are no longer available.

As an example of differential attrition, assume that in Maria's study the educational group is found to be uninteresting and ineffective by participants and that 10 women drop out of this group, while only 2 members of the multifaceted group leave. Thus, if Maria found that the educational group showed significant reductions in inappropriate eating behaviors relative to the multifaceted group, this difference would not necessarily be due to the independent variable. Instead, those subjects who might have responded most negatively on the dependent variable remove themselves. That is, bulimic women who are not affected by the educational treatment leave the study. This creates the erroneous impression at posttest that the educational treatment was more effective than it actually was. This problem is diagrammed in Table 5-6.

Instrumentation

Instrumentation refers to the procedural process, variations in which systematically bias research results. As just one of many possible examples, suppose that two therapists were hired to each conduct two groups of therapy for children with attention disorders. What if the therapists, although equally trained and experienced, actually vary greatly in implementing the cognitive-behavioral treatment? What if one is much more skilled than the other? If the results of the four cognitive-behavioral therapy groups are combined, the results will be misleading because only two of the groups will be optimally conducted. Specifically, the results will be systematically biased toward the null hypothesis—that is, the treatment and comparison groups will not differ. This case of instrumentation is illustrated in Table 5-7.

TABLE 5-6   Hypothetical effect of differential attrition in Maria's research study.

Pretest	Treatment	Posttest	Effect on conclusions
BULIT-R scores	Educational (N = 25) (10 least responsive to treatment drop out)	BULIT-R scores	Educational group outcome enhanced because move unresponsive subjects dropped out of this group than the multifaceted one
BULIT-R scores	Multifaceted (N = 25) (2 least responsive to treatment drop out; 8 other low-responsive stay because of perceived peer pressure existing in multifaceted treatment)	BULIT-R scores	

TABLE 5-7 Potential instrumentation effects in a study of cognitive-behavioral treatment for children with attention deficit disorders.

Subjects randomly assigned to treatment groups	Posttest mean on hyperactivity	Effects on conclusions
Group 1 Cognitive-behavioral:	6.1	If results from less-skilled therapist are combined with results from skilled therapist, analysis may falsely conclude no significant difference between cognitive-behavioral and no treatment. Cognitive-behavioral may well be found to be superior in reducing hyperactivity if implemented by skilled therapist
Group 2 skilled therapist	6.3	
Group 3 Cognitive-behavioral:	10.1	
Group 4 less-skilled therapist	10.3	
Group 5 Comparison group of no treatment	8.2	

Regression

Regression is a statistical artifact in which individuals who score at the extreme on one occasion (high or low) tend to produce scores closer to the mean on the second occasion. Unfortunately, this can be mistaken for a treatment effect. Scores that are low at first become higher just through regression, not necessarily because the treatment works. Regression could be eliminated by selecting perfectly reliable measuring instruments. In the absence of any error of measurement, there can be no regression and scores would remain the same across repeated testing. Until the day comes when such error-free measurements are available, however, regression remains a concern.

Using Maria's study to illustrate regression, assume that Maria wants to sample only women who have severe bulimia. Because these women initially report a high number of bulimic episodes, these same women on retest might show a reduction in bulimic frequencies due to regression toward the mean.

In studies in which two groups are exposed to different treatments, *differential regression* can be a concern. For example, if Maria sampled hospital subjects with severe bulimia and assigned these subjects to an educational treatment group, regression might occur for this group. In contrast, a university group of bulimic women with less severe bulimia could be assigned to the multifaceted group. This group would show less regression. Therefore, an improvement for the educational group relative to the multifaceted group could actually be the result of differential regression.

FACTORS INFLUENCING EXTRANEOUS VARIABLES

Knowing what research factors influence extraneous variables is important for two reasons: (1) this information can reveal when the different extraneous variables are most pronounced and (2) researchers can use this material either to control for an extraneous variable or assess its severity after the study is concluded. In general, the degree to which the nine extraneous variables influence a particular study depends on the research type and research method used.

Research Type

In Table 5-8, we provide a list of three general research types—correlational, quasi-experimental, and experimental—indicating how each type is related to each extraneous variable. (These and other research types are discussed more extensively in Chapters 8 and 9.)

Briefly, correlational researchers control for history because subjects are measured on variables X (for example, self-concept) and Y (for example, introversion) in immediate succession. Without a passage of time, neither history nor mortality can exert influence. Further, because the X and Y dependent measures are different, testing and regression effects do not occur. As for selection bias, in true correlational studies scores on X are not used for classification, so no selection takes place. The extraneous variable most pronounced in correlational studies is maturation, since the order of X and Y can artificially produce change in Y as a function of subject fatigue or boredom.

As for quasi-experimental research, researchers typically pretest two **intact groups**—groups already formed on some existing basis. Already existing groups are pretested and then exposed to different treatments. One group is a comparison group (C); the other group receives the treatment of interest (X).

TABLE 5-8 Relationship of research type to extraneous variables.

	Research type		
Extraneous variable	**Correlational** X Y	**Quasi-experimental** O X O O C O	**Experimental** R X O R C O
Selection bias		?	+
Subject bias			
Researcher bias			
History	+	?	+
Maturation	−	?	+
Testing	+	?	+
Mortality	+	?	+
Instrumentation			
Regression	+	?	+

NOTE: +   = research type reduces extraneous variable
  −   = research type makes extraneous variable more pronounced
  blank = research type not specifically related to extraneous variable
  ?   = depends upon similarity of intact groups
  0   = dependent variable,   X = treatment,   C = comparison,   R = random assignment

After treatment, each group is posttested. In Chapter 9, we refer to this design as the **nonequivalent comparison group design**.

Because quasi-experimental researchers use intact groups, the following may be either made more pronounced or reduced: selection bias, history, maturation, testing, mortality, and regression. The key factor in making this determination is the similarity of the intact groups. (This is why question marks are inserted for relevant extraneous variables in Table 5-8.) An example of dissimilar groups could be nurses in day and night rotations; or nurses who may differ in terms of demographic characteristics such as whether or not they have children, their marital status, or their ambition to pursue continuing education. These already existing differences between groups may artificially create differences in other extraneous variables. On the other hand, intact groups may not differ significantly. Suppose an educational researcher exposes two different classrooms of students to different instructional techniques. If both are third-grade, regular education classes and both contain children of similar demographic composition, the number of relevant extraneous variables is probably reduced.

At the very least, the quasi-experimental researcher should provide information on the comparability of the groups, such as their demographic composition. In this way, the consumer of research can better decide whether groups are similar. Or, the quasi-experimental researcher can include the intact groups as a level of another independent variable and assess the impact of this variable on the critical manipulation. We will expand on this concept, known as blocking, later in this chapter.

The final research type shown is experimental. The researcher randomly assigns (R) subjects to either a treatment or a comparison group. Subjects are then posttested (O). As we mentioned in Chapter 3, the beauty of random assignment is that it controls for many extraneous variables by reducing the chance that groups will be dissimilar. Thus, if groups are different at the end of treatment, it is more likely that the experimental manipulation caused the difference.

Research Method

Another factor influencing the relevance of any extraneous variable is research method, namely research procedure, sample, and context. Examples of research procedures, sample, and context are shown in Table 5-9.

Most of the research methods are self-explanatory. Further, the relationship between each method and extraneous variable is straightforward. For example, if the researcher who develops the hypotheses collects the data, researcher bias is pronounced. Or, the longer the study, the more extraneous variables increase in relevance. The exception to this is testing, since initial effects of the pretest probably wear off with time.

The sampling method known as homogeneous sampling requires some elaboration. In some studies, researchers study **homogeneous samples**, assuming that similar subjects will not differ systematically on any extraneous variable. To obtain a homogeneous sample, researchers require participants to meet specific inclusion and exclusion requirements. For example, if subject characteristics

TABLE 5-9 Relationship of research methods to extraneous variables.

	Research Method						
	Research procedure				Sample		Context
Extraneous variable	Researcher collects data	Different data collectors	Longer duration studies	Low reliability of measure	Homogeneous sample	Younger subjects	Laboratory setting
Selection bias					+		
Subject bias			−				−
Researcher bias	−		−				
History			−		+		
Maturation			−		+	−	
Testing			+		+		
Mortality			−		+		
Instrumentation		−			−		
Regression				−	−		

NOTE: + = research method reduces extraneous variable
       − = research method makes extraneous variable more pronounced
   blank = research method not specifically related to extraneous variable

like psychological adjustment, education, and age relate to the number of bulimic episodes, Maria should ensure that her treatment groups are similar on
these qualities. To do this, she could restrict participation to subjects who (1)
score high on a test of psychological adjustment, (2) have at least a high school
education, and (3) are between the ages of 18 and 24. By including only subjects
who meet these requirements, Maria can be fairly sure that her two groups will
be similar.

CONTROLLING OR ASSESSING EXTRANEOUS VARIABLE

To control for an extraneous variable means to prevent its influence before the study even begins. The information presented in Table 5-10 can be helpful in this endeavor. For example, when planning research, the selection of a measure with high reliability and validity is important in the control of instrumentation and regression effects. Reducing the length of a study can prevent subject and researcher bias, history, matura-tion, and mortality. Unfortunately, reducing the length of a study can also increase the relevance of testing.

Sometimes, extraneous variables cannot be controlled before a study begins
so they must be assessed after the study. For example, after her study is over,
Maria could ask subjects how the death of a famous person from bulimia affected
them. An analysis of subjects' responses would help her determine whether or
not this historical event biased her research results.

In Table 5-10, we provide several methods for controlling and assessing extraneous variables. The table shows whether the recommended method is used to assess, control, or is irrelevant to each extraneous variable. We begin by describing recommendations not previously encountered, then note how these terms control or assess extraneous variables.

Matching

When **matching**, researchers match subjects in groups on some variable known to be related to the dependent measure, which in turn controls for selection bias. While the purpose of matching is similar to that of random assignment, the difference is that subjects are matched on a single variable extremely well—intelligence, economic status, or previous treatment experience, for example. With random assignment, subjects are said to be matched approximately on all possible preexisting sources of differences.

Matching requires two procedural events: (1) obtaining data on the variable to be matched using questionnaires or previous records and (2) using subject status on the variable as a means of assigning subjects randomly to groups. For example, assume that general psychological adjustment is related to bulimic episodes and that for her data to be more valid, Maria needs to ensure that her two groups are similar with respect to general adjustment. To do this, she could (1) pretest her 50 subjects on a measure of psychological adjustment, (2) rank order subjects in terms of their status (score) on the meas-

TABLE 5-10   Recommendations for controlling and assessing extraneous variables.

	Recommendation					
Extraneous variable	Blocking	Statistical control	Post investigative inquiry	Standardize conditions	Reduce study length	Select reliable and valid measures
Selection bias	A	C				
Subject bias			A	C	C	
Researcher bias			A	C	C	
History			A		C	
Maturation			A		C	
Testing	C	C	A			
Mortality			A		C	
Instrumentation				C		C
Regression	C					C

NOTE: A = can Assess influence
       C = can Control extraneous variable
       Blank = not applicable

Matching can control for selection bias. Using a placebo control can control for mortality. Unobtrusive observation can control for subject bias. Making subjects blind to expectations can control for subject bias. Making researchers blind to hypotheses can control for researcher bias. Counterbalancing measures can control for maturation.

ure, (3) take the most adjusted and second most adjusted subjects and randomly assign each of these individuals to the multifaceted and educational groups. This process would be repeated for the next pair and continue until all 25 pairs of subjects were similarly placed in the two treatments. Upon completion of matching, Maria can be fairly confident that her two groups are roughly similar with respect to psychological adjustment. This example of matching is illustrated in Table 5-11.

Blocking

Blocking occurs when the researcher includes an extraneous variable in a study so that its effects on the dependent variable can be assessed. The blocked variable thus becomes a second independent variable. As an illustration, Maria could arbitrarily decide to label subjects as either most-adjusted (block 1), middle-adjusted (block 2), or least-adjusted (block 3) based on their psychological adjustment scores. The highest 17 scores could be used to define most-adjusted, the next 17 to constitute the middle-adjusted, and the bottom 16 individual scores could represent the least-adjusted group. She would then have two independent variables: treatment type with its two levels and psychological adjustment with three levels—a factorial design we will discuss in Chapter 9. Again, the advantage of blocking is that the effects of treatment and psychological adjustment on eating behavior can then be independently and interactively assessed. The use of blocking is illustrated in Table 5-12.

TABLE 5-11   Hypothetical use of matching in Maria's research study.

Pretest	Rank order of psychological adjustment scores (highest to lowest)		Random assignment of matched pairs to treatment groups
Psychological adjustment score	Pair 1	Highest	Multifaceted
		Second highest	Educational
	Pair 2	Third highest	Educational
		Fourth highest	Multifaceted
	Pair 3	Fifth highest	Multifaceted
		Sixth highest	Educational
	Pair 4	Seventh highest	Educational
		Eighth highest	Multifaceted
	Pair 25	Second lowest	Educational
		Lowest	Multifaceted

TABLE 5-12   Maria's hypothetical use of blocking on psychological adjustment.

Treatment	Psychological adjustment		
	Block 1 (most-adjusted)	Block 2 (middle-adjusted)	Block 3 (least-adjusted)
Multifaceted			
	(N = 17)	(N = 17)	(N = 16)
Educational			

As a means of assessing selection bias, consider the earlier example of how Maria could create bias by selecting hospital subjects to receive the educational treatment and university subjects to get the multifaceted approach. Using a blocked design, Maria could assess the significance of being in a particular group—hospital or university—by including type of sample as an independent variable. Specifically, Maria would give hospital and university subjects both multifaceted and educational treatments, which would result in the blocking design given in Table 5-13. In this design, type of sample becomes the blocked variable, with two blocks—hospital and university. The effectiveness of each treatment can be examined for each type of sample. In other words, the researcher can independently assess the influence of type of sample according to the independent variable of most interest, treatment type. This type of design is very appealing, as we will show in Chapter 9.

Statistical Control

Statistical control of extraneous variables requires the researcher to pretest subjects and then to use various statistical techniques to adjust for group differences on the posttest measure. For example, if Maria finds the hospital and university samples different in degree of pretest bulimia, she can compensate for these differences statistically. Statistical control techniques will be elaborated on in Chapter 10.

Placebo-Control

With a **placebo-control** treatment, subjects receive treatment they believe is genuine but that lacks merit. For example, a placebo control is operating when biofeedback researchers connect children to a biofeedback apparatus and then engage in small-talk without using the biofeedback machine to provide feedback to the children. Using placebo groups can control for subject bias because subjects in these groups believe they are getting a legitimate treatment. This belief may negate subject biases related to demand for equal treatment or possible subject demoralization. These types of subject bias will be expanded in Chapter 9. In addition, if subjects believe that their placebo treatment is valid, they may

TABLE 5-13   Assessing selection bias with a blocked design.

| Treatment | Type of Population | |
	Hospital	University
Educational		
Multifaceted		

be less likely to drop out of the group. Therefore, a placebo control treatment can lessen the probability of differential attrition.

Unobtrusive Measurement

Unobtrusive measurement refers to measurement or observation of subjects who do not know they are being observed or measurement that is done before research participation begins. In the former case, an example would be watching driver behavior from behind a wall. In the latter case, data may consist of historical information like a school cumulative folder or hospital records. When subjects are unaware they are being observed, there is no Hawthorne effect, and there are no demand characteristics—which effectively eliminates subject bias.

Subject-Blind Method

At the outset of this chapter, we discussed concealment, which means that subjects are uninformed about critical aspects of the research—hypotheses or treatment groups. This is referred to as the **subject-blind method**. The purpose of keeping subjects uninformed about critical aspects of a research investigation is to control for subject bias.

Researcher-Blind Method

Similarly, even the data collectors may be unaware of the research hypotheses. The reason for this is to keep those who interact with participants free of bias. This strategy is called a researcher-blind method. Problems may arise when those who develop a research hypothesis and design the study also collect the data.

Finally, both subjects and data collectors may be unaware of the purpose of the study. This procedure is aptly referred to as the **double-blind method**.

Postinvestigative Inquiry

Postinvestigative inquiry refers to obtaining information from participants after their research involvement concludes. Researchers may use informal interview techniques or a structured questionnaire to get specific information about participants' experiences during the research study. Information can be collected to assess most extraneous variables, as Table 5-10 shows.

Standardized Conditions

Researchers can standardize conditions before the actual conduct of the investigation. This is one purpose of pilot research. When conditions are standardized, the administration of variables is systematic and unchanging across different researchers, subjects, or groups of subjects. For example, if two researchers are measuring a variable, the accuracy of their measures should be standardized. One way to do this is to establish interrater reliability, as noted in Chapter 4.

Using our original example of instrumentation effects, recall that a researcher was interested in the effectiveness of cognitive-behavioral therapy for children with attention deficit disorders. To collect the data, she used therapists who, unbeknownst to her, exhibited different skills in implementing cognitive-behavior therapy.

To standardize data collection procedures in this example, the researcher could videotape each therapist in a therapeutic interaction with the same child, then ask two experts in cognitive-behavioral therapy to rate the researchers on specific cognitive-behavioral therapy skills. If the experts' ratings were similar, the researcher could tentatively conclude that the therapists are roughly equivalent in skill and that the data they collect will have been obtained in a standardized fashion.

When conditions are standardized, investigators will be less likely to systematically bias the results, thus controlling for researcher bias. Further, when researchers are unbiased, subjects have one less clue for determining the true purpose of the study. Therefore, standardizing conditions can control subject bias.

Counterbalance Measures

When different tests are used to measure subjects, the order in which the tests are presented can systematically influence research outcomes. For example, subjects may become more tired or bored as testing continues, so later measures will become less accurate. To avoid these maturation effects, researchers can **counterbalance** measures by presenting subjects with different orders of tests. As a result, some subjects receive test 1, then test 2; others receive test 2, then 1.

MARIA REVISITED

Let us return to Maria's research, noting (1) the basic plan she outlined in Chapter 3, (2) her selection of a measuring instrument in Chapter 4, and (3) how she evaluated each source of invalidity in designing her study.

Maria's first decision was the formulation of her final research question, which affects internal validity indirectly by determining the related hypotheses. Her research hypotheses clearly delimit what methods can be used to answer the question. Maria's research design calls for two groups, with subjects assigned randomly to each, and a posttest. Thus, her hypotheses require a particular research design—the two-group (multifaceted vs. educational) experimental design. Note how this design controls for many extraneous variables.

The selection of her dependent variable, the focus of Chapter 4, relates to measurement error. In fact, Maria selected her test of bulimia because it showed adequate levels of reliability and validity.

Maria considered internal validity in terms of MAXMINCON. First, since her study is experimental, Maria will maximize the differences between her two treatments.

Second, Maria considers how to minimize error. Again, a reliable and valid test will minimize measurement error. Also, Maria will pilot her two treatment groups with faculty supervision and will develop a list of goals and formats for each session in both treatment groups. She will then have her faculty supervisor rate her on how well she meets these goals in two different sessions for each treatment group. If the ratings show consistency across sessions for each treatment format, she will have evidence that she is administering the treatments consistently. This will reduce procedural error. Also, Maria will meet each group at approximately the same time, for the same amount of time, and will space the meetings at 2-week intervals. By standardizing the timing of the groups, she hopes to further reduce procedural error.

Finally, Maria considers the effects of extraneous variables. In Table 5-14, we show each extraneous variable, her evaluation of its impact, and her method for controlling or assessing each extraneous variable.

Table 5-14 summarizes most of the principles previously discussed. The extraneous variables of most concern to Maria are subject bias, researcher bias, mortality, and instrumentation. (Note that except for mortality, the other three relevant variables cannot be controlled by research type.) We briefly summarize Maria's evaluation and adjustment to these extraneous factors.

First, Maria considers subject bias. It will be difficult for her to keep subjects in the two groups from communicating with each other. For example, all of Maria's groups will be conducted at the Counseling Center—thus increasing the likelihood that subjects in the different groups might communicate. If there is communication between experimental groups, several potential subject biases may develop. We will discuss these further in Chapter 9. To reduce the possibilities for communication between groups, Maria will run the groups on different days. The educational and multifaceted groups will never meet on the same day. Also, she will make her consent form less explicit to reduce the demand characteristics inherent in informed consent.

Researcher bias is also a concern for Maria. Since she designed her study and is collecting the data, she is at-risk for biasing the results in the direction her research hypothesis predicts. It would be advisable to have other counselors collect the data for her, but Maria prefers not to do this. She is concerned about (1) not having the time to train other counselors in the multifaceted method (a training she has independently obtained) and (2) using other counselors to conduct the educational groups—the method of treatment already in use by center counselors. She does not want to introduce instrumentation error, which is possible, given that she would be comparing two different treatments run by different counselors.

Similarly, Maria is at-risk for introducing an instrumentation effect. She may run the multifaceted group more optimally than the educational group, biasing her results in the expected direction.

To deal with both researcher bias and instrumentation, Maria will make the following procedural adjustment. She will develop a brief rating form so her faculty supervisor can evaluate how well she follows the techniques, format, and objectives required for each treatment program. During a pilot test of her treatment groups, Maria's faculty sponsor will observe Maria on two different occasions for each treatment group. Ratings show that Maria consistently follows the philosophy of each treatment across different sessions will be used as evidence that she is not biasing the treatment programs and she is not running one group any better than the other. If ratings reveal that Maria significantly departs from either treatment regime or changes the way she runs the groups over time, her faculty adviser will let her know so she can make the appropriate adjustments. Finally, after her pilot research is concluded, a similar observation and rating procedure will be implemented during her actual thesis research.

Last, Maria is prepared for the possibility of differential attrition. This is a concern because participants in the educational group may find this approach less useful and therefore will not be compelled to complete the program. During her thesis study, Mary will try to obtain follow-up information on why subjects did not complete the treatment. A comparison of reasons why subjects in either group leave the study can be used to assess whether differential attrition occurred. For example, Maria may find that 10 subjects in the educational group and 4 in the multifaceted group leave for personal reasons—they move, a family member dies, and so on. The similar reasons for departure, would suggest that one treatment was not perceived as more valid than the other, if participants who do leave report honestly. However, as the discrepancy between numbers leaving each group increases, the mere fact of the discrepancy suggests differential attrition, despite the reasons subjects give for dropping out.

TABLE 5-14 An evaluation of extraneous variables in Maria's study.

Extraneous variable	Evaluation	Method to control or assess
Selection bias	No intact groups; random assignment to groups	Controlled by research type
Subject bias	Demand characteristics in consent form; duration may increase between-group talk	Reduce explicitness of consent form; must keep duration or will not get a treatment effect
Researcher bias	Researcher aware of hypotheses and will lead the groups	Faculty ratings of congruence with each treatment philosophy across two different sessions
History	No intact group; random assignment to groups	Controlled by research type
Maturation	Older subjects; random assignment to groups	Controlled by research type
Testing	No pretest; random assignment to groups	Eliminated without pretest
Mortality	Random assignment will reduce but may be differential attrition if educational perceived as less valid	Assess subject loss during study; determine why subjects drop out
Instrumentation	Treatment may be conducted differently, with multifaceted more appropriately administered than educational	Use faculty ratings described under researcher bias
Regression	No pretest; not a homogenous sample in terms of bulimia	Eliminated with no pretest and heterogeneous sample

CONCLUDING COMMENTS

We conclude this chapter with two forms to use in critiquing the internal validity of existing studies or as a general guide in decision-making when planning your research. In Form 5-2, we combine the first two principles of MAXMINCON—maximizing the effects of the independent variable and minimizing error factors. Form 5-3 is the same as Form 5-2, except that it evaluates the control or assessment of extraneous variables.

EXERCISES

1. Suggest ways to maximize the dichotomy of the following independent variables:
   a. Depression treatment
   b. High school teaching methods
   c. Counselor theory
   d. Substance abuse treatment
   e. Modality of client contact
2. Analyze Forms 5-1, 5-2, and 5-3. Discuss how the figures are related to the concepts of reliability and validity discussed in Chapter 4.
3. Analyze the following study concerning dental hygiene. Subjects are ran-

FORM 5-2 A form for evaluating maximization of independent variable and minimization of error.

1. Is research type quasi-experimental or experimental? If yes, continue with #1a. If no, go to #2.

   1a. How are levels of the independent variable (e.g., treatment) maximized?

   _____
   _____
   _____
   _____

2. How is error minimized?

	Method to minimize	Evaluation
Subject error		
Procedural error		
Measurement error		

FORM 5-3 A form for evaluating extraneous variables.

Extraneous variable	Method to control or assess	Evaluation
Selection bias		
Subject bias		
Researcher bias		
History		
Maturation		
Testing		
Mortality		
Instrumentation		
Regression		

domly assigned into two groups. X, the treatment group, receive four seminars in proper eating, brushing, and other healthy dental hygiene habits. Another group gets four seminars in which films are shown of patients with different dental pathology (such as tooth decay, gum disease, and so forth). The idea is that subjects viewing the films will be "scared" into proper dental hygiene. Finally, a third group is simply requested to continue their dental habits as usual knowing that in two months they will receive a free dental exam. This free exam is true for the other two treatment groups as well. With this information, specify the:

a. Research design (X and O).
b. Extraneous variables relevant to the design.
c. State recommendations for assessing or controlling the variables you identified.
d. Demonstrate the technique of blocking that would help you assess and control one potential extraneous variable.

4. Consider the White and Franzoni paper in Appendix E in terms of:
   a. Was the independent variable dichotomized? Why or why not?
   b. Identify any relevant sources of error.
   c. Of the nine extraneous variables, identify the three you believe most relevant. Why do you think they are most relevant?
   d. With your answer in mind, what are your recommendations for assessing or controlling these variables?

5. In evaluating your potential thesis topic, complete Form 5-1.

6

EXTERNAL VALIDITY

MARIA IS CONCERNED about the generalizability of her study, realizing that others might be interested in how her results apply to their situations. She believes that other researchers and practitioners will be interested in her study only to the extent that it applies to their subjects, in their setting, and with their ability to replicate her methods.

Maria wonders whether she should have included hospitalized subjects. Should she have sought out African American subjects? Was investigating only females a severe limitation? Was relying on volunteers a fatal flaw as far as other researchers are concerned? Should she have spent more money to train other providers than herself, conduct the sessions somewhere other than the counseling center, and purchase additional measures of change in bulimic behavior? Will the multifaceted treatment be as effective with other providers and with bulimic women several years in the future? Could she have omitted some components of the multifaceted treatment and still obtain as much success?

Maria considered some of these questions while designing the study and concluded that since she had limited financial resources, she could only devote one year to her study and that either she could investigate these questions in further studies or other researchers would have to provide the answers. Maria concluded that she would do as good a job as she could to identify her population and conduct the study so that the results were generalizable to that population; other researchers could decide for themselves how valid the study would be for their own populations. She would carefully define and report her population, describe how she conducted the study, and report how the results were obtained.

Maria decided to include in her report the following *characteristics* of her *population:*

1. Female
2. University-enrolled
3. Hispanic American and Anglo-American
4. Attending university in the southwest
5. Volunteer

She also reported the following characteristics of the *setting* in which the study was conducted:

1. Time of study (spring of 1993)
2. Location of the group meetings
3. Time of day of the group meetings
4. Frequency of the group meetings

Finally, Maria detailed the *methods* she used, specifically describing the independent variables and dependent variables:

1. Detailed description of both the educational and multifaceted treatments
2. Description of how the implementation of those treatments deviated from the planned implementation
3. Description of unusual or unexpected events that occurred outside the treatment (movie star dies of bulimia)
4. Report of unusual or unexpected events that occurred within the treatment (groups bonded more than was expected from the literature)
5. Copy of the BULIT-R; report of its reliability and validity for Maria's population

RELATIONSHIP BETWEEN INTERNAL VALIDITY AND EXTERNAL VALIDITY

In the previous chapter, we discussed the various threats to the internal validity of a study, as well as the procedures and designs that could either assess, eliminate, or drastically reduce those threats. While it is important to have internal validity—confidence in the integrity of results of the study—science can only be advanced if we can generalize those results to other situations. That generalizability is referred to as **external validity**.

Internal validity is a necessary but not sufficient condition for external validity—necessary because internally invalid results cannot be validly generalized and not sufficient because external validity is a higher-order conclusion, as depicted in Figure 6-1.

Figure 6-1 indicates three possible situations. In case A, the study lacks internal validity; we are not confident that the results are a function of the treatments. Therefore, we would not prefer one treatment over the other, even with another sample from the same accessible population. In case B, the researcher is confident that the sample represents the target population and therefore would use that treatment in another sample from the same target population. Since the treatment has not been investigated for, or found applicable to, other populations, we limit our recommendation of use to that target population. In case C, research with this treatment on other populations has shown the viability of the treatment for those populations. Therefore, we would recommend its use in those populations.

Figure 6-2 resembles Figure 6-1, with Maria's study used as the example. Note in case C that once the multifaceted treatment was shown to be successful with Anglo-American and Hispanic American volunteer males, the multifaceted treatment would be recommended for use with other Anglo-American and Hispanic American university males. The treatment in case C, then, has external validity for Anglo-American and Hispanic American university male volunteers but not for other populations such as African Americans, volunteer hospital males, or any population of nonvolunteers.

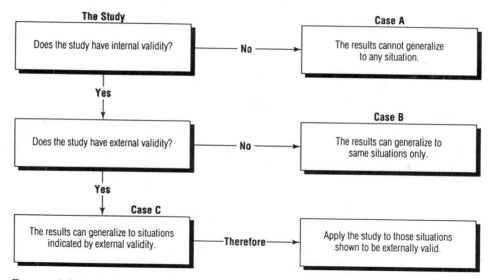

FIGURE 6-1 Comparison of permissible generalizations under (case A) no internal validity, (case B) internal validity only, and (case C) internal and external validity.

When a researcher conducts a study, his or her biases, whether or not the researcher is aware of them, may lower internal validity, or they may influence decisions about the design of the research. Doing a credible study means exercising control over the choice of subjects, the setting, and the measuring instruments. The more control is used, the more likely it is that high internal validity will be obtained; but the more control there is, the more limited the results will be to a particular setting. If the treatment is sterile as compared to the outside world, there will generally be little external validity with regard to setting. Because the ultimate goal of research is to make generalizable statements (external validity), we must first establish a firm grasp of what happens in a particular situation (internal validity).

The researcher's primary responsibility is to provide assurances that the study produced the results it did and that the attribution of cause is defensible. These components all relate to internal validity. The researcher also must provide information about the determination of external validity. The researcher should discuss the effects of the various threats to validity and state a belief about the degree of the external validity for the researcher's population. After all, the researcher should be in the best position to do that. But since the consumer's population will rarely be the same as the researcher's, the consumer must assess the applicability (external validity) of the research to the consumer's population.

Once we are confident that the study's results are internally valid, we must determine to what other situations we can generalize these results. Such external validity demonstrations are often the prompts for additional research. For in-

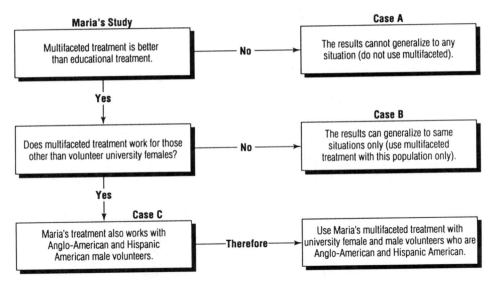

FIGURE 6-2 Comparison of permissible generalizations under (case A) no internal validity, (case B) internal validity only, and (case C) internal and external validity for Maria's study.

stance, a treatment may work with a certain population, but a researcher may wonder what it would do for a slightly different population—possibly in a different setting or with a different way of measuring the outcome. Any one of these questions can point the researcher to a fruitful inquiry.

Campbell and Stanley (1966) did the pioneering work on both internal validity and external validity, which was more fully treated by Bracht and Glass (1968). We divide the concept of external validity into three major areas, following the lead of Smith and Glass (1987). Each of the following is expanded upon in the next sections:

1. **Population external validity**—the population of subjects that one can generalize to.
2. **Ecological external validity**—the settings that these same results also would occur in.
3. **External validity of operations**—whether other researchers could obtain the same results using similar operational definitions of the independent variable and dependent variable.

Keep in mind that inferences about external validity must be made by both the researcher and the consumer of the research. The researcher has three kinds of responsibilities. First, the researcher must select all research procedures and then describe exactly what population, setting, and methods were used. This description will help the reader understand how the research was conducted. Research can be conducted in many different ways, some of which are less tolerant than others of threats to internal and external validity.

Second, the researcher must make an estimate of the study's external validity to the researcher's population. Random selection from the target population followed by random assignment to treatment groups is the most defensible procedure and thus gives the best estimate. Notice that random assignment to treatment groups is an advantage for internal validity but is not a sufficient condition for external validity. In Maria's case, subjects were randomly assigned to the two treatment groups, but were subjects randomly selected first from the population of all bulimics at her university? No, they were not. Maria had no access to people who were unaware of her study, nor to those who did not want to change their behaviors, nor to those who chose not to volunteer. If she did have access to all bulimics and all cooperated with her, then she could have randomly sampled from the bulimic population and randomly assigned subjects to treatments.

Third, the researcher should make estimates of external validity for other situations that would be of high interest. While these estimates must also be made by consumers of research, the researcher is closer to the procedures and may have some insights about the validity (or lack of validity) of such inferences.

Each consumer of research must make an independent inference about how applicable the research results are to his or her situation. This inference requires a careful and critical reading of the research. An inference about external or internal validity would be based on common sense, logic, theory, and a person's knowledge base. Even better than making inferences, however: the consumer of research can become a researcher and obtain empirical evidence supporting the inference. Indeed, empirical demonstration is usually more defensible than logical inference.

Research that is attempted in real-life settings is sometimes called **analogue research**. In such research, small modifications are usually made in otherwise real-world settings. This type of research is the ultimate goal of researchers who want to identify the real effect of some manipulated variable. Although analogue research is intended to approximate real situations, this method is also based on a high degree of experimental control. Thus, while many variables contribute to the outcome in helping profession interactions, the analogue researcher is interested in isolating one or two of these variables, while attempting to hold all other factors constant. In this way, analogue researchers try to scientifically assess the impact of one or two experimental manipulations.

To illustrate analogue research, assume that an investigator is interested in this research question: Does social worker interpersonal style affect client perceptions during a home visit? The analogue researcher could stage a home environment and have subjects read a standardized vignette describing the purpose of the visit, and the qualifications and background of the social worker. Subjects could then be assigned to one of three conditions: passive, aggressive, or assertive social worker interpersonal style. After a 30-minute interaction, subjects could rate the social worker's effectiveness. The analogue researcher would try to hold all other variables affecting social worker effectiveness constant. For example, the vignette would contain identical purposes of the visit, similar social worker background and qualifications, and same home environment. Finally, the social worker in each condition could be the same person (to hold elements like physical attractiveness, gender, and ethnicity constant).

TWO ASPECTS OF EXTERNAL VALIDITY

As indicated in Figures 6-1 and 6-2, there are two aspects of external validity: (1) the appropriateness of the generalization from the study to the target population, setting, and operations and (2) the identification of other populations, settings, and operations to which these results can be generalized. The first aspect is a necessity. We need to know where these results will occur. Is there some systematic difference between the sample and the target population? Will these same results occur only on the second floor of the research building? Will they occur only with Researcher A as the experimenter?

Being able to generalize results to other populations, settings, and operations is of great benefit. People tend to search for general statements rather than specific statements for each situation. Although it is too much to expect general statements to apply in all situations, we want to expand the boundaries of each statement we do make as much as possible. In the following sections, we will examine this idea.

POPULATION EXTERNAL VALIDITY

Although random sampling has been highly touted in previous chapters, human service providers seldom have the luxury of obtaining a random sample. When they do, it is usually from an accessible population, not the target population. An **accessible population** is one that is readily available to the researcher. If subjects do not volunteer, or refuse to finish the research, or do not even know about the study, they do not comprise the accessible population. Only those who know about the study, who do volunteer, and who finish the research can provide data. Therefore, two assertions must be made: (1) that the sample represents the accessible population and (2) that the accessible population represents the **target population:** the population to which one wants to generalize.

If random selection from the target population has been accomplished and internal validity satisfied, then one can legitimately generalize to the target population; but researchers usually cannot sample from all the target population and therefore must investigate the possibility of differences between the accessible population and the target population. The study of hyperactive boys discussed earlier is a good example of the differences between the studied sample of the accessible population and the target population. Samples that are obtained from telephone, newspaper, or word of mouth may have subtle differences from those randomly sampled from the population. In fact, it is often a good idea to identify characteristics of the sample. Form 6-1 is a form that we find useful in recording information which makes consumers aware of sample characteristics.

FORM 6-1   Consumer's guide to evaluating population external validity.

DEMOGRAPHIC VARIABLES
   Gender
   Age
   Ethnicity
   Geographic location
   Income
   Religion
   Political
   Other
TIME (designed by researcher):
   AM/PM, end of semester, during national debate over topic, during war, and so on.

CONDITIONS OF PARTICIPATION
   Volunteers
   Restricted range on some variable
   Climate of accessible population's environment relative to other environments
   Other

TASK CONSTRAINTS
   Practice effects
   Threatening to some
   Interview, multiple-choice, or essay preferred by some
   Understanding level of the subjects

INTERACTION OF ANY OF THE ABOVE

AUTHOR'S STATED TARGET POPULATION
_____

MARIA REVISITED

Maria will report the gender (female only), age (university student), ethnicity (Anglo-American and Hispanic American), geographic location (southwest), and educational level (undergraduate) of her subjects. She deems income, religion, and political party affiliation to be irrelevant to the study. Maria will report conditions of participation as volunteers, nonhospitalized, and receiving no course credit or remuneration. Subjects were in fact enticed to participate by being told that they would probably change their behavior if they attended the sessions. Maria's target population is thus Anglo-American and Hispanic American female southwestern university undergraduate volunteers.

THE ACCESSIBLE POPULATION

Often, a sample is obtained from a restricted subset of a target population—those subjects who are available for one reason or another—so the accessible population is probably different from the target population to which the researcher wishes to generalize the results. (Researchers usually claim a much broader target population than is realistic, which will entice more readers, but the results will not be applicable to the population of interest of all those readers.) The differences between the sample and the target population seriously call into question the validity of generalizing the sample results. Figure 6-3 shows the two kinds of populations and how a researcher goes about generalizing the results from a sample to the accessible population and then from the accessible population to the target population.

As indicated in Figure 6-3, random sampling is the basis for the generalizability of sample results to the accessible population. If random sampling has not been used, generalization depends on judgment, which can be formed by knowing the process by which subjects were chosen, characteristics of the subjects, and how those characteristics compare to the characteristics of the target population. That is why researchers often report demographic and other quantitative information about the sample such as percentages of males and females, mean age, percentages of single and married subjects, and percentages of ethnic minorities. Unfortunately, researchers seldom report parallel information for the accessible population or for the target population. Members of an accessible population are different from the target population in two major ways: they are willing to participate in the study, and they are at the right place at the right time.

Volunteers

One way to increase response rate is to make participation in the study as enjoyable, convenient, and inviting as possible. Trying to increase participation

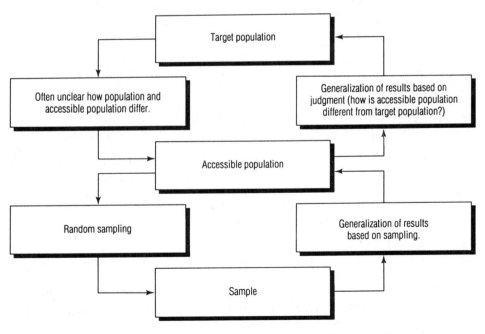

FIGURE 6-3   The process of generalizing from the sample to the accessible population.

by force or by conniving will usually lead to either no data or data with systematic error or random error. On the other hand, restricting the target population to volunteers is sometimes not a concern. In many helping profession situations, those who receive help have sought out the help—that is, they volunteer. Furthermore, one of the elements of successful job counseling, personal counseling, and nursing is that the subject wants to improve. It is very difficult to provide services to those who do not want to be helped, and when such services are provided, they are usually not successful.

Maria sampled from an accessible population. She could not force women to undergo her treatments, so she was only able to treat volunteers. Would the results of her study generalize to nonvolunteers? Applying the treatments to nonvolunteers would be the only way to answer the question. Short of replicating the study on nonvolunteers, Maria can only attempt to make a guess. If the nonvolunteers simply did not hear about the study, then they probably would respond in about the same way as the volunteers. However, if women did not volunteer because of the gravity of the condition of their health, their commitment to continue binging and purging, or their inability to acknowledge a problem, these women might be expected to respond less positively to treatment. Because research is usually not conducted on nonvolunteers, such guesses should be made by the researcher.

Location

When a university-based researcher recruits subjects, members of the accessible population are usually members of the same university as the researcher. However, in order for research to have meaning to researchers or practitioners at other sites, a target population would have to be larger than just that one university. Is that university different in some ways from other universities? Are undergraduate students different from people of the same age who are not in school?

Maria's study involves university students only. Would the results generalize to women who have graduated, or to those who have dropped out, or to those who have never gone to college? Each of these potentially different populations may be different, that is, women in each of these populations may respond differently to treatment. The study would have to be replicated on these populations to see whether they really are different in terms of the effectiveness of the multifaceted treatment.

Two other major population constraints are evident. Maria's study was conducted at a university in the southwest. Would bulimics in other parts of the country respond similarly? Probably they would, but we would feel more confident in making this statement if the study were replicated elsewhere. Secondly, there were no African American women in the study. Would these women respond the same way to treatment or would they constitute a different population? A thorough knowledge of the population, the treatment, the dependent variable, and bulimia is needed in order to answer this question subjectively. Empirical replication is the way to answer it objectively, that is, from a scientific point of view.

Let us imagine that members of an accessible population work at a health provider's institution whose administrator approved a research project after the researcher was turned down at several other institutions. Is the climate in this institution the same as the climate in other institutions? Are the staff members cooperating with the study? If they are, are they cooperating willingly or under duress? These factors would all have to be known before the validity of the study results for the target population of all institutions could be estimated.

EXAMPLE OF SAMPLE, ACCESSIBLE POPULATION, AND TARGET POPULATION

Peterson (1991) conducted a study of social workers' knowledge about AIDS. She obtained a random sample of 500 names from the central membership directory of the National Association of Social Workers (NASW), stratified by fields of practice. While she reported the responses by field of practice, she did not report the initial percentages that were mailed out. Since only 76% ($N = 379$) responded (prodded by two follow-up mailings), we do not know if certain fields of practice tended not to respond (not volunteer). Peterson does report that 71% of the respondents were female and that the average age (of the 309 agreeing to report age) was 42.7 years. The majority of the respondents had a master's degree in social work (84%), and 87% of those who indicated race ($N = 330$ out of 379) indicated that they were Caucasian, 3% black or Hispanic, and 3% Native American. Respondents were from all areas of the United States, with 34% from the North, 26% from the Midwest, 24% from the South, and 16% from the West. (Since Peterson provided neither operational definitions of these geographic locations nor population percentages, we do not know for sure that all areas were proportionately sampled. We might feel reassured, though, that there were some respondents from all areas.)

Peterson did provide an approximation of some target population data by referencing a national survey of the same association. That survey (also on volunteers) had responses of 74% female (similar to 71% in the Peterson study) and 10% ethnic minorities. Peterson asserted that the differences in the two studies appear to have been small. Note that although both of the studies obtained a random sample of names, the fact that not everyone responded resulted in a nonrandom sample of the target population. While the target population of members of the NASW was of interest, the two studies actually reported results from an accessible population of volunteers.

Target Population

From the consumer's viewpoint, the target population is of primary interest, but the target population of interest to the consumer is often different from that envisioned by the researcher. Therefore, it is the consumer's responsibility to make the judgment as to whether or not the results would be applicable to the consumer's population. Looking at the actual sample is thus critical for the consumer. The consumer must determine that, for example, what works in the inner city will also work in the suburbs, what works for adolescents also works for young adults, or what works for bulimics also works for anorexics.

Determining Population External Validity

A consumer of Maria's research results would be aware that Maria sampled from one university in the southwest. Looking at the demographics supplied by Maria and understanding the extent of regional differences would help a consumer make an inference about generalizability to another nonsouthwestern university. That consumer may feel comfortable in generalizing Maria's results to another university setting, but another consumer, working with bulimics in a hospital setting, may not be comfortable. Feeling that hospital bulimics are in more immediate medical danger than university bulimics, that consumer would probably require a different mixture of the multifaceted treatment components.

A researcher cannot anticipate all possible populations and therefore should not be required to determine external validity for all those populations. In early stages of research on a particular issue, the target population might be limited. Once the mechanisms are determined within the specific target population, research would be extended to other target populations. Let us assume that Maria's multifaceted treatment is very effective for bulimics at her university. Practitioners at another university may be interested in trying her multifaceted treatment, hoping that it will work but realizing there may be differences in the two universities that might reduce its effectiveness. Until validated in the new situation, Maria's multifaceted treatment must be considered as possibly valid rather than definitely valid. Other university counseling centers might use the multifaceted treatment until they fail to find results. Then, research should be undertaken to determine the factors that result in success with one target population and failure with other target populations.

Representation of Population External Validity

One way to envision the external validity of Maria's study is depicted in Figure 6-4. The circle depicts Maria's study; it is divided into seven major slices: Gender, Location, Time, Geographic location, First initial of last name, Ethnicity, and Volunteer vs. Nonvolunteer. Each slice is further divided into segments that are closer to the center, indicating that Maria's study is probably more externally valid for that segment. The generalization of Maria's study to segments at the edge of the circle (1995–96, nonvolunteers, and African Americans) is more tenuous. Other slices, such as age and hair color, could be considered. Potential users of Maria's study probably would not be concerned about hair color or first initial of last name, although they may be concerned about generalizing the results of Maria's study to younger or older women.

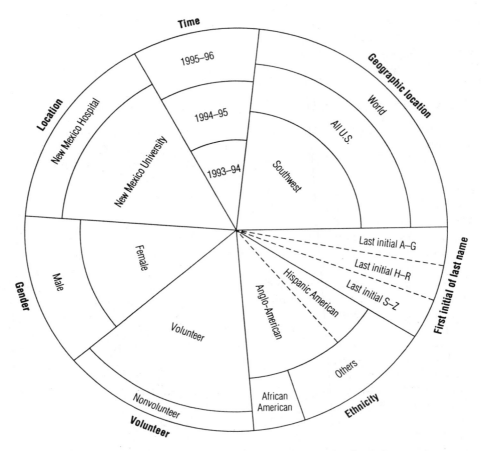

FIGURE 6-4   Example population external validation for Maria's study.

SELECTING A SAMPLE TO ANSWER THE RESEARCH QUESTION

In helping profession research, we inevitably rely on human subjects to provide the data to answer our research questions. As we will discuss in later chapters, the way we select subjects for research is of vital importance because it directly affects the internal and external validity of research results. The next sections expand on the sampling techniques first discussed in Chapter 3.

Samples and Populations

A **sample** is any group on which information is obtained. Since it is extremely rare to collect information on all members of a group, a sample represents one subset of a larger group called the **population**. When we speak of how samples are selected from populations, we refer to **sample selection procedures**.

Regarding samples and populations, the first conceptual step for a researcher is to determine the population of which each subject is a member. This is not as easy as it may seem because it is not always clear what defines the larger group. For instance, a researcher investigates the question: Is behavior modification or Ritalin more effective in reducing the hyperactive behaviors of fifth-grade boys? The researcher samples 100 hyperactive fifth-grade boys to study this question empirically. What is the larger group in this case? Is it every boy in the universe who has ever been hyperactive, is currently hyperactive, or will ever be hyperactive? Is the larger population all fifth-grade boys in the United States or just the state from which the sample is drawn?

Again, the target population is the group to which we wish to generalize the results. While the researcher initially defines this group, this definition is partly subjective. The most conservative way to define a target population is to limit the population to the larger group from which the sample is selected. For example, if 50 hyperactive children were sampled from all hyperactive boys in School District X, which has 200 children, then the target population is all hyperactive fifth-grade boys in School District X. Because School District X lies in a unique geographic, cultural, and ethnic setting, the results of the study are appropriate to just this target population. Whether they are generalizable to another population of hyperactive fifth-graders is unknown; that question could generate a new research study.

Restricting the target population to the larger group from which the sample was drawn is important, because it is very common to see target populations defined as some larger group to which the researcher wishes to generalize the results, such as all hyperactive fifth-graders in the state, in the United States, or in the world. Thus, be wary of statements in reports like, The results show that hyperactive children tend to respond better to behavior modification than Ritalin. Note that the target population is no longer confined to the 200 fifth-graders in School District X but now implies a much larger group—larger geographically, and larger with regard to gender, age, and socioeconomic status.

Let us illustrate the paradox of simple random sampling using Maria's proposed research study as an example. Assume that Maria wants to use simple random sampling to select 50 subjects from the target population, which she defines as all southwestern university women with bulimia. Because every member of this population must have an equal chance of being selected, Maria must somehow locate all southwestern university women with bulimia and make these women aware of the research study she is conducting. In her attempt to achieve this goal, she aggressively advertises her study by (1) printing a flier about the study, (2) going to every faculty meeting in all university departments to request that each faculty member circulate the announcement to students, (3) putting the flier on all campus bulletin boards, (4) setting up daily radio airings of the study for one week, and (5) putting a full-length advertisement in the student newspaper.

Now consider whether or not Maria has made all southwestern university bulimic women aware of the study. Even with the amount of time and money Maria spent recruiting, we could never assume that every member of the population was aware of the study. Perhaps some bulimic women were away from their university during Maria's advertising, or some instructors never announced the study, or another student covered her bulletin board announcement with another flier. Because it is nearly impossible to assume that all population participants had an equal chance of selection, simple random sampling is nearly impossible—nearly impossible, that is, if the researcher defines a population that is large and difficult to reach. However, recall that target populations are arbitrarily specified by the researcher. Note that Maria could change the definition of her target population so that simple random sampling could easily be employed. For instance, she could redefine her larger group as all southwestern university bulimic women who were aware of her study. If she located 200 such subjects, she then could use simple random sampling to select her final sample of 50. The disadvantage of this narrower target population is that Maria can only generalize the results of her study to a smaller group of bulimic clients. Her results can no longer be generalized to all southwestern university women—specifically, not to those who were unaware of her study.

One final nuance about random sampling techniques: While each population member must have an equal probability of being selected to participate in a study, there is no guarantee that once selected, subjects will consent to participate. For example, in the hyperactivity study, the researcher may have found that upon requesting family consent to participate, only 50 of the first 100 randomly selected families consented. Yet, since every member of the target population had an equal chance of being selected, there is no violation of simple random sampling.

It is equally clear that the target population is no longer all hyperactive fifth-grade boys in School District X if half these children do not participate in the study. The researcher must redefine the target population as all hyperactive fifth-grade boys in School District X whose families volunteered to participate in this study. The children who do not volunteer would define another target population. The researcher could now accurately state that simple random sampling occurred for this redefined target population. Although simple random sampling also occurred for the nonparticipating target population, this is no longer a meaningful fact because this group is not being measured and conclusions drawn from the study do not pertain to the nonparticipating group. As we will discuss later, one major issue in human subjects research is that those who volunteer to participate in a research study form one group that usually differs from the group that does not voluntarily participate. Here again, the question is whether the results obtained with one group (volunteers) are generalizable to the other group (nonvolunteers).

Stratified random sampling occurs when the target population has various levels of a characteristic that the researcher wants represented in the sample. Suppose that 60% of the School District X fifth-grade boys are Anglo-American and the remaining 40% are African American. A random sample of 200 would not likely result in 60% (120) Anglo-American and 40% (80) African American. Stratified random sampling would first randomly sample 120 (60%) Anglo-Americans and then randomly sample 80 (40%) African Americans, thus guaranteeing that the sample percentages match the target population percentages.

Either simple random sampling or stratified random sampling is ideal because these procedures increase the applicability of drawing conclusions to the population from which the sample was drawn. Unfortunately, their use is hindered by practical issues, such as the time and money involved to employ them. Consider the hyperactive study. If all the hyperactive children in School District X are to be sampled, it is time-consuming and expensive to travel to the various schools in School District X, visit different classroom teachers, and meet parents to seek their children's participation. Sampling the hyperactive fifth-graders from one school is much easier and less expensive.

Convenience Sample

Because of time and money concerns, the most common sample in human subjects research is the **convenience sample.** As the name implies, a convenience sample is simply a group of subjects who happen to be most available for participation in a research study. Since there is no systematic selection in a convenience sample, it is less representative of the target population. Examples of convenience samples are (1) an outpatient group of hyperactive children seen in hospital X, (2) a group of high school students who come to counselor Y for career counseling, (3) students of Professor Z's psychology 101 class who fill out a survey, and (4) mall shoppers selected to answer questions about the quality of products. Sometimes convenience samples cannot be avoided, but whenever they can, we recommend that simple random sampling or its stratified counterpart be implemented.

It is difficult to define the population from which a convenience sample comes. For instance, samples of beginning psychology students are classic examples of convenience samples. The question is, which target population do beginning psychology students represent? One narrowly defined target population is other psychology students at the same university. However, since these are beginning psychology students, it is doubtful whether the sample would accurately represent even other psychology students at a particular university. You can see that the convenience sample would be even less representative of the general population of students at the university and would not represent students attending other universities at all.

Random Assignment

Random assignment is not a sampling procedure but a method for assigning each member of the selected sample to a group. Random assignment uses simple random selection to assign each final sample member to a particular group. If every member in the final sample has an equal probability of being assigned to each group and each member is independently selected to the group, subjects are said to be randomly assigned to groups. Random assignment is a critical concept that assumes extreme importance in ascertaining internal validity.

In Figure 6-5, we illustrate the relationship between the target population and two sampling techniques—random and convenience. We also indicate that random assignment occurs when the researcher places the selected subjects into experimental groups.

Target population

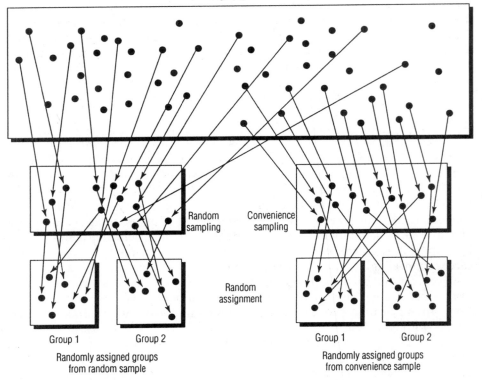

FIGURE 6-5 Comparison of random sampling and convenience sampling.

MARIA REVISITED

Maria's goal is to select 50 bulimic women for participation in her study. She will randomly assign 25 to one type of counseling and 25 to the other type of counseling. Currently, Maria is seeing 12 women at the University Counseling Center who have bulimic symptoms. She informs her adviser of her intent to recruit 12 of her clients as subjects. However her adviser is concerned that Maria's clients may participate in her study because of their prior relationship with Maria. In other words, Maria would have a dual relationship; one with her clients, another with her clients as subjects. After her meeting with her adviser, Maria agrees to exclude subjects who are her personal clients. She knows that other center staff members have contact with 30 bulimic clients, and she gets permission to contact each of these women, 25 of whom agree to participate in her study. To obtain the 25 additional participants, she advertises in the student newspaper; with the consent of some psychology, nursing, and social work professors, she makes presentations to their classes in an attempt to enlist subjects for her study. Within 2 weeks, she has her 50 subjects and is ready to conduct her study. What is Maria's target population? What is the sample? What is the sampling procedure Maria used? Try to answer these questions now before reading any further.

Maria defines her target population as university bulimic women who were aware of her study.

Note that her population neither includes bulimic women in the university who were not aware of her study nor bulimic women outside the university, since she did not recruit subjects from any other setting.

Her sample of the university population consists of the 50 bulimic women enlisted for participation in her study. She sampled them through convenience, since 25 subjects were already seeking services at the University Counseling Center, and the additional 25 were located through selected class presentations and newspaper responses. Note that her convenience sample may not even be representative of university women who were aware of her study. There could have been many women who were eager to participate, but she took only the first 25 to achieve her goal of recruiting 50 subjects. In this case, the first women to participate may differ from those coming to her attention after she met her goal. For example, early volunteers may be more highly motivated, or since recruitment began in one college, the required 25 women all came from that college.

The populations of aware and unaware bulimic university women are likely to differ as well. Maria recruited subjects more actively from human service courses (aware population) and thus missed bulimic subjects enrolled in classes in other academic disciplines such as the physical sciences, engineering, and business (unaware population).

To review briefly: The researcher is responsible for assessing external validity for the accessible population and the target population. The person doing the research can make some guesses about external validity to the other populations, but it is the responsibility of other researchers to determine validity empirically. We should not require every research finding to be generalizable to a broad range of populations. While it would be advantageous for one treatment to be effective for all populations, a treatment that is effective for only one specific population is also valuable. One treatment that is very effective for one population should not be applied to other populations. The treatment would probably be ineffective. The goal is to find a treatment that is the most effective for each population.

ECOLOGICAL EXTERNAL VALIDITY

Ecological external validity is concerned with the setting in which the study was conducted and whether the research results could be generalized to other settings. These other settings could be field settings other than the laboratory, other researchers, other demand characteristics, or new or disruptive settings. Again, the researcher must do two things: (1) describe the setting of the research precisely and (2) make some inferences about the other settings in which the researcher could be expected to obtain the same results.

Description of the Experimental Treatment

After describing the research environment in detail, the researcher should provide assurances that there were no features of the setting that other researchers could not replicate in a similar setting. For instance, if several subjects dominated a therapy group in a positive way, the same domination may not occur again. Another example would be if research treatments were conducted in a spacious and inviting meeting room. These facilities could have contributed to treatment effects, and since other practitioners may not have such facilities, they may not observe the same effects.

As an example of how a research setting can affect results, Mitchell and Frederickson (1975) showed slides of four male counselors, three of whom were identified as having a physical disability. Subjects were asked to read 20 counseling situations and to identify the one counselor they would be most likely to choose. Subjects were to select a counseling situation, even if it did not apply to them. The choices subjects would make in an experimental situation like this may very well be different from ones they would make in real life, particularly if the subject had the problem described and was seeking help. We might guess that some subjects would simply distribute their choices among the four counselors. Others may have chosen a handicapped counselor because they thought they were supposed to do so. Since in the laboratory there is no commitment to see one of the counselors, choices do not have ramifications. Therefore, any conclusions from such research would be tentative and would have to be followed up with more costly designs in more life-like situations.

MARIA REVISITED

Maria's study included the multifaceted treatment, which she defined as a set of specific activities completed in sequence, each requiring a specified amount of time. Thus, the multifaceted treatment could be replicated in another setting by another researcher. Maria was careful to include only activities that were widely available; she did not incorporate any procedures that required special training or certification.

Researcher Effects on External Validity

Researcher effects occur when the treatment effect is partly attributable to the person conducting the research. Perhaps this person has particularly good counseling skills, or the researcher's personality may be more in line with one therapeutic treatment than another. The researcher may favor one treatment—this is usually called researcher bias. For instance, Maria must be careful to present both treatments equally well. Her subjects must find them equally convincing.

Researcher effect was discussed in Chapter 5 as a threat to internal validity. Clearly, the researcher should have no effect on the outcome of the study. Even though the original researcher's characteristics may be congruent with both original treatment groups, these same characteristics may keep researchers with different abilities, skills, styles, and personalities from being able to replicate the original research. The replicating researcher would influence the results differently than the original researcher, which would create a problem with researcher effect as it relates to external validity.

It has also been widely documented that researcher effect can result from researcher expectancy (Rosenthal, 1976). This expectancy can occur in many ways, from the choice of the dependent variable, to the choice of the treatment, to communications with subjects or research assistants, to scoring and interpreting results. A design that produces an estimate of this effect is presented in a later section.

Novelty and Disruption Effects on External Validity

Novelty and disruption effects can occur when a treatment is different from one that subjects usually receive. Often, when a new treatment is provided to subjects who are used to the standard treatment, the subjects will do better just because it is a new treatment. Most people react to new treatments by acquiescing and trying to do better. Here, initial results with a novel treatment will be positive. For the novel treatment condition, there is internal validity—the treatment really does work—but there may not be external validity. When other researchers use the novel treatment for a longer period, the treatment's effects may erode as the novelty erodes. On the other hand, some people will be very confrontational and deliberately try not to do well. With confrontational subjects, the new treatment probably will not be better than the usual treatment.

An opposite problem occurs when a new treatment is disruptive. The results may be negative initially, but once the subjects routinely implement the new treatment, results may become positive. A researcher should always plan the length of the treatment to be long enough for the treatment to take hold—for disruptive influences and novelty influences to wear off—so that the treatment is effective. Also, the effects of the treatment should be long-lasting, not elevated for the benefit of posttesting.

In Maria's study, the novelty of acknowledging bulimic behavior or the novelty of one of the multifaceted components might wear off after a period of time. If the subjects are still experiencing this novel effect during the posttest immediately after treatment, the treatment's effects will be recorded as higher than on a posttest that is administered several months later.

On the other hand, some components of Maria's multifaceted treatment may be difficult for some subjects to understand or to implement. Often, the mechanics of something new (new machine, new card game, new counseling process) may get in the way of what newness is supposed to accomplish. Maria must determine the length of her study based on these and other novelty and disruption factors.

Interaction of Setting and Treatment Effects

The researcher must be aware of and describe any peculiarity of the setting. For example, when a new drug prevention program is implemented in a school district, it would be valuable to know that the school personnel (1) have failed miserably with their first program, (2) are being raked over the coals in the media, and (3) are desperately searching for any new procedure that is better than what they currently have. In this situation, school personnel are motivated to implement the new drug program and to see that it works. This setting is very different from one in which a school district is looking for their first program as a preventive program. If the research was done in the first setting, we would expect positive results, but we would not expect the same magnitude of results in the second setting because of the historical difference of the two situations.

Let us suppose that Maria's study was conducted during a time of little national news regarding bulimia. Thus, she could afford to ignore history as a threat to the internal validity of her study. Although she could generalize the results to similar, uneventful times, to what extent can she generalize to more eventful times? Maria probably should not generalize to such times, for if her multifaceted treatment were implemented, for example, at the time a celebrity dies from bulimia, we might expect (1) more women coming forth to volunteer, (2) more attention to the various treatments by the subjects, and (3) more effect at posttest for both treatments. On the other hand, if the treatment coincides with renewed emphasis on slim models and a new government report decrying the obesity of its citizens, then all treatments for bulimia might be ignored or be ineffective.

EXTERNAL VALIDITY OF OPERATIONS

External validity of operations focuses on the research procedures and the operational definitions of the variables, both independent and dependent. While most researchers discuss constructs, they must use specific measures of those constructs, and the various specific measures are not all equally good. Just because the developers of a measure say that it measures a construct, that does not mean it measures the construct perfectly—or even measures it well. Other researchers and practitioners may prefer to operationally measure a construct differently, and the results may be different.

Measurement of the Dependent Variable

Scientific generalizations are desirable and are based on constructs such as mental health, IQ, and anxiety. Since we can never measure these constructs directly, we use operational definitions of these constructs to do so. As we discussed in Chapter 3, there is one construct of anxiety, but there are many ways to measure anxiety.

To measure anxiety, we could employ any one of many paper and pencil measures. Some of those are multiple-choice, some are essay, and some are fill-in-the-blank. We could use projective measures, sociological measures, or physiological measures. If we measured one individual with each of these measures, we might find very different levels of anxiety.

A researcher must select an operational definition for each dependent variable. Other researchers might choose other operational measures; thus the consumer must decide (1) whether the chosen operational definition really measures the construct and (2) whether the results of using that operational definition will generalize to other operational definitions that the consumer might be interested in.

In Chapter 4, we discussed Maria's choices for her dependent measure of bulimia. Although Maria discusses the results in terms of the construct bulimia, she (and her consumers) should never forget that she operationalized bulimia in terms of the scores on a paper and pencil self-report measure—BULIT-R.

Pretest Sensitization Effects on External Validity

In Chapter 5, we discussed the influences of the pretest on treatment outcome. If a pretest is administered in a study, subjects may become sensitized to what the study is about. This might not happen without a pretest. Pretest sensitization does not automatically occur when a pretest is used; it will occur only when the subjects are influenced by the pretest. The more general the pretest, the less likely there is to be a problem. If pretest sensitization does occur in a study, the results of that study cannot be generalized to a situation in which no pretest is administered. That is, the treatment is not the sole cause of the changes; the pretest is part of the cause. Thus, the treatment lacks internal validity.

It should be noted that a researcher can take advantage of pretest sensitization. That is, the treatment can be defined to include the pretest as part of the treatment, which means that the results can only be generalized to situations in which there is a pretest and not when there is no pretest. Since the pretest is usually inexpensive, requires little inconvenience, and is usually such a crucial component of the treatment, including the pretest makes good sense. Although such a treatment cannot be validly generalized to the nonpretest situation, this may not be an issue for the research and consumer communities.

In Maria's study, a pretest is a good idea because the subjects are likely to be at varying levels of severity. There would be no concern about pretest sensitization in Maria's study because the subjects had to be aware of their bulimic behavior and had to want to control it. Also, the treatment would remind them of their behavior and would encourage them to desist from binging and purging. Thus, practitioners and other researchers can generalize Maria's treatment only to pretest situations, but that caveat is of no concern.

Posttest Sensitization

Posttest sensitization means that the results will be influenced by the particular dependent variable used. Posttest sensitization can occur in several ways. First, the expectation of the posttest can cause better performance during the treatment and therefore, higher scores at posttest. Second, the posttest may be a learning experience—the initial items on the test may cause understanding of the treatment to solidify for the subjects. Certain items can also tip off the purpose of the study or the answers the researcher wants. In a sense, the posttest becomes part of the treatment; when that happens, the researcher must communicate that to the consumer. The results of the research then can only be generalized when the posttest is included. (The expectation of taking a posttest and the integrative powers of a posttest could also be included as part of the treatment.)

In Maria's study, if the subjects know they will be held accountable at a specific posttesting time, they may make more effort to reduce or stop their binging and purging. On the other hand, if subjects go to the treatment sessions thinking they will just gain information and possibly change their behavior, without any expectation of a posttest measure, we might expect less treatment effect. Since Maria's subjects will know they will be posttested, her study can only be legitimately generalized to other situations that include subjects' expectation of that same posttest. If a therapist chooses not to use the BULIT-R or any other measure at posttest, different results might occur, simply as a function of the subjects' knowledge that there will be no posttest.

Measurement of the Independent Variable

The same comments about operationalizing the dependent variable apply to operationalizing the independent variable. Attaching a name to a particular treatment communicates something concrete only if the treatment has been fully delineated and followed. Treatment identifiers such as "group counseling" or "individual Rogerian counseling" are not sufficient because different researchers have very different ways of implementing those treatments. Each researcher should provide a clear description of the treatment, including location, pretest procedures, information provided to the subjects, length of each session, total number of sessions, general procedures within each session, general goals of the study, and criteria for termination and posttest assessment. All the procedures should be defined so that another researcher could conduct the same study.

In Chapter 5, we discussed Maria's choices for the definition of her treatments and the length of the treatments. Her multifaceted treatment identifies a specific treatment and is not one that other researchers can put together in a haphazard way. The term *multifaceted* does not define the treatment components; we need to look at Maria's specific treatment procedure.

Posttest Administration

The timing of the posttest administration can be an important factor. Some treatments produce immediate effects that are measurable after treatment but dissipate shortly after that. Most consumers (also most subjects) would be interested in a treatment that has a long-lasting, rather than a temporary, effect. So, researchers who include a delayed posttest in their design provide more evidence of the effectiveness of their treatment than those who provide only an immediate posttest. The delayed posttest might even uncover a delayed effect, one that was not evident at immediate posttest but which developed after treatment. Counseling treatments that encourage clients to use their existing skills in new ways would be one such possibility. Here, there might be more effect several months after treatment than immediately following treatment because the clients would have several real-world opportunities in which to try out the new skills; implementation of the new skills might become more routine and thus more effective.

A follow-up measure of the binging and purging behavior in Maria's study would be a valuable addition to the study. Long-term improvement would be important. Recidivism has been documented with some bulimic subjects; therefore, any treatment should have as one of its goals the reduction or elimination of recidivism.

Multiple Treatment Interference

Some subjects receive what can be considered multiple treatments. This can occur in one of three ways. First, there may be other naturally occurring treatments that subjects either receive automatically or search out. For instance, some subjects might receive counseling through their religious affiliation in addition to the experimental counseling. Second, a researcher may purposefully design a treatment to include two or more major components, as Maria did. Third, researchers sometimes counterbalance treatments by giving treatment A and then treatment B to one group, while giving treatment B and then treatment A to a second group. Without these additional groups, a researcher cannot identify the true effect of either treatment A or treatment B.

Not only is it difficult to disentangle the various treatments, but it is usually unclear whether the same results would occur if only the one target treatment were administered. It is usually best to have each subject receive only one treatment, which simplifies the determination of the effects of that treatment. Some of the single-subject designs discussed in Chapter 9 separate out the effects of the various treatments.

Maria's study is a good example of the researcher incorporating various treatments—Maria calls them components—into one multifaceted treatment. If Maria finds that the multifaceted treatment is better than the educational approach, she cannot conclude that each component of the multifaceted treatment is a valuable and necessary component. The most she can conclude is that if all the components are used (in the same order and for the same length of time), treatment will be effective. Follow-up research can determine if certain components can be omitted—this is called **decomposition**—thus saving time and money. If such subsequent research determines that components 1 and 2 are necessary but that component 3 is not, then we will have a new definition of multifaceted. We will also have found a less expensive treatment that results in the same effectiveness.

METHODS FOR INCREASING EXTERNAL VALIDITY

External validity is lacking when nothing is known about how the results of a study relate to other populations, settings, or operations. External validity knowledge is gained when an internally valid study is conducted on another population, setting, or operation. Such a study could be considered a replication of the original study with a slight change in population, setting, or operation. The next section details what the researcher can do to increase external validity with respect to a target population, as well as other populations. The subsequent section details what other researchers can do to extend the external validity to populations of interest to them.

External Validity Methods Under the Control of the Researcher

The primary method the researcher has is random selection from the target population. Given random selection, the (internally valid) results of the study can be generalized to the target population. If random selection was not possible, as is usually the case, the sample should be described in detail. By doing this, the researcher is making an inference about the population to which the results are applicable.

Other sampling procedures can increase the external validity of a study. If a researcher wants to generalize to all subpopulations of a particular variable, then subjects should be sampled from each of those subpopulations and tested to see if the results are any different. In Maria's study, ethnicity is one such variable on which the subpopulations of Anglo-Americans and Hispanic Americans are to be tested. If these two subpopulations should be found to react similarly to the treatments, they really are the same subpopulation with respect to bulimic treatment.

Sometimes, **purposive sampling** can be used to make sure that particular types of people are included in the research. Examples would be (1) selecting only so-called typical people, (2) selecting from across the entire range of some variable, and (3) selecting only the extremes on some variable.

For example, Cowdery, Iwata, and Pace (1990) were interested in finding alternative ways of treating self-injurious behavior. Their only subject was exhibiting self-injurious behavior. This single-subject study focused on various reinforcement strategies. Even though the results are generalizable only to that one subject, other researchers and consumers may get some useful ideas from what these researchers accomplished.

The third example for purposive sampling is when limited funds lead the researcher to focus on the two extremes of a continuous variable. Such studies are usually undertaken when researchers are first investigating that variable. If a difference cannot be found between the extreme groups, there would probably not be differences between less-extreme groups.

Designs for Increasing External Validity

A researcher is only responsible for establishing the external validity of a study's results to the target population, in same setting and using same procedures. But many researchers want to extend the applicability of their study to other situations. Several designs can help the researcher accomplish this task.

TABLE 6-1   Design to assess Hawthorne effect and researcher expectancy.

Group 1	R	X	I_p	O_1	(Treatment X; Implementer thinks positively)
Group 2	R	X	I_n	O_2	(Treatment X; Implementer thinks negatively)
Group 3	R	H	I_p	O_3	(Hawthorne comparison H; Implementer thinks positively)
Group 4	R	H	I_n	$O4$	(Hawthorne comparison H; Implementer thinks negatively)

RESEARCHER EXPECTANCY DESIGN.   Researcher expectancy can be controlled for in a design that expands on the traditional treatment-comparison design. Each of these two treatments has two conditions, one in which the implementer believes the treatment will be effective and one in which the implementer believes the treatment will be less effective. The design is illustrated in Table 6-1.

The first two groups in Table 6-1 are treatment groups (treatment X), and the last two groups are comparison groups (treatment H). Group 1 is the usual treatment group in which the implementer understands (correctly) that the implementation is in fact the treatment. It is thus reasonable to assume that the implementer will have a positive expectation about the results and that the results may be inflated because of these positive expectations.

The Group 2 implementer is led to believe that the treatment is a comparison treatment, and thus it is reasonable to assume that the implementer will have a negative expectation about the results and that the results may be deflated because of those negative expectations.

The Group 3 implementer is led to believe that the Hawthorne comparison treatment (H) is really a new treatment. It is thus reasonable to assume that the implementer will have a positive expectation about the results and that the results may be inflated because of these positive expectations.

The Group 4 implementer is led to believe that the Hawthorne comparison treatment is really the traditional comparison group. Thus, it is reasonable to assume that the implementer will have a negative expectation about the results and that the results may be deflated because of those negative expectations.

O_1 minus O_2 is one estimate of the researcher effect, while O_3 minus O_4 is another estimate of the researcher effect. O_1 minus O_3 and O_2 minus O_4 are two estimates of the treatment effect. The two estimates of the researcher effect should be similar, as should the two estimates of the treatment effect. The value of the design in Table 6-1 is that it allows the determination of what the effect might be in a real situation where the Hawthorne treatment effect and researcher effect are nonexistent.

MARIA REVISITED

Maria felt that she did not need to use the above design for several reasons. First, she was comparing her multifaceted approach with the existing standard approach for treating bulimia. Second, while she thought she had developed a better way to treat bulimia, until some data support her supposition, she can honestly tell the educational group that they are receiving the best treatment available. She realizes that if she could afford to hire other therapists to conduct treatment groups, the resulting experimenter-blind design would be preferable. Since she was short of cash, though, Maria decided to make every effort to hide her expectations.

SINGLE-ORGANISM DESIGNS.   Each subject is the best control for herself or himself. Many elaborate single-subject designs have been developed to take care of various threats to both internal and external validity. The fact that only one subject has been studied must always be kept in mind, as external validity can only be determined for that one subject. (Single-subject designs will be discussed in Chapter 9.)

FACTORIAL DESIGNS.   When subpopulations are investigated, the design can be expanded to include the variable that identifies those subpopulations. For instance, Maria is interested in the treatment effects in both Hispanic American and Anglo-American women. Ethnicity thus becomes a second independent variable. Maria has expanded her design from one independent variable (treatment) to two independent variables (treatment and ethnicity). Such a design not only allows for treatment and ethnic effects but also the interaction of treatment and ethnicity (discussed in Chapters 9 and 10). Such a design could produce results showing that the relative effectiveness of the multifaceted approach over the educational approach is greater for Hispanic Americans than for Anglo-Americans.

MULTIPLE DEPENDENT VARIABLES.   One way for the researcher to investigate external validity to other measures is to incorporate those other dependent measures in his or her own design. Statistical techniques exist that can be used to analyze the set of dependent measures simultaneously. (These are described in some detail in Chapter 10.) One of the results of such a study is the determination of whether or not these dependent variables measure the same construct. The results can then be generalized to all dependent variables that measure the same construct.

External Validity Methods Under Control of the Consumer

The consumers of research can either accept the constraints and estimates provided by the researcher, or they can investigate the validity generalizations they are interested in that the researcher did not report.

REPLICATION.   Replicating a study is one way to verify that the results are stable in that population. A true **replication** repeats all aspects of a study on a different sample from the same target population. In reality, most researchers do modify one or more aspects of a study; therefore, when they find similar results they provide empirical support for internal validity and external validity. No one study should be expected to be externally valid in all ways, but a knowledge base is formed by knowing to what populations, settings, and operations the results are and are not generalizable.

META-ANALYSIS. The researcher usually conducts a literature review before beginning a research project, and consumers usually try to get as much information as possible before making a decision. Since each research study is susceptible to differing threats to internal validity, seldom do research results (even strict replications) yield the same conclusion. Most literature reviews briefly state the findings, providing at best a general, subjective impression.

Meta-analysis is a computational way to combine the results of many similar studies (Glass, McGaw, & Smith, 1981; Light & Pillemer, 1984; Rosenthal, 1984). One treatment effect is calculated for each study. The **effect size** is the difference between the treatment and comparison groups, divided by the standard deviation (usually of the comparison group). The division by the standard deviation removes the score scale from each difference between treatment and comparison. Thus, each study is on a common scale and the results for all the studies can be aggregated, even though different operational measures might have been used. Thus, one index can portray the general magnitude of effect.

An additional value of meta-analysis is that a variable that was not investigated in each study can be investigated across all the studies. For instance, assume that there have been 40 studies investigating the effectiveness of the home delivery of newborns. While each study may have shown more success for home delivery than hospital delivery in general, the results are varied. Suppose there is reason to believe that the distance from a major hospital makes a difference and that home deliveries closer to major hospitals are less successful. The results of the 32 studies that reported distance from major hospital could appear as in Figure 6-6.

Note that the initial variation in effect size can be accounted for partially by this added variable—distance from major hospital. No one study looked at the variable of distance, but since 32 of the 40 studies reported the distance, that variable could be compared to the effect size of the study (see correlation in Chapter 10).

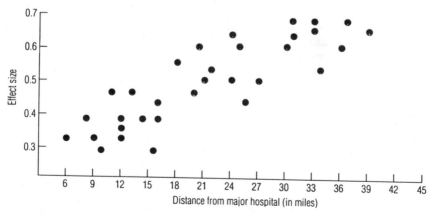

FIGURE 6-6 Relationship between distance from major hospital and effect size.

EXTERNAL VALIDITY AS IT RELATES TO THE KNOWLEDGE BASE

In Chapter 1, we introduced the notion of the knowledge base. Of course there are many knowledge bases—one for each issue within each content area. Because there are three components to external validity (populations, settings, and operations), we propose conceptualizing the knowledge base as a rectangle as shown in Figure 6-7.

The specific building blocks in any knowledge base will be a function of (1) what needs to be known and (2) what is known regarding that issue in that content area. What needs to be known can be illustrated, for example, by understanding that testicular cancer can be contracted by males and not females. Thus, the population of females need not be investigated for external validity. With respect to settings, one research issue may be reasonably limited to hospitals, while another may be expanded to include both inpatients and outpatients.

Some knowledge base blocks will be larger than others, indicating more general applicability. Some blocks will be filled more than others, indicating more certainty. Some blocks will be missing entirely, as research has yet to commence in that area. Some blocks that should be there may be missing because researchers do not yet realize those issues are relevant.

CONCLUDING COMMENTS

As you have probably surmised, there are many concerns related to external validity. No one study can adequately respond to each threat. Also, there is no index of how well a study deals with external validity. This is a judgment call.

External validity is a major concern because we want our research to have meaning, not only for the target population but for other similar populations, settings, and operations. The best way to establish meaning is to replicate the research in the places desired, under conditions desired, with the specific populations desired, and with the various operational definitions desired.

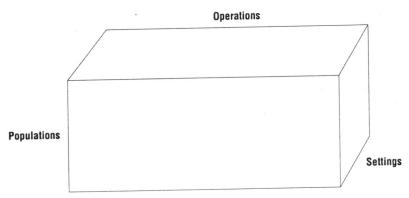

FIGURE 6-7   The knowledge base conceptualized as a rectangle.

TABLE 6-2   Threats to internal and external validity according to time in the research process.

SELECTION OF SUBJECTS
  Selection bias (internal)

PRETEST
  Testing (internal)
  Instrumentation (internal)
  Statistical regression (internal)
  Pretest sensitization (external)

TREATMENT
  DUE TO THE RESEARCH CONTEXT
    History (internal)
    Maturation (internal)
    Interaction of history and treatment effects (external)
    Novelty and disruption effects (external)
    Experimental treatment diffusion (internal)
  DUE TO RESEARCHER'S ACTION
    Explicit description of the experimental treatment (external)
    Multiple treatment interference (external)
    Researcher effect (external)
  DUE TO SUBJECT'S ACTIONS
    Experimental mortality (internal)
    Hawthorne effect (external)

POSTTEST
  Testing (internal)
  Instrumentation (internal)
  Statistical regression (internal)
  Posttest sensitization (external)
  Measurement of the dependent variable (external)
  Timing of posttest administration (external)

One way to review all the threats to internal and external validity is to consider them in terms of the paradigm in Table 6-2. The major research activities in an experimental research study occur in the order of (1) selection of subjects, (2) pretest, (3) treatment, and (4) posttest. Since the bulk of the threats occur during treatment, we have further divided those threats into three categories: (1) threats due to the research context, (2) threats due to the researcher's actions, and (3) threats due to the subjects' actions. Since there are so many threats, they can become confusing and overpowering. You may want to refer to this table when determining what threats are applicable at what times. No one study, of course, can avoid all threats, but a well-designed study eliminates most of them, assesses the extent of the threat with some, and minimizes the remaining. You—the researcher—should report how each of these threats affects the study.

MARIA REVISITED

Maria's literature search identified bulimia as a major problem for many adults. She identified components of a new treatment that she felt would be better than the traditional educational treatment. Although she would have liked to demonstrate its effectiveness with all young adults, she

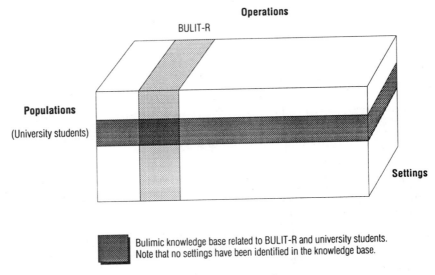

Operations

BULIT-R

Populations

(University students)

Settings

Bulimic knowledge base related to BULIT-R and university students. Note that no settings have been identified in the knowledge base.

FIGURE 6-8   Selected aspects of Maria's knowledge base.

realized that she was limited by time and financial resources. Therefore, she had to build certain limitations into her study. The knowledge base that Maria relied on with regard to external validity is partially represented in Figure 6-8. Maria's study is based on the accumulated knowledge that she discovered in her literature review. Her study fills in some gaps in the knowledge base.

With respect to the populations side of the rectangle, Maria studied subjects who were in a university setting. To keep this figure simple, we do not include the ethnic groups that she investigated.

The operations side of the rectangle in Figure 6-8 indicates the dependent variable—BULIT-R. Again, other operations Maria used are left out of the knowledge base at this time. The intersection of University and BULIT-R indicates one aspect of the knowledge base she would review and contribute to.

Consider now an expanded version of Maria's knowledge base in Figure 6-9. The populations side of this figure reflects the fact that Maria had access to both Anglo-Americans and Hispanic Americans. Since few African Americans attended her university, she decided to limit her study to just Anglo-Americans and Hispanic Americans. While most of the literature dealt with Anglo-Americans, she felt that it was also applicable to Hispanic Americans. She also knew she was making a contribution to the knowledge base by including Hispanic Americans in her study. She hoped that other researchers would study the effectiveness of the multifaceted treatment with African Americans.

The settings side of the rectangle in Figure 6-9 indicates that Maria conducted her research on bulimia in a university counseling center in New Mexico. An even more expanded knowledge base would include other settings, such as individual treatment and group treatment. In addition, hospitals and clinics could be included as setting variables. Maria's literature review determined that previous researchers have considered these settings different from the university counseling center setting, primarily because of the severity of the bulimic condition found within hospitals and clinics. Therefore, what works in one setting may not work in another. Once Maria finds that her new

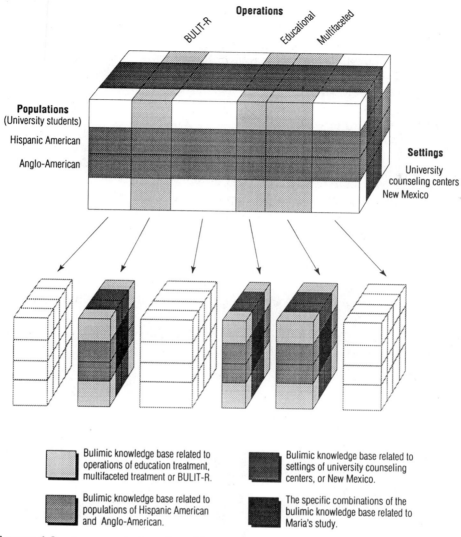

Operations

BULIT-R   Educational   Multifaceted

Populations
(University students)

Hispanic American

Anglo-American

Settings

University
counseling centers
New Mexico

Bulimic knowledge base related to
operations of education treatment,
multifaceted treatment or BULIT-R.

Bulimic knowledge base related to
populations of Hispanic American
and Anglo-American.

Bulimic knowledge base related to
settings of university counseling
centers, or New Mexico.

The specific combinations of the
bulimic knowledge base related to
Maria's study.

FIGURE 6-9   An expanded version of Maria's knowledge base.

multifaceted treatment works in the group setting at the university, she might recommend researching the new treatment in hospitals and clinics. Since group treatment is less expensive than individual treatment, there is little reason to research the effectiveness of the multifaceted treatment in the individual setting. (Indeed, the multifaceted treatment relies on group processes, so it would not be feasible to apply it in the individual situation.)

The third side of the rectangle is concerned with operational definitions. Maria identified her dependent variable of BULIT-R. Maria also identified the independent variables of educational and multifaceted. She chose to omit from the rectangle all the rectangle treatments that have been investigated, since there has been little observed effectiveness for those other treatments. The darkened rectangles indicate the part of the knowledge base that Maria would particularly have to include in her literature review, and ultimately make a contribution to from her findings.

The next two chapters explore various designs that Maria could use to answer her research question. While she has a good idea of her design, she realizes that there are several ways her research question could be answered.

EXERCISES

1. Assume you are conducting a study on the most effective way to psychologically treat battered women. You are working in a shelter located in a small southwestern town. The population is mainly Hispanic American. Identify three threats to external validity from this situation.

2. In selecting groups for an experiment, how do random selection and random assignment differ?

3. How do internal validity and external validity differ? Can a piece of research have a high degree of internal validity and low external validity?

4. Compare and contrast the target population and the accessible population in the two articles in Appendix E.

5. For those planning on doing a thesis, how could you modify your research so as to increase the external validity?

7

CULTURAL FACTORS
RELATED TO RESEARCH

IN HER LITERATURE REVIEW, Maria identified many studies of college women being treated for bulimia. Maria noted, though, that most of the studies included only Anglo-American women. Since Maria was attending a university that had almost as many Hispanic Americans as Anglo-Americans, she wondered if the results reported in the studies she read would also apply to Hispanic Americans.

Having become aware of the problems surrounding external validity, she decided to include in her study not only Anglo-Americans but also Hispanic Americans. However, Maria was concerned that including these two groups might affect both the conduct and the internal validity of her study. She was also concerned that the two groups of subjects might respond to her differently, since she was clearly identified with one group—Hispanic Americans. She wondered what she could do to minimize these effects.

Finally, Maria wondered whether or not her cultural identity focused her research in some way. Was she making decisions about the conduct of her research on the basis of her culture—decisions that other researchers might not make?

B oth the cultural diversity of the United States and the ethical guidelines developed by the American Psychological Association require practitioners to recognize that differences with respect to age, sex, socioeconomic status (SES), and ethnic background can affect relationships in the helping professions. Cross-cultural research may in fact be an area of interest for some helping professionals; in any case, researchers need to be aware of issues that may surface when they conduct or evaluate cross-cultural research. As a potential researcher and evaluator of research, you should know about strategies for dealing with those issues.

DEFINING AND IDENTIFYING CULTURAL GROUPS

To conduct cross-cultural research, the investigator must develop a strategy for identifying cultural groups. In this section, we discuss these strategies and the potential difficulties in identifying cultural groups. We then suggest ways to reduce these difficulties.

The United States is a culturally diverse country, so government agencies, social scientists, and members of the helping professions may be accustomed to using cultural categories or labels—generic labels that facilitate the description and classification of large numbers of people into distinct groups. However, it may be erroneous to assume that the people being classified are familiar and comfortable with, or accepting of, those labels. People who immigrate from less culturally diverse countries may not have given much thought to racial, ethnic, or cultural labels, particularly the ones employed by social scientists in the United States. Thus, asking such people to categorize themselves may be a novel and confusing experience for them. For example, an international student from the Middle East was asked to identify his race when registering at a southwestern university. Since he had never been asked to do this, he expressed some confusion. The registration clerk finally advised him that he must be Caucasian because he was neither Negroid nor Mongoloid.

Researchers often use race, nationality, ethnic culture, and religion to establish the identity of groups. Confusion can arise, however, when these terms are used incorrectly. *Race* is sometimes confused with ethnicity, nationality, or religion; in fact, race is based on physical attributes and is subdivided into the Caucasoid, Negroid, and Mongoloid races. *Nationality* refers to country of origin. *Ethnicity* implies a common ancestry and cultural heritage and encompasses customs, values, beliefs, and behaviors (Kumabe, Nishida, & Hepworth, 1985). However, at times a person is asked to respond to a question about race using national, ethnic, or religious categories. For example, the terms Mexican, Hispanic, and Jewish are sometimes mistakenly used to describe a person's race.

Generic labels are used to classify groups of people who share certain characteristics. While these labels are convenient, they have inherent disadvantages, including confusion about who does and does not fall under the rubric of the label. Also, disagreements about labels, about the population for whom the label is intended, and about the clustering of heterogeneous groups into a single homogeneous one are common among social scientists.

The generic term Hispanic was developed by a federal agency—the Office of Management and Budget (OMB)—in 1978 to describe people who are perceived to have a similar ethnic background (Federal Register, 1978, p. 19269). The OMB defined a Hispanic as "a person of Mexican, Puerto Rican, Cuban, Central or South American or other Spanish culture or origin, regardless of race." While the OMB definition may be generally satisfactory, it also poses some problems. For example, while Brazil is a South American country, Brazilians are excluded from the OMB definition of Hispanic because they are not of Spanish origin and descent. Indigenous tribes in Mexico and Central and South America speak their own native languages and are not of Spanish descent either. On the other hand, the Spanish did have a significant cultural impact on Filipinos, but these people are not considered Hispanic.

While an investigator may be satisfied with a certain generic label, there may be disagreement among social scientists about it. Further, those who are labeled may not concur with the generic term; in fact, they may dislike being categorized as belonging to such a group (Marin & Marin, 1991). For example, the term Hispanic American may be preferred in some regions of the country, while Latino may be the term of choice in other areas. Hayes-Bautista and Chapa (1987) and Perez-Stable (1987) have argued that Latino is more appropriate than Hispanic American because it makes explicit the Latin American origins of the people it describes. However, the problems identified with the term Hispanic American also apply to Latino. Other terms such as Raza, Chicano, and Mexican American have been used when conducting research with Hispanic Americans of Mexican ancestry, but they are not appropriate when studying other Hispanic American groups.

Participants' identification and comfort with the label employed by the researcher can affect their willingness to participate in a research study as well as their response style (Marin, 1984). For example, if participants are accustomed to describing themselves as Mexican or Honduran, they may resent a researcher who categorizes them as Hispanic American or Latino. They may have a different perception of what the term implies or may feel that nationality is more important than ethnicity. Marin and Marin (1991) interviewed Hispanic Americans in San Francisco and found differences in preference for the Latino and Hispanic American labels as a function of acculturation. More acculturated individuals preferred the latter term. Only 3% of the respondents interviewed by these researchers assigned no importance to the label employed to describe them.

The problems discussed so far are not exclusive to Hispanic Americans; similar issues may be encountered when studying other cultural groups. For example, in a course on family ethnicity and diversity, students were asked their opinions about labels. Some students objected to being classified as Anglo and expressed a preference for a term that denoted nationality, such as Irish, Italian, or Polish. There was also a debate on the appropriateness of terms such as Black, African American, Black American, and Negro. Some students were surprised to discover that persons from the Middle East are from Asia because they thought the terms Asian and Asian American referred primarily to persons of Chinese or Japanese descent. One Asian student, for instance, was only familiar with the term Oriental.

Using surnames to determine cultural or ethnic classification can have advantages as well as disadvantages. If a researcher wants to target a specific cultural group, the use of last names can be an initial step in the process. It is highly likely that a significant proportion of subjects will identify themselves as belonging to that group. The researcher cannot rely completely on surnames to determine ethnic culture, however. A person with a Spanish last name may be Hispanic American, Native American, Portuguese, Italian, or Filipino.

Simply asking subjects to identify their own cultural group may lead to misclassification. In addition to the problems with labeling already discussed, it is possible that some subjects' self-identity may differ from their social identity. For example, highly acculturated individuals may consider themselves to be American and not identify with an ethnic or cultural group, even though society may perceive that they do.

Another problem inherent in the use of generic labels has to do with the generalizability of research findings when culturally diverse people are subjects. The terms Hispanic American and Asian American, for example, describe groups of people who share commonalities but who may be diverse with respect to language, nationality, immigration history, SES, acculturation, and religion—all of which affect values, attitudes, and behaviors. Participants' responses to research would consequently be affected. Cross-cultural researchers need to provide information about the cultural subgroups they study and discuss the generalizability of their findings to similar groups.

Given the difficulties we have discussed, you can probably see how important it is for researchers to familiarize themselves with the various labels used to describe the specific group they plan to study. It may also help to find out whether or not the group of interest has shown a preference for a particular cultural label. For example, if the researcher is conducting an investigation in an area in which the term Latino is more prevalent than Hispanic American, the researcher may consider using the former rather than the latter term. Additionally, Marin and Marin (1991) recommend that researchers ask participants to indicate national origin or ancestry in order to make a more accurate identification. If generic labels are used initially, subjects can then be asked to elaborate further and provide information about nationality or ancestry. This will allow the researcher to describe the cultural group more accurately and better address the generalizability of any findings.

A MULTICULTURAL APPROACH TO RESEARCH

In this section, we will discuss the importance of cross-cultural research, the methodological factors that have limited the use of cross-cultural research, and recommendations for enhancing the meaning of this type of research.

Researchers usually sample college students or middle-class Caucasians. While this practice provides valuable information and implications for practice, it does not add significantly to the understanding of cultural diversity (Atkinson, 1987; Ponterotto, 1988). Overemphasis on one subpopulation contributes to the development of theories and implications that lack cultural relativity (Pedersen, 1987).

Members of the helping professions acknowledge the influence of cultural diversity on human behavior and the need for multicultural research that can enhance the understanding of diversity as it relates to their professions (Pedersen, 1991; Sue, Arredondo, & McDavis, 1992). In recent decades, graduate training programs have taken a proactive stance and have made changes in their programs to facilitate the development of culturally skilled professionals (Sue et al., 1992). Research is a powerful force in the development and testing of theories that facilitate the understanding of human behavior and the development of helping strategies (Borg & Gall, 1989). In a call specific to the counseling profession, Sue et al. (1992) issued the following statement:

Research and counseling may become a proactive means of correcting many of the inadequacies and problems that have plagued us for years. . . . Research would become a powerful means of combating stereotypes and correcting biased studies. Studies would begin to focus on the positive attributes and characteristics of minorities as well as biculturalism. (p. 480)

However, if multicultural research is to enhance the understanding and appreciation of diversity, investigators must take certain steps to avoid the pitfalls that reduced the effectiveness of prior research and promoted stereotypes that added to the confusion and misperceptions.

A number of factors have limited the efficacy of cross-cultural research. Among these are: (1) cultural encapsulation—or assuming that differences between groups represent some deficit or pathology—(2) overemphasis on between-group differences without sufficient attention to between-group similarities as well as within-group differences, and (3) failure to take important socioeconomic variables into account.

Cultural Encapsulation

Cultural encapsulation occurs when people depend entirely on their own values and assumptions and define reality through those cultural assumptions and stereotypes (Pedersen, 1988; Wrenn, 1962). Pedersen (1987, 1988) identified ten assumptions that can contribute to cultural encapsulation and reduce effective relationships in the helping professions. Pedersen (1988) also discussed reasonable opposites that can enhance effective resource delivery by helping professionals. Several of these assumptions, as well as their reasonable opposites, have relevance for multicultural research.

Some assumptions that can lead to cultural encapsulation (Pedersen, 1987, 1988) are (1) everyone shares a single measure of what constitutes normal behavior; (2) individuals are the basic building blocks of society; (3) abstract words and concepts can be used that everyone will understand in the same way; and (4) we assume that we are culturally aware and that we already know what all of our assumptions are. If any one of these assumptions is incorrect, the research process can be adversely affected.

DEFINING NORMAL BEHAVIOR.   The first of these culturally biased assumptions is related to determining what constitutes normal behavior. If the researcher fails to examine his or her own values and assumptions and to see how they affect the conceptualization of normal behavior and thus the constructs employed in the research, there is a danger that between-group differences (such as those between African Americans and Anglo-Americans) can be perceived as pathological because they deviate from the researcher's idea of normalcy. We examine next how cultural definitions of normal behavior can contribute to misperceptions and limit the usefulness of cross-cultural research.

BIAS TOWARD INDIVIDUALISM.   Individualistic societies emphasize the independence and autonomy of individuals, whereas collectivistic societies stress interdependence that ensures the welfare and survival of the group rather than of the individual (Gibbons, Stiles, & Shkodriani, 1991). Normal behavior would naturally be defined differently in each of these societies. While some psychological tests define and measure normal behavior and identify deviations from this norm as pathological, using this strategy in cross-cultural research can be dangerous because cultural differences do not necessarily constitute deviations.

For example, imagine that a researcher is examining family functioning within a culturally diverse group. If the researcher's beliefs are consistent with those found in an individualistic society, the researcher may conceptualize healthy, normal functioning as the fostering of independent, autonomous behaviors among the children and may then proceed to measure this construct by noting the degree and intensity of physical contact between grown children and their parents. But if the researcher examines family functioning in a group that stresses *inter*dependence rather than independence, the researcher may erroneously interpret "too much" closeness, for example, as a deviation. The (interdependence) cultural group may simply espouse a worldview that emphasizes group rather than individual welfare, and close contact between grown children and their parents may represent their use of a natural support system rather than enmeshment or pathological dependence. Again, if the researcher makes certain assumptions regarding what constitutes normal behavior, and if these assumptions have limited cultural relevance with the population of interest, then the validity of the results is questionable.

ASSUMING CONSTRUCTS ARE UNIVERSALLY UNDERSTOOD.   Another kind of mistake can occur when the researcher is familiar with and accustomed to using certain constructs or abstractions and assumes they are universally understood (Pedersen, 1987, 1988). If the cultural group of interest is not familiar with the constructs or interprets them in a different way, however, the results of the research may not be valid (Marin & Marin, 1991).

Decision-making, for example, has often been examined using a definition of the construct that is derived in one culture—and considered the norm—and then used with groups that are culturally quite different. The results of these studies have added confusion rather than understanding of cultural diversity and have fostered stereotypes that have negatively affected the helping professions (Amaro & Russo, 1987; Andrade, 1982; Cromwell & Ruiz, 1979; Marin & Marin, 1991; Vega, Patterson, Sallis, Nader, Atkins, & Abramson, 1986).

Ponterotto (1988) identified the lack of a conceptual framework to guide cross-cultural research as a limiting factor. When assumptions about what constitutes normal behavior and constructs and abstractions are applied universally to culturally diverse groups, investigators may unwittingly be approaching cross-cultural research from a social deficit or pathology conceptual framework (Atkinson, 1987; Cromwell & Ruiz, 1979; Sue et al., 1992).

Pedersen (1991) proposed multiculturalism as a generic approach to counseling and research in the helping professions. Multiculturalism is currently considered by some to be the potential "fourth force" in the helping fields; its impact may equal that exerted by the first three forces: psychodynamics, behaviorism, and humanism. The underlying philosophy of multiculturalism is an acceptance and appreciation of diversity. From a multiculturalistic perspective, diversity can be perceived as an attribute rather than a symptom of pathology.

ASSUMING THAT WE ARE CULTURALLY AWARE. Pedersen (1988) discussed another assumption that can interfere with the effective provision of services, namely, that we already know what all of our assumptions are. Pedersen proposed that social scientists (1) engage in self-exploration, (2) gain awareness of their own values and beliefs and the relevance these may have in counseling, and (3) challenge their assumptions by considering alternative assumptions. The exploration of assumptions can be facilitated by understanding cultural relativity.

Cultural relativity refers to the idea that behavior must be understood within the context of the culture in which it occurs (Axelson, 1985; Hall, 1976). In other words, researchers should attempt to understand behavior from the viewpoint of the cultural group they are studying rather than from their own cultural perspective. Taking this approach may reduce the danger associated with encapsulation. Mistaken assumptions about what constitutes normal behavior can be avoided, thus facilitating the development of a multiculturalistic approach to research that sees diversity as a strength rather than a limitation or a sign of pathology.

Marin and Marin (1991) offer additional recommendations for facilitating cultural relativity and avoiding some of the pitfalls discussed in this section. If feasible, researchers can profitably immerse themselves in the ethnic culture of the group they are interested in studying. This experience can help the researcher develop a better understanding of what is considered normal behavior in the culture, as well as the relevance of constructs and abstractions that the researcher plans to use. The benefit of the experience can be enhanced if the researcher also learns to consider alternative worldviews.

Marin and Marin (1991) and Ponterotto (1988) encourage social scientists to seek information directly from cultural minorities and not rely too heavily on majority values and perceptions of normal behavior. Insight into another culture can be gained through collaboration with key informants who are members of the cultural group of interest prior to doing the research. This type of collaboration can provide valuable information that can increase the validity of the research project and help the researcher anticipate and deal with potential difficulties. Through a collaborative effort, a researcher may obtain information regarding the relevance and appropriateness of constructs, abstractions, instrumentation, and methodology. This information can affect all of the planning stages described in Chapter 3.

Overemphasizing Between-Group Differences

Another factor that has limited the usefulness of cross-cultural research has been the overemphasis on between-group differences—differences between two culturally diverse groups—without sufficient attention to between-group similarities or within-group differences (Lloyd, 1987; Ponterotto, 1988). Woodworth (as cited in Stagner, 1988) cautioned against the danger of neglecting the overlap in distribution when comparing two groups.

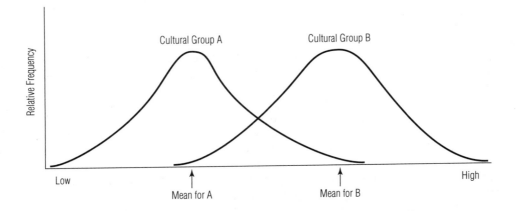

Figure 7-1 indicates how a behavioral trait might be distributed within each of two groups. Assume that the trait has been measured and each person now has a score on that trait. There clearly is a difference in the means (average scores) of the two groups, which indicates a between-group difference; but there are also within-group differences—the variability within each of the distributions. In other words, not all people in Group B are alike. The two distributions overlap; some subjects in Group A have higher scores than those at the Group B mean. Indeed, some people in Group A are closer to the Group B mean than are some members of Group B.

Lloyd (1987) also questions the value of focusing only on between-group differences and reports from his own experience that doing so has limited his ability to work with culturally diverse groups. Axelson (1985) defines cultural universals as fundamental similarities or universal themes that underlie diverse cultural patterns. The expression of those themes may vary in different cultures, but certain underlying commonalities remain. For example, human beings have basic physiological, emotional, and spiritual needs, but how they go about meeting those needs may vary across cultures. Axelson (1985) notes that overemphasis on the differences to the exclusion of the commonalities can increase the potential for bias and prejudice. Cross-cultural research that is biased does not enhance the understanding and appreciation of diversity and can contribute to misperceptions and confusion.

Within-group differences are the variations within a cultural group, which may be found with respect to such variables as nationality, religion, language, SES, immigration history, and acculturation level (Axelson, 1985; Lee & Richardson, 1991). All of these factors can influence how subjects respond to research; consequently, the external validity of the research findings is affected. Axelson (1985) describes three groups of Black Americans with different immigration experiences and historical backgrounds. The experiences of the free blacks differed from those of the freed slaves, who, in turn, differed from West Indian immigrants and Haitian Americans. The experiences of each group of

Black Americans affected their perceptions of themselves and their perceptions of the world, and consequently, their values, beliefs, behaviors, and goals.

Within-group differences can be found even within a specific group. For example, the early Cuban immigrants, known as the "Golden Exiles" differed from the "Marielitos" who immigrated later. These differences, which were related to class, race, and degree of acceptance into the United States, affected their worldview (Suarez, 1993). Differences like these may influence how subjects respond to research.

Neglecting Socioeconomic Variables

The neglect of important socioeconomic variables such as power, prestige, and money (Axelson, 1985) can also confound research findings because investigators may mistakenly attribute between-group differences to ethnic culture rather than to SES. Axelson (1985) differentiates SES from culture by explaining that socioeconomic variables affect perceptions of locus of control and, therefore, people's beliefs regarding the attainability of goals. People with similarly high aspirations may differ in their expectations of being able to realize their goals as a function of SES. Frustration with the inability to achieve desired goals can contribute to the development of what Axelson calls a stretched value system, which is accompanied by a low degree of commitment to those values. While the expression of values may vary between groups as a function of socioeconomic factors, these between-group differences are environmentally influenced rather than culturally rooted. As income, power, and prestige change, so may the expression of values. Figure 7-2 represents these concerns.

Failure to account for socioeconomic variables can compromise the validity of cross-cultural research. For example, suppose that a researcher compares family roles, family functioning, and psychological well-being between a group of middle-class Anglo-Americans and a group of low-income African Americans. Any differences found between these two groups may be related to cultural diversity, or they may be associated with socioeconomic factors. Bowman (1993) shows that employment and income have a significant effect on the way African Americans perceive fulfillment and satisfaction with family roles and family functioning. Therefore, any observed differences between these groups may disappear when the socioeconomic variable is considered in the research design, that is, when middle-class Anglo-Americans are compared with middle-class African Americans. (In this case, SES is used as a selection factor—only middle-class subjects are selected. In Chapter 5, we discussed the resulting sample as homogenous with respect to SES.) A researcher could, on the other hand, use SES as a blocking variable, resulting in six groups: lower-class Anglo-Americans, middle-class Anglo-Americans, upper-class Anglo-Americans, lower-class African Americans, middle-class African Americans, and upper-class African Americans.

There is a need for well-designed, cross-cultural research that can facilitate the understanding and appreciation of diversity, particularly given the cultural composition of the United States. Poorly designed cross-cultural research can contribute to confusion, misperceptions, and stereotypes.

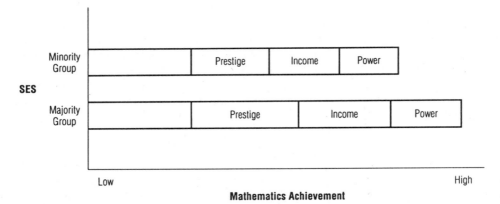

FIGURE 7-2   Figural representation of the confounding effects of socioeconomic status (SES) on Mathematics Achievement.

CULTURAL VARIABLES: IMPLICATIONS FOR CROSS-CULTURAL RESEARCH

Although common themes such as affiliation, communication, and esteem needs may tran-scend culture, the way those needs are met may vary as a function of culture (Axelson, 1985). Cross-cultural differences may be found in the expression of values and in the behaviors used to satisfy needs. Theories that help researchers explain and predict behaviors, and ultimately facilitate change when necessary, should take the effect of diversity in the helping professions into account. Cross-cultural researchers also need to be aware of the impact that diversity in values, attitudes, and behaviors can have on the way populations respond to the research process.

There are only a few studies using culturally diverse populations, but the information these studies have provided is valuable. In this section, we will examine some variables found among culturally diverse groups and show how they contrast with the mainstream culture. We will also discuss how these variables can affect the research process. The variables discussed in this section have been found to be particularly relevant for certain cultural groups, but because of within-group differences, individual subjects may vary in their adherence to cultural values. These variables may also be found to a lesser extent among individuals belonging to the mainstream culture.

Collectivism versus Individualism

In an earlier section, we discussed the impact of collectivism and individualism on the conceptualization of normal behavior, on the constructs and concepts employed in cross-cultural research, and on the conclusions that can be drawn from research findings. Collectivism and individualism also influence the way people relate to each other, the manner in which subjects respond to research, and the way research data are gathered. Again, *collectivistic cultures* emphasize the welfare of the group over that of the individual and are associated with interdependence, readiness to be influenced by others, preference for conformity, and cooperation in relationships (Gibbons, Stiles, Schnellmann, & Morales-Hidalgo, 1990; Marin & Marin, 1991). *Individualistic cultures* stress independence, personal rather than group objectives, competition, and power in relationships; these cultures measure achievement through individual success (Axelson, 1985; Marin & Marin, 1991; Stiles, Gibbons, & Schnellmann, 1990). Collectivism has been associated with Hispanics, Native Americans, and Asians (Axelson, 1985; Marin & Marin, 1991; McAdoo, 1993).

Because cooperation in interpersonal interactions is emphasized in collectivistic cultures, individuals who adhere to these values may respond more favorably to a research procedure that includes a personal rather than an impersonal approach. In other words, personal invitations to participate, interviews, and case studies would be preferred over mailed invitations or questionnaires. Personal contact with subjects may increase the rate of participation with collectivistic groups. However, the emphasis placed on cooperation may pose a threat to the internal validity of the findings. Participants might provide socially acceptable responses in order to avoid interpersonal conflict (Marin & Marin, 1991)—a more likely response than with those who espouse individualistic values (Marin & Marin, 1991).

Deference for both authority and older people are emphasized in collectivistic cultures. Researchers may be regarded with respect because of their social position and educational attainment and viewed as authority figures. Consequently, participants from collectivistic cultures may be more inclined to show respect for the researcher by providing socially acceptable responses. Marin and Marin (1991) suggest that the researcher's respect for subjects—acknowledging their expertise, for example—may reduce the power differential between researcher and participant and facilitate the research process.

Communication Style

Communication appears to be an important factor in people's lives, regardless of cultural differences. Communication styles, however, may vary across cultures; styles may be derived from collectivistic or individualistic values. In individualistic societies, the preferred communication style may be verbal, open, direct, and confrontational if necessary. The assertive expression of ideas and affect is encouraged; people say what they mean and mean what they say. In collectivistic cultures, the preferred communication style may be nonverbal and indirect, and confrontation is avoided whenever possible because it can disturb relationships and lead to the loss of face. The direct expression of ideas and affect is discouraged, and the establishment of rapport and the development of trust are prerequisites for the discussion of such taboo topics (in that culture) as sex, illness, and death (Attneave, 1982).

Shon and Ja (1982) for example, note that the rules of communication within most Asian cultures are determined by factors such as age, sex, occupation, education, social status, family background, marital status, and parenthood. A researcher interested in examining the grieving process or sexual functioning, for example, among a traditional Asian group should consider a research methodology that would take into account the cultural variables that affect self-disclosure in that group. The procedure for obtaining data from the Asian group may be different from one that would be used if the group of interest were Anglo-American and middle-class. Whereas a mailed questionnaire or direct questions may be effective ways to obtain data from the Anglo-American group, the Asian group may require the use of personal contact with an interviewer who can inspire trust and be alert and responsive to nonverbal cues.

Time Orientation

Time orientation is another important cultural factor to consider when conducting cross-cultural research. The ordering of time into past, present, and future varies as a function of culture. Middle-class Anglo-Americans are described as being future-oriented, and time is conceived in this group as future > present > past (Spiegel, 1982). Punctuality, organization, and planning are emphasized because they facilitate the accomplishment of future goals. Time may be broken down into orderly blocks or schedules.

Among several other cultural groups, the ordering of time is present > past > future. This latter time orientation may be found in Hispanic Americans, African Americans, Native Americans, and Asians (Marin & Marin, 1991; McAdoo, 1993; McGoldrick, Pearce, & Giordano, 1982). It can also be found in some white ethnic groups: Italian Americans and Irish Americans (Spiegel, 1982) and Appalachian Americans (Axelson, 1985). Individuals who are present-oriented may not be as preoccupied with punctuality and may organize their time according to day-by-day needs rather than a prescribed agenda.

Cross-cultural researchers who develop a time line for their study need to be aware of differences in time orientation among different groups and exhibit some flexibility in order to accommodate those differences. For example, a researcher who is future-oriented and emphasizes punctuality may be discouraged when subjects do not respond in a timely manner. Subjects who are present-oriented may arrive late for an interview, or may not show up at all if something they see as more important arises. The researcher may find subjects' lateness or lax attitude toward time offensive or interpret it as an indication of their reluctance to participate. However, these perceptions may not necessarily be accurate and may merely indicate differences with respect to time orientation. Researchers should be aware of these differences and be prepared to make modifications in their time lines or schedules as necessary.

Summary of Cultural Variables

The entire range of values (for example, from collectivism to individualism) is possible within groups because of between-group similarities and within-group differences. In this section, we have discussed the impact that cultural variables may have on cross-cultural research. The researcher needs to be aware of these cultural variables and make an assessment regarding how well the specific group of interest adheres to them. For example, the researcher may need to employ different procedures for data gathering when studying the behaviors of highly acculturated, Mexican American college students than when doing so with working-class Mexican nationals or when comparing upper-class Anglo-Americans with lower-class Appalachian Americans or middle-class Italian Americans.

MEASUREMENT IN MULTICULTURAL RESEARCH

The efficacy of cross-cultural research can be facilitated with the use of measuring instruments that are written in the primary language of the research participants. The nonequivalence of research instruments, however, can limit the internal validity of cross-cultural research. In this section, we will discuss some problems with translation as well as strategies that can enhance the equivalence of research instruments.

Translating research instruments into another language can be a difficult process. The constructs and the instruments used to assess those constructs must be culturally relevant. The instruments must include content and concepts that ask the same questions as the original and are interpreted in the same manner by subjects from a different culture. Cultural bias, misinterpretation of items, and nonequivalence of assessment instruments may pose difficulties that limit the utility of the research (Fouad, Cudeck, & Hansen, 1984; Mayberry, 1984; Scheuneman, 1979).

Before attempting a translation, researchers should be aware of their own values and how these affect their research interests and their conceptualization of behavior and constructs. As stated previously, the false assumption that others define normal behavior and constructs in the same way as the researcher may lead to the development of encapsulated instruments and biased studies. A researcher can consult with members of the group of interest and see whether the constructs of interest are culturally relevant or not and whether the instruments can accurately assess or measure those constructs.

For example, suppose that a researcher wants to examine egalitarianism between spouses. The researcher defines egalitarianism as equality in the relationship between the wife and the husband and decides to assess the degree of egalitarianism by using a task-sharing scale. Influencing that decision is the researcher's assumption that the person with less power takes more responsibility for household chores. The definition of the construct and the method of assessing it may be relevant with some groups, such as couples who both work but who do not employ housekeepers, but the assessment method may be of limited value with another group. Examples would be working couples who employ housekeepers or couples who do not associate household chores with power in relationships. While direct questions may be useful in one instance, observation of a process may be required in another. How the researcher defines and measures constructs can affect the findings obtained and the conclusions drawn from those findings.

The researcher must take into account any cultural factors that may affect the assessment of the constructs and see to it that the instruments used are culturally equivalent. Even an accurate translation of an instrument may still be biased if cultural variables are ignored. For example, Valencia and Rankin (1985) discuss problems with the assessment of auditory short-term memory and attention among Mexican American children using a translated Spanish version of the McCarthy Scales of Children's Abilities. These researchers note that Mexican American children scored lower than their Anglo-American counterparts on subtests that measured auditory short-term memory and attention through word recall. A language analysis of the English and Spanish versions of the scale revealed important differences between the two languages that affected the construct being measured. With few exceptions, Spanish words contain more syllables than their English counterparts, as depicted in Table 7-1.

The researchers report that the number of syllables on the Memory I subtest items was 66% higher on the Spanish version than on the English version. The Numerical Memory I subtest contained 71% more syllables on the Spanish version than on the English version. Therefore, even though both versions of the scale require that children recall essentially the same words or numerals, children who took the Spanish version were required to remember more syllables (and therefore more information) than children who completed the English version. The effect of word length as a function of language differences contributed to bias in the way the construct was measured. Thus, even though the original and translated versions of an instrument appear to be the same, they may not be culturally equivalent.

Conventional translation methods typically consist of three steps: (1) translation, (2) back-translation to the original language, and (3) establishing equivalence of the two forms using bilingual samples (Fouad et al., 1984; Hansen, 1987; Harrington, 1989; Mayberry, 1984). Each step, however, can have problems that can threaten the equivalence or usefulness of the instrument with certain populations.

Translation of Instruments

The first step—translation from the first to the second language—is usually done by skilled, bilingually fluent translators working individually, sequentially, or as a team (Hansen, 1987; Harrington, 1989; Mayberry, 1984). One person translates the instrument and gives the translated version to a second person, who

TABLE 7-1 Selected words from the Valencia and Rankin (1985) study of the McCarthy Scales of Children's Abilities.

English	Spanish
kiss	beso
cowboy	vaquero
man	hombre

makes revisions and gives it to a third person, who continues this process (Hansen, 1987). The team approach involves either joint translation through a committee or independent translations that are then merged after translators meet and reach a consensus (Hansen, 1987). The problem with this process is that skilled translators may produce a translation that is accurate but inappropriate for the population of interest. Translators often fail to take relevant socioeconomic and cultural factors of the target population into account, or they use words and phrases that may not be easily understood by the target population. Translators may be from a higher socioeconomic level and may translate the word "x" into the Spanish "y." Although this could be an appropriate translation for a person of higher SES, a person of lower SES might interpret the Spanish "y" as the Spanish "z."

Back-Translation of Instruments

Back-translation is usually done by skilled, bilingual translators (Fouad & Bracken, 1986; Fouad et al., 1984; Hansen, 1987). The back-translation is then compared to the original version and assessed for accuracy as well as for potential difficulties in comprehension. A problem at this stage is that the back-translation can have reasonable conceptual similarity to the original, but the original translation may be of poor quality (Mayberry, 1984). Even skilled translators can infer concepts mistakenly from poor translations as they translate back to the original language.

Establishing Equivalence of Instruments

The translated instrument is field-tested using bilingual subjects in order to establish equivalence. Correlation coefficients are examined between parallel forms or between the original and translated forms (Hansen, 1987). A problem here is that using bilingual subjects in field-testing the translated version assumes that these subjects represent the monolingual target population—an assumption that is not always correct (Mayberry, 1984). As an example, Diaz (1988) points out that differences exist between the Spanish spoken in the United States and Spanish spoken in Latin American countries; Spanish spoken by bilingual subjects residing in the United States is often interspersed with Anglicisms (English words given a Spanish sound) that are not used by monolingual Hispanics. This problem is not unique to the Spanish language and can be particularly difficult with research that uses international samples.

Problems in Developing a Multicultural Instrument

Gross and Scott (1989) identify a problem with overreliance on bilingual subjects in the translation process, that is, the overestimation of bilingual fluency. These researchers translated a professional certification test to another language and used a small bilingual sample in the field-test. One of these subjects obtained the highest score on the original version and the lowest score on the translated

TABLE 7-2   A serial approach to translating family science instrumentation.

STEP 1: TRANSLATION

1.   Have two or more translators experienced with the target population produce separate translations, taking the socioeconomic factors of the population of interest into account.

2.   Have translators review and merge the translated versions to arrive at a product they feel will be most appropriate and reliable for the target population.

3.   Have the translated version further reviewed for grammar.

STEP 2: ASSESSMENT OF CLARITY AND EQUIVALENCE

1.   Assess reading comprehension with subjects representative of the target population. Have subjects read the translated instrument and identify words or phrases that are difficult to understand.

2.   Administer each item orally to monolingual subjects representative of the target population and ask each subject, What does this question mean to you? and What are the instructions asking you to do?

3.   Record and compare the impressions of the subjects with the items and instructions as they are worded in the original language.

4.   Make changes as necessary and repeat the process until the intent of the items and instructions in the translated version are accurately conveyed.

STEP 3: BACK-TRANSLATION

1.   Audiotape the back-translations of bilingual persons of varying educational levels.

2.   Have a skilled translator listen to the tapes and make changes as necessary in the translated version of the instrument.

STEP 4: FIELD-TESTING

1.   Pretest and posttest with a group using the instrument in the original language to establish a baseline reliability index.

2.   Pretest and posttest using the translated version of the instrument with monolingual representatives of the target population to determine the reliability of the translated instrument with the target population.

3.   Pretest and posttest with two bilingual groups and control for administration order effects.

STEP 5: ASSESS RELIABILITY

1.   Determine the amount of error due to the reliability of the instrument. If the baseline reliability is low, the instrument itself may not be reliable.

2.   Consider the amount of error that can be attributed to translation problems. Compare the baseline reliability index to the test-retest correlations obtained in the monolingual and bilingual groups. (See Chapter 10 for more discussion of correlation.) If the baseline reliability index is high and the other correlation indices are low, this usually indicates translation problems. (See Chapter 4 for more extensive discussion of reliability.)

3.   Examine the translated instrument for reliability, using the target population. This is accomplished by comparing the test-retest correlation index of the monolingual group (Group 2) with the baseline reliability index (attained from Group 1) and the test-retest correlations of the bilingual groups. If the reliability index of the monolingual group is low and the others are high, the translation may be accurate but nevertheless inappropriate and unreliable with the target population.

STEP 6: INTERPRETATION

1.   Determine extraneous factors that affected each reliability index by interviewing members of the bilingual and monolingual groups.

2.   Discriminate between extraneous factors and translation problems.

version—a discrepancy attributed to the subject's lack of fluency in the second language.

Another problem with translation occurs when the original instrument is developed with a sample that is not representative of the target population, especially with respect to SES. Thus, the translation may be adequate, but the relevance of the instrument may be questionable with subjects whose socioeconomic background differs from that of the original population (Hansen, 1987). Finally, verification of the effectiveness of the translation with the population of interest is usually not done until the translated instrument is administered to members of the target population.

Because the relevance of translated instruments is reduced when socioeconomic and cultural factors are ignored or when testing of the translated version is performed with subjects who are different from the original monolingual population, researchers should consult with subjects throughout the translation process in order to enhance instrument equivalence and relevance.

Serial Translation Process

We have listed potential problems that can occur during each step of the translation process. Herrera, DelCampo, and Ames (1993) discuss a serial translation process that may address these difficulties and facilitate the development of an equivalent, culturally sensitive instrument. These steps are listed in Table 7-2. While the steps listed in the table do not guarantee cultural equivalence, they can facilitate the process by helping researchers obtain information from members of the target population throughout the translation process. They can thus take into account cultural and socioeconomic factors that are relevant with the target population.

GATHERING DATA

The researcher who has consulted with members of the target population or with persons who have experience with and knowledge of the culture of the population of interest may obtain information throughout the process regarding strategies that can enhance the participation rate. We have discussed some of these strategies already.

Personal versus Impersonal Approach

Personal contact with members of some groups may be a more effective way of obtaining data than an impersonal strategy such as mailing them a request to participate. The personal approach may involve direct contact to explain the nature of the research. Data may be obtained through face-to-face interviews or personal delivery and collection of research instruments.

Three factors—collectivism, time orientation, and lack of experience as research participants—may make personal contact a more effective way of obtaining data (Marin & Marin, 1991). Subjects who come from collectivistic cultures may respond more positively if contacted in person and may fail to respond to a mailed invitation to participate. Subjects who are present-oriented may delay responding to an invitation to participate in research and eventually forget about it. College students—a population that is often used in research—may be accustomed to requests to participate in research, but other groups may not understand what is being asked of them, or they may have negative expectations based on previous experience. In some instances, subjects may need more extensive instructions and assistance in order to respond to the research instrument.

Personal communication with subjects may place more demands on the researcher's time. The researcher can employ assistants or a research team that can help in the data collection process. While assistance with data gathering can have certain benefits, it can also pose some potential problems with respect to instrumentation, interrater reliability, and researcher bias. (These issues were discussed in Chapter 5.)

Using Culturally Similar Research Aides

Marin and Marin (1991) note that there are benefits associated with the use of same-ethnicity data collectors. The similarity of backgrounds between data collectors and research participants can facilitate the development of rapport, trust, and effective communication. Rapport is particularly important with individuals from collectivistic cultures. Trust may be of special significance when the researcher is interested in obtaining information on subjects that may be taboo (sex, family problems, death) with the group of interest.

Trust is also essential when the group of interest has any reason to doubt the purpose of the research, for example, if subjects have any concerns regarding the effect of research participation on their legal status in the country. Marin and Marin (1991) also note that some immigrants who come from politically troubled countries may have had negative experiences that can lead to distrust and reluctance to participate in any type of research in which personal information is disclosed or documented.

Speaking the Language of the Subject

Communication with culturally diverse subjects can be enhanced if the researcher or research aide speaks the subjects' language, that is, communicates in their native or primary language. However, speaking the same language implies much more than the use of a common language. It also involves knowing both verbal and nonverbal forms of communication. The data collector should be aware of differences in dialects or cultural variations in the meanings assigned to the same words. Variations within the same language were exemplified in a television commercial that showed three Hispanic youths from three different parts of Latin America joking about the different terminology each of them used for "bus"—camion, gua-gua, and bus—and for "soda"—gaseosa, refresco, and soda.

Speaking the same language also implies taking into account socioeconomic variables that can affect the communication process. The investigator or data collector may need to employ different terminology depending on the participant's level of education. Failure to do so may contribute to confusion or resentment and ultimately to noncompliance.

Knowing the Culture of the Subjects

Knowledge of a group's culture may also make it easier to understand and process nonverbal communication; as we said earlier, some cultural groups do not emphasize direct communication but depend more on intuition and sensitivity to nonverbal cues. Valuable information may be lost when the data collector is not attuned to these nonverbal messages. Nonverbal cues may also signal a participant's readiness to disclose personal information.

Compensation in the form of a monetary reward, services (for example, medical services), or a gift that can benefit either the subject or the community may increase participation with some cultural groups and convey both respect and appreciation for their willingness to be in a research study. Marin and Marin (1991) indicate that compensating subjects for their participation in research does not appear to increase selection bias, and it does serve as an incentive for participation. Once again, consultation with persons who know the culture of the target group can help the researcher determine the propriety of compensation, the type of compensation to employ, and the amount that is appropriate. This reduces the potential for the compensation to be perceived as offensive or as a bribe.

BECOMING A CULTURALLY SKILLED RESEARCHER

Members of the helping professions can take steps to facilitate their development into culturally skilled researchers. Since research contributes to the understanding of human behavior and the factors that promote well-being, the development of culturally skilled researchers seems paramount. Three process models for the development of cultural awareness will now be presented.

Bennet's Model for the Development of Cultural Sensitivity

Henderson, Sampselle, Mayes, and Oakley (1992) discuss Bennet's (1986) developmental model for promoting cultural sensitivity—a model similar to the white racial and minority identity development models discussed in the counseling literature (Atkinson, Morten, & Sue, 1983; Helms, 1984; Ponterotto, 1988; Sabnani, Ponterotto, & Borodovsky, 1991). The process described in these models is associated with the development of awareness, understanding, and appreciation of self and of others. Therefore, these models have relevance for cross-cultural researchers as well.

Bennet's (1986) model for the development of cultural sensitivity (as cited in Henderson et al., 1992) involves six stages: denial, defense, minimization, acceptance, adaptation, and integration. We will integrate aspects of Bennet's model with information presented by Pedersen (1987, 1988).

According to Bennet's model, the individual moves from ethnocentricity to multiculturalism as described by Pedersen (1991). In the first stage (denial) the person makes assumptions about normal behavior that are based on his or her own cultural framework without taking cultural relativity into account. In the second stage, cultural differences are conceptualized as pathological because they deviate from the person's definition of normal. In the third stage, there is a recognition of cultural differences and a beginning awareness that the person's own assumptions may have limited relevance in different cultures. However, despite this awareness, there is a continued reliance on encapsulated research measures and methods. Individuals in the fourth stage begin to challenge their assumptions and consider alternate constructs. In the fifth and final stage, the person can validate cultural differences and perceive the world from a different cultural perspective. In the final stage, the individual can recognize between- and within-group differences and similarities and can understand and appreciate diversity.

White Racial Identity Model

The white racial identity model (Atkinson et al., 1983; Helms, 1984; Ponterotto, 1988) focuses on awareness, understanding, acceptance, and appreciation of self and others; the paradigm involves movement through five stages. In the first stage (preexposure or precontact), a person lacks self-awareness as a racial being, denies his or her own ethnicity, and lacks awareness of the impact of culture on the research process. The danger at this stage is that cultural differences will be seen as pathological and that the procedures used in a study will have little or no relevance to culturally diverse groups. Hence, the findings that researchers at this stage obtain may have little or no validity at best and contribute to negative stereotypes at worst.

In the second (conflict) and third (prominority or antiracism) stages, the person examines his or her own cultural values. However, this recognition contributes to cognitive dissonance, rejection of self, and a paternalistic attitude toward persons of diverse cultures. Individuals at this stage may have good intentions, but their depreciating attitudes toward their own culture and paternalistic attitude toward the culturally diverse may contribute to bias in the research process.

In the fourth stage (retreat into white culture), the individual may retreat from multicultural issues, including from multicultural research. This stance does little to further the development of multiculturalism and, given the cultural composition of the United States, can limit the development of the helping professional.

In the final stage (redefinition and integration), the individual develops an appreciation and respect for diversity (both in self and in others) that may permit the recognition of the impact of culture on the research process. The individual at this stage is able to consult and collaborate with culturally diverse persons and is flexible enough to adapt research methods and procedures in order to make them more culturally relevant. The individual at this stage also recognizes the effect of research findings on potential clients, practitioners, and on the counseling profession as a whole.

Minority Identity Development Model

The minority identity development model describes a process that members of the nondominant group may experience. Specifically, the stages here deal with how minority members perceive (appreciate or depreciate) themselves, members of their own group, members of other culturally diverse groups, and members of the dominant group. Regardless of the researcher's cultural background, the researcher's level of awareness and attitude toward diversity can have an overt or covert effect on the research process from the topic that is chosen to the conclusions that are drawn. This process, as described by Atkinson et al. (1983), also involves five stages: conformity, dissonance, resistance and immersion, introspection, and synergetic articulation and awareness.

Becoming Culturally Sensitive

Sabnani et al. (1991) describe several tasks that may facilitate movement through the stages of the white racial identity model. These tasks have relevance for multicultural researchers of diverse backgrounds since they foster the awareness and appreciation of diversity. The tasks associated with stage one (preexposure or precontact) include participation in cultural experiences such as ethnic dinners, intercultural sharing, case studies, ethnic literature reviews, and value statements exercises. These tasks can increase understanding of one's own and others' cultural heritage and how this heritage affects values, beliefs, behaviors, and goals.

Tasks associated with stage two (conflict) include exploring one's own stereotypes and prejudices and seeing how these can affect the research process. Examining the roots of racism and the effect of discrimination on race relations are also part of stage two. At stage three (prominority or antiracism), individuals are encouraged to participate in cross-cultural encounter groups, cultural immersion, and consultation with members of culturally diverse groups in order to further increase awareness of the effect of paternalistic attitudes on the research process. Individuals at stage four (retreat into white culture) are encouraged to participate in cross-cultural encounter groups and develop an understanding of minority and white identity development. Tasks associated with stage five (redefinition and integration) include participation in feedback-related exercises and cross-cultural practices in order to facilitate the development of a cultural identity that allows the individual to value cultural richness and diversity.

Summary of Process Models

The models discussed in this section describe a process of growth. Culturally sensitive researchers continually challenge their beliefs and assumptions and make adaptations in order to promote the validity and relevance of cross-cultural studies. Culturally sensitive research can create enrichment opportunities for the researcher, the cultural group, and the counseling profession.

If a researcher is unsure of a situation (whether for cultural reasons or other reasons), an intensive case study might be appropriate. Such an intensive study allows the development of understanding that might not occur in the types of research that are described in later chapters.

MARIA REVISITED

As a Hispanic American Maria was familiar with many of the concerns about cultural factors, but she realized that she needed to do a self-check on the various issues. She tried to take an impartial look at her reasons for studying bulimia and the reasons for choosing the methods she did. Was she predisposed to think of bulimia only as a female, Anglo-American disease? Was she open to the possibility that Hispanic Americans might also have the disease? Was her cultural background leading her to make any research decisions that would predispose some of the results? She reasoned that although her parents lived in Mexico, they were educated in the United States, as was she. English and Spanish were spoken interchangeably in her home. She felt comfortable in both cultural worlds. More importantly, she felt she understood both cultural worlds.

Maria felt that since she was a master's degree student at the same institution as the subjects, there would be a natural level of trust. Trust was also generated through her association with the institution's Counseling Center. Although Maria planned to implement all of her treatments in English, she was prepared to answer individual questions in Spanish if she felt that would provide a more precise answer to the participant. Her knowledge of the culture would be a guide in making this decision and in the kind of information provided.

Maria also considered cultural factors related to the subjects. First, were the causes of bulimia different for Hispanic Americans than for Anglo-Americans? There was no literature on Hispanics with bulimia, so she had no research base. She intended to keep notes on this issue during treatment, and she planned to discuss this issue with subjects at the conclusion of her study.

The willingness of Hispanic American women to undergo treatment could partly be assessed by the proportion of women who, upon reading the consent form, agreed to participate. Also, Maria planned to compare the proportion of Hispanic American women who dropped out of the study to the proportion of Anglo-American women who dropped out.

Finally, the effectiveness of the two treatments on these two cultural groups was of concern. Maria decided to include a research hypothesis that would test whether or not the multifaceted treatment was equally superior to the educational treatment in the two cultural groups.

CONCLUDING COMMENTS

We have discussed factors that can threaten or enhance the validity and usefulness of cross-cultural research. Table 7-3 provides a summary of the factors discussed in this chapter.

EXERCISES

1. Pick five of the assumptions leading to cultural encapsulation and identify the extent to which you make those same assumptions.

TABLE 7–3 Steps to take when conducting cross-cultural research.

DEFINE THE POPULATION

1. Use labels such as race, nationality, ethnicity, religion correctly.
2. Be familiar with the cultural labels used to describe the group of interest.
3. Determine whether the group of interest has shown a preference for or resentment of any particular label.
4. Ask subjects to indicate national origin or ancestry.

ENHANCE THE EFFICACY OF CROSS-CULTURAL RESEARCH AND AVOID PREVIOUS PITFALLS

1. Consider multiculturalism versus social deficit or pathology framework to guide cross-cultural research.
2. Review Pedersen's (1987, 1988) ten assumptions that can contribute to cultural encapsulation.
3. Explore reasonable opposites to biased assumptions.
4. Use cultural relativity to conceptualize behavior.
5. Use constructs and concepts that are culturally relevant with the group of interest.
6. If feasible, become immersed in the target group's culture.
7. Procure cultural information through consultation or collaboration with the group of interest.
8. Attend to between- and within-group differences and similarities such as race, gender, class, nationality, historical background, language, and acculturation.
9. Factor in socioeconomic variables to reduce confusion about whether differences are cultural or socioeconomic.

DETERMINE THE EFFECTS OF CULTURAL VARIABLES ON THE RESEARCH PROCESS

1. (Collectivism Versus Individualism)
   If the group of interest demonstrates collectivistic tendencies, consider a personal rather than impersonal approach. for example, send a personal invitation to participate, conduct interviews, do case studies.
2. (Communication Styles)
   If the group of interest uses a nonverbal and indirect communication style, consider personal contact, development of rapport and trust with participants, mutual respect, and the use of culturally similar research aides.
3. (Time Orientation)
   If the group of interest is present-oriented, understand and accept differences in time orientation and be flexible with resspect to time lines and scheduling.

USE ACCURATE MEASUREMENT

1. Ensure the cultural relevance of constructs and concepts.
2. Use an instrument that employs the same language, that is, one that takes into account language, dialect, fluency, and socioeconomic variables, of the group of interest.
3. Use a translation process that includes minority cultural information gained through consultation or collaboration and testing.

GATHER DATA

1. Find out about the culture of interest through consultation or collaboration.
2. Use the personal rather than the impersonal approach.
3. Use culturally similar research aides.
4. Engender trust.
5. Speak the language of the subject.
6. Know the culture of the subject.

BECOME A CULTURALLY SKILLED RESEARCHER

1. Become familiar with cultural sensitivity and white racial and minority identity development models.
2. Assess your own developmental stage.
3. Participate in activities that can promote movement toward the integration stage in which diversity is recognized, valued, and respected.

2. Why is it important to realize that there are within-group differences as well as between-group differences?

3. What are some ways that make it difficult for a 50-year-old to "speak the same language" as a 20-year-old?

4. Review the paper by White and Franzoni in Appendix E. How might the ethnicity and gender of the researchers influence the study at any of the eight stages of empirical research? How might the ethnicity or gender of the subjects sampled influence the outcome? Did the researchers make any effort to include elements of multicultural research in their study? Explain.

5. For those pondering a thesis, identify how your own cultural beliefs may impact your study at each of the eight stages of empirical research. Using Chapter 7 as your guide, what steps would you take to integrate multicultural research methods?

8

DESCRIBING EVENTS: NONEXPERIMENTAL RESEARCH

SUPPOSE THAT MARIA BEGINS her research project with a completely different focus than originally stated. Instead of trying to determine which of the two treatments is most effective, assume that Maria asks clients to complete the BULIT-R, a background information survey, and a measure of personality traits. Further, she asks that clients complete all needed information upon initial intake interview, allotting roughly 90 minutes to finish all measures. Her sample is 50 subjects, just like her original sample, with all subjects appropriately informed.

She reformulates her research question and hypotheses as follows. Her new research question is, What background variables and personality descriptors are related to bulimic symptoms? While in reality the hypotheses she develops would be based on existing literature, imagine that two of her hypotheses are (1) clients who come from higher-income families will have more severe bulimic symptoms than clients from lower-income families; and (2) clients showing the most bulimic episodes will be more passive-aggressive in personality type than clients with fewer episodes.

There are five basic types of descriptive research: (1) **case study**, (2) **survey research**, (3) **correlational research**, (4) **ex post facto research**, and (5) **developmental research.** In this chapter, we detail each of these approaches; we include a definition of each, give examples from the literature, state advantages and disadvantages associated with different approaches, and finally, offer recommendations for descriptive study design and implementation.

Researchers often combine elements of different descriptive methods. For example, they might do a survey study in which correlations are used or conduct an ex post facto study in which the researchers collect data by administering a survey questionnaire. We hope that by the end of the discussion, you will be able to recognize examples of each descriptive design and identify research that combines different designs—or different descriptive modes. After reading about each descriptive method, try to form a mental prototype of each. Then, as subsequent methods are developed, you might compare and contrast the different methods. This should improve your comprehension. You can also check your understanding toward the conclusion of the chapter, because the final section will show how the different descriptive methods overlap and differ.

DESCRIPTION AND EXPERIMENTATION

To understand the essential nature of all descriptive research, and better yet, to be able to contrast descriptive research with more experimental approaches noted in the next chapter, consider the following exercise. Assume you are asked to describe a friend. You might use physical descriptors like tall, short, heavy, thin, blond, dark, bearded, long nose, bushy eyebrows, and so on; or you could resort to personality descriptions such as talkative, quiet, mannerly, shy, defensive, happy, angry, sensitive, detached, and so on. At the conclusion of your description, the listener will have a clear mental picture of your friend.

Suppose you are then asked whether any of your friend's characteristics can be changed. For example, if you described him as short, stocky, sensitive, and happy, you reasonably conclude that his height is likely to stay the same, but he could engage in various weight-loss behaviors and become less stocky. Further, if the person you described wished to be less sensitive, it is conceivable that through psychological therapy, he could achieve this goal. You assume that while a person's happiness could be changed, no one would want to change from happy to unhappy.

This situation is analogous to descriptive and experimental research. Descriptive research is much like describing a friend—it relates, portrays, and recounts variables the way they are. Descriptive investigation provides something like a snapshot of variables, informs us about the incidence of events, and indicates the nature of the relationship between events. One outcome of a descriptive study would be statistics on the incidence of schizophrenia in the United States.

On the other hand, researchers using **quasi-experimental** and **experimental methods** are not as interested in description. Rather, quasi-experimental and experimental researchers seek to manipulate variables. For example, in your description of a friend, imagine that a known relationship exists between weight and sensitivity, such that heavier people (relative to their height) are generally more jovial and happy than thinner people, who tend to be more brooding and seemingly less happy. Knowing this relationship exists, the quasi-experimental researcher would be most interested in manipulating weight to determine the effects of weight change on mood. For example, some subjects would engage in weight-loss behaviors, while a control group would not.

In essence, the difference between descriptive and experimental research studies is the difference between **correlation** and causation. Again, researchers employing descriptive methods describe things as they are—the incidence of a single variable or the correlation between two or more variables. On the other hand, quasi-experimental and experimental researchers determine whether the manipulation of one or more variables causes changes in another variable.

You may recognize a logical order between description and experimentation. Typically, descriptive research necessarily precedes experimental research. If a relationship does not exist between two variables, then manipulating one or the other would be senseless. Yet, knowing a relationship exists does not reveal whether or not one variable causes changes in another. Similarly, the investigative agendas of researchers may begin with description and proceed to the manipulation of variables to examine cause and effect.

For example, recall the chapter vignette and suppose that Maria's data reveal two high associations. Perhaps individuals reporting the most bulimic episodes have higher-income parents than those reporting fewer episodes. The second relationship might show that the more bulimic episodes a person has, the more the person tends to be passive-aggressive, while a person with fewer episodes would tend to be less passive-aggressive. Maria describes two important relationships. The experimental researcher would next ask, What would happen if either (or both) variable were altered?

From an experimental perspective, Maria must first consider whether or not the variables can be manipulated. The family income variable cannot, since Maria would not have much luck asking parents to give up high-paying jobs so she can determine the effects of income on bulimic episodes. However, she might be able to influence passive-aggressiveness. For example, she could engage clients in an assertiveness training program and subsequently measure the effects of this training on frequency of bulimic episodes. We will describe the specific types of experimental and quasi-experimental studies in Chapter 9.

In the sections that follow, we focus on the five basic descriptive approaches, beginning with case study research. As we said in Chapter 7, this type of research is particularly useful when cultural differences might threaten the validity of a research study.

CASE STUDY RESEARCH

In applied settings, the term *case* is commonplace, as in caseloads, case assignment, and case presentation. In the applied context, case means client, and professional duties like taking a case history refer to duties regarding specific clients.

In contrast, the case study in research connotes a more in-depth, intensive study of a particular unit, such as an in-depth description of history, symptoms, or treatments. For instance, Sigmund Freud (1920, 1963) reported numerous, detailed case studies in his pioneering work on psychoanalysis. Similarly, Jean Piaget (1952) conducted intensive case studies of his children in order to describe the development of human intelligence and cognition. While the term case always refers to a single unit, that unit is not necessarily one person. It could be some other discrete entity like a single ward, a single company, or a single tribe.

Criteria for defining case studies in research are given below; they closely approximate those described by Yin (1984). First, a researcher must select a theoretically significant case. For example, Freud (1961) selected a child named

Little Hans as a case study to document the development of phobia. The case was theoretically significant because it allowed Freud to explain the child's fear of horses as a function of Freud's psychosexual theory, specifically, the Oedipus and castration complexes. If Maria were less interested in an empirical study, and were, for example, more interested in explaining a particular client's bulimic symptoms from a particular theoretical perspective, she could select a case that clearly shows how a relevant theory accounts for the client's disorder.

Another component of case study research is the development of one or more research questions. For instance, Maria could select a single case and ask a different research question: Will a combination of therapeutic techniques reduce a person's bulimic symptoms? (Note how this rephrased question differs from her original research question posed in Chapter 3.) To answer this question, Maria could describe the client's history and detail specific techniques and procedures she implemented to reduce the client's symptoms.

The third element is collecting evidence about the research question. Although the term "evidence" does not specify how to collect data, the definition suggests that however information is collected, it must be done so intensively—for example, in detailed descriptions of background. Methods used in obtaining case study data are broad, ranging from making detailed notes about phenomena, the way Piaget did to describe how cognitive processes change during childhood, to self-report procedures like those Maria could adopt to answer her case study research question.

In fact, the collection of evidence gives case study researchers great flexibility in collecting and analyzing data. The generic classification of case studies as descriptive, or even quasi-experimental, depends entirely on the amount of control and structure researchers exert in collecting and presenting case study data. The more control exerted, the more quasi-experimental the case study; less control makes it more descriptive.

For example, to be considered a case study, the essential prerequisite is rich description, usually gathered from interviews, observation, and sometimes patients' self-reports. The work of Freud and Piaget provides classic illustrations of the descriptive case study, since both collected information from observation and interview, leading to their respective detailed descriptions of human behavior. Although rich in description and detail, Freud and Piaget were less formal and systematic in how their data were collected and presented. Further, even when a treatment approach is pioneered in a case study, the gains from treatment are described anecdotally by the researcher rather than systematically, for example, by using standardized tests.

Illustration from the Literature

Daniels (1977) reports psychotherapeutic techniques he used to treat a client with severe migraine headaches. He first reviews the literature pertaining to the treatment of migraine headaches, noting (1) the symptoms associated with migraine headaches, such as nausea, vasoconstriction, and throbbing pain; (2) commonly employed treatments for migraine headaches, such as hypnosis, biofeedback, and systematic desensitization; (3) practical problems with previous treatments, like the need for expensive equipment (for example, with biofeedback) and an inordinate amount of clinical service; and (4) the purpose of his case study, which was to describe a combination of clinical techniques requiring only 6 hours of treatment time and minimizing the need for costly apparatus.

The second section of Daniels' paper is a case history of the client, including pertinent treatment information such as age, gender (female), current and past frequency of migraines, medications, symptoms associated with migraines, antecedent precursors to migraine episodes, and consequences of migraine attack.

Treatment techniques, essentially those that were behavioral and cognitive in nature, are outlined in the third and final section of the paper. Behavior therapy was systematic desensitization; the client first received training in deep muscle relaxation. Daniels then had his client use a cue-controlled relaxation procedure in which the client subvocally uttered a cue word (calm) at the conclusion of each deep muscle relaxation response. In addition, a hypnotic induction recorded on a cassette tape was given the client in order for her to practice relaxation at home. She was given specific instructions to warm her fingers and cool her head. The cognitive therapy employed was rational-emotive therapy, since the author noted that an antecedent to the client's migraine headaches was her unrealistic expectation of others. Daniels explained the client's illogic to her, demonstrated adaptive reasoning processes, and required the client to accept a more logical thinking style. Daniels reports that in just 5 weeks and after only three sessions, the combined use of deep muscle relaxation, cue-controlled relaxation, hypnosis, and logical thinking allowed the client to produce peaceful sensations at her own volition. No further migraine headaches were noted a year later in a follow-up visit.

Advantages and Disadvantages of Case Study Research

As with all types of research, the case study presents unique research advantages and disadvantages. Advantages are the (1) development of preliminary hypotheses for further explanation, (2) potential to capitalize on natural contexts, (3) depth of description, and (4) focus on idiographic inquiry.

For some researchers, the case study is a vehicle for further investigative inquiry. Again taking Daniels' study as an example, since preliminary results suggest the efficacy of cognitive-behavioral treatment for patients with migraine headaches, a larger, more elaborate experimental research study could next be designed to determine whether or not patients will benefit from cognitive-behavioral therapy compared to a no-treatment group.

Second, as the total antithesis of controlled laboratory research, case and field studies rely on behavior as it occurs in natural environments, like a school, home, or work setting. For instance, a social worker may visit a client's home and recognize an entirely different set of family relationships and interactions than when this family visits the agency. When used with larger units like tribes or with particular cultures, this research is called *field study* or **ethnographic observation**.

The potential depth of description is another advantage of the case study approach. The case study researcher is free to detail fine points of the behavior or treatment procedure so that the reader can be completely privy to all aspects of the case and thus better able to understand, or even replicate the case study.

Finally, the case study is rooted in the idiographic tradition. By focusing on single cases and not groups, case study researchers continually center on the uniqueness of subjects. The case study approach does not allow the generalization of results to a different subject.

Ironically, some of the advantages of case studies are also disadvantages. For instance, the primary concern about case study research is that by being idiographic, case study results cannot be validly generalized to other cases. In other words, general principles, rules, or descriptions cannot be established using case studies, since every case is unique and the descriptions derived are specific to that case. However, the extent to which case studies can in fact be generalized to other, similar cases depends on how many times the researcher replicates the results of the case. For example, the researcher treating six hyperactive children with biofeedback who subsequently presents results individually for each child has, in essence, replicated (assuming the results are favorable for each child) the case six times, thus improving generalizability of results to other, similar hyperactive children.

A second delimiter of case study research is, again, the flip side of an advantage, namely the possibly contaminating effects of researcher bias. Because case study researchers observe subjects in natural settings, without concern for control of factors that might affect a behavior of interest, it is difficult to remove bias in selecting and measuring variables. In other words, in the absence of control, researchers are at-risk for observing and reporting relationships between variables that confirm hypotheses, while ignoring other factors that may not support the initial predictions. Researcher bias is most pronounced in case studies.

Recommendations

Based on the preceding discussion, several recommendations can be offered for the conduct of descriptive case study research. The quality of descriptive case studies is improved when data are collected from multiple observers. For example, in the Daniels (1977) study, reports about the client's migraines could have been collected from her husband and a close contact in the work setting. By using multiple sources, the problem of observation bias is reduced because the confirmation of positive results from several sources removes some of the inherent bias if just one researcher is collecting information.

Also, it is recommended that case study researchers employ reliable and valid measuring and observational techniques. For example, Daniels (1977) should provide evidence that the measurement of migraines is reliable and valid. If the measure is an observational one (like migraines), then it would be necessary to establish interrater reliability—the extent to which different data gatherers agree about the specific behaviors that constitute a migraine headache. Further, validity data would also be required, such as determining if observational measures agree with, for example, self-report questionnaire data. In the absence of this information, the quality of the case study is severely diminished.

Finally, whenever possible, the descriptive case study researcher should attempt to replicate results obtained with a single case. For example, Daniels (1977) could have selected a patient with a roughly similar constellation of background data and presenting problem, employed the same intervention, and sought a second confirmation of treatment utility.

SURVEY RESEARCH

How often have you heard an advertisement that includes a statement like, "Four out of five dentists recommend . . ." or "Three out of four doctors prescribe . . ."? Or how often have you picked up the telephone and heard, "Mrs. Smith, my name is Bob and I am conducting a survey about . . . ; do you have a minute to answer a few questions?" These examples suggest the nature of survey research.

Survey research is aimed at describing some variable by indicating its frequency in a particular population. Therefore, the terms *epidemiological, prevalence,* or *incidence research* are sometimes used synonymously with survey research. The types of variables examined are many, including general attitudes, opinions, values, and beliefs, as well as specific questions about service and product use. The measurement process requires the researcher to use questions from existing instruments or to construct topic-related questions if no instrument is germane to the purpose of the study.

One of the first tasks in survey research is to develop the format of the survey and to write pertinent questions. Recall from Chapter 4 the various ways of constructing test questions. The researcher must consider the clarity of the instructions, readability of the questions, and the potential for the respondent to answer questions in socially desirable ways.

Although careful attention must be given to defining the target population and clearly stating sampling procedures in all research types, these factors take on added importance in survey research. To illustrate why this is so, consider the polls frequently conducted by television networks to determine, among other things, a presidential candidate's popularity. The target population could be as large as all registered voters in the United States. For example, researchers might have access to computerized listings of the names and the telephone numbers of all registered U.S. voters, then randomly generate a list of 3,000 names. Polling these voters would then indicate a candidate's national popularity. However, different results could occur if the candidate were a southern Democrat and the pollster surveyed the opinions of the first 500 telephone callers in Alabama. If the target population and sampling technique are not stated explicitly, voters might be misled about the candidate's popularity.

Finally, survey researchers must also select the method by which the survey will be administered. Survey data may be retrieved in one of four ways: mailing the survey, administering the survey directly to groups, conducting telephone surveys, or conducting personal interviews. Fraenkel and Wallen (1990) have developed a useful table that compares each survey administration procedure across several factors. With minor alterations to their table, we show it in Table 8-1. Here, two major considerations are apparent in all research— time and cost. Both are saved by the direct administration of surveys. On the other hand, with personal interviews in which the researcher individually administers the questionnaire to participants, the time and cost factors become procedural liabilities.

Table 8-1 also addresses a matter of great relevance to survey researchers, namely *return rate*, which is defined as the percentage of completed surveys to all survey administrations. To illustrate why return rate is a primary concern of survey researchers, the authors of this text routinely receive requests (probably one a week) to complete mailed surveys about such matters as book adoptions, organizational affiliations, professional practices, and so on. Although we try to respond to all surveys, questionnaires are occasionally discarded by accident or buried under other papers, and their return to the expectant researcher is delayed. Note that across the four administration techniques, return rates for direct administration and personal interview are (predictably) the highest. On the other hand, return rate is a major concern when surveys are mailed. Unfortunately, 100% return rates are almost impossible to obtain; researchers typically aim for a 75% return of mailed surveys.

TABLE 8-1   Considerations in the selection of survey administration procedure.

Consideration	Direct Administration	Telephone	Mail	Interview
Comparative cost	1[a]	2.5	4	2.5
Facilities needed	yes	no	no	yes
Training of questioner	yes	yes	no	yes
Data collection time	1	2	3	4
Return rate[b]	1.5	3	4	1.5
Group administration	yes	no	no	yes
Follow-up to questions[c]	no	yes	no	yes
Degree of subject bias	2.5	2.5	4	1
Degree of experimenter bias	2.5	2.5	1	4
Objectivity of responses[d]	1.5	3	1.5	4

[a]Rank-ordered administration procedures: 1 = most positive; 4 = least positive; decimals indicating a tie
[b]The percentage of completed surveys to total participants surveyed
[c]Whether the administrator can request additional information about responses to survey questions
[d]Ease of scoring

Illustration from the Literature

An excellent example of survey research is a study conducted by Watkins, Campbell, and McGregor (1989). Because previous investigators had focused on master's-level clinical psychology samples, Watkins et al. were interested in professional issues surrounding master's-level counselors, specifically, their institutional affiliation, theoretical orientation, training and career satisfaction, professional activities, and self-view.

The researchers defined their population as all master's-level American Psychology Association (APA) members who identified counseling as their specialty. The size of this population, as located in APA computer files, was 560. The researchers were interested in sampling the entire target population and had an initial return rate of roughly 75%. Unfortunately, the number of usable questionnaires dipped to 59%, mainly because many master's-level respondents possessed the doctorate or were in doctoral training by the time they completed the survey.

A 9-page questionnaire containing 72 items was constructed—an instrument that paralleled an earlier questionnaire used to survey a doctoral-level sample of APA counseling psychologists. The instrument included items regarding demographic variables like gender, age, ethnicity, and exposure to personal counseling. Of most importance, the questionnaire contained multiple-choice and *Likert-type* items (for example, 1 = very satisfied; 6 = very unsatisfied) regarding professional matters. A packet including the questionnaire and an explanatory letter, along with a return envelope, was sent to all 560 APA, master's-level counselors. A reminder postcard was mailed 2 weeks later to nonreturnees. At 2-week intervals, two more complete packets were sent to nonrespondents. Even with these prompts, only 75% of the sample eventually returned the instrument.

A brief summary of the main findings is as follows. First, concerning professional activities, 80% of master's-level counselors did psychotherapy and counseling and spent the most time in this area, as expected. When compared to a doctoral-level sample of APA counselors (data obtained in an earlier study by Watkins, Lopez, Campbell, & Himmel, 1986), master's-level counselors did more therapy and counseling, as compared with the doctoral-level respondents, among whom an academic view—interest in research and teaching—predominated.

As for institutional affiliations, the master's-level participants were mainly affiliated with applied settings such as private practice and counseling centers, whereas the doctoral sample frequently affiliated with academic departments. Similarly, the master's-level participants viewed themselves largely as practitioners, contrary to the doctoral-level sample in which an academic self-view predominated.

Eclecticism was viewed as the primary theoretical orientation for the master's-level respondents. Most sample respondents identified their approaches as a synthesis of several theoretical choices.

Most master's-level participants (66%) felt satisfied with their general academic training; about 75% thought their graduate training prepared them for their vocation; and almost 85% of the sample felt some degree of satisfaction with their career. For these same items, no differences were obtained between the doctoral and master's-level samples. Although 85% of the sample indicated some degree of satisfaction with their career choice, only 46% said they would select counseling psychology as their field of choice if life could be lived over again. Clinical psychology was the most frequently selected alternative. Finally, almost 80% of the master's-level respondents believed that the labor market was either fair, bleak, or poor for those entering the profession with a master's degree in counseling.

In discussing their results, Watkins et al. (1989) note many similarities in the data provided by master's-level counselors with other applied samples of survey respondents drawn from the APA, namely that the practitioner viewpoint predominates and that most practitioners believe in an eclectic theoretical perspective. To explain career satisfaction results, the investigators note that their master's-level sample does not see parity between counseling and clinical psychology, and this inequity leads to an unfavorable perception of job prospects, as well as to the desire to choose clinical psychology if a second life were available.

Perhaps the most pressing issue raised by the researchers is the role of master's-level counselors in the APA, particularly in Division 17 (Counseling Psychology). Since Watkins et al. (1989) found that respondents held a dim view of job prospects and were not happy with the APA organization, the most important question is whether to continue training master's-level counselors. Further, if the master's degree is retained, what should the APA and Division 17 do to serve the professional counselor with a master's degree better? To pursue these questions, the researchers called for renewed discussion and examination of these critical points.

Advantages and Disadvantages of Surveys

The single greatest advantage of survey research is the amount of information that can be collected from many participants at the same time. In a relatively quick and cost-effective manner, survey researchers can learn a great deal about values, attitudes, socioeconomic factors, and demographic data from large samples of respondents.

A related advantage of survey research is the potential to sample respondents from extremely large, arbitrary populations. For example, consider the population in the Watkins et al. (1989) survey, which was all master's-level, APA-affiliated counselors. These surveyors had access to a national population—quite an advantage over researchers who use methods that limit their access to larger populations.

Finally, survey research can be of great practical utility. For example, in the Watkins et al. (1989) study, knowing the high percentage of APA-affiliated, master's-level counselors who identify with a practice but not an academic orientation is very relevant for those who teach and train these graduate students. The data suggest that program trainers need to design research courses for students who place a higher premium on applied counseling skill.

As is true with all research methods, survey research has inherent limitations. One notable issue is the accuracy of survey data, since respondents may not see the importance of survey questions, or equally disturbing, may respond in biased ways. This latter concern is especially salient when survey questions cover sensitive topics such as patterns of sexual behavior, drug habits, or AIDS awareness.

As mentioned earlier, another liability of survey research is return rates, especially when mailing surveys. The result is not only a lower number of subjects, but the subjects who do not return surveys probably differ from those who do.

Recommendations

To improve the quality of survey research, we offer several recommendations. First, survey researchers must develop clear and detailed descriptions of the arbitrary population and the sampling procedures used to select members from this population. With reference to the Watkins et al. (1989) study, it is clear that the survey results pertain only to APA-affiliated, master's-level counselors. Initially, the investigators thought their target population consisted of 560 members, but after excluding those in pursuit of or already obtaining the doctoral degree ($N = 125$), the population shrank to 435, of which 245 were actually sampled.

Sample representativeness is mostly a function of sampling procedure. In the example study, random sampling was not used because the researchers attempted to observe the entire target population; the population was defined by APA computer records, and surveys were sent to all potential participants. Unfortunately, as with most mailed surveys, only some of the target population responded, so representativeness is an issue in cases in which return rates dip below 75%. Thus, despite the vigorous efforts of the researchers to solicit a higher return rate, the question remains whether the selected sample ($N = 245$) represents the beliefs of the initial target population ($N = 435$).

Many suggestions for question writing and item formats are given in Chapter 4, and potential researchers should consider some of these methods useful in constructing a new survey. One critical consideration, often overlooked by survey researchers, is the rationale for using the questions they do on surveys. For example, in the Watkins et al. (1989) study, there is no explicit rationale for including the six areas of opinion it surveyed. The authors say their purpose was to clarify issues and controversies surrounding master's-level training for counselors, but why are these six areas used? Are these six the only debatable ones? One way investigators can justify the content of their survey questionnaire is through the literature review, which should provide clues about what questions, or sets of questions, should be included. The author of survey research can then use previous literature to develop a rationale for using particular items on the survey.

In constructing survey items and selecting response formats, the researcher must account for the literacy level of the respondents. Further, items on questionnaires must consist of clearly defined terms to reduce different interpretations of each items. For instance, a term like egalitarian could be uniquely interpreted, misinterpreted, or simply unknown to many respondents. The data derived from such a question would be useless.

A third recommendation is to evaluate the degree to which sample respondents might answer questions dishonestly. Usually, the degree of dishonesty relates to the purpose of the research, as well as to the type of attitude or behavior being surveyed. Consider the increased likelihood of getting false responses to a survey given to company employees when these employees know they can be fired if they have drug or alcohol problems. On the other hand, lying would be at a minimum when a university researcher wants to determine the types of epistemological attitudes held by graduate students in the helping professions.

When the accuracy of subjects' responses is likely to be highly questionable, researchers have several tactics available. First, titles should be removed if they state the survey purpose. Titles that use more socially acceptable terms should be substituted. For instance, the Drug and Alcohol Survey could be changed to the Survey of Recreational Habits. Or, when measuring socially undesirable traits, a measure of shyness could be titled the Social Reticence Scale. Other strategies are (1) using preexisting survey instruments that contain response bias scales, (2) including distractor items not relevant to the survey that will disrupt the development of response sets, and (3) alternating positive and negative statements like, I like professors who stick to the facts, and I find it annoying when professors tell anecdotes.

Finally, it is crucial that survey researchers pilot the administration and practical utility of the survey before conducting a full-fledged study. Researchers should administer the instrument and request feedback from pilot participants after they complete the measure. Feedback should be given about the clarity of directions, the clarity of the items, and if relevant, the degree of response bias.

When direct administration is used, the surveyor should practice delivering standardized instructions to respondents and should develop a standardized proctoring procedure. In other words, the survey should be administered the same way each time, much like any standardized test such as the SAT or GRE. Such standardized delivery will reduce procedural error.

CORRELATIONAL RESEARCH

Imagine you are observing two people sitting on a bench in the park. One person is named Tom, the other Tina. Amazingly, you observe that every time Tom stands up so does Tina, and every time Tom sits down so does Tina. After one hour and 50 occurrences of sitting and standing, you reason that these events occur together for Tom and Tina. This type of observation defines the basic premise of correlational research, which is determining whether two or more events occur together. In other words, correlational researchers examine the way variables co-vary, or co-relate.

We use correlational or associational logic frequently. When parents say that their daughter is well-behaved around children except for one friend, the implication is that the daughter's misbehavior and that friend go together. When we go to work and our boss greets us upon first sighting with "hello," we come to believe that first sightings by the boss and hello go together. Such associations are many, and if stretched further, it could be argued that our daily lives are predominantly dictated by associations—or correlations. In fact, all correlational techniques are rooted in the basic idea that two events go together. Researchers in the helping professions extend this idea to include variables of interest such as intelligence and achievement, depression and anxiety, case load and quality of service, and so on. As with other methods discussed in this chapter, correlational research qualifies as a descriptive method because of its emphasis on describing relationships.

A secondary purpose of correlational research is to predict an event given a preceding event. In prediction, it is assumed that a statistical estimate of correlation exists so that when future scores on variable X (the predictor) become known, researchers will be able to predict scores on Y (the criterion). A classic example is the use of scores on the GRE to predict students' GPAs in graduate school. Since this correlation is known, researchers can predict a student's graduate school GPA if they know his or her GRE score.

After collecting correlational data, the results may be presented as in Table 8-2, which shows a hypothetical correlational outcome for two variables. In this situation, Table 8-2 shows that the subject's name (or some other identification

TABLE 8-2 Data required to determine correlation between social worker case load and quality of service.

Social Worker Name	Case Load[a]	Quality of Service[b]
Tom	22	36
Fred	15	46
Susie	20	41
Mary	26	45
Rick	18	43
Carrie	32	24
Alice	12	48
Bob	22	35
Peggy	17	44
Julie	28	27

[a]Number of active cases
[b]Supervisor rating of quality; 10 = poor quality and 50 = excellent quality

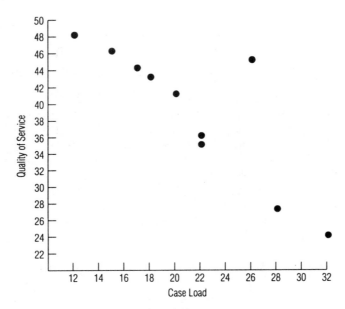

FIGURE 8-1   Scatterdiagram for the data in Table 8-2.

code) is placed on the far left of the diagram, and the two variable names head two additional columns to the right of the subjects' names. Each subject has data for both variables. For example, Tom has 22 active cases and a service quality rating of 36.

The degree of correlation derived from these data can be estimated in two ways. One method is by calculating the Pearson product-moment correlation coefficient, a statistical concept that estimates correlation on a scale from –1.00 to 1.00. This correlation coefficient will be discussed further in Chapter 10. The other method is to graph the correlational data using a scatterdiagram. A scatterdiagram for the data given in Table 8-2 is presented in Figure 8-1.

The estimation of correlation leads to three outcomes. When a correlation is significantly high-positive, as X goes up so does Y. In the helping professions, examples of high-positive correlations are many and include intelligence and achievement, height and weight, blood alcohol and alcohol consumed, family income and value of family home, to name a few. If a correlation is perfectly high-positive, its value is 1.00, as shown in the scatterdiagram in Figure 8-2.

Figure 8-2 also shows a lack of correlation ($r = .00$). Here, there is no systematic relationship between variables, and knowing the value of the predictor variable (X) tells us nothing about the criterion variable (Y). More simply, if Tom stands up, we do not know what Tina will do; she may stand or remain seated—we cannot predict with any certainty. Demonstrated research examples of zero correlations are eye color and intelligence, job satisfaction and job performance, and length of psychotherapy and therapy outcome.

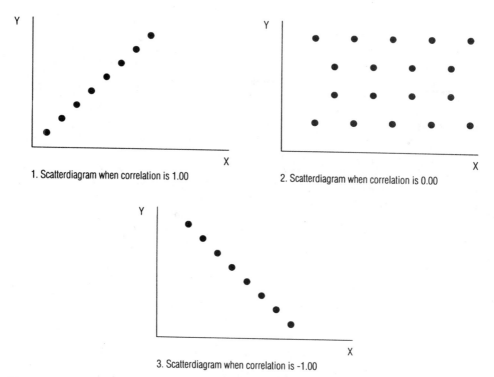

1. Scatterdiagram when correlation is 1.00

2. Scatterdiagram when correlation is 0.00

3. Scatterdiagram when correlation is -1.00

FIGURE 8-2   Scatterdiagram of three correlational outcomes.

The final correlational outcome represented in Figure 8-2 is high-negative, a value approximating –1.00. This type of correlation means that as variable X goes up, Y goes down and that as X goes down, Y goes up. Drawing a parallel to Tom and Tina, if their behavior were perfectly negatively correlated, whenever Tom stands up, Tina sits down and when Tom sits down, Tina stands up. Examples in research are time-out-of-seat and academic productivity, and age and vision. Note that the fictitious data given in Table 8-1 represent a negative correlation: case load high, quality of service low; case load low, quality of service high. To verify this fact, look at the numbers in Table 8-1 and note that as individual case loads rise, quality suffers and that as quality increases, case loads drop.

While the concept of correlation is most understandable when two variables are studied, human behavior is not that simply determined; therefore, correlational researchers rarely isolate just two variables for study; instead, they examine many variables at once. For example, items on a personality questionnaire can be defined as single variables so that if the instrument contains 50 items, each item could be correlated with each of the others—a total of 1,225 correlations. Any time more than two correlations are studied simultaneously, the term **multiple correlation** is used. Several commonly employed multiple correlation methods are **multiple regression** and **factor analysis**.

Illustration from the Literature

In a rare instance when only three variables were examined, Bowman and Reeves (1987) used Pearson product-moment correlations to study the relationships between empathy (both experimenter and supervisor) and moral development. Their review of the literature revealed that the relationship between empathy and moral development had yet to be studied among counselors in training, despite the importance of empathic skills in the counseling process. A total of 35 students from three sections of a counseling practicum in facilitative skills at San Francisco State University participated. Participants completed a Defining Issues Test (DIT) measuring moral development and the Empathic Understanding (EU) scale. Students completed the DIT before the course, then completed the 12-week training module, which was designed to increase facilitative action through in-class practice and feedback. Upon completion of the program, students gave supervisors a set of videotapes of counseling sessions for evaluation, and the supervisors rated the tapes using the EU scale. Also, the participants viewed a videotaped counseling interview (with counselor responses deleted) and responded in writing to the client's statements. These written statements were assessed by the researchers using the EU instrument.

Results showed that all correlations were significant; supervisor ratings of EU and DIT scores ($r = .36$), researchers' EU ratings and DIT ($r = .61$), and the researchers' and supervisors' ratings ($r = .40$). The authors note that while moral development is related to empathy, a confounding variable like intellectual ability may also associate with empathy. Further, the authors discuss the need to increase moral development, since those low on this dimension will be likely to possess less empathy.

Advantages and Disadvantages of Correlational Studies

Correlational methods provide the researcher a means for analyzing many variables—a particular advantage for this descriptive method. Unlike any other statistical technique, correlation allows the investigator to analyze simultaneously how many variables co-relate.

A second advantage is that correlational methods are useful for a vast array of research questions; as we said earlier, associations are the essence of life, and it is equally conceivable that all researchers have as their goal the identification of co-relationships among variables. If researchers keep their research questions in this format, correlational methods will provide the desired answers. A good example of this type of research can be drawn from the study we cited by Bowman and Reeves (1987), who tested the research question, What is the relationship between moral development and counselor empathy?

The negative side of correlational research pertains to a single theme: Conclusions drawn from correlational research are limited, and all correlational conclusions should be accompanied by provisos. Note that the occurrence of two events together does not mean that one event caused the other. One of the more famous sayings in science is, Correlation does not imply causation.

However, it is easy to cross the border between correlation and causation.

As one classic example, research to determine the effect of genetics and environment on intelligence is entirely correlational, because a researcher cannot manipulate these variables experimentally. A researcher cannot separate twin siblings at birth and expose one sibling to an enriched environment and the other to a deprived environment. Instead, researchers have focused on correlational techniques and estimated the relationship between IQ scores of full siblings and compared that correlation with the correlation between the IQ scores of identical twins. As genetic similarity increases, so does the correlation, so that the correlation between full siblings is roughly .50, increasing to almost .90 for identical twins. Based on these data, it would be easy to presume that intelligence is largely caused by genetics, but this conclusion is incorrect because correlational research methods cannot be used to prove cause and effect relationships. It may be that the genes do indeed exert a causal effect on intelligence, and the available research suggests this conclusion. Yet, such a conclusion can never be scientifically proved—it must simply remain a tantalyzing association.

A final point is that correlation can be considered exploratory research, possibly leading to more experimentally derived investigations. Consider the interesting association between attitudes and behavior. Often, attitudes do not predict subsequent behaviors. For example, a belief in the conservation of natural resources does not necessarily mean the believer will use less water than other individuals. First, the association between a belief (in water conservation) and a behavior (daily residential water use) must be established. If the correlational data show that high belief in water conservation goes with low daily water use and low belief in water conservation goes with high daily use, then experimental studies can be designed to alter the latter group's beliefs and subsequent behavior—if all agree that conservation of natural resources is important. In this example, an experimental study might expose low believers in conservation to a 2-week course in the importance of conservation of water and then compare subsequent water use of course participants with low-believer, nonparticipants. Note that without the initial correlational study, the experimental study would be meaningless because we would not know how water use varies with conservation beliefs.

Second, correlational outcomes highlight the difference between nomothetic (group) and idiographic research positions, since correlation necessarily involves group data. The problem is that while there may be a relationship between variables, there will often be an exception to the rule. As an example, if you reexamine the data in Table 8-2, you will note that in general as case loads go up, quality of service goes down. The one exception to this rule is Mary, who seems able to keep a high case load and maintain quality service to her clients.

Third, as with all nonexperimental designs, the lack of control in correlational research is a weakness. The main concern in correlational research, highlighted in the study by Bowman and Reeves (1987), is that variables not examined in a study may influence the variables of interest. Humans are complex, and rarely is one construct like empathy solely related to one other variable like moral development. As the authors note, cognitive development is highly related to moral development, and if moral development is highly related to empathy, empathy can also be presumed related to cognitive skill. Further, cognitive skill is also related to a host of other variables. Do these variables also enter the empathy equation? The point is that the astute researcher should use correlational research when considering the complexity of human behavior so that other variables that might influence the selected variables can be taken into account.

Finally, correlational outcomes require making a distinction between strength of the correlation and **statistical significance**. The problem is that correlations can be statistically significant, yet meaningless. For example, with 10 subjects, a statistically significant correlation at the .05 level of significance is .63 and yet, with 102 subjects and using .05 as a significance level, the correlation required for significance is roughly .20. Unfortunately, a correlation of .20 is trivial, as you will see in Chapter 10, although a correlation of .60, while not meeting significance standards, is quite high. Without reference to statistical significance, Best and Kahn (1989) suggest that correlations between .00 and .20 be viewed as negligible, .20 to .40 as low, .40 to .60 as moderate, .60 to .80 substantial, and .80 to 1.00 as high to very high.

Recommendations

As with all forms of research, the use of high-quality measuring tools is essential in correlational research, especially considering that constructs selected for correlational study are operationally defined through measurement. That is, the constructs are defined by the tests selected.

Consider the Bowman and Reeves (1987) study. The EU scale was reported to have interrater reliability of .88 to .91, good enough for research purposes, while the test-retest reliability of the DIT was given as high .70s to the .80s—also sufficient for investigation. Given this information, we know that different raters tend to agree in assigning empathy scores to trainees and that a person's moral development tends to be stable. Because of the reliable measures used, participants' scores contain less error, which means the correlation contains less error. Simply put, by using reliable measures, researchers increase the likelihood that an obtained correlation would occur again with similar subjects, researchers, and procedures.

What about validity? The authors do not mention validity data, so it is difficult to determine whether the data truly reflect participants' moral development and empathy. In other words, while we know the data are somewhat dependable, we must assume the results are meaningful.

A statistical theme pervades the remaining recommendations for conducting correlational research. Many of these components will be discussed later in Chapter 10, but one suggestion can be discussed in terms of sampling and involves the problem of **truncation**—obtaining a limited range of scores on any of the measured variables. A limited range of outcomes for a particular variable will usually lower the correlation.

The problem can be illustrated by altering the example study used in Chapter 3 to describe samples, populations, and sampling procedures. Recall that 200 children were identified as hyperactive, but let us change the research question so that the investigator is now interested in the correlation between parent and teacher reports of hyperactive behavior, as measured by a scale for this purpose. For whatever reason, the investigator chooses to study only the most hyperactive children (therefore a more homogeneous sample). Based on pediatrician reports, the researcher selects the 50 most hyperactive children. A correlation of .30 is obtained, and the researcher is perplexed by the apparently small relationship between parent and teacher reports of hyperactive symptoms.

Truncation is the likely culprit, since parent and teacher ratings were probably restricted to the high range of the measuring device, thus lowering the obtained correlation. Ironically, the sample of interest to the research—those most severely hyperactive—resulted in the most truncation. Further, by restricting the sample to severely hyperactive students, the results cannot be generalized to other, less hyperactive children.

The remedy for truncation seems obvious—select samples based on random sampling procedures and sample from the entire range of the population (as we suggested in Chapter 5). However, neither remedy may be practical or even desirable. For example, the case could be made that truncation is a healthy side-effect of the desire to study specific samples. The researcher interested in agreement between parent and teacher ratings for the most hyperactive children probably had a reason for selecting a restricted sample.

Further, while the aim in correlation is to randomly sample all variable values in the population, this is often impossible. Take for example the correlation between the GRE and the graduate school GPA. This correlation is lowered because graduate students are typically required to score above the mean on the GRE, thereby reducing the potential range of values (both GRE and GPA) that could be studied if graduate schools randomly accepted individuals regardless of their GRE score. Obviously, random selection of individuals from the population of those taking the GRE would be foolish and costly because many students who were accepted would not finish the program; they do not possess the skills to do so that are measured by the GRE. A researcher would have to select subjects randomly from a naturally restricted population—those scoring high enough on the GRE to gain admission to graduate study. Again, truncation is a factor.

In sum, the correlational researcher can avoid truncation by random sampling of an unrestricted population. If the investigator is practically prohibited from doing so or has a research question requiring the use of a restricted sample, a statistical correction for truncation is available.

DEVELOPMENTAL RESEARCH

What is more obvious than the fact that humans change over time? We mature physically, our interactions with peers change, and we think differently as we grow older. Those aspects of human behavior that change in time are of most interest to developmental researchers, who include some of the more famous scientists like Freud and Piaget. In developmental research, time-related change can be operationally defined in different ways, such as by chronological age, when the researcher employs individuals of different age groups. Time-related also can refer to such milestones as grade in school or years of experience. Developmental researchers typically treat the time factor as an independent variable that is presumably related to some dependent measure such as intelligence, moral reasoning, empathy, height, or recreational activities. Because time is a variable that cannot be manipulated, developmental research is classified as nonexperimental. As with all other nonexperimental approaches, age is presumed to be related to selected behavior changes but not causally so.

Sometimes, confusion about what constitutes developmental research arises when researchers (1) include age or grade as one of several independent variables and (2) observe subjects more than once. As an example of the former, consider a study in which the self-concept of two groups of 5-year-old subjects is measured every 6 months for a 5-year period. One group is made up of children with an alcoholic parent; the other childrens' parents are not alcoholic. As another example, what if Maria Gonzalez collected posttest data immediately following treatment, then again at 6 months, and again at 1 year? Are either of these studies developmental?

The answer is that the study of children of alcoholic parents is developmental, while Maria's is not. In the first example, age is an independent variable, presumed to be related to the changes in the emotional functioning of children with alcoholic parents. Whether the children have alcoholic parents or not is a second independent variable. On the other hand, Maria is not using age as an independent variable; instead she is interested in the lasting effects of treatment for individuals with an eating disorder. While many researchers collect follow-up data, this is not developmental research because the research question pertains entirely to the lasting effects of treatment but not to naturally occurring, time-related changes in behavior. However, Maria would have a developmental study if she removed the treatment entirely and focused on age-related changes in eating behavior for a nondisordered eating population. She could not study a disordered eating population, because this population would presumably seek treatment, and it would be unethical to withhold treatment for extended periods from those who desire it.

There are three basic types of developmental research designs; each is represented in Table 8-3. The table shows that when using a **longitudinal design**, the same subject group (A) is repeatedly studied over time; here, an age span of 6 years is used. On the other hand, investigators using a **cross-sectional design** study different age groups, or cohorts, (A, B, C) at a single time. Finally, a compromise strategy is the **cross-sequential** approach in which groups are different age groups; each is measured repeatedly (age-group A at 12 and 15 and age-group B at 15 and 18). Before we discuss the pros and cons of these three developmental designs, we provide an illustration of a cross-sectional design.

Illustration from the Literature

A study by Post-Kammer (1987) shows how a single piece of research can cross different research types. She asked three research questions, one requiring a developmental method, the other an ex post facto design (to be discussed next), and still another, a correlational procedure. However, at least one aspect of her study clearly illustrates the use of a cross-sectional design—the reason for including it here. The developmental research question posed by Post-Kammer (1987) was, Do 9th- and 11th-grade boys and girls differ in their work values and career maturity? The author justified the importance of the question by referring to career development theory and the desirability of helping high school counselors better understand students' changes in career values.

To answer the question, the author cross-sectionally sampled 885 students constituting an entire 9th- and 11th-grade graduating class of a suburban high school in a large midwestern city. During class meetings, the researcher administered two different career inventories—the Career Maturity Inventory (CMI) and the Work Values Inventory (WVI). The CMI is a 75-item inventory on which test-takers receive one total score measuring general attitude about career choice and five subscale scores: Decisiveness, Involvement, Independence, Orientation, and Commitment. The author gives one study of CMI test-retest reliability and refers the reader to the technical manual of the CMI for further information about validity data. The WVI is a 45-item inventory measuring two global dimensions of work: (1) *internal* (Achievement, Altruism, Creativity, Esthetics, Intellectual Stimulation, and Management) and (2) *external* (Associates, Economic Returns, Independence, Prestige, Security, Supervisory Relationships, Surroundings, Variety, and Way of Life). Test-retest reliability is reported, while two different references are given as support of the instrument's validity.

Again, because three different questions were asked, different data tables and statistical procedures were employed. To answer the ex post facto question (discussed later in this chapter) about sex differences, the author provides a table containing results for both genders, including means, standard deviations, and a statistical comparison of the means for each of 21 scores obtained on the two career inventories. To answer the question about how the two instruments correlate, another table lists the correlations between CMI total score and the 15 work value scales.

Of most importance here is the cross-sectional data that consisted of means and standard deviations on all 21 scales for 9th- and 11th-graders, with statistical comparison across grade groups. Of the 21 total comparisons, 5 proved signifi-

TABLE 8-3   Longitudinal, cross-sectional, and cross-sequential developmental designs.

Longitudinal Design:	Age	Group
	12 (1983)	A
	15 (1986)	A
	18 (1989)	A
Cross-Sectional Design:	12 (1989)	A
	15 (1989)	B
	18 1989)	C
Cross-Sequential Design:	12 (1983)	A
	15 (1983 & 1986)	B & A
	18 (1986)	B

cant, with the 11th-graders showing greater intrinsic job values—Achievement, Altruism, and Creativity. As for extrinsic values, the grade groups did not differ on seven of the nine extrinsic scales, with one scale higher for 11th-graders (Variety) and one higher for 9th-graders (Associates). No differences for any of the six CMI scales were obtained.

In discussing the grade differences, the author notes that some support is provided for a change in career values from extrinsic to intrinsic with the passage of time between freshmen and junior high school grades. Both 9th- and 11th-graders showed similar extrinsic orientations, revealing that extrinsic values are somewhat stable for this high school sample. Similar stability was noted in the career maturity data, which revealed no significant differences between grades, suggesting that, contrary to intuition, career maturity develops earlier than expected, at least for this sample. In terms of practical implications, the author suggests that high school counselors should not expect the career values of high school students to change, especially maturity values, and that to increase maturity during high school, specific curricular activities such as group sessions that stimulate career thinking and values clarification may need consideration.

Advantages and Disadvantages of Developmental Research

Developmental researchers have the distinct advantage of sampling human behavior at different times rather than at a single time as most other researchers do. Indeed, a strong case can be made that for certain research areas, developmental research is the most meaningful investigative approach because human potential naturally develops with maturation and experience. Developmental research provides a sound method for understanding the powerful influences of maturation and learning on behavior.

More specifically, each developmental research design has associated benefits and costs. To keep this discussion focused on a particular design, the advantages and disadvantages of each design will be presented successively. Starting with the longitudinal approach, the greatest advantage of this design is that the comparability between the groups across time should be perfect. After all, how much more equivalent can different age groups be if the same subjects are measured as they pass through selected age periods?

Unfortunately, longitudinal research has major liabilities. A 3-year longitudinal study necessarily requires 3 years to collect all the data; a 6-year longitudinal study 6 years, and so on. Similarly, the longer the time frame, the more practical concerns about internal validity accrue. The two most profound internal validity threats to longitudinal research are attrition (subjects move, lose interest, or die), and history. As more time elapses, it is more likely that other events can occur to alter participants' standing on the dependent variable. Testing effects may also reduce internal validity, especially if the researcher does not use at least one parallel form of the instrument.

In contrast to the longitudinal design, the cross-sectional approach requires a single measurement point and uses three different age groups. This clearly reduces the time and financial costs associated with longitudinal research. At the same time, the three age groups may not be equivalent with regard to other variables that could affect the dependent variables. For example, consider the study we mentioned earlier examining the relationship between age and an alcoholic parent on self-concept. If a cross-sectional design had been used, how could we be sure that groups of 5-, 7-, and 9-year-olds were initially (at age 5) equal with respect to other factors related to self-concept such as SES and motivation. Without knowing the comparability of different age groups on variables also related to the dependent variable, the results of cross-sectional research must be interpreted cautiously.

The cross-sequential design represents a compromise. This approach has some of the advantages and disadvantages of each approach, but none are as extreme. (See Table 8-3.)

Recommendations

For researchers who want to conduct a purely longitudinal or cross-sectional developmental design, we offer the following advice. First, consider exactly how long subjects will be observed. Developmental theory can usually guide the researcher in making this decision. For example, a longitudinal study on the effects of pubescence on self-esteem may include a 4-year period from, for example, ages 10 to 14. Many language studies focus on developmental periods when language ability develops rapidly, typically from 1 year of age to about 4 years, by which time children approximate adult language. Thus, we recommend that longitudinal researchers select a time span based on developmental theory and research.

As for threats to the internal validity of longitudinal designs, the researcher can deal with these threats as with any other piece of research—by explicitly indicating how the threat occurred and how much of a concern it presents. Take the threat of attrition as an example. If the researcher has data on the subjects who discontinued participation, the investigator should present, or at least summarize, these data to see whether discontinued subjects differ from remaining participants. If the two groups do differ, which usually can be determined through statistical comparison, then attrition is a clear threat. If no differences are found, the threat of attrition is not so great. In either case, attrition lowers the size of the sample, which is always unfortunate. Even history can be accounted for if the researcher can provide some evidence that no historical threat occurred that would invalidate study results.

As for cross-sectional research, the main concern is for the comparability of the groups on potentially confounding variables. The researcher must ensure comparability among the subjects composing the age groups by measuring any potential confound and presenting these data in the research paper. Returning to the self-concept study, if cognitive ability is related to self-concept, to equate the groups on cognitive skill, the researcher could review school folders to see what type of cognitive skill data exist. Perhaps some quantification of report card information could be used to see whether or not the different age groups are roughly equivalent in terms of school achievement.

Ethnicity and socioeconomic data could also be presented. In the absence of any differences between age groups on those factors related to self-concept, the researcher can safely proceed. And thanks to statistics, even when the groups do differ on some important variable, the statistical procedure discussed in Chapter 10 called analysis of covariance can statistically remove these differences.

EX POST FACTO RESEARCH

Whereas developmental researchers focus on time-related subject attributes, ex post facto (also known as causal-comparative) researchers study a vast array of other subject attributes. The term *ex post facto* means after the fact and denotes that subjects already possess the independent variable of interest before the research study begins. Sometimes, a variable of interest (such as ethnicity) cannot be manipulated; others would be unethical to manipulate. For example, a researcher could not examine the effects of diet on children's intelligence by asking one group of parents to feed their child foods high in sugar and the other parents to keep their child on a highly nutritious diet. Again, because the variables studied are preexisting subject attributes and cannot (or sometimes should not) be manipulated, ex post facto research is classified as nonexperimental.

As do developmental researchers, ex post facto researchers treat attribute variables like smoking, ethnicity, and religious preference as levels of an independent variable. In the first example in Table 8-4, smoking is treated as an independent variable with two levels—smoker and nonsmoker; examples two (ethnicity) and three (religious preference) both have five levels. Thus conceptualized, the purpose of ex post facto research is to locate between-group differences on the dependent variable. Possible variables that may be studied in ex post facto research are presented in Table 8-4.

Illustration from the Literature

Burbach, Kashani, and Rosenberg (1989) conducted an ex post facto study using diagnostic condition as an independent variable and a measure of parental bonding as the dependent variable. Specifically, these researchers were interested in how three different groups of adolescents—depressed, psychiatric-controls, and normal-controls—would differ in their self-reported feelings regard- ing how they bonded with their parents. In the introduction section of the paper, the authors note that disturbances in parental bonding have long been associated with disturbances in psychosocial development, and ultimately, psychopathology. For example, the authors cite research that shows that depressed adults consistently self-report their parents to be low in parental care and highly overprotective, a pattern called "affectionless control."

The authors suggest that the following are improvements in their methods over previous research: (1) use of structured diagnostic interviews to determine diagnostic condition, (2) examination of depressed adolescents currently living with their parents instead of adult depressives, the latter being the sole focus of previous investigators, and (3) inclusion of a psychiatric-control group, which had been omitted from prior study.

The researchers had access to a list of adolescent students attending public schools in a midwestern U.S. community of roughly 65,000. From this list, they solicited participation from 150 adolescents and their families, selecting 25 male and 25 female adolescents from each of three age groups: 14- , 15- , and 16-year-olds. To obtain the desired equality in gender for each of the three age groups, the researchers initially contacted 214 families; 70% of the contacted families agreed to participate.

During a home visit to each consenting family, a research assistant administered a structured diagnostic interview to both parent and adolescent, along with a 25-item Parental Bonding Instrument (PBI). The structured interviews followed the DSM-III, with the final decision about diagnostic grouping based entirely on the adolescent interview. This resulted in 12 adolescents being considered depressed; 16 were eligible for the nondepressed, psychiatric-control group—for example, they had conduct, oppositional, or anxiety disorders; and 75 adolescents qualified for the normal-control group. The PBI required the test-taker to self-report attitudes about the parental relationship by responding to statements like, My parents spoke to me in a warm and friendly voice, on a three-point, Likert-type scale. The PBI provides two scores, one for parental care and the other for parental overprotection, which results in four unique combinations of parental bonding: (1) optimal bonding (high care—low overprotec-

TABLE 8-4   Representation of different ex post facto studies.

	Independent Variable	Dependent Variable
Example 1	(Smoking Status) Smoker Nonsmoker	(Hand Strength) Score on Pressure Grip Test Score on Pressure Grip Test
Example 2	(Ethnicity) American Hispanic American African American Native American Anglo-American Asian	(Family Values) Family Values Survey Family Values Survey Family Values Survey Family Values Survey Family Values Survey
Example 3	(Religious Preference) Catholic Protestant Jewish Other None	(Health Habits) Health Beliefs Health Beliefs Health Beliefs Health Beliefs Health Beliefs

tion), (2) weak bonding (low care—low overprotection), (3) affectionate constraints (high care—high overprotection), and (4) affectionless control (low care—high overprotection). Reliability and validity data were neither provided nor referenced for any of the instruments.

As for data analyses, the authors' first goal was to assess how equal the three groups were with respect to other variables that could influence the ratings of parent bonding. The variables initially assessed were demographic and consisted of gender, age, grade, race, and SES. Initial comparison across the three groups revealed only one difference—there was a significant preponderance of females in the depressed group (10 females and 2 males). A separate analysis was then conducted to see if gender influenced parent bonding self-report. No gender differences emerged, enabling the researchers to continue with their primary analyses.

The primary analysis was conducted to determine how the three diagnostic groups (the ex post facto variable of most interest) differed on the PBI dimensions of parental care and overprotection (recall the earlier expectation about the outcomes for depressed adolescents). Contrary to expectations, the parental bonding pattern known as affectionless control was noted for the nondepressed psychiatric-control group but not for the depressed or normal-control group. Instead, the depressed group revealed patterns of bonding that were less optimal than those of the normal-control group but not as destructive as those revealed in the self-reports of nondepressed psychiatric-control participants.

In addition, the authors looked at whether the three diagnostic groups differed on any of the 25 PBI items, and they provide a table including each PBI item and the mean response ratings for each of the three groups. On none of the items did the depressed subjects differ from the control groups. However, when compared with normal controls, the depressed subjects did report less help from both parents and poorer parental understanding of their problems and worries; they also felt less wanted. Further, when compared to the nondepressed psychiatric-control group, the depressed adolescents reported more frequent parent-child discussions, more parental enjoyment of parent-child discussions, and being more frequently singled out for parental smiling.

The authors' first point of discussion is to note that the affectionless control variable expected in the depressive subjects was not found. Instead, this bonding dynamic was more characteristic of the nondepressed, psychiatrically disturbed patients. When considered together, all psychiatric groups differed from normal-control adolescents in terms of parental care; specifically, disturbed patients felt their parents were less understanding, and this group also felt less wanted by their parents than did normal-control subjects. In sum, the authors note that the exact role of parental bonding is difficult to assess, given the obtained results. For example, it could be that psychiatric disturbance leads adolescents to rate their parents negatively, thus casting doubt about the validity of subjects' perceptions. The researchers say other factors, like a child's temperament, could also relate to how parents bonded with their children and that further investigation will be needed to disentangle the unique contribution of other related factors.

Several limitations to the study were noted, including the fact that adolescents reported the bonding of both parents at the same time rather than by making separate self-reports for maternal and paternal care. The other noted weakness was combining different types of depression into a single group (major depression and dysthymic disorder), thus affecting the composition and diagnostic purity of the depressed group.

Advantages and Disadvantages of Ex Post Facto Research

Researchers use ex post facto methods to investigate the many human factors not amenable to experimental manipulation. The types of human subject variables of interest are endless, including demographic variables like gender, ethnicity, income, occupation, grade, or school type; variables such as type of psychopathology, medical condition, or school handicap; and all kinds of attitude, personality, and cognitive differences such as career typology, personality traits, and self-concept. Clearly, ex post facto researchers play an important role in the investigative enterprise.

Because the number of relevant variables is so enormous, the possibility of examining many variables in one study is increased. To capitalize on this fact, many ex post facto researchers include three or four attributes in a single study so they can study the unique and interactive effects among attributes. For example, the attributes given in Table 8-4 could be collapsed into a single study of the effects of religious preference, ethnicity, and smoking status on health beliefs.

Finally, similar to correlational researchers, ex post facto researchers can use this method as a precursor to experimental study. The same logic applies. If high associations are found between the independent variable (conservation belief, which is now classified as low, middle, or high) and the dependent variable (daily water use), then experimental studies can be designed to alter beliefs to see if these altered beliefs have an effect on the behavior—daily water use.

Unfortunately, the parallel with correlational research also translates to similar disadvantages; most of the advantages center on the interpretive value of ex post facto results. Even more than with correlational outcomes, ex post facto researchers seem to be treating subject attributes like real experimental manipulations—mainly because the independent variable is partitioned into various levels—to compare different groups. The independent variable is still an attribute, and in the absence of experimental creation, the relationship between variables is just that—an association. Statements about causality cannot be made using ex post facto methods.

As an example of the greater temptation to draw incorrect causal conclusions when using ex post facto methods, consider the highly controversial association between ethnicity and intelligence test scores. Suppose that a researcher studies children in one of four ethnic groups (Anglo-American, Hispanic American, African American, and Asian) and compares intelligence test scores for the groups. The researcher finds that Hispanic Americans and African Americans score about 15 points lower than Anglo-Americans and that Anglo-Americans score about 7 points less than Asians, and that these differences are statistically significant. What can we conclude? An incorrect conclusion is that ethnicity is causally related to intelligence. Two interpretive limitations become apparent. First, even if the ex post facto differences are accurate (ethnic groups do differ in intelligence), it is problematic to explain why. In other words, what about ethnicity is associated with differences in intelligence? By focusing on global, diffuse subject attributes like ethnicity, questions about why differences emerge simply cannot be addressed, thus limiting the interpretative usefulness of results.

A more fundamental problem in the interpretation of ex post facto data is confounding, because through the artificial creation of nonequivalent groups, differences on the dependent variables may be to due to just about anything. Nonequivalence occurs whenever subjects self-select to levels of the independent variable by virtue of a particular attribute they possess. In a complete antithesis of random assignment, Anglo-Americans self-select to the Anglo-American group, African Americans to the African American group, and so on. Because each ethnic group constitutes a unique blend of environment, values, and traditions, the limitation is that any one of many between-group differences may explain the results. For example, in the ethnicity and intelligence test score study, it may be that the African American and Hispanic American samples contained a preponderance of lower-income families, so that differences in intelligence may be unrelated to ethnicity but rather to income status.

Recommendations

As gleaned from the aforementioned disadvantages, most of the major criticisms of ex post facto research pertain to data interpretation. To increase the accuracy of conclusions, we recommend the following.

First, although all researchers must guard against conclusions that go beyond the data, such conclusions are particularly tempting in ex post facto investigation. For example, suppose that the investigator interested in ethnicity and family values finds that Native Americans have the highest family values, Anglo-Americans the lowest, and the other ethnic groups are somewhere between these two extremes. Given these data, the investigator may conclude that ethnic groups' differences in family values are due to sociological factors such as income level or rural residence or to psychological factors such as parenting style. However, such conclusions cannot be derived from the study itself, since the purpose of the research was to describe differences, not explain why the differences exist. While speculation about why there are differences is permissible, researchers should not transform speculation into conclusions based on ex post facto procedures.

Second, because of the ease with which research questions can be formed using ex post facto methodology, investigators must not simply pick variables out of thin air. Instead, the investigator should read previous research carefully and plan the study accordingly to reduce the likelihood that ex post facto outcomes will be used to answer poorly developed, vague questions such as Will groups differ? Through the careful analysis of previous literature, researchers can link results to well-conceived and precise expected outcomes, thereby reducing the possibility of misinterpreting data.

Another issue surrounding clarity and precision is the problem of operationally defining the levels of the independent variable. The ex post facto researcher must clearly define each between-group attribute so that membership in the group is readily apparent. The clearer the definition of group membership, the less likely it is that the data can be inaccurately generalized to a population not represented in the study. Using the smoking study as an example, consider what defines a smoker and a nonsmoker. Suppose that nonsmokers are defined as those who have never smoked, and the results show that nonsmokers have stronger hand grips than smokers. Can these results be generalized to people who did smoke but who stopped smoking in the last year or the last 5 years? These questions would not exist if the researcher had defined nonsmokers as those who have not smoked for the last 5 years.

Variables like ethnicity also require precise definition. What defines a Hispanic American? Does this group include only those with Hispanic surnames? Does it include Hispanic American females who adopt Anglo-American surnames? Does it exclude Anglo-American women who adopt Hispanic surnames? Does it include Puerto Ricans, Central Americans, or Cubans? To improve the clarity of demographic variables, ex post facto researchers can provide several categories defining ethnicity so that when identifying ethnicity on a form or a questionnaire, the participant will be more likely to identify their ethnic origin. Further, when using tests to define groups, such as a test of shyness to define high- versus low-shyness groups, the ex post facto researcher must carefully consider how valid (accurate) the test is with respect to classifying people's shyness.

As with all research types, use random sampling from a population, if possible, which in ex post facto research is the population of each group defining the levels of the independent variable. For example, if the ethnicity study in Table 8-4 revealed that there were 100 Hispanic Americans, 120 African Americans, 75 Native Americans, 90 Anglo-Americans, and 70 Asians, the researcher could randomly select 25 members of each of these groups. Again, the advantage is increased accuracy in generalizing the results to the target population specified.

One of the most significant problems with ex post facto research is the lack of internal validity—attributing the outcomes to group membership and not to other variables associated with group membership that might also explain the data. To improve the internal validity of ex post facto research, the researcher must identify (usually in the literature) potential confounds and then take steps to control for them. As one example, suppose that previous research shows that hand grip is highly correlated with diet and exercise regimes—the healthier the diet and exercise plan, the stronger the grip. Further, suppose that smokers have less healthy diets and exercise plans than nonsmokers. If the researcher conducted the study without controlling for group differences in diet and exercise, study results could be a function of diet and exercise group differences rather than the group difference selected for examination—smoking status.

To control for possible confounds, many of the strategies discussed in Chapter 5 are relevant. With respect to ex post facto research, several control methods are discussed briefly in the following paragraphs with reference to the studies in Table 8-4.

Before devising control methods, the researcher should demonstrate that the potential confound variable is indeed a confound for the sample under investigation. In other words, the researcher should conduct a statistical analysis to verify that groups differ on the supposed confound variable. If no group differences emerge, there is nothing to control for; on the other hand, if group differences on the confound do emerge, the researcher can resort to the following strategies.

One strategy is *matching*, which requires the identification of equivalent scores on the confounding variable across all groups of interest. As an example, suppose that health beliefs are related to health status—the more chronic the health problem, the more negative our beliefs about health. Since health status is a confound here, the researcher must identify similar health status outcomes for particular members of each group. Specifically, suppose that a subject with a Catholic preference obtains a health status score of 50 (extreme good health); another subject with an identical or very similar score would need to be identified in each of the other four groups. This process continues throughout the score range for health status until the researcher is confident that each group contains roughly equal distributions on the health status variable, thus eliminating it as a confound. The problem with matching is that if we know the groups differ on health status to begin with, it is difficult to find similar matches throughout all religious preferences. That is, if those with no religious preference have lower health beliefs, then matching individuals in the no-religion group with other religious groups that contain individuals with high health status is impeded.

Another control strategy is **homogeneous sampling**—or studying groups that are similar on the confound variable. For example, the researcher could select for study only those with high health status across the various religious groups. The major concern with this approach is that it limits generalization of results, in this case, to only those with high health status.

Finally, the ex post facto researcher can obtain data on the control variable and subsequently remove this variance from the dependent variable through the statistical process referred to as ANCOVA. This method is discussed in Chapter 10.

CONCLUDING COMMENTS

Having presented five unique descriptive research types, our purpose in this concluding section is to compare and contrast each of the descriptive methods. To begin this task, Table 8-5 presents a brief summary of key components of each descriptive method. The key elements are (1) type of research question usually asked, (2) how data collection typically proceeds, and (3) how statistical analysis may be accomplished.

Again, all descriptive researchers depict relationships between variables; none of the variables studied are manipulated by the investigator. Further, a third global similarity appears in Table 8-5, that is, the methods used to obtain data may be similar across the different descriptive types. For example, all descriptive researchers can collect data by administering a questionnaire or conducting a personal interview.

With regard to contrasts, Table 8-5 reveals that different descriptive researchers (1) focus on different research questions, (2) depict relationships in different ways, and (3) use different statistical techniques to analyze data. With respect to research questions, one basic distinction between descriptive methods is the explicit (or implicit) research question the researcher develops. Table 8-5 shows how various descriptive researchers seek to answer fundamentally different research questions. However, note that researchers can include different descriptive research questions within a single study, as Post-Kammer (1987) did, in combining the features of correlational, developmental, and ex post facto research.

While data may be obtained in a similar manner, the type of descriptive design determines how the data will be analyzed statistically. For example, a survey, correlational, and ex post facto researcher can obtain data using direct administration of a questionnaire. However, the data must be analyzed statistically in a way that is consistent with the research question and the descriptive method used to answer it. In the case of the survey data, statistical analysis is the calculation of percentages within categories, such as Watkins et al.'s (1987)

TABLE 8-5   Key elements of the five descriptive methods.

Descriptive Type	Research Plan Element		
	Research Question	Data Collection	Statistical Analyses
CASE STUDY	What is the condition? What is the treatment? How does behavior occur in natural environment?	Single case; repeated case; data collection via observation or patient report	None; anecdotal; subjective interpretation by researcher
SURVEY	What is the incidence? What is the prevalence? What percentage of the sample holds a particular belief?	Large sample; direct administration of questionnaire by mail, telephone, or personal interview	Percentages; frequencies
CORRELATIONAL	How do two or more variables relate?	Can be same as survey but usually direct administration; at least two scores obtained for each subject	Pearson correlation; multiple regression; factor analysis
DEVELOPMENTAL	What are time-related changes in human behavior differing on some time-related variable such as age, grade, or years on job?	Diverse methods— standardized tests, observation, interview	ANOVA; ANCOVA; t tests
EX POST FACTO	How do categories of independent variable relate to dependent variable?	Can use any survey method; sample consists of people differing on attribute of interest	Same as with developmental

display of percentages of the sample with various beliefs and practices. In contrast, the correlational researcher asks a different kind of question, such as, What is the relationship between theoretical orientation and view of practice? The correlational method therefore requires a correlational statistical technique. The ex post facto researcher could ask, Are there gender differences in theoretical orientation? In this case, a t test could be used with gender of the sample treated as an independent variable with two levels (male and female) and theoretical orientation as the dependent variable.

EXERCISES

1. Assume you are interested in whether a child's ethnicity is related to placement in special education classes. Select a descriptive research method to study this potential relationship and defend your choice.

2. For each of the four major descriptive methods, name the single extraneous variable you believe most relevant to internal validity. Defend your choices.

3. Jane is a master's-level counseling student and is employed part time at a state funded outpatient drug and alcohol facility which serves children and adolescents. Jane notices after working with this population that the majority of clients exhibit low self-esteem, particularly in the area of physical image. None of the clients participate in any type of extra-curricular activities after school. The only type of social event these clients engage in is "partying" with their friends after school and on weekends. Jane begins to wonder if there is a relationship between her clients' inactive lifestyle and corresponding low self-esteem and poor body image. Given this research scenario, do the following:
   a. Identify potential independent and dependent variables.
   b. Describe how Jane could use correlational research to assess whether physical exercise is related to self-esteem.
   c. Assume Jane follows an adolescent group of 20 subjects, 10 getting the physical fitness training, the other 10 acting as a no-treatment control. Identify variables which may be threats to the internal validity of her study.

4. Examine the White and Franzoni paper in Appendix E, and determine why it is a descriptive study. To which category of descriptive research does it belong? Does it belong to just one descriptive category?

5. For those exploring a thesis, determine if your proposed research is descriptive. If any aspect of the research is descriptive, which type is it? What are the primary advantages and disadvantages in your case? How can you remedy any negative features?

9

UNDERSTANDING AND DESIGNING QUASI-EXPERIMENTAL AND EXPERIMENTAL RESEARCH STUDIES

MARIA'S ORIGINAL RESEARCH PLAN required her to administer different treatments to subjects in one of two groups—educational or multifaceted. Maria's plan now meets the three general criteria defining experimental research. First, she plans to manipulate at least one independent variable—the group counseling format. Second, she will do her utmost to control the various sources of invalidity she now knows about. For example, she might have another therapist run the two groups to reduce experimenter bias. She might also eliminate the pretest so as to cancel testing effects. She might also monitor the two groups closely to ensure that each group is being treated in the standardized fashion she initially envisioned. Finally, once Maria has selected her sample of 50 subjects, she will randomly assign 25 subjects to each of the two counseling groups. Maria knows that random assignment to groups is a process unique to experimental research and one that sets experimental and quasi-experimental investigations apart.

In Chapter 8, we noted one central theme of experimental research, namely, manipulating variables to determine cause and effect relationships. That is, in experimental research, the levels of the independent variable are deliberately constructed by the investigator to examine how these levels affect the dependent variable.

In the helping professions, the number of variables that can be manipulated is seemingly limitless. Variables range from global conditions like counseling format or office environment to more subtle manipulations like verbally praising clients' positive self-statements or altering a single sentence in giving feedback to student trainees. Of course, not all variables can be manipulated; height, for example, cannot be changed. As we have noted also, many variables could be manipulated, but subjects would never consent to such manipulations. A researcher would not succeed, for instance, in getting parents to give up their newborns so the effects of environment and heredity on intelligence could be examined.

ADVANTAGES AND DISADVANTAGES OF EXPERIMENTAL RESEARCH

Experimental researchers can increase the internal validity of their studies by maximizing the effects of the independent variable, minimizing extraneous variables, and controlling for error variables. Since experimental researchers manipulate the independent variable, they define how the levels of this variable will be delivered. For example, Maria can create the multifaceted and educational groups to follow prescribed techniques that define each of these two formats. Her goal would be to keep the multifaceted group just that—a mixture of cognitive therapy, empowerment, self-esteem building, and all other elements that define the multifaceted treatment approach. On the other hand, Maria wants to inform and teach people about proper dieting in the educational group. Thus, by defining the approaches and techniques in each group, Maria can differentiate the two levels of her independent variable. Thus, she can maximize the influence of this variable on her dependent variable.

Another advantage of experimental research is the amount of control the researcher can exert. However, this systematic administration of variables in experimental research conjures up stereotypes associated with an experiment: images of the laboratory—investigators in white coats, rooms with strong lighting and white walls, no posters, plants, or windows, and fixed temperatures. The aim of control, though, is to reduce inconsistencies in the research environment that lead to error in subjects, procedures, or measurement.

Experimental researchers in the helping professions often conduct studies outside the laboratory; therefore, they cannot control all environmental stimulation such as sound, temperature, or different clothing. However, the ideal of standardized data collection always exists in experimental research whether the study is performed in a laboratory or in a more natural setting. For example, although Maria will conduct her study in a nonlaboratory setting, she will still be responsible for ensuring that the treatment process is as standardized as possible.

Finally, experimental researchers randomly assign subjects to levels of the independent variable. As noted in Chapter 5, this procedure is effective in controlling for many extraneous variables. Random assignment is a unique procedure in experimental study, one that highlights the difference between experimental and quasi-experimental research.

Typically, subjects are randomly assigned to either an experimental or a control group. We prefer to call it a comparison group because the term control group implies that extraneous variables are controlled by this procedure. Specifically, cause and effect relationships are strengthened if the group receiving the experimental manipulation improves relative to the comparison group.

All experimental investigators face several conspicuous problems. Ironically, these problems are created by the very themes that contribute to the advantages of experimental research. For example, because independent variables are manipulated, some sources of invalidity are particularly threatening: subject bias, experimenter bias, and mortality.

With respect to subject bias, the major concern in experimental research is between-group communication. This occurs when subjects in different experimental groups learn of differences in their treatment protocol. Neale and Liebert (1986) cite three subject coping strategies that may develop from between-group communication. One is **compensatory equalization of treatments,** when subjects in one group perceive that subjects in the other group are receiving more beneficial experiences. This perception may lead them to demand that their group receive similar treatment. Using Maria's study to illustrate, members in the educational groups may learn that in the multifaceted sessions clients are encouraged to discuss feelings about body image. Because self-exploration of feelings is not an aspect of the educational group, members of this group might insist that Maria allow members to express attitudes about body image. If she acquiesces and allows the educational group to self-explore, she equalizes the groups and masks the true differences between the variables.

Another subject attitude is **compensatory rivalry.** This occurs when subjects in a comparison group learn that subjects in the treatment group are expected to do better than they are. Such knowledge often results in the comparison subjects working extra hard to see that the expected effect does not occur. If, for instance, Maria compared the multifaceted group with a wait-list comparison group, subjects in this latter group may try to reduce the expected superiority of the treated group by regulating their eating patterns. Therefore, the relationships between variables would no longer be valid as originally proposed, because the comparison group is no longer a comparison group but a self-treated group.

Finally, the exact opposite of compensatory rivalry can occur, which is **resentful demoralization.** As with compensatory rivalry, this happens when comparison subjects learn that another group is receiving more beneficial treatment. However, instead of compensating, subjects in the comparison group become angry, disillusioned, and less motivated—attitudes that can adversely affect their status on the dependent variable. Instead of masking the effects of the independent variable on the dependent variable as the other three subject biases do, this problem creates artificial differences between groups on the dependent measure. For example, if Maria were to use a wait-list comparison group, these subjects might become bored and unmotivated during the course of the study. These feelings might result in a worsening of eating behavior. Maria's measures of eating habits after the study might then show a spuriously great difference between the multifaceted and wait-list group. Again, these subject attitudes can become extraneous variables that affect study results.

Besides subject bias, experimenter bias can be a concern, especially if the experimenter is administering different levels of the independent variable. For example, if Maria conducts both multifaceted and educational groups, she could easily become more enthusiastic, energetic, and interested in the multifaceted group. In contrast, she might approach the educational group in a more unappealing, disinterested manner. Thus, differences between the two groups might not reflect the real meaning of the groups but rather how the therapist's attitude prevented her from conducting the groups as originally intended. Recall that in Chapter 5 we discussed how Maria's experimental bias could result in an instrumentation effect if she runs one group more optimally than another. Even if Maria does have other researchers run the groups, however, an instrumentation effect could still be possible. In the absence of data showing the equality of treatment providers throughout the course of the study, instrumentation effect is always a possibility.

A possible result of subject and experimenter biases, especially resentful demoralization, is that subjects in the group of less interest may become disillusioned by the effectiveness of the other group. This may result in subjects dropping out of the study, thus increasing the potential for mortality effects.

Finally, one potential disadvantage of experimental research is the lack of generalizability of results from an experimental environment such as a laboratory to the real world. When levels of the independent variable are so tightly defined and controlled, the situation loses its meaning as a real-life analogue. In other words, by being too controlled, the setting of the study becomes increasingly contrived and artificial and is not likely to be relevant to a real counseling setting, a real classroom, or a real family interaction. As we noted in Chapter 6, making the research context more lifelike is the purpose of analogue research.

In Table 9-1, we summarize the advantages and disadvantages of experimental research.

RECOMMENDATIONS

The following recommendations are provided to help reduce potential problems with experimental research. There are unique types of subject bias related to experimental research, and we provide strategies related to between-group communication first.

TABLE 9-1 Advantages and disadvantages of experiments.

Advantages	Disadvantages
Maximize effects of independent variable	Demand characteristics Compensatory equalization Compensatory resentment Resentful demoralization
Minimize systematic error	Experimenter bias Instrumentation effect Mortality
Control extraneous variables through random assignment	Generalization

One strategy is related to the duration of treatment. If the researcher is studying different treatment approaches, the treatments should be given in the smallest amount of time needed to be effective. The longer the study, the more likely subjects are to discuss group formats. Another tactic is to treat groups in different geographical areas, reducing the chance that members of different groups will communicate.

Further, using a placebo-comparison group can minimize the possibility of between-group communication, because when subjects in a wait-list control group learn that they are being compared with an experimental treatment, they will demand equality, play the underdog with compensated energy to improve dependent variable status, or become demoralized. Therefore, rather than using a no-treatment group, the researcher can use a placebo group. A **placebo group** is one that gets some form of treatment, perhaps a comparison treatment, or several components of the experimental treatment but not the critical ones. In this way, subjects' tendencies to equate, play the underdog, or be demoralized will be reduced.

Experimenter bias is also a problem in experimental research. The most common way of preventing that is to have someone other than the principal investigator—research assistants or data collectors—run the experimental groups. By keeping those responsible for administering the groups unaware of the research question and hypotheses, that is, **data collection-blind,** the chance that the data collector will contaminate the groups is lessened.

With regard to instrumentation, it is useful to collect information about how well the groups are conducted and to collect these data at different times in the treatment program. Recall that Maria had her supervisor rate her counseling effectiveness for each treatment at two different times in the study.

As for mortality, keeping the possibility of between-group communication to a minimum should lessen the chance that negative attitudes will develop in the comparison treatment group. Further, the use of a placebo group should reduce perceived discrepancies between subjects in different groups. Even if some subjects in the comparison group do prematurely end their participation, these subjects may not differ from subjects still participating in either group. As noted in Chapter 5, pretest data or other information about subjects who discontinue can be used to see whether or not there are systematic differences between subjects who end participation and subjects who continue.

The degree to which data in an experiment can be generalized to other settings requires resolution through continued research. Specifically, researchers can conduct further studies that more closely approximate a natural context. It is nonsensical to request that experimental researchers relinquish the control sometimes afforded by a laboratory setting. However, the more controlled the environment, the more artificial this setting may become. In trying to find a balance between controlled environments and natural settings, some researchers conduct **field experiments,** which have all the qualities of experimental research but are conducted outside the laboratory. Maria's research study is best classified as a field experiment, because she is conducting experimental research in the field—in the University Counseling Center.

To facilitate the understanding of experimental research, we divide experiments into two categories—simple and complex. The distinction between these categories is based on a single, easily identifiable criterion—the number of independent variables studied.

SIMPLE EXPERIMENTAL DESIGN

Experimental studies vary on a continuum ranging from very simple to very complex. When conducting a **simple experiment,** the researcher studies the effects of one independent variable with two or more levels (groups), on one or more dependent variables. Maria's study is an example of a simple experiment. She will examine one independent variable (type of counseling) with two levels (multifaceted or educational) and one dependent variable (BULIT-R). On the other hand, a complex experimental study would be the manipulation of two or more independent variables, with subjects randomly assigned to the levels of at least one of these variables. While the number of dependent variables is not important in categorizing experimental research, the addition of a second independent variable, whether manipulated or not, makes the design more complex and allows the researcher to examine several different effects. We now discuss a commonly encountered, simple experimental design.

Posttest-Only Comparison Group Design

A frequently employed simple experimental design is the **posttest-only comparison group design,** in which the investigator uses a comparison group that receives no form of intervention. The design can be represented as:

R   X   O
R   O

R = random assignment to group
X = intervention
O = dependent variable

The design calls for random assignment of subjects to two groups—one getting X, the other not getting X—and then measuring the two groups on some dependent variable. Maria's design is very similar; the only difference is that her comparison group receives some form of treatment, as shown below:

R   X1   O
R   X2   O

R   = random assignment to group
X1 = multifaceted intervention
X2 = educational intervention
O   = dependent variable

There are many variations of simple experimental designs. For example, a researcher could study two treatments and a no-treatment group, producing three levels of a single independent variable—type of treatment. Further, most researchers who study a single independent variable look at the effects of this variable on several dependent variables, like scores on different tests. An example of this type of simple experimental design is presented next.

Illustration from the Literature

White, Williams, Alexander, Powell-Cope, and Conlon (1990) examined the effectiveness of different types of bedtime routines for hospitalized children. Specifically, these researchers were interested in the effects of bedtime stories on hospitalized children's length of time to fall asleep, incidence of distress, and duration of self-soothing behaviors. The outcomes of the study were seen as important to the nursing staff, especially in their effort to make children's hospital stay as comfortable as possible.

Subjects were 94 children and their parents, with the children's ages ranging from 3 to 8 years. Children were included in the study if their hospitalization was to last at least two consecutive nights and if they had received no medications that might affect their sleep 24 hours before hospital admission. Children were randomly assigned to one of four groups, three of which required that parents not be present at bedtime. These groups were defined as follows: (1) 16 children heard a parent-recorded story (PRS) before bedtime; (2) 14 children listened to a stranger-recorded story (SRS); and (3) 17 children did not listen to a story (NOS). The fourth group of 47 children and parents was also included and the parents were required to be present at bedtime, although no story was included (PPB).

The groups were hypothesized to affect three variables: (1) length of time to fall asleep, a variable referred to as sleep onset latency (SOL); (2) the incidence of distress, such as whimpering or the aggressive handling of self or toys; and (3) frequency and duration of self-soothing behaviors such as the purposeful touching of self or objects.

The results of the study showed that the groups differed for SOL and distress behaviors but not for self-soothing indicators. For sleep onset, the pattern was PRS > PPB > SRS = NOS. In other words, children who heard a parent-recorded story (PRS) took the greatest amount of time to fall asleep. While children in the PPB condition required significantly less time to fall asleep than the PRS group, both these groups took significantly more time than children who heard no story (NOS) or heard a stranger-recorded story (SRS). As for distress, the group outcomes were PRS > SRS = NOS = PPB, showing again that when children heard their parents' voices they were in more distress than children in any of the other groups. More impressive is that these differences remained when other potentially confounding variables such as SOL at home, observers, child's age, and first night SOL were controlled for statistically.

Advantages and Disadvantages of the Simple Experiment

The advantages of the simple experimental design pertain to just that—simplicity. When experimental researchers manipulate a single independent variable, both the practical factors of time and cost are lessened. For example, relative to more complex experimental designs, researchers conducting simple experiments typically do not require as many subjects; thus they spend less time locating and recruiting subjects, and they save money in materials.

Simple experimental studies are easier to read and understand than more complex experiments. Readers of simple experimental research are usually able to recognize the lone independent variable and the dependent measure (or measures), which helps in accurate comprehension of the major findings of the study. One disadvantage of simple experimental design is that being simple means reducing the number of variables under investigation. Thus, the researcher is restricted to conclusions regarding one variable, although any of several other potential independent variables may interact with the variable under study. Since human behavior is so complex in nature, it may be more prudent to study the effects of several different variables—which is precisely the rationale for conducting complex experimental studies.

Recommendations

The simple experiment serves a useful purpose. Maria's study is a case in point. If the research question is supported by current literature, researchers should adopt a simple experimental design. As always, the tenets of MAXMINCON (see Chapter 5) need consideration, and hence the researcher must design the study to increase internal validity. Note that blocking cannot be achieved in a simple experiment, because the blocked variable becomes a second independent variable, which identifies the design not as a simple design, but a complex design—discussed next.

COMPLEX EXPERIMENTAL DESIGNS

Human behavior is the result of a complex interaction of variables, and when only one variable is studied, conclusions are necessarily limited. Thus, some researchers choose to examine several independent variables at once. This type of experiment is known as a **complex experiment** or **factorial** design. Complex experiments occur when an investigator examines the effects of at least two independent variables on one or more dependent variables. Of course, the investigator must also meet the three general criteria of experimental research: (1) the manipulation of at least one independent variable, (2) minimization of error by systematic data collection, and (3) random assignment of subjects to different levels of at least one independent variable. In terms of the second independent variable, this variable may or may not be manipulated. Again, since the basic requirement for an experiment is manipulation of at least one independent variable, it is not necessary for the second variable to be manipulated.

In complex experiments, the reader will often see references to designs that are 2 × 2 or 3 × 2 × 3, and so on. These numbers define the number of independent variables and the number of levels of each independent variable.

Treatment Type

	Educational	Multifaceted
SES Low		
High		

FIGURE 9-1   A 2 × 2 experimental design.

For example, in a 2 × 2 design, there are two independent variables (the number of numbers), each with two levels. In the second case, there are three independent variables—two with three levels and one with two.

To illustrate the complex experiment, suppose that Maria wants to include SES as a second variable. (Assume that previous research pertains to this variable.) SES is an attribute of subjects and therefore is not manipulated, so her purpose would be to examine the separate and interactive effects of SES and treatment type on her dependent variable (bulimic episodes). Her new design is represented in Figure 9-1. Contrast her new design with her simple experiment, which if represented in box format, would look like Figure 9-2. Note that by adding a second independent variable (SES) with two levels (high and low), Maria has doubled the number of **cells** in her study. Each cell refers to the particular combination of the levels of independent variable(s) the subject receives (more simply, the number of boxes). Each cell is unique in her study, because it represents a separate combination of levels of each independent variable. This design is also referred to as a completely **between-subject** design, because subjects are placed in one of the four cells. In other words, subjects in her study will get just one of the following four combinations:

Low SES—Educational
Low SES—Multifaceted
High SES—Educational
High SES—Multifaceted

The opposite of between-subject designs are **within-subject** designs in which each subject passes through at least two cells. In other words, in a within-subject design, the same group of subjects is always measured at least twice, hence the descriptor, **repeated measures.**

Treatment Type

Educational	Multifaceted

FIGURE 9-2   A one-way experimental design.

There are two basic within-subject designs. First, researchers can construct a within-subject independent variable and then measure the effects of this variable on the dependent variable. Suppose, for example, Maria included, in addition to her two treatments, an additional independent variable—the gender of each group leader. She might have subjects in the multifaceted group receive this intervention from first the male, then the female group leaders. The educational subjects would also receive treatment in the same male, female therapist sequence. This design is illustrated in Figure 9-3. Note that Maria is combining both between- and within-subject elements. For example, treatment type is a completely between-subject variable; leader gender, the added independent variable, is a within-subject variable. As the design shows, subjects pass through two cells within each treatment so that group leader gender is said to be **nested** within treatment type. This design is also a 2 × 2, with treatment type completely between-subject and group leader gender within-subject, nested in treatment.

In our review of the current periodicals in human service professions, we found that researchers rarely adopt this type of within-subject design. It is easy to see why. In Maria's study, subjects would receive essentially the same treatment program twice, either multifaceted or educational, with only leader gender differing in the second treatment application. This may increase several threats to internal validity. The obvious benefit is the increase in external validity, since the treatment is replicated with leaders of different genders.

Researchers should consider nesting a within-subject variable in a completely between-subject variable if they feel it will answer their research questions. For Maria, this design makes little sense. If she did want to include group leader gender, she could more appropriately determine the effects of gender with the completely between-subject design.

The second application of within-subject design is commonly encountered in helping profession research. Note that since the primary characteristic of within-subject designs is the repeated measurement of subjects, pretest and posttest designs technically qualify as within-subject designs; subjects are measured at least twice. Thus, the second type of within-subject design includes studies with repeated measurement of the dependent variable but no creation of a second independent variable. Rather, time of measurement is the second independent variable, with at least two levels—time 1 (pretest) and time 2 (posttest).

As an example, assume that Maria pretests and posttests her bulimic subjects. From a complex, factorial perspective, her design is represented in Figure 9-4. Again, her design is referred to as a 2 (treatment type) × 2 (time) design, with treatment type completely between-subject and time nested within treatment. The BULIT-R is still Maria's dependent variable; the time of measurement of the BULIT-R becomes the second independent variable. Because this design is frequently encountered in the human service literature, we next provide an example.

Illustration from the Literature

A study by Gift, Moore, and Soeken (1992) nicely illustrates a complex, factorial design as it pertains to nursing research. The researchers studied three inde-

Treatment Type

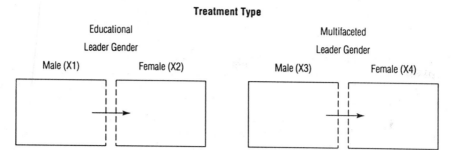

FIGURE 9-3   One between-subject independent variable (treatment type), one within-subject independent variable (leader gender).

pendent variables, one between-group, the other two repeated measures. A summary of the study follows.

The researchers were interested in reducing dyspnea, the sensation of difficult breathing, among a sample of chronic obstructive pulmonary disease (COPD) patients. In their literature review, they note that dyspnea is the most frequently cited problem among COPD patients and yet, very few obtained relief for this symptom. The authors believed that anxiety exacerbates dyspnea and that a treatment program targeting anxiety might simultaneously improve dyspnea. Thus, since relaxation training is proven to be effective in lowering anxiety, the authors describe the purpose of their study as testing the effectiveness of a taped relaxation message in reducing dyspnea and anxiety in COPD patients.

The authors used a convenience sample of 26 subjects (8 subjects left the study) from the patient population of 3 private physicians. All subjects met the diagnostic criterion for COPD, currently experienced dyspnea, and had an average age of 67. The group was predominately female.

The 26 participants were randomly assigned to one of two groups. In the treatment group, 13 subjects were seen individually at their physician's office. They viewed a prerecorded tape that showed them progressive relaxation techniques for tension release in 16 muscle groups and were given the tape to take home to practice. By contrast, the 13 comparison subjects were told to

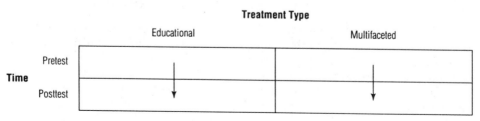

FIGURE 9-4   Design for two-group, pretest and posttest.

relax and sit quietly for 20 minutes and to do the same at home. After their initial visit, all subjects returned to their physician's office three times at weekly intervals.

Two sets of dependent variables were measured. The first set, consisting of skin temperature, heart rate, and respiratory rate were taken at the beginning and the end of each of the four sessions. The researchers used these measures to assess the relative effectiveness of the relaxation tape, setting specific pre- and posttreatment criteria as documentation that relaxation had been achieved. For example, skin temperature elevations of 2° F indicated that relaxation had occurred. Similar criteria were set for heart and respiratory rate; both decrease with relaxation.

Analyses on the first set of dependent variables consisted of a $2 \times 2 \times 4$ factorial analysis of variance. The three independent variables were Group (treatment versus comparison), Time (pre versus post), and Session (one through four). Statistical analyses revealed that, relative to the comparison group, (1) the treatment group had elevated skin temperature for all four sessions, while the comparison group did not; (2) the treatment group had lowered respiratory rates for all four sessions, while the comparison group lowered their respiratory rates for only one session; and (3) both groups were able to lower their heart rates for all four sessions.

The researchers analyzed a second set of dependent variables, those related to dyspnea, relaxation, and airway obstruction. Anxiety was assessed using the Spielberger Anxiety Inventory, a self-report scale designed to measure state anxiety (transitory feelings of tension and apprehension) and trait anxiety (enduring disposition to perceive situations as threatening). Each of these two scales is measured by a 20-item inventory in which subjects indicate how they feel right now (state) and how they usually feel (trait). Respondents rate each statement on a scale in which 1 = not at all and 4 = very much so. The examinee receives a total score for each of the two scales.

The second group of dependent variables was measured at the beginning and conclusion of the study. Thus, the researchers were interested in pre-post changes between the two groups, analyzing these data using a 2×2 repeated (pre and post) measures analysis of variance. In sum, the treatment group, when compared to the comparison group, showed significant pre to post reduction in anxiety and dyspnea and were able to increase Peak Expiratory Flow Rate (PEFR), thus reducing airway obstruction.

Advantages and Disadvantages of Complex Experiments

As with simple experimental research, more complex experimental studies share the advantage of using manipulated independent variables, control, and random assignment. In comparison to simple experiments, complex experiments provide more information about the individual and interactive effects of independent variables. Basically, complex studies provide more information than do simple experiments. The Gift et al. (1992) study illustrates just how much information can be obtained from a complex experiment.

Similarly, consider Maria's completely between-subject design noted earlier.

By adding the SES variable, she would be combining two separate studies in one—a simple experiment with treatment type and an ex post facto study (the attribute of SES). If she had manipulated the second independent variable, for example, used brief versus long-term therapy and assigned subjects randomly to one of the four cells, then she would have been conducting two simple experiments in one study—one examining treatment type, the other length of therapy. Clearly, complex studies provide much information in a single investigation.

Unfortunately, since complex experimental research yields a large amount of information, this type of study is more costly and requires more time to complete than a simple experiment. Similarly, the more independent variables there are, the more difficult it can be to understand the content of the research report.

Specific advantages and disadvantages also can be outlined for between-subject and within-subject designs. Completely between-subject designs capitalize on random assignment, minimize the time required to complete the study, and also allow for the determination of an experimental effect. The beauty of any between-subject design is that it affords the opportunity for random assignment to groups, and, as we noted in Chapter 5, random assignment is the single most effective way to increase the internal validity of a study.

Compared to within-subject designs, between-subject designs do not require as much time to complete. This is clearly noted in a contrast of Maria's completely between-subject versus completely within-subject plans. If we assume, as Maria originally proposed, that 3 months is the amount of time required for the treatment to affect the dependent variable, then in her between-subject design, 3 months is the amount of time needed as long as both groups are run concurrently. On the other hand, assuming the same amount of time was needed in her within-subject plan, Maria would need 3 months for each cell. Since subjects pass through two cells, a total of 6 months would be required for subjects to participate in each treatment phase.

Finally, in studies in which two or more between-subject groups are formed, the researcher can determine the magnitude of the effectiveness of the group of most interest. For example, Maria could determine exactly how effective the multifaceted treatment was relative to the educational treatment. This numerical index of experimental treatment effectiveness is referred to as *effect size* and was discussed in Chapter 6.

Unfortunately, by assigning subjects to different levels of the independent variable, the researcher is also setting up a situation in which the groups can differ on extraneous variables. This may reduce the internal validity of the study. Although we noted that random assignment is the single most effective way to reduce extraneous influences, even random assignment does not entirely eliminate between-group differences; it only minimizes the chances of large differences.

Also, between-subject designs require more subjects than within-subject designs. For example, in Maria's completely between-subject design, four cells are formed, and it is usually agreed that each cell requires at least 20 subjects. That means Maria will need 80 subjects—probably more to compensate for dropouts. Further, depending on the general SES level of the community where she conducts her study, she might have to screen many more subjects than she actually needs to get the same number (40) in each SES group (high versus low). On the other hand, in Maria's within-subject design, if subjects pass through two cells, only 40 subjects would be required instead of 80.

One advantage of within-subject designs is the need for fewer subjects: but the most important benefit is that each subject serves as his or her own control. That is, when subjects pass through each cell, they are being compared with themselves, leaving only the levels of the independent variable to account for changes in the dependent variable. The logic in within-subject studies is that the best way to assure that groups are equal is to have the same subjects in each group.

The disadvantage of within-subject designs, as previously noted, is the amount of time needed for subjects to complete all cells. However, there is another major disadvantage for within-subject designs, namely that of **order effects**. This occurs when treatment effects are due to the order in which treatment is received and not to the treatment per se. For example, having received one treatment, subjects may be more tired, disappointed, and less motivated when they receive the second treatment. If this occurs, the second treatment will show less positive effect when compared to the first condition, even though the second treatment might actually be more positive if received either first or by itself. For example, if subjects in Maria's study receive male, then female leaders, measurement after the female-led groups may show more negative effects simply because the female group leaders followed male group leaders. In our recommendations section, we provide a procedure for overcoming order effects indigenous to within-subject designs. Table 9-2 summarizes the general advantages and disadvantages of complex experiments, as well as the specific pros and cons of between- and within-subject complex experiments.

Recommendations

Clearly, a researcher has many options when considering a complex, factorial study. In fact, while the disadvantages of complex experiments are the same

TABLE 9-2 Advantages and disadvantages of simple and complex experiments.

	Advantages	Disadvantages
SIMPLE	Less time and cost Easier to comprehend	Limited conclusions
COMPLEX	Unique and interactive effects of independent variables	More time and cost More difficult to understand
1. Between-subject	Random assignment Less time than within-subject	Extraneous variables More subjects needed than for within-subject
2. Within-subject	Each subject is own control Fewer subjects needed than for between-subject	More time needed than for between-subject Order effects

Client Problem

	Relationship	Vocational
Directive		
Nondirective		

Social Worker Style (row label)

FIGURE 9-5 Example of one fixed independent variable (client problem) and one random independent variable (social worker style).

disadvantages relative to simple experiments, concerns like time, cost, and readability vary greatly with the type of study. Sometimes these disadvantages will be minimal. For example, consider a clinical social worker who wants to study the interaction between client problem and counselor style and designs a three-page script for subjects to read, after which they rate counselor effectiveness. This researcher develops four packets, each with a unique combination of independent variables as indicated in Figure 9-5.

After sampling from a target population, the researcher will have subjects read a script and then rate the hypothetical counselor on counseling effectiveness. Note that much of the cost will be for obtaining and producing materials such as scripts and the rating scale of counselor effectiveness. Upon entering the room, groups of subjects can be randomly assigned a packet so that data collection may be completed in a week, perhaps less. And, if the researcher can understand the results and write them clearly, the previously listed disadvantages are greatly reduced.

However, as previously noted, one perpetual difficulty when using a within-subject design is order effects. The problem was illustrated when we considered what would happen if Maria nested leader gender, a within-subject variable, in her completely between-subject variable, treatment type. Here, Maria could **counterbalance** the order of leader gender, by randomly assigning subjects to different orders. Some could get a male leader first, the others a female first. In essence, order of treatment would become another between-subject variable, as illustrated in Figure 9-6.

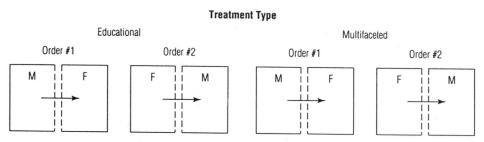

FIGURE 9-6 A counterbalanced two between- (treatment type and order) and one within-subject (leader gender) design.

By randomly assigning subjects to one of two different treatment orders, Maria can assess the effects of order. For example, if we presume that females followed males, as indicated earlier, and that female-led groups suffered because of this arrangement, this new design would allow Maria to assess the effects of female-led groups when subjects receive this condition first. In essence, Maria can examine order effects because each within-subject condition is reversed for both groups.

Besides the random assignment of subjects to orders, another common method for evaluating order effects is called the **Latin square design.** In this approach, the researcher systematically orders the levels of the independent variable so that no level appears twice on the same row or column for each group. The Latin square approach is used when designs are completely within-subject, which occurs when subjects pass through all conditions. This happens when, for example, one independent variable is manipulated with three levels, and subjects are measured after receiving each level. An example would be measuring subjects' perceptions of social worker skill after exposure to a worker having each of three disability types—social workers with an amputated limb (X1), social workers who are blind (X2), and social workers who have no physical disability (X3).

Like the counterbalancing procedure described earlier, researchers can use the Latin square design to assess the effects of order by systematically arranging conditions as shown in Figure 9-7. Note how the Latin square method of ordering conditions precludes conditions from appearing twice in the same row or column.

A final note about Latin square and completely within-subject designs is necessary. First, the Latin square design can be used in complex, factorial designs, but for simplicity of explanation we chose a simple experiment with one independent variable.

Also with respect to completely within-subject designs, if the previously mentioned researcher interested in client perceptions of social workers did not use a method for counterbalancing the order of disability types, the study would not qualify as an experiment, because subjects would not be randomly assigned to levels. Instead, all subjects would pass through all conditions in the same order, eliminating the use of random assignment. However, researchers usually use counterbalancing techniques; by doing so, they create "between-group" on the order subjects receive each condition. For example, three between-group orders were created by using the Latin square in the social worker disability study, and subjects could be randomly assigned to each of these orders.

Concluding Comments About Complex Experiments

Although we presented several subtle manipulations in experimental design, there are seemingly endless nuances in experimental procedures. We cannot cover the large number of experimental designs, but we hope you can accurately represent independent variables and their levels and can comprehend both simple and complex experimental research.

All experimental researchers, whether they are using simple or complex

Group			
1	X1	X2	X3 **0**
2	X2	X3 **0**	X1
3	X3 **0**	X1	X2

NOTE: Observations would be obtained after each treatment. "0" indicates the three that would be averaged to determine the effectiveness of X3.

FIGURE 9-7 Latin square design.

designs, share the advantage of random assignment of subjects, because, as we noted in Chapter 5, this method best increases the internal validity of the results. Unfortunately, random assignment is sometimes difficult in the helping professions. We now discuss a group of research types in which random assignment does not occur, but the other two criteria of experimentation are met—an independent variable is manipulated and data are collected systematically.

QUASI-EXPERIMENTAL DESIGNS

To illustrate quasi-experimental research, let us return to Maria's study and slightly alter her procedure for recruiting subjects. Assume that Maria obtains 25 bulimic subjects from the University Counseling Center and another 25 bulimic subjects from a mental health agency in town. Assume further that the mode of treatment for bulimic subjects at the mental health center is educational. In this situation, Maria already has a preexisting group that can be used for comparison to her multifaceted treatment groups.

What is the major difference between this situation and her simple experiment? The difference is random assignment. The only difference between true experiments and quasi-experiments is random assignment, which occurs only in the former. Quasi-experiments thus define all situations in which (1) the researcher manipulates at least one independent variable; (2) the researcher exerts control in the form of standardized data collection and possibly the use of a control group; and (3) random assignment of subjects to groups is not possible because of practical or ethical constraints.

Random assignment is of course a great advantage, but it is not always possible, especially in the helping professions. One practical impediment to random assignment is that preexisting groups already exist, which the researcher lacks authority to alter. Examples of intact groups would be workers in one of three shifts (morning, evening, graveyard), students in different types of graduate programs (school, general counseling), students of different classroom teachers (Mr. Jones, Ms. Smith), or patients in psychiatric wards (schizophrenic, mood, substance abuse). Since intact groups are frequently encountered by researchers, quasi-experiments serve a useful purpose.

Consider the case of a researcher interested in the effects of group consultation on psychiatric nurses' (PN) job morale and satisfaction. Suppose that administrators of a psychiatric hospital decide that only the morning shift will employ a new weekly PN group consultation practice, while the other two shifts (evening and graveyard) will maintain current practice. The researcher must take the groups as they exist and compare the morning group with one or both of the unchanged groups. Random assignment is not possible here; the researcher cannot put all the nurses' names in a hat and randomly select nurses to receive group consultation. Some nurses may be working other jobs or have other commitments that preclude their participation in the morning shift. In sum, intact groups exist for various reasons, and the researcher may have no authority to change these groups.

A second impediment to random assignment is that the use of comparison groups who receive no treatment, such as a wait-list group, is sometimes unethical. For example, if Maria compared multifaceted treatment with a wait-list group and randomly assigned subjects to these two groups, a subject with serious, life-threatening bulimia may, through random assignment, be selected for the wait-list group. Clearly, having the subject wait for treatment would be unethical.

In terms of the MAXMINCON principle (see Chapter 5), quasi-experiments, like true experiments, share the advantage of maximizing the effects of the independent variable and minimizing error. For example, the quasi-experimental researcher, by manipulating the independent variable, exerts some control over how the levels of this variable will influence the dependent measure.

As for minimizing error variables, quasi-experimental researchers typically cannot manage the research environment to the same degree as true experimental researchers. This is because quasi-experimental researchers, by virtue of using preexisting groups, tend to conduct investigations in more naturalistic settings. For example, rather than having subjects participate in laboratory settings, quasi-experimental researchers may examine variables in the field—in counseling clinics, hospitals, and classrooms. As previously mentioned with true experiments, this can be viewed as both an advantage and disadvantage.

Of course, without random assignment, the major drawback of quasi-experimental research is the lack of control over extraneous variables. Specifically, when intact groups are used, selection bias is automatically created, because the researcher administers different levels of the independent variable to different groups. Thus, naturally occurring differences between the groups may explain the results. These alternate explanations compete with the desired conclusion—that the independent variable, and nothing else, caused changes in the dependent variable.

As an example, consider the group consultation study with psychiatric nurses. The researcher will administer the group consultation to one sample—the morning shift—and not to the other two samples—the evening and graveyard shifts. However, reasons that PNs select particular shifts may reflect a host of potential extraneous variables related to job morale and satisfaction. For example, suppose that PNs who want morning shifts have family commitments in the late afternoon and early evening, while evening and graveyard PNs tend to have fewer family commitments. Suppose that many evening and graveyard PNs are concurrently enrolled in graduate degree programs, while this is not so with the morning shift. Already two differences between the samples are noted—family involvement and amount of education. If these variables are related to job morale and satisfaction, extraneous variables are operating to reduce the internal validity of the study.

Further, preexisting differences between naturally occurring samples exacerbate selection bias, because the experiences of people in different groups will not be the same during the investigation. That is, by self-selecting a particular shift, PNs will necessarily have different work experiences that can affect the dependent variable and thus blur the meaning of the data. Quasi-experimental researchers face the additional problem of selection bias interacting with history and attrition.

As an example of selection bias interacting with history, assume that members of each of the three shifts will differ in the amount of interaction with psychiatric patients; both morning and evening shifts may have more interactions than the graveyard PNs. At issue is whether the amount of interaction with psychiatric patients could influence job morale and satisfaction independently of group consultation. Again, an extraneous variable is introduced because intact groups were employed. Methods quasi-experimental researchers can use to deal with extraneous variables emanating from preexisting groups will be discussed later.

Although there are many quasi-experimental designs (cf. Campbell & Stanley, 1966), we focus on two general quasi-experimental approaches—the nonequivalent comparison group design and single-subject investigations. While both approaches meet the general quasi-experimental criteria, the procedures and rationale behind each method are very different. We now discuss the specific methods associated with nonequivalent comparison group design and single-subject designs.

Nonequivalent Comparison Group Design

A commonly encountered quasi-experimental research design is the nonequivalent comparison group design, diagrammed below with a no-treatment group and with a comparison treatment group:

(no-treatment group)	O	X	O
	O		O

and

(comparison treatment group)	O	X1	O
	O	X2	O

The diagram illustrates that subjects are pretested, treated, then posttested. The diagram could be altered by dropping the pretest, but without a pretest, the internal validity of this design is greatly reduced. In the diagram, X versus no-X or X1 versus X2 represents the manipulated independent variable. This again reveals the crucial difference between this design and a true experimental design—nonequivalent groups are preexisting, having already been formed through some sort of selection process. We next provide an illustrative nonequivalent control group design.

ILLUSTRATION FROM THE LITERATURE.   A study by Christopher and Roosa (1990) provides an excellent example of a nonequivalent control group design. These authors refer to their study as a "quasi-experimental pretest-posttest control group design; random assignment to conditions was not possible" (p. 69). A brief description of their study follows.

The researchers were interested in the effectiveness of an adolescent pregnancy prevention program titled, Success Express Program. The program required middle school students to complete six sessions, five of which were designed to "teach behaviors, attitudes, and skills consistent with the abstinence theme . . ." (p. 68). Goals and objectives for each of the first five sessions were identified as (1) self-esteem, (2) knowledge of the reproductive system, (3) coping with peer pressure to be sexually active and benefits of abstinence, (4) communication strategies for just saying no assertively, and (5) examination of future goals and goal setting skills. During the sixth session, participants completed a graduation ceremony, and posttest data were collected. The program lasted 6 weeks.

The sample consisted of 320 adolescents, 191 of whom participated in the abstinence program; the other 129 served as comparisons. The sample was primarily minority (69% Hispanic American, 21% African American). The average age of the participants was 12.8 years, and most students came from low-income families. The average participant's family income was $12,688. Program participants were sampled from five schools in which the abstinence theme was part of a health curriculum, as well as from various community sites. Comparison subjects were selected from the same schools as the program participants, but the comparison subjects did not receive the program during the study. The authors did point out that many comparison participants received the program in school later.

The primary analyses concerned the following dependent variables: a scale of self-esteem, two scales of adolescent perception of family communication, lifetime sexual behavior of self and best friend as measured by a series of items progressing from kissing and concluding with coitus, and premarital attitude about best age for first coitus, age expected to have first coitus, and best age to be married. The independent variable was treatment type—abstinence program versus no program—and the researchers also chose to analyze results by gender of the participant. Gender thus became a second independent variable with two levels. Finally, time of testing—pre versus post—was treated as a third independent variable with two levels.

Although many analyses were reported, we summarize only the findings regarding the equivalence of two groups on pretest dependent variables, followed by the effects of the program. First, of central importance to the researchers was the potential for the nonequivalent groups—abstinence participants and comparison participants—to be different with respect to pretest scores on the dependent variables. Thus, the authors performed a series of analyses to determine the pretest equivalence of the two groups.

Two significant differences between the groups emerged. First, the program participants were a half-grade more advanced than comparison subjects. Because the researchers note that advanced maturation could affect the dependent measures—the likelihood of engaging in sexual behavior increases with age—the researchers used analysis of covariance to adjust scores so that the two groups would be equated on the grade-level variable. Also noted was that participants began dating at a slightly earlier age than did comparison subjects. Unfortunately, the researchers could not adjust age at first dating statistically because many students had yet to start dating.

Of major interest was the effect of the program. Pretest-posttest changes by gender and program revealed no differences for self-esteem, communication problems, openness of family communication, best age for engaging in sex for first time, age expected to have sex, best age for marriage, attitudes about premarital sexual intercourse, and best friend's lifetime sexual interaction. Only one difference emerged—participants differed significantly from the comparison students on posttest, lifetime sexual behavior. Specifically, data revealed that program participants increased the level of their sexual interaction during the study, while the comparison students did not.

The authors note the perplexing and disturbing finding that participants increased their sexual activity during the study. The opposite finding would be expected, since the program is designed to prevent (or at least decrease) sexual activity. It seemed to have the opposite effect. The authors note that because the increase in sexual activity for the participants was especially high for males, the possibility of false reporting by male participants could explain this finding. However, the researchers gave several refutations of this explanation. If false reporting was a problem, then male comparison subjects should show similar posttest increases in sexual activity, which they did not. The authors also question the effectiveness of a sexual prevention program that stresses a single theme, abstinence. They suggest that for any program to be successful, it must consider the complex interaction of factors (family, social, personality) that affect adolescent sexual activity.

ADVANTAGES AND DISADVANTAGES OF QUASI-EXPERIMENTS. The Christopher and Roosa (1990) study highlights many pros and cons of the nonequivalent comparison group design. An advantage of this design is the inclusion of the pretest. By including a pretest, the researcher can determine the similarity between supposedly nonequivalent groups. When no preexisting differences are found, the nonequivalent groups are said to be equivalent, at least with respect to those variables pretested. Therefore, in the absence of random assignment, the use of a pretest is the main method by which quasi-experimental researchers ensure that their naturally formed groups are as similar as possible.

If pretest differences do emerge, as they did in the Christopher and Roosa (1990) study, the researcher is faced with intact groups that already differ on dependent measures. However, even if group differences show up on a pretest, the researcher can still proceed; additional techniques like analysis of covariance must be employed. These will be discussed in more detail in Chapter 10.

The Christopher and Roosa (1990) study highlights a general advantage of all quasi-experimental research, that is, the more naturalistic setting in which quasi-experimental researchers conduct their investigations. This means that subjects participating in quasi-experimental research are less likely to react to the demand characteristics that are inherently troublesome for true experimental researchers.

Two related disadvantages of nonequivalent comparison group designs can be given. First, there is the possibility of selection bias interacting with differential attrition. In other words, already existing differences between participants may uniquely affect the likelihood that the groups will have different dropout rates. In fact, just such a finding was observed by Christopher and Roosa (1990)—41% of the program participants dropped out, compared with 30% of the comparison subjects. The researchers subsequently performed a series of analyses simply to find out why a higher percentage of subjects in the program dropped out of the study than did comparison subjects. Their findings revealed that compared with comparison dropouts, program dropouts expected sex earlier, believed the best age of coitus was younger, and engaged in more sexual activity. Thus, since the program subjects were dating earlier and were generally more advanced than the comparison subjects, program participants may have perceived the message of abstinence as irrelevant. They may even have perceived it negatively and dropped out in greater proportion than the comparison group subjects. Again, because the two groups were not entirely equivalent to begin with, differential attrition was more likely to occur.

There is another problem with the nonequivalent control group—the interaction of selection bias and history. The problem is that while nonequivalent groups may be equivalent at pretest, differences on the posttest may be due not to the treatment but to some unique historical event that only one group is aware of.

To understand the problem further, consider the group consultation for psychiatric nurses study noted earlier. Assume the researcher finds no pretest differences among the three shifts. The group consultation model is implemented for the morning shift but not the other two shifts. Thus, we think any difference in posttest data is due to the consultation effects, but this is not necessarily true, because subjects in each of the three shifts have unique job responsibilities, demands, and situations. For instance, suppose that during the consultation study, wages are increased for the graveyard shift—a strategy designed to reduce turnover among PNs who select this shift. Additionally, what if the evening shift complains to management that they should not have to prepare and clean up after dinner? Suppose the administration concedes, hiring support staff to be responsible for evening meals. Both shifts might now show a dramatic increase in morale and satisfaction, but these increases, when compared with increases in morning shift morale brought on by the consultation program, would mask real differences between the groups. Thus, selection bias offers the opportunity for subjects to have unique histories once the study begins. Unfortunately, demonstrating no pretest differences between groups does not prevent this type of interaction.

RECOMMENDATIONS. When using a pretest in the nonequivalent control group design, the problem of testing effects could be viewed as a disadvantage. However, not using a pretest is far more problematic, since the results of a posttest alone cannot be meaningfully interpreted. Our advice is to keep the pretest and use other methods, such as alternate forms, for reducing testing effects.

When pretest differences do occur, the analysis of covariance procedure used by Christopher and Roosa (1990) is recommended. The procedure statistically adjusts groups to make them more equivalent.

Concerns about selection bias (intact groups) interacting with attrition and history are more difficult to overcome. Perhaps the key is in prevention, or making the nonequivalent groups as equivalent as possible. This seems odd, since this type of research refers to nonequivalent groups. However, nonequivalence, again, simply refers to the fact that random assignment did not occur, and instead, intact groups were used for assignment to levels of the independent variable. However, a researcher should try to select groups that are as equivalent as possible. By doing so, the potential of selection bias to interact with attrition and history will be less likely, because the groups will be similar in initial attitudes and their experiences during the study will probably not differ.

Again, refer to the group consultation study. By using the three different shifts, the researcher has selected three nonequivalent groups. As we have noted, each shift will have unique work attitudes and opportunities. In this situation, the researcher must be careful in interpreting the degree to which results on the posttest are due solely to the effects of having, or not having, group consultation.

On the other hand, what if the psychiatric hospital had enough beds to house different morning shifts in separate wards? Here, the researcher could compare the morning shift (Ward A) receiving group consultation with the morning shift (Ward B) not receiving group consultation to determine if group consultation affects job morale and satisfaction. By comparing two different morning shifts operating in the same psychiatric hospital (and with the same type of patient population), the researcher has the advantage of comparing two groups that are more equivalent than would be possible when comparing three different shifts. The major point here is that the researcher should select a comparison group that is as equivalent as possible to the group receiving the treatment of interest. Care in selecting the comparison group is the best method for reducing the interaction of selection bias with attrition and history.

When a researcher is concerned about the interactions of selection bias with attrition and history, the following recommendations (previously noted in Chapter 5) will be reiterated. Regarding differential attrition, using placebo comparison groups rather than a no-treatment group should reduce attrition that can occur in greater proportion in the comparison group. (Interestingly, just the opposite problem occurred for Christopher and Roosa.) Also, reducing the length of the study will help minimize attrition.

Gaining more information about the unique experiences of each group following participation can explain the degree to which history is a serious threat. Also, since history depends on the length of the study, shortening the duration of the investigation will be likely to reduce the effect of history.

Single-Subject Design

Single-subject research qualifies as a type of quasi-experimental design, because single-subject researchers (1) manipulate an independent variable, (2) gather data in a systematic, controlled manner, and (3) do not randomly assign subjects to groups. This latter feature is obviously impossible for the single-subject researcher, because there are no groups.

To illustrate how single-subject researchers manipulate the independent variable consider the design in Figure 9-8. The figure shows that during A, the baseline period, the subject revealed a high frequency of behavior, relative to B, the manipulated variable. After B was introduced, behavior decreased; further, when B was withdrawn, the subject's behavior returned to baseline conditions. The manipulated variable (treatment) was created by the researcher and has two levels—A and B. Closer examination reveals that single-subject research is another application of the repeated measures design, because the target behavior is repeatedly measured. Similarly, single-subject research can be conceptualized as a completely within-subject design, since a single subject passes through all study phases. The design depicted in Figure 9-8 is known as an ABA design.

One way single-subject researchers control extraneous variables is through research design. The design of the single-subject study in Figure 9-8 is itself one method of increasing the likelihood that the independent variable, and not some other variable, caused the change in behavior. For example, assuming the data in Figure 9-8 were real, it is likely that B caused the change in behavior frequency. Before B was implemented, behavior was high; it decreased only when B was instigated and rose again when B was removed.

In addition to care in design, single-subject researchers collect many measures of behavior and are concerned about the accuracy of behavior measurement. For example, in Figure 9-8 the accuracy of behavior observation might be measured by having two different observers tally the frequency of the target behavior to check the degree of interrater reliability. Further, behaviors other than the one graphed in Figure 9-8 are likely to be collected.

ILLUSTRATION FROM THE LITERATURE.   To treat the severe self-injurious behavior (SIB) of a 9-year-old boy, Cowdery, Iwata, and Pace (1990) demonstrated the effectiveness of differential reinforcement of other (DRO) behavior. The authors propose that DRO interventions for SIB have been minimally documented, and allude to the importance of empirically establishing the legitimacy of DRO. A summary of their report is given below.

The subject was a 9-year-old boy presenting with a severe and long-established SIB, which was scratching and itching. The problem was so severe that upon participation in the study, the child wore bandage wraps on most of his body, including his head, neck, arms, legs, and feet. Lesions were noted on his face, back, and penis. Background information revealed that the SIB was at least

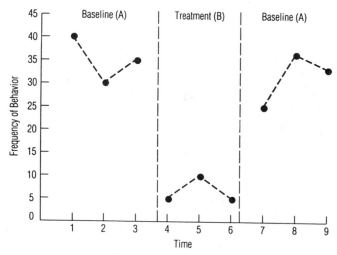

FIGURE 9-8 A single-subject design.

6 years in duration and for the past 2 years, the subject spent most of his time with medical specialists. Medical data did not reveal a physiological cause for his SIB. The subject's intelligence was low-average, but the child had never attended school because of the severity of his SIB. A previous intervention of applying a cold pack contingent upon SIB was deemed inadequate.

To treat this subject, the authors began by operationally defining the target behavior of SIB as scratching or rubbing one body part against another or rubbing a body part against a stationary object. An unexpected behavior developed during the study—crying—and this behavior was also defined and recorded. Observers recorded the percentage of intervals in which the behaviors occurred; interrater reliability, obtained for over half the sessions, was above 90% for all phases and behaviors.

Before treatment was introduced, the authors conducted a functional analysis of the subject's behavior in an attempt to determine what situations provoked SIB. The baseline conditions studied were (1) *attention*—the researcher attended to the subject only upon SIB and ignored him the remainder of the session; (2) *demand*—the subject was asked to perform some task and was given time-out contingent upon SIB; (3) *alone*—the subject was observed while alone in a room with no access to toys; (4) *play*—the researcher engaged in toy play and gave attention to the subject only in the absence of SIB, and (5) *alone with toys*, to measure the subject's SIB with nonsocial stimulation.

The most important finding during baseline observation was that SIB occurred entirely in the alone condition and not at all during the other four conditions. In other words, providing almost any type of continuous one-to-one supervision or nonsocial stimulation reduced SIB. Given this pattern of baseline data, the researchers concluded that the participant's SIB was entirely self-stimulatory in nature, although why it was reinforcing could not be specified.

The authors noted that two common treatments for SIB were not practical for this subject. For example, weakening the self-stimulation by bandaging his hands had already proven to be ineffective; the subject could still self-stimulate by rubbing bandaged parts of the body together. Further, while almost any form of social or nonsocial stimulation would reduce SIB, expecting hospital staff or caretakers to engage the subject in a continuous, supervised manner would be unrealistic. Even though the alone with toys condition also competed with SIB, it was equally unlikely to expect that toys would maintain reinforcement value over time.

As an alternate strategy, the researchers proposed a DRO treatment involving a token—a penny to be exchanged for activities or food—for increasing the duration of time the subject did not engage in SIB. Results showed that this procedure effectively suppressed SIB for up to 30 minutes at a time. During a brief reversal period when the DRO program was not in effect, the subject's SIB increased to initial baseline percentages. However, upon a second implementation of DRO, SIB was suppressed, and again for intervals as long as 30 minutes. Crying, which was not noted during baseline, appeared only when the DRO program was in effect. The authors noted that crying only occurred when the subject did not earn tokens; in other words, when SIB occurred and the DRO was in effect, the subject cried because of nondelivery of reinforcement.

The final phase of the study was an attempt to extend the DRO program from isolated treatment sessions to longer periods of daily activities in the hospital clinic. The researchers noted that while SIB was under control in the treatment sessions, it remained high throughout the day.

To address this problem, the authors instructed hospital staff in the token program. A timer was set for 30 minutes; staff were instructed to give the subject a penny for each 30-minute period without SIB. In addition, the authors introduced a simpler procedure that did not require tokens; instead, social reinforcement (praise, hugs) was given for each period of no-SIB. Also, data were collected when neither the token nor social programs were in effect. After seven baseline sessions, social, token, and baseline periods were alternated. Unexpectedly, the social reinforcers did not produce any change in SIB behavior relative to baseline, while the token program maintained its effectiveness. Thus, the token procedure was maintained and extended to include the participant's entire waking day. He was subsequently discharged to his parents, who were also taught the token procedure.

Advantages and Disadvantages of the Single-Subject Design

The advantages of single-subject research are in the idiographic approach to research and the natural context in which single-subject research is typically conducted. In essence, single-subject researchers extend case histories by making these histories more like experiments and thus, they are more scientific. Indeed, as we noted at the outset of this discussion, single-subject researchers want to improve the internal validity of their data by selecting a particular single-subject design, repeatedly measuring the dependent variable, and using only measures of behavior that are reliable.

An asset of single-subject research is the number of different designs that give the researcher greater flexibility in answering novel research questions. For example, the researchers of the study just cited used an ABAB design. Note that the subject's self-injurious behavior was high in the first baseline, lowered by the treatment, rose again during the absence of the treatment, and was suppressed again during the second treatment phase. By using the ABAB design, the researchers strengthen their conclusion that the treatment program caused the decrease in the subject's behavior. Other single-subject designs include AB, ABA'B; more complex designs involve at least two different treatment phases like ABCABAC. (C is the second treatment.)

Still another commonly encountered single-subject procedure is called **multiple-baseline design.** As the name implies, several baselines are obtained and generally consist of different subjects. If one subject is used, different situations or behaviors are included. The researcher then systematically applies the treatment to one baseline at a time. We illustrate multiple-baseline design by altering the procedure and findings of the Cowdery et al. (1990) study.

Assume the researchers selected three different conditions from their functional analysis—attention, demand, and alone. Also assume that the subject's behavior was almost equally high in all three conditions (it was not). Suppose the researchers obtained multiple baselines across the three conditions (they did). They could implement the treatment in the attention-only condition, while leaving the other two conditions untreated. If the investigators later treated the alone condition and, still later, the demand condition, a multiple-baseline design would be in effect. Logically, the subject's behavior should decrease in the treated condition (attention) but remain high in the other two conditions until the treatment is implemented in each successive situation. As the treatment is implemented, the behavior should respond accordingly. For example, the pattern of expected data for this multiple-baseline design across situations is illustrated in Figure 9-9. Another advantage is that researchers can use single-subject methods to explore innovative treatment methods or equipment. For example, Schulman, Stevens, Suran, Kupst, and Naughton (1978) examined the effectiveness of a biomotometer in reducing the over-activity of an 11-year-old boy. The biomotometer was then a new device sensitive to physical movements, and when the intensity of movements reached a certain level, the meter would provide immediate feedback as an auditory signal. Thus, Schulman et al. reported on how the biomotometer could be combined with positive reinforcers (tangible rewards for keeping the signal off) to treat over-activity.

A related advantage is using single-subject procedures to **decompose** interventions to study their parts individually. For example, if a treatment includes using (A) positive reinforcement (B), time-out (C), and corrective feedback, the researcher might want to know how much of the package is required to change behavior. The researcher could systematically study each combination of parts in a design like ABC, the complete package, then its parts, such as AB, AC, and BC. If the data reveal that AB, but no other combination, is as effective as ABC, then the intervention procedure can be made more economical by eliminating C.

As for disadvantages, common limitations include generalizability, use of weak designs, reliance on the visual inspection of data rather than statistical

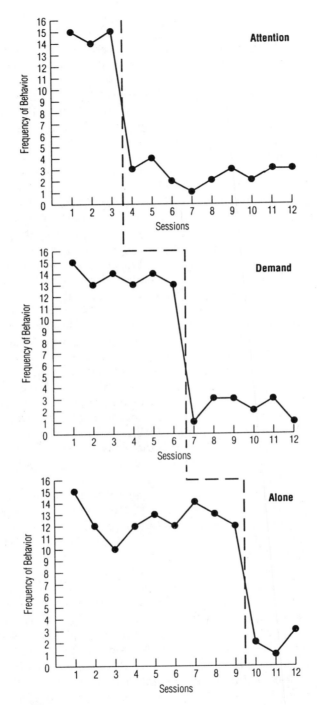

FIGURE 9-9 Multiple-baseline design.

tests, researcher bias, and instrumentation. Each of these disadvantages is discussed next.

Perhaps the most frequent criticism of single-subject design is that generalizability of the results to other subjects, situations, and behaviors may be limited. For example, the Cowdery et al. (1990) data may only apply to a similar subject. This means that for those results to be potentially generalizable to another subject, the subject would have to be similar with respect to age, gender, duration of SIB, type of SIB, no medical cause for SIB, low-average intelligence, no school attendance, and most importantly, that SIB only occurs when left alone and in no other condition. Clearly, the chances of finding a subject to which the results may be relevant are extremely limited.

For single-subject researchers, recall that generalizability is less important, because this type of research is born from the idiographic perspective. Again, idiographic investigators are more concerned about the accuracy of conclusions to one subject than the generalizability of conclusions from samples to populations. This latter concern is of most interest to nomothetic (group focus) researchers.

Although a variety of single-subject designs exist, researchers sometimes have to use weaker designs (in controlling for extraneous variables) out of practical necessity or because the variables cannot be changed. The ABAB design, like that in the Cowdery et al. (1990) study or in multiple-baseline designs—the very methods that most effectively guard against extraneous variables—often cannot be used because these methods are neither ethical nor relevant.

For example, if the subject in the Cowdery et al. (1990) study presented with SIB so severe that it was life-threatening, a B-only design would be required. Clearly, it would be difficult to justify baseline observations (A) because of the life-threatening circumstances involved. However, the results of a B (treatment-only) study cannot be meaningfully interpreted.

Further, there are also occasions when treatments require the subjects to learn a behavior that cannot be unlearned. In these instances, baseline observations of the behavior can be obtained and the subsequent effects of treatment compared to baseline in an AB design. For example, clinicians could observe parents verbally praising their child. After baseline, parents could be taught how to use response-contingent reinforcement (B) and the effects of this instruction assessed in an AB design. Unfortunately, an AB design like this remains vulnerable to extraneous variables, namely history and maturation. The researcher cannot return to baseline because the parents have learned a skill that many cannot forget.

A third weakness of many single-subject investigations is the practice of simply eye-balling data to determine the meaningfulness of the results. That is, single-subject researchers may rely on the visual inspection of trends in the data to support their hypotheses. This is why graphs (like the figures given earlier in this section) are so frequently encountered. The graph is the primary means of data analysis. Although several different traditional statistical techniques have been offered (Kazdin, 1982; McNeil, Newman, & Kelly, 1996) as a means to analyze single-subject data, such techniques are not as widely used as visual inspection of graphed data.

Researcher bias is a noteworthy problem in single-subject studies. Specifically, because the researcher knows the most about a particular treatment or is the only one trained to handle special equipment, it is the researcher who frequently collects single-subject data. This, combined with the typically frequent and intensive contacts between researcher and subject, creates the opportunity for researcher bias to develop.

Finally, instrumentation is of particular concern in single-subject studies because many observations are obtained. Since data are collected through observation, problems can occur with what the observer sees as an instance of the target behavior, or observers may become more or less skilled as observation proceeds. With respect to the former, if two researchers agree to observe SIB, there must be a mutually agreed-upon definition of this behavior. However, even a single instance of a behavior like scratching can vary in terms of intensity, duration, frequency, and topography so that even the most well-conceived definition of scratching will not be complete. If data collectors have difficulty agreeing that an instance of scratching has occurred, the results of the study can be rendered meaningless.

A more subtle problem is a systematic change in observer skill as the observations proceed. For example, observation and recording skill may gradually increase as the study progresses. This instrumentation effect would result in differences in observer agreement (less skill) during baseline but perhaps fewer differences in agreement during treatment (more skill). The net result would be a meaningless comparison of accurately obtained treatment data with inaccurately obtained baseline data.

RECOMMENDATIONS. We provide the following recommendations for addressing each of the aforementioned disadvantages. Beginning with the generalizability problem, many single-subject researchers choose to replicate their results with more than one subject. By replicating results with different subjects, the results of the study become increasingly generalizable to other, similar subjects. Thus, it is not surprising to see single-subject researchers present individual data for two, and sometimes more, subjects. In this format, subjects are selected on the basis of similar demographics and presenting behavior. The researcher usually obtains baseline data on subjects and then applies treatment, frequently in an AB design. Researchers can simultaneously collect data on subjects, so that subjects are observed at different points in the investigation. An alternate approach is to collect data successively, that is, each subject completes the study before initiating data collection for the next subject.

With due consideration of ethical considerations and relevancy, single-subject researchers should opt for designs most likely to reduce the influence of extraneous variables. For example, Cowdery et al. (1990) chose an ABAB design instead of an AB design, probably because the ABAB design reduces the chance that treatment effects are due to history or maturation. Because of their pattern of data, it is highly unlikely that history or maturation were problems; if they were, the behavior of the subject would not have risen or dropped in the second baseline and treatment, respectively.

The criticism of single-subject researchers' overreliance on visual inspection can only be satisfied by employing relevant statistical techniques. (For more information, see Kazdin's [1982] text on single-subject research or the statistical text by McNeil, Newman, and Kelly [1996].)

The issue of experimenter bias can be treated the same as with group designs—by using experimenter-blind procedures. To implement experimenter-blind procedures effectively in the case of single-subject research, the researcher must thoroughly train the data collector in observation and recording skills, as well as in implementing the treatment procedure. Sometimes this is not as difficult as it sounds, since potential data collectors may already be proficient with observation, recording, and treatment techniques, especially if these individuals are part of a trained clinic staff.

Finally, with respect to instrumentation, single-subject researchers typically place emphasis on data collection skill. This is evident in the inclusion of data regarding the interrater agreement of at least two different data collectors. Typically, if agreement data, however it is obtained, equals or surpasses 80% agreement, it is safe to conclude that the observers were recording the same behavior. Further, if agreement data are provided across different phases of the study (A and B), as it usually is, then changes in observer skill level can be determined. If agreement remains similar throughout the different phases of the study, the observers are not systematically changing in observational skill.

CONCLUDING COMMENTS

The essential features of the experiment—a manipulated independent variable and the element of control—separate the types of research discussed in this chapter from the previous chapter. Yet, within this chapter, we noted that an experiment can have many manifestations, ranging from simple experiments to complex experiments and from group designs in which subjects cannot be randomly assigned to experiments with single subjects. Indeed, the diversity of experimental procedures is a tribute to the ingenuity of researchers in answering a variety of research questions.

EXERCISES

1. Look at the following list of potential independent variables:
   a. learning style (auditory or visual)
   b. income level (low, middle, high)
   c. text type (large or small print)
   d. size of group (2, 3, 4, or 5 persons)
   e. drug use and type
   State whether each of these variables can be manipulated or not. Justify your position.

2. You are interested in assessing the time needed for Steven, a sixth grader, to

become accepted by his classmates after enrolling in a new school. You note salient facts, such as that seven school days were needed before other children sat down with Steven for lunch and ten school days before they chose him for a P. E. team. What steps could you take to transform this case study into single-subject research?

3. Tom is interested in determining the effects of communication skills training on patient satisfaction with nursing staff. Tom's sample will be nurses in the local hospital. Nurses in the treatment group will attend a series of workshops aimed at improving interpersonal skills (such as empathic listening, warmth, reflection, and so forth). Nurses in a comparison group will receive no training. His dependent measure will be an instrument he develops in which patients will rate nurses on various interpersonal dimensions. Both the treatment and comparison group will be rated by patients before and after the treatment group completes the training. With this research vignette in mind, do the following:
   a. Determine whether Tom's study is simple or complex and explain your rationale.
   b. If Tom were concerned about the potential of the control group exhibiting subject coping strategies (such as compensatory equalization of treatment, compensatory rivalry, and so forth), how might he design a placebo control group to eliminate this phenomenon?
   c. With only the information provided, determine whether Tom's study is a quasi-experimental research design or an experimental research design. Explain your reasoning.
   d. If Tom were to consider the time between the pretest and posttest to be an independent variable in his study, what type of research design would he be employing (within-group or between-group design)? Explain your rationale.

4. In examining the study by Daley et al. in Appendix E, determine if it is a simple or complex experiment. Why? Is it a between- or within-subject design? Defend your answer.

5. With respect to your possible thesis, consider the following:
   a. Is your study descriptive or experimental?
   b. If it is descriptive, how could you redesign it so it is experimental?
   c. If it is already experimental, is it simple or complex?
   d. Is it a between- or within-subject design?
   e. Will you use a pretest? Why or why not?
   f. Can you use random assignment? Why or why not?
   g. Will you administer a posttest? If so, when?

10

MAKING SENSE OF RESULTS: ANALYZING RESEARCH DATA

C hapter 10 is divided into five major sections. In the first, general research procedures are discussed, along with descriptive and inferential statistics. The second section includes a discussion of the most widely used descriptive statistics: measures of central tendency, measures of variability, skewness, and correlation. In the third section, inferential statistics are discussed. We present the general steps in hypothesis testing and the procedures that allow researchers to make inferences from the data. In the fourth section, we briefly discuss the procedures that are appropriate when multiple dependent variables are of interest to the researcher. In the final section, we discuss how these procedures are related.

Appendix B contains Maria's fictitious data and selected descriptive analyses. Appendix C contains various possible research hypotheses related to Maria's study and the requisite computer set-up and results.

GENERAL RESEARCH PROCEDURES

Human behavior researchers are not usually interested in how a particular person behaves but in how people like that particular person might behave in the future. For example, human service providers are not interested in knowing how Maria's 25 subjects in the multifaceted group react but in how other bulimic women will react if given that treatment. Science is built upon general findings obtained from studying groups of people.

Statistics play two roles in making those general statements about behavior. First, **descriptive statistics** are used to describe the sample that the researcher investigated and to communicate the nature of the sample to the reader. **Inferential statistics** deal with the process whereby statements are made about the population of interest, either the population sampled or a larger population a researcher might make an inference to in the future. The knowledge base in any field is based on the results derived from inferential statistics; therefore, inferential statistics and the conclusions drawn from them are of utmost importance.

In the next section, we will discuss descriptive statistical procedures. In the section after that, we will describe inferential statistics.

DESCRIPTIVE STATISTICS

Descriptive statistics are used to provide a general idea about the scores in a particular sample. Rather than display all the scores, researchers provide a measure of where the **average** score is and the **variability** around that score—or how different the scores are from the average. Many distributions of scores in the behavioral sciences are **normal**, but some are not. When scores are bunched at the bottom or top of the distribution, we say the distribution is not normal. A distribution of scores is normal when it looks like a bell-shaped curve with most of the scores near the middle (the mean) and a few tapering off to the sides, that is, deviating either above or below the mean. The degree of skewness shows how far the shape of the distribution is from being normal. Figure 10-1 shows a normal distribution as well as two

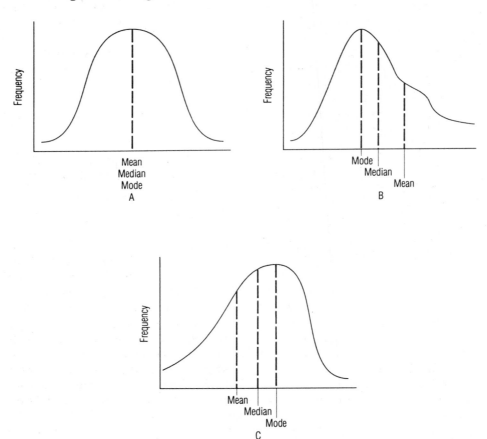

FIGURE 10-1 Schematic drawings of (a) a normal distribution, (b) a positively skewed distribution, and (c) a negatively skewed distribution.

distributions that are not normal. These figures are discussed in more detail later. Finally, if the relationship between two variables is of interest, the researcher would investigate the correlation between those two variables.

Measures of Central Tendency

When a researcher wants to know where scores tend to fall on the scale, he or she can check a single score that is used to represent all the scores. That single score can be calculated in three different ways, that is, there are three **measures of central tendency: mode, median,** and **mean.**

The **mode** is the most frequently occurring score. As such, the mode could be the highest score if more people had that score than any other score. Likewise, the mode could be the lowest possible score. The mode simply depends on how the scores of the sample of subjects are distributed. If two different scores occur an equal number of times and these are the most frequent scores, the distribution is called a **bimodal distribution;** one with a single mode is called a **unimodal distribution.** Changes in the score distribution will not necessarily change the mode. For example, if 10 people with extremely high (but different) scores are added to a distribution, the mode does not change.

The **median** is that point on the score scale at which half the scores fall below and half fall above. Thus, the median is the 50th percentile. The median is influenced, to some extent, by all the scores. If the two highest scores in a distribution are found to have been collected erroneously and are actually two of the lowest scores, then the revised median will be lower than the original median. The mode, on the other hand, would not be likely to change in this situation.

The **mean** is the most widely used measure of central tendency and is calculated by adding all the scores and then dividing by the number of scores. Most readers have come into contact with the mean in sports (batting average = .303), economics (Dow Jones average = 1303.65), and sociology (average number of children = 2.4). The mean depends on all the scores, so if a score is changed, the mean will change. If a score higher than the mean is added to the distribution, the mean will increase. If a score below the mean is subtracted from

TABLE 10-1   Data with one outlier.

John	3	Median	= 3
Sam	3	Mode	= 3
Sally	6	Mean	= 7.0 (42 + 6)
Jerry	1		
Luisa	26		
Frank	3		

the distribution, the mean will increase. If a score equal to the mean is added or subtracted, the new mean will be the same as the original mean. One disadvantage of the mean is that one extremely high or low score (an **outlier**) will have a large influence on it.

The data in Table 10-1 show a situation in which only one high score is above the mean. This is not to imply that the mean was incorrectly calculated but that it might, in this case, be a poor indicator of where the scores tend to bunch up. For the data in Table 10-1, the mode (and median) of 3 would be a much better indicator of where the scores bunch up than would the mean of 7. Table 10-2 summarizes the advantages of the various measures of central tendency.

Measures of Variability

While the measures of central tendency provide a single *point on the score scale* at which the scores tend to bunch up, **measures of variability** show the degree of spread of the scores or a *distance on the score scale*. The three commonly used measures of variability are *range, interquartile range,* and *standard deviation.*

The **range** is the easiest measure to calculate and is found by subtracting the lowest score from the highest, and adding 1. The 1 is added to obtain the spread of all the score values. Suppose there were only two scores, and they were adjacent scores of 3 and 4. The range would be $[(4 - 3) + 1] = 2$, which indicates that the scores range over two units on the score scale. Since the range is determined from only the highest and lowest scores, it is influenced by only those two scores. All the other scores could be bunched up at the middle, bunched at one extreme, or evenly distributed. In all three cases, the range would be the same.

TABLE 10-2   Advantages of measures of central tendency and variability.

Measures of Central Tendency	Advantages
MODE	Not influenced by extreme scores Only applicable measure when scores not normally distributed
MEDIAN	Most easily interpreted by naive readers Not influenced by extreme scores
MEAN	Function of all scores Used in subsequent statistical calculations
Measures of Variability	
RANGE	Identifies total score scale
INTERQUARTILE RANGE	Easily interpreted by naive readers Not influenced by extreme scores
STANDARD DEVIATION	Function of all scores Used in subsequent statistical calculations

The **interquartile range** is used with the median, because it is calculated from percentiles. By subtracting the score at the 25th percentile from the score at the 75th percentile, the distance on the score scale that encompasses 50% of the people can be calculated. If this distance is short, we know that the scores are bunched tightly. If, on the other hand, the distance is long, we know that the scores are not bunched tightly but are spread out over the score scale. Since the interquartile range is calculated from only the 25th percentile and the 75th percentile, none of the other scores affect that calculation.

The **standard deviation** is calculated from all the scores and is therefore influenced by all those scores. The standard deviation shows just what the name implies—the standard amount that scores deviate from the mean. As such, when the mean is reported as the measure of central tendency, the standard deviation should be reported as the measure of variability. Because all scores are considered in the calculation of the standard deviation, if there are one or two outliers, the standard deviation might not be the best statistic to report. The interquartile range would be better. With all subsequent statistical procedures, though, use the mean and the standard deviation. The advantages of each measure of variability are summarized in Table 10-2.

Measures of Skewness

Most inferential statistics rely on the assumption that distributions are normal. Although most behavioral science variables cannot be seen and therefore cannot be verified—no one has actually seen an IQ—most scores are derived so that they follow a normal distribution.

The **normal distribution** is actually a mathematical function that is beyond the scope of this text. Suffice to say that a normal distribution is symmetrical, that is, there is a mirror image about the center of the distribution. Because of this symmetry, the mean, median, and mode all fall at the same score point. In addition, scores in a normal distribution tend to bunch up at the center of the distribution and taper off at the tails. Because the normal distribution is a mathematical function, the percentage of people represented at each point along the score scale can be determined, as shown in Figure 10-2.

As indicated in Figure 10-2, a z score of 0.00 on a normal distribution is associated with the 50th percentile. Also, a deviation IQ of 115 is 1.00 standard deviation above the mean, and therefore 84% of the people are below that IQ score. Someone who has a deviation IQ score of 130 has an IQ that is higher than that of 98% of the population.

Not all distributions are normally distributed. While most standardized measuring instruments yield normally distributed scores for the population they were normed on, using such an instrument with a different or a restricted population may yield a non-normal or **skewed distribution**. An example of a skewed distribution would be scores on an extremely easy test. Scores would be piled up at the top end of the distribution; a few people would score low. Such a distribution is called a **negatively skewed distribution**. (See Figure 10-1 for schematic drawings.) On the other hand, an extremely hard test might result in a **positively skewed distribution** if only a few students obtain high scores

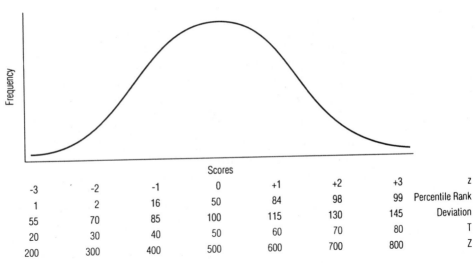

			Scores				
-3	-2	-1	0	+1	+2	+3	z
1	2	16	50	84	98	99	Percentile Rank
55	70	85	100	115	130	145	Deviation
20	30	40	50	60	70	80	T
200	300	400	500	600	700	800	Z

FIGURE 10-2   Relationship between score scales on the normal distribution.

and most obtain very low scores. Since the mean is compiled from all scores, and the median is affected by many scores, the mean (and to some extent the median) will move toward the tail of the distribution as in Figure 10-1.

Measures of Relationships: Correlation

Often a researcher suspects that subjects who have high scores on one variable also have high scores on another variable. (This may also be true for low scorers.) To see whether or not this is the case, the relationship between the two variables must be computed, using subjects who have scores on both of the variables. The relationship is referred to as the correlation between the two variables. While several kinds of correlations can be investigated, the **linear correlation** is investigated most often. This linear correlation is referred to as the **Pearson product-moment correlation.** The correlation coefficient is represented by r and is the highest positive at 1.00 when there is a perfect positive correlation, highest negative at –1.00 when there is a perfect negative correlation, and is equal to 0.00 when there is no relationship between the two variables. Figure 8-2 depicted these three extremes.

One outlier (either an erroneous score or some atypical individual) can drastically affect the value of the correlation coefficient. The second author of this text once erroneously recorded an IQ score of 55 as 555, which resulted in an erroneous correlation between IQ and Math Achievement of –.60. When the error was discovered and corrected, the correlation turned out to be more in line with what other researchers were finding—a correlation of .80. Care should always be taken when working with numbers, as calculators and computers cannot tell whether a score is an outlier or not.

The Pearson correlation is used in approximately 95% of the correlation

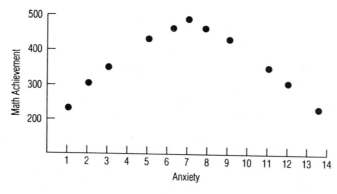

FIGURE 10-3   Nonlinear relationship between Anxiety and Math Achievement.

literature, but note that this index reports a linear relationship. If the data have some systematic, nonlinear relationship, that relationship will not be discovered with the Pearson correlation, and the Pearson correlation will yield a linear relationship that will underestimate the real nonlinear relationship. The relationship between anxiety and math achievement may be as shown in Figure 10-3. That is, students who are extremely anxious will do poorly, as will students who care so little that they neither pay attention in class nor study for the test. Those who are psyched up for the test (but not too much) will likely do the best.

If the Pearson correlation (straight line relationship) in the Figure 10-3 data were calculated, the correlational value would be close to 0.00. While it is correct to conclude that there is no linear relationship, there is clearly a systematic relationship in the data—a second degree relationship. There are many other nonlinear relationships that can be investigated, but they go beyond the scope of this text. (See McNeil et al. 1996, for ways to investigate various nonlinear relationships.)

Sometimes, the range of one variable will be restricted, as often occurs with entrance examination tests when only those making above a minimum qualifying score will be accepted. Another example is with screening tests when the lowest scoring applicants are to be accepted for treatment. Whenever selection is based on one of the variables, the resulting correlation will be reduced, or attenuated (a term used in the statistical literature).

Types of Scores

The scores collected originally are referred to as **raw scores** because nothing has been done to them. Raw scores do allow for crude comparisons on the same test but usually do not allow for equal-interval comparisons on the test. When comparing results from two different tests, raw scores cannot be used; some transformation is necessary.

Subtracting the mean from the raw score produces a **deviation score**, that is, the number of raw score units a person deviates from the mean. In Table

10-3, James has a raw score of 90 on variable X and a raw score of 80 on variable Y. On which test did he do better? If the question is whether or not he did better than the rest of the class, the raw score is of no value. The raw score must be transformed into another score. James deviates 10 units above the mean on variable X ($\overline{X}$ = mean of X) and 5 units above the mean on variable Y. Until we consider the variability in the data, however, we cannot unequivocally say which score is better.

The most common and useful measure of the spread of scores is the standard deviation. When the X and the Y scores for James are depicted in terms of standard deviation units (see last two columns), we note that James is 1 standard deviation unit above the mean on both X and Y. That is, his deviation score on X is 10 and the standard deviation is 10; therefore, he is 1 standard deviation unit above the mean. The standard deviation unit scores are referred to as standard scores in general and when calculated in this fashion, they are called **z scores.** The mean of these scores is 0, and the standard deviation is 1. Table 10-4 presents other forms of standard scores.

Another type of standard score is the Z score, which has a mean of 500 and a standard deviation of 100. Tests administered by the College Entrance Examination Board, including the Scholastic Aptitude Test and the Graduate Record Examination, use such scores. The lowest possible score on these tests is 200, and the highest possible score is 800, so all scores are positive and all are three-digit scores. The T scores have a mean of 50 and a standard deviation of 10, so T scores have two digits and range from 20 to 80. Examples of tests using T scores are the Miller Analogies Test and the Minnesota Multiphasic Personality Inventory-2.

IQ scores are constructed so they have a mean of 100 and a standard deviation of either 15 or 16, depending upon the arbitrary choice made by the test developer. The WISC is an example of a deviation IQ score that uses a standard deviation of 15.

Percent correct and **percentiles** are terms often confused. The percent correct is simply the number of correct answers divided by the total number of items. Thus, if Susan got 24 out of 25 items correct, her percent correct would be 24/25—96% correct. This tells us how she did on the test but nothing about how she did relative to other students in the class. She may have had the highest score

TABLE 10-3   Raw scores and transformed scores for four individuals.

Individual	X	Y	$\overline{X}$	$\overline{Y}$	x	y	S_x	S_y	z_x	z_y
James	90	80	80	75	10	5	10	5	1	1
Rachel	90	90	80	75	10	15	10	5	1	3
Rena	80	75	80	75	0	0	10	5	0	0
Ramon	70	70	80	75	−10	−5	10	5	−1	−1

NOTE: X is raw score on X; Y is raw score on Y; $\overline{X}$ is mean of X scores; $\overline{Y}$ is mean of Y scores; x is deviation from mean of X; y is deviation from mean of Y; S_x is standard deviation of X scores; S_y is standard deviation of Y scores; z_x is standard score on X; z_y is standard score on Y.

TABLE 10-4   Examples of three standard scores.

Individual	X	Y	x	y	z_x	z_y	Z_x	Z_y	IQ_x	IQ_y
James	90	80	10	5	1	1	600	600	115	115
Rachel	90	90	10	15	1	3	600	800	115	145
Rena	80	75	0	0	0	0	500	500	100	100
Ramon	70	70	−10	−10	−1	−1	400	400	85	85

NOTE: $\bar{X} = 80$; $\bar{Y} = 75$; $S_x = 10$; $S_y = 5$; x is a deviation score $(X - \bar{X})$; Z_x is a standard score with a mean of 0 and a standard deviation of 1; Z_x is a standard score with a mean of 50 and a standard deviation of 100; IQ_x and IQ_y have means of 100 and standard deviations of 15.

in the class or the lowest. On the other hand, a percentile shows how a person does relative to others. If Susan is in a below-average class, then her score of 96 might be at the 90th percentile, showing that she did better than 90% of the students in her class. If she were in an above-average class, her score of 96% would be at a lower percentile. If she were at the 50th percentile, she would be doing better than half the class and less well than the other half of the class.

MARIA REVISITED

The data Maria might have collected appear in Appendix B-1; these are based on the assumption that she treated a total of 50 bulimic women. Table 10-5 contains the computer symbols (limited to 8 characters) for each of the variables.

Her design was a pretest-posttest with random assignment. The BULIT was the primary measure of bulimia obtained at pretest and at posttest. Measures of family typologies—Family Environment Scale (FES) and Psychological Adjustment (PSYCHADJ) were also obtained at pretest; another measure of bulimia, Eating Attitude Test (EAT), was obtained at posttest.

TABLE 10-5   Computing symbols for each variable.

Variable	Computer Symbol
Pretest BULIT	PREBULIT
Posttest BULIT	POSBULIT
Change in BULIT	CHANGE
Treatment	TREAT
	(1 = educational)
	2 = multifaceted)
Family Environment	FES
Psychological Adjustment	PSYCHADJ
Eating Attitude Test	EAT

TABLE 10-6   Descriptive information from Maria's study.

Variable	Educational Treatment M	Educational Treatment SD	Multifaceted Treatment M	Multifaceted Treatment SD
PREBULIT	110.2	3.70	110.2	3.71
POSBULIT	103.0	3.81	94.6	4.07
CHANGE	−7.2	2.07	−15.6	2.75
PSYCHADJ	2.0	.71	2.1	.86
EAT	53.8	5.61	44.2	4.86

NOTE: The APA *Manual* requires *M* when reporting means and *SD* when reporting standard deviations. Means are to be reported to one more decimal place accuracy than in raw data. Standard deviations are to be reported to two more decimal place accuracy than in the original data.

Table 10-6 contains the descriptive measures Maria might want to report. These were obtained from the computer set-up in Appendix B-3. We note in Appendix B-2 that there were a few more FES level-1 women in the educational treatment and fewer FES level-2 women in the educational treatment. This information is presented in Appendix B-2 in a bar graph, a pie chart, and a block chart. (We do this to make the information as clear as possible, but most journals require tabular material because it is easier to typeset.)

INFERENTIAL STATISTICS

When a researcher wants to make a statement about a population, she or he usually does not have access to that population. Either the population is too large to test or it will only exist in the future. The best a researcher can do is to take a sample from a current (accessible) population and make an inference to a desired target population. The inference could be correct, or it could be incorrect—the researcher cannot know for sure.

In this section, we outline the steps in hypothesis testing; then we discuss several statistical techniques that allow researchers to make inferences about their results. These techniques are grouped according to the nature of the independent (or predictor) variables. Continuous variables—those falling on some continuous dimension like IQ—are discussed first. Categorical variables—those forming distinct groups such as male-female, treatment comparison, or low SES-high SES—are discussed next. The section concludes with an overview of statistical techniques that can be used when several dependent variables are of interest.

Steps in Hypothesis Testing

Hypothesis testing relies on the method of indirect proof. To obtain support for a desired hypothesis, a researcher actually tests the antithesis of that hypothesis. If the researcher can reject the tested hypothesis (the antithesis), then the desired hypothesis can be held as tenable. If the researcher cannot reject the tested antithesis, then the desired hypothesis cannot be held as tenable.

Most statistics texts refer to the desired hypothesis as the **alternate hypothesis,** as it indeed is an alternate to the tested hypothesis. We prefer the term **research hypothesis,** because it is the hypothesis that the researcher wants to establish. Once the research hypothesis is specified, it guides the remaining process, so it must contain certain components, namely the

1. Population to which the researcher wants to generalize
2. Predictor variable(s)
3. Criterion variable(s)
4. Parameter of concern (usually means or correlations)
5. Parameter value (such as the population mean > 0; or symbolically, $\mu > 0$).

The parameter values can be nondirectional, such as $\mu \neq$ or directional, such as $\mu > 0$. As hinted in previous sections, we strongly favor directional hypotheses because they provide for definitive conclusions.

The statistical hypothesis is the antithesis of the research hypothesis in that only one population value is specified. All other components are the same in the two hypotheses. This hypothesis is often referred to in the literature as the **null hypothesis,** but we think since null implies nothing or zero, it is a misleading term in many applications. (For example, the following hypothesis might be of interest: $\mu > 100$; population correlation $> .40$.) Table 10-7 contains Maria's research hypotheses. Some hypotheses do refer to a zero value, but others refer to a nonzero value and therefore have nothing to do with the idea of null.

Figure 10-4 contains the various possibilities for testing a statistical hypothesis in a sample and then inferring those results to a population. In the population, the statistical hypothesis may either be true (column on the left) or false (column on the right). Based on the sample data, the researcher may conclude that the statistical hypothesis is false and reject the statistical hypothesis (top row) or may fail to reject the statistical hypothesis and act as if it is true (bottom row). Since the population is never known, the researcher never knows if the decision is correct.

The probability of making a mistake can be controlled through the specification of **alpha**—the proportion of times that the researcher is willing to make a mistake by rejecting a true statistical hypothesis. Values of alpha are specified by the researcher and are commonly .05 and .01 in research in the helping professions. The value of .01 requires the sample results to be more discrepant from the statistical hypothesis than does the value of .05, but with an alpha of .01, the researcher has 1 chance out of 100 of making an erroneous conclusion; with an alpha of .05, the risk increases to 5 chances out of 100. If the researcher wants to take much less risk, alpha could be set at some lower value, perhaps .001.

For example, if a researcher is investigating the ability of various fuels to get people to the moon, he or she would set alpha at a very stringent level, because incorrectly accepting the fuel as a good fuel would have drastic conse-

TABLE 10-7 Maria's research hypotheses.

RH #1 For the population of bulimic women, the multifaceted treatment is more effective than the educational treatment in decreasing bulimia from pretest to posttest. (treatment effect)

RH #2 For the population of bulimic women, the multifaceted treatment is more effective than the educational treatment at the endo f treatment. (treatment effect)

RH #3 For the opoulation of bulimic women, there is a positive correlation between Psychological Adjustment and change in BULIT score. (predictive validity)

RH #4 For the population of bulimic women, there is a positive correlation greater than .60 between posttest BULIT and posttest EAT. (concurrent validity)

RH #5 For the population of bulimic women, there is a positive correlation greater than .70 between the two administrations of the BULIT for subjects not receiving treatment. (test-retest reliability)

RH #6 For the population of bulimic women, the rank correlation between the pretest BULIT and the posttest BULIT is greater than .70. (rank correlation).

RH #7 For the population of bulimic women, Psychological Adjustment and FES are predictive of change in BULIT from pretest to posttest. (multiple correlation)

RH #8 For the population of bulimic women, the mean pretest BULIT score is greater than 104. (testing a single population mean)

RH #9 For the population of bulimic women, the mean decrease from pretest BULIT to posttest BULIT is more than 0. (repeated measures)

RH #10 For the population of bulimic women, the mean decrease from pretest BULIT to posttest BULIT is more than 8. (repeated measures, with value other than 0)

RH #11 For the population of bulimic women, the multifaceted treatment will result in a posttest mean that is more than 6 units lower than the educational treatment. (difference between two means, value other than 0)

RH #12 For the population of bulimic women, the EAT posttest means for the three FES groups will not be the same. (one-way ANOVA)

RH #13 For the population of bulimic women who receive the educational treatment, there is a difference between the pretest BULIT scores of the women who remain for the full length of the treatment and those who leave during the treatment. (missing data test).

RH #14a For the population of bulimic women, the three levels of FES do not have the same posttest BULIT means when averaged over the multifaceted and educational treatments. (main effect for one independent variable)

RH #14b For the population of bulimic women, the multifaceted treatment is superior to the educational treatment in terms of posttest BULIT means averaged over the three FES levels. (blocking, or main effect for one independent variable)

RH #14c For the population of bulimic women, the difference on posttest BULIT means between the multifaceted and educational treatments is not the same across the three FES levels. (interaction between two independent variables)

RH #15 For the population of bulimic women, the multifaceted treatment BULIT change is greater than the educational treatment change, over and above pretest Psychological Adjustment. (covariance)

---

quences. Testing substances that could poison a city's water supply would be another example in which a very conservative alpha would be desired.

If the rejection of a true statistical hypothesis is not crucial, an alpha of .05, .10, or even a less stringent .20 may be used. Unfortunately, many human service providers do not consider their research to be crucial and often adopt these more liberal alpha levels, which are based on the argument that human behavior is more variable and less predictable than behavior in the hard sciences. We do

Reality

	Statistical hypothesis is true.	Statistical hypothesis is false.
Reject the statistical hypothesis.	type I error	correct decision
Do not reject the statistical hypothesis.	correct decision	type II error

Decision

FIGURE 10-4   The four possible outcomes in hypothesis testing.

not agree with that position. We think human behavior is predictable and certainly important to investigate.

Type I error occurs when the researcher thinks there is significance but there is not. We know how often this happens—the probability of its happening is equal to alpha. If alpha is chosen to be .05, then 5% of the time the researcher will make a Type I error. Once alpha has been specified, the data can be collected and the test statistic calculated. Commonly used test statistics are the t test for one- and two-group applications—two levels on the independent variable—an F test when there are more than two groups—more than two levels on the independent variable or more than one independent variable—and χ^2 when all variables are categorical. Table 10-8 specifies the test statistic for each of the various techniques that will soon be discussed.

The calculated test statistic is compared to what the test statistic would be under the statistical or null hypothesis using different alphas. For example, if alpha is .05, then the calculated test statistic is compared to the largest 5% of the test statistics calculated under the statistical hypothesis. Tables have been constructed depicting the range of values of these test statistics. If the calculated test statistic is larger than the tabled value for the value the researcher has chosen, we say that significance has been obtained. That means the statistical hypothesis can be rejected, and the research hypothesis can be held as tenable. If the calculated test statistic is smaller than the smallest test statistic based on alpha, significance has not been obtained, the statistical hypothesis cannot be rejected, and the research hypothesis cannot be held as tenable.

Many researchers use computer programs such as SAS (SAS Institute, 1985) used in Appendix B-3 and Appendix C. One of the values of such programs is that they provide the exact probability of the sample results occurring under the statistical hypothesis, thus circumventing the need to refer to the test statistic (t, F, χ^2, or z). This probability value can be compared to the chosen alpha, and if less than alpha, the statistical hypothesis can be rejected and the research hypothesis can be held as tenable. The advantage of this procedure is that the exact probability can be reported in a journal article and any reader can use his or her own alpha as the yardstick for comparison. That is, if probability is reported to be .04, it would be significant for the author who has an a priori alpha of .05, but for a more conservative reader who has an alpha of .01, the results would not be significant. Since the choice of alpha is personal and somewhat arbitrary, the publication in journals of the exact probability (in conjunction with the author's a priori specified alpha) is a welcome trend.

Continuous Variables as Predictors

Whenever continuous variables are used as predictors, researchers use some kind of correlational analysis. Although the ideas and procedures are the same, different names have been attached to techniques used in different situations. The three situations discussed in this section are (1) both variables are continuous—Pearson product-moment correlation, (2) both variables are ranked—Spearman rank correlation, and (3) there are multiple predictors—multiple regression or multiple correlation.

BOTH VARIABLES CONTINUOUS. The **Pearson** product-moment correlation was discussed earlier as a descriptive statistic. The population correlation could be investigated and tested for various values. Maria's research hypotheses RH #3, RH #4, and RH #5 are examples of testing a population correlation. Again, Maria's RH #3 was:

TABLE 10-8 Relationship among all the statistical procedures.

Number and nature of predictor variables	Technique	Test statistic	Number and nature of criterion variables
none	single population proportion	t	one dichotomous
none	single population mean	t	one continuous
one continuous	point biserial	t	one dichotomous
one continuous	Pearson product-moment correlation	t	one continuous
one ranked	Spearman rank correlation	t	one ranked
one dichotomous	two-group proportion	t	one dichotomous
one dichotomous	difference between two means	t	one continuous
many dichotomous	ANOVA	F	one continuous
many continuous	multiple regression	F	one continuous
multiple dichotomous	chi-square	χ^2	multiple dichotomous
multiple dichotomous	discriminant	F	multiple continuous
multiple continuous	factor analysis	none	none
none	factor analysis	none	multiple continuous
many continuous	canonical	F	many continuous

For the population of bulimic women, there is a positive correlation between Psychological Adjustment and change in BULIT score.
Symbolically: $\rho > .00$

where ρ is the Greek letter rho, which represents the population correlation. Statisticians use Greek letters to represent population parameters. This analysis is an attempt to establish the predictive validity of the measure, Psychological Adjustment. Maria can make this directional hypothesis because the literature consistently reports that those female bulimics who are more psychologically adjusted respond better to treatment for bulimia. Maria's systematic expectation is shown in Figure 10-5.

Appendix C-1 contains the computer set-up and results; the calculated correlation between Psychological Adjustment and change in BULIT is $r = .02$. The test of significance, when testing this sample correlation against the hypothesized population correlation of 0, yields an associated probability from the computer printout of $p = .8468$. Since the sample correlation was positive as hypothesized, the computed probability (which is always reported as nondirectional on computer printouts) must be divided by 2, resulting in an effective probability of .4234. (See McNeil [1994] for a more thorough discussion of adjusting computer generated nondirectional probability.) Given an alpha of .05, the calculated probability is not lower; Maria cannot reject the statistical hypothesis and she cannot accept the research hypothesis. She must conclude that there is not a positive correlation between level of Psychological Adjustment and change in BULIT score.

Maria's RH #4 was:

For the population of bulimic women, there is a positive correlation greater than .60 between posttest BULIT and posttest EAT.
Symbolically: $\rho > .60$

This research hypothesis is an attempt to establish, to some extent, the validity of the BULIT. If the BULIT and the EAT both measure bulimia, they should be highly correlated. Here, establishing that the population correlation between

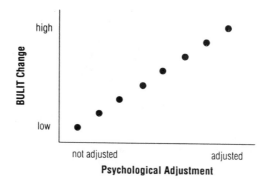

FIGURE 10-5   Schematic drawing representing the expected relationship between Psychological Adjustment and BULIT change.

these two measures is greater than .00 is too weak. Maria chose the value of .60 because she really believed that these two measures were measuring the same construct. Appendix C-2 contains the computer set-up and results; the calculated correlation between BULIT and EAT is $r = .80$. The test of significance, when testing this sample correlation against the hypothesized population correlation of .60, has an associated probability of .0027. Since the sample correlation was positive (therefore in the direction hypothesized), and using an alpha of .05, Maria can reject the statistical hypothesis and accept the research hypothesis. She can conclude that for the population of bulimic women, there is a positive correlation greater than .60 between posttest BULIT and posttest EAT.

Maria's RH #5 is one way to determine the reliability of an instrument. Here, she is investigating test-retest reliability:

> *For the population of bulimic women, there is a positive correlation greater than .70 between the two administrations of the BULIT for subjects not receiving treatment.*
> *Symbolically:* $\rho > .70$

Note that this is a directional hypothesis, because for a test to be reliable, the subjects should be ranked fairly similarly at the two occasions. Note also that Maria chose a nonzero value to use as the hypothesized benchmark for her reliability. Although most studies simply report their obtained reliability, Maria chooses to say that her test is more reliable than .70. Although this hypothesis should have been tested on subjects not receiving treatment, we proceed with the computer analysis on each of Maria's two treatment groups to show how each type of statistic can be analyzed by the computer program.

Appendix C-3 contains the computer set-up and results indicating that the obtained reliability for the educational group (TREAT = 1) is .84 and the likelihood that this high correlation was obtained by chance from a population whose correlation is .70 is less than .05. Therefore, Maria can accept her research hypothesis for the educational group. The obtained reliability for the multifaceted group (TREAT = 2) is at the end of Appendix C-3 and is .75, with an associated probability greater than Maria's alpha. Maria cannot reject the statistical hypothesis and cannot accept her research hypothesis that the BULIT is more reliable than .70 for the multifaceted group.

BOTH VARIABLES RANKED.   We discussed earlier how outliers systematically increase or decrease the mean. Also, outliers can have a large effect on the correlation coefficient. Outliers often result from errors in recording data. They also can be valid data points from subjects who are indeed different or who respond in an unusual way to the data collection procedure. On many tests, subjects can answer falsely or in ways they think make them look good. In unusual cases, subjects can deliberately make themselves look bad. If any one of the above reasons leads to an unusually high (or low) score, some of that score is due to error and the statistical analysis will compound that error, resulting in an overestimate or underestimate. Outliers systematically bias the analysis in one direction or the other.

Another occasion for ranking is when the researcher is unsure of how the variable should be scored. In the physical sciences, most variables are observable and often easily measured. Since we cannot see psychological and behavioral variables, we do not know exactly how to score them—we do not know their metric. For instance, should every intelligence item be scored as equally important? Probably not, but someone who answers one more item right than anyone else is probably a little smarter than everyone else—that person is top-ranked.

If the researcher knows that there are some outliers in the data, or if the researcher is not sure about the metric of the variables, subjects can be ranked on each variable and the correlation between those ranks calculated. Ranking reduces the systematic effect of the outlier, since the outlier is no longer so discrepant from the rest of the data.

Although there is a hand calculation formula developed by Spearman called the Spearman rank correlation, the same correlational value would be obtained if the ranked values were submitted to the regular Pearson product-moment correlation formula.

Because the BULIT is a self-report measure, it is susceptible to faking. Therefore, RH #6 might make more sense, particularly if outliers were observed in the data:

For the population of bulimic women, the rank correlation between the pretest BULIT and the posttest BULIT is greater than .70.
Symbolically: $\rho > .70$

Appendix C-4 contains the computer set-up and results. Again, we use Maria's data, although the research hypothesis would have to be tested on subjects who did not receive any treatment. The obtained rank correlation within the educational treatment is $r = .81$, with an associated test statistic of $z = 1.88$ and an associated probability between .05 and .10. Since the rank correlation is greater than .70, the computed probability can be divided by 2 and reported as less than .05.

MULTIPLE PREDICTORS. Many people believe that most behaviors are complexly related, and the two techniques we have discussed employ an extremely limited view of predicting that complex behavior. Why study complex behavior in as simple a way as possible? Why not investigate other variables simultaneously? This is in fact what is accomplished with **multiple correlation** or **multiple regression**. A researcher can entertain multiple (continuous and categorical) variables simultaneously in the attempt to predict the criterion.

The measure of correlation obtained with multiple correlation is indexed by R, which ranges from 0.00 to 1.00. A more interpretive measure is the square of that index—R^2—which is the proportion of sample criterion variance accounted for by the set of predictors. Since R is a decimal value, R^2 will be an even smaller decimal value. Although much research produces extremely small R^2 values, many statisticians believe that R^2 should be routinely reported.

Maria's RH #7 is a multiple correlation kind of hypothesis:

For the population of bulimic women, Psychological Adjustment and FES are predictive of change in BULIT from pretest to posttest.
Symbolically: Population $R^2 > .00$

Here, two variables—FES and Psychological Adjustment—are being considered simultaneously as predictors of change in BULIT. RH #3 considered only Psychological Adjustment in the prediction of change in BULIT. Appendix C-5 contains the computer set-up and results. The R^2 value (R-square on the printout) is .1096. The multiple correlation resulting from FES and Psychological Adjustment predicting change in BULIT is thus the square root of .1096, or .3311. Note that a capital letter is used when multiple predictors are used, whereas the small letter r was used when only one predictor is used. The test statistic here is $F = 2.892$, with an associated probability of $p = .0654$. Assuming an alpha of .10, we conclude that these two variables, considered simultaneously, predict change in BULIT. We do not know that both are necessary. All we have done is to compare the utility of both of them to the utility of neither of them. All we can conclude is that, as a set, these variables do predict a nonchance amount of the variability of BULIT change.

On the other hand, assuming an alpha of .05, we conclude that these two variables, considered simultaneously, do not predict change in BULIT. We conclude that both are not necessary. All we can conclude is that, as a set, these variables do not predict a nonchance amount of the variability of BULIT change. As shown in Appendix C-5, the correlation between FES and CHANGE is .33 and has an associated probability value of .0190. In this multiple correlation application, the significance of one variable by itself (FES) is different than when considering the two variables (FES and Psychological Adjustment).

Categorical Variables as Predictors

When a researcher is interested in knowing the difference between intact groups or artificially contrived groups, the researcher is looking at categorical variables. That is, there are no meaningful scores on the variable that defines the groups, only group membership designations. Examples include treatment-control, male-female, and old-young. Treatment-control is a grouping artificially contrived to test the viability of a new treatment. Male-female is a dichotomy that is easy to identify. Old-young on the other hand is an artificial dichotomy determined by the researcher from the continuous variable of age. In all the above examples, each subject will be a member of one and only one group. Sometimes, subjects will be assigned to groups; in other cases, subjects bring their group membership to the data collection.

SINGLE GROUP. The simplest design is when there is only one measure on one group. Here, the researcher has some information about what the standard should be and applies that standard to the one group. An example of a research hypothesis for a single group is Maria's RH #8.

For the population of bulimic women, the mean pretest BULIT score is greater than 104. Symbolically: $\mu > 104$

In Maria's study, RH #8 is actually a tautology because she used the BULIT pretest score as a way to select subjects for her study. But we use this hypothesis because it shows how a researcher might choose a standard using a single population mean. In this study, a standard of 0 would not make sense, nor would any standard below 100. A cutoff of 104 was used to include subjects; therefore, it makes sense that the population mean would be above 104 at pretest time, particularly on an immediate retest on the BULIT-R.

Appendix C-6 contains the computer set-up and results. The pretest sample mean for all subjects in the study was 110.22—6.22 units more than the hypothesized value of 104. When this mean is tested against the hypothesized mean of 104, a t of 11,9969, with an associated probability of .0001, results. Since the pretest mean is greater than 104, the nondirectional, computed probability can be divided by 2 to yield the directional probability of .00005. Therefore, Maria can reject the statistical hypothesis that the population BULIT pretest mean is 104 and can accept the research hypothesis that the BULIT pretest mean is greater than 104.

TWO DEPENDENT GROUPS. Often, the researcher wants to know what subjects were like before treatment started, or what their baseline status was. Or, there might not be a good source of information about what the population value should be. In Maria's study, the subjects had to have a BULIT score above 104 to be included in the study. The real interest is what their BULIT score is after treatment, as compared to their pretreatment level. In other words, Maria wants to know whether or not the BULIT score has decreased.

If a researcher is concerned about pretest status (and most should be), a pretest observation should be built into the study design. The traditional statistical literature refers to this analysis as a **repeated measures design.** This design allows the researcher to determine the gain (or the decrease as in Maria's case) from pretest to posttest and attempt to attribute that gain (decrease) to the treatment. An eample research hypothesis for a pretest and posttest for Maria is RH #9.

> For the population of bulimic women, the mean decrease from pretest BULIT to posttest BULIT is more than 0.
> Symbolically: $\mu_{post} > 0$

If Maria wanted to demonstrate a more substantial decrease, perhaps of 8 units, she would test RH #10:

> For the population of bulimic women, the mean decrease from pretest BULIT to posttest BULIT is more than 8.
> Symbolically: $\mu_{pre} - \mu_{post} > 8$

The computer set-ups and results for RH #9 and RH #10 are in Appendix C-7. The mean decrease is 11.4. When comparing this decrease with the hypothesized decrease of 0, the resulting t is 16.63, with a calculated probability of .0001. Since the results are in the hypothesized direction, the calculated probability must be divided by 2, yielding the directional probability of .00005. Therefore, Maria can state that the population decrease is more than 0. But how much more than 0 cannot be determined with RH #9.

RH #10 does provide a more definitive estimate of the decrease. The mean decrease was 11.4 (3.4 more than the hypothesized decrease of 8.00), and the computed t is 4.96. Since the mean decrease is more than 8, the computed probability must be divided by 2, yielding a probability of .00005. Thus, Maria can say that bulimics treated with her two treatments would decrease more than 8 points on the BULIT over the 3 months of the treatment. But could that decrease be equally attributable to the multifaceted and educational treatments? Or is one treatment more effective than the other, as originally posited by Maria? RH #10 does not indicate which one is more effective. We next turn to an analysis that specifically tests that question.

TWO GROUPS.   As we discussed in Chapter 5, a researcher might be concerned that a competing explainer of the results is maturation or historical events. Reducing the interval between pretest and posttest reduces the likelihood of these competing explainers being valid but also reduces the amount of time the subject has to receive treatment. A better solution is to include a comparison group.

If there is no information about what the standard should be, particularly for the population the researcher is interested in, a comparison group should be considered. A comparison group avoids competing explainers of differences in populations, time, and testing conditions because the two groups measured are from the same population. If subjects are randomly assigned to a treatment and a comparison group, then the researcher can be fairly safe in assuming that the two groups are similar at pretest. Using a comparison group increases the sample size, but the benefit usually outweighs the cost of the increased number of subjects. An example of a research hypothesis for two groups is:

For the population, the Experimental Method will produce a higher mean on the criterion Y than will the Comparison Method.
Symbolically: $\mu_E > \mu_C$

An example of comparing two groups resulted from Maria's literature review. The review revealed that the multifaceted approach should be more effective in reducing bulimic episodes than the educational approach. As a result, she decided to test RH #2:

For the population of bulimic women, the multifaceted treatment is more effective than the educational treatment at the end of treatment.
Symbolically: $\mu_{MF} < \mu_E$

Appendix C-10 contains the computer set-up and the results. The multifaceted treatment had a posttest BULIT mean of 94.6, while the educational treatment group had a posttest BULIT mean of 103.0. These means appear to be different, but the significance test indicates the likelihood of these two samples coming from a common population. If vagaries due to random sampling can be ruled out, then Maria can attribute the difference to the kind of treatment received. For these data, the t is 7.49, with an associated nondirectional probability of .0001. Since the results are in the direction hypothesized, Maria must divide the computed probability by 2, resulting in a directional probability of .00005. Since the directional probability is less than her stated alpha of .05, Maria can reject the statistical hypothesis of no difference between the two treatments. She accepts the research hypothesis that the multifaceted treatment is more effective than the educational treatment. Since Maria's alpha was .05, she knows that the probability that this statement is in error is .05.

If the researcher anticipates that the Experimental Method will cost more than the Comparison Method (or if the developer of the Experimental Method wants to hold the Experimental Method to a higher standard than the Comparison Method), then the researcher could require that the Experimental Method generate, for example, a mean more than 5 units higher than the Comparison Method. Here the research hypothesis would be:

For the population, the Experimental Method will produce a mean more than 5 units higher on the criterion Y than will the Comparison Method.
Symbolically: $\mu_E > (\mu_C + 5)$

The conclusion from testing Maria's RH #2 is not as definitive as if Maria had tested RH #11:

For the population of bulimic women, the multifaceted treatment will result in a posttest mean that is more than 6 units lower than the educational treatment.
Symbolically: $\mu_{MP} < (\mu_E - 6)$

The above hypothesis might have been derived from the literature, or it might have been specified by Maria after doing an analysis of the cost of the multifaceted treatment. The multifaceted treatment may require more resources, more training of the therapist, or more storage space. To convince other therapists that any additional costs are tolerable, a larger effect should be shown. In any case, the value chosen (whether zero or some nonzero value) is a result of a cost-benefit analysis that is extremely subjective and difficult to do.

Appendix C-9 contains the computer set-up and results for RH #11. The posttest BULIT mean for the multifaceted treatment (adjusted for the hypothesized value of 6) is 100.6, and the posttest BULIT mean for the educational treatment is 103.0. The calculated t is 2.11 and the nondirectional probability is .0395. Since the means are in the hypothesized direction, the directional probability is .0198 (.0395/2). Since the directional probability is less than Maria's alpha of .05, she can reject the statistical hypothesis and accept the research hypothesis.

Random assignment does not guarantee that the two groups will be equivalent, or even similar. Some randomly assigned groups will be very different. Therefore, it is usually advisable to obtain pretest measures on subjects, even when subjects are randomly assigned. If pretest and posttest measures on the same variable for two groups are available, the following research hypothesis could be tested:

For the population, the gain from pretest to posttest for the Experimental Method is greater than for the Comparison Method.
Symbolically: $(\mu_{post\ E} - \mu_{pre\ E}) > (\mu_{post\ C} - \mu_{pre\ C})$

Maria's RH #1 was of this structure, comparing the gain (actually the decrease) attributable to one treatment relative to the other treatment. The design is amenable to the t test of the difference between the means of two gains. Appendix C-8 contains the computer set-up and results. The multifaceted mean decrease is 15.56, while the educational mean decrease is 7.24. The mean decreases are in the hypothesized direction, so the computed nondirectional probability of .0001 can be divided by 2 to produce the desired directional probability of .00005. Since this directional probability is less than Maria's alpha of .05, she can reject the statistical hypothesis and hold RH #1 as tenable.

This kind of hypothesis can also be used to test to see if the subjects who dropped out of the study are different from those who stayed the entire time. If there is a difference, the population to which the researcher wants to generalize needs to be altered. In an earlier chapter, we posited that 10 women in the educational treatment might have dropped from the study. If this did happen, we might be concerned that those we will call the leavers were different from the stayers. The pretest BULIT scores of the 10 leavers could be compared with the pretest BULIT scores of the 15 women who remained in the educational treatment. Maria decides to test this question as RH #13:

> For the population of bulimic women who receive the educational treatment, there is a difference between the pretest BULIT scores of the women who remain for the full length of the treatment and those who leave during the treatment.
>
> Symbolically: $\mu_{STAYERS} \neq \mu_{LEAVERS}$

Appendix C-12 provides the computer set-up and the results. The calculated t is .38 with an associated nondirectional probability of .7034. The two means of 110.5 and 109.9 are different but not enough different for Maria to think they are from different populations. Those who left the educational treatment were not different on the pretest BULIT from those who remained in the study.

MORE THAN TWO GROUPS. All the research hypotheses discussed above can be tested with the t statistic. When more than two groups are being considered, the more general F statistic must be used.

Often, a researcher wants to investigate more than two groups simultaneously. Perhaps three different curricula are being investigated or the effects of a new therapy are being explored on four different patient groups. When more than two groups are being investigated, the more general technique of **analysis of variance (ANOVA)** must be employed. All the one-group and two-group designs discussed above could have been tested with ANOVA, but the t test is a computationally and conceptually simpler approach. An example of a research hypothesis with four methods is:

> For the population, after treatment the posttest means for the four methods will not be the same.
>
> Symbolically: $\mu_1 \neq \mu_2 \neq \mu_3 \neq \mu_4$ for at least one pair

A major problem with this research hypothesis is the vague question being tested and the vague answer that will result if statistical significance is found. To conclude that all means are not the same is not very informative. Therefore, there has been a proliferation of **post hoc techniques** that attempt to isolate where the differences are, for example, the Scheffe, Tukey, and Newman-Keuls tests.

These post hoc techniques all control for the potential increase in making a Type I error when performing multiple tests on the same data (see Hinkle et al., 1994). Unfortunately, post hoc tests neither allow for directional hypotheses nor directional conclusions. At best, the post hoc analysis allows for the identification of groups that are different; future researchers can examine the differences directionally. Particular groups could be compared, with a directional expectation, an approach called *a priori planned comparisons*. The expected direction should not be determined from the data but from the literature review or theoretical expectations.

Maria's RH #12 is an example of more than two groups:

> For the population of bulimic women, the EAT posttest means for the three FES groups will not be the same.
>
> Symbolically: $\mu_{FES1} \neq \mu_{FES2} \neq \mu_{FES3}$, for at least one pair

The above research hypothesis can be diagrammed as in Table 10-9. Notice that the groups in Table 10-9 were not randomly assigned, because family typology, which is the construct FES is measuring, is something subjects bring with them to the study, not a variable that can be easily manipulated.

Appendix C-11 contains the computer set-up and the results. The means for the three groups are: FES group 1–52.6, FES group 2–46.5, and FES group 3–47.8. The computed F is 3.89, and the associated nondirectional probability is .0273. Because the computed probability is less than Maria's alpha of .05, Maria can conclude that all means are not equal. Which means are not equal are indicated in the middle of Appendix C-11 (the Student-Newman-Keuls). This analysis indicates that the FES level-1 group is different from both FES level-2 and FES level-3. The post hoc analysis at the end of Appendix C-11 (the Tukey) indicates that only FES level-1 is different from FES level-2. In neither case can we tell which group is higher or lower. Although Maria knows the means and therefore knows which groups have higher means, she cannot make a directional conclusion, because she did not initiate this analysis with a directional hypothesis. She can use these results as a basis for a follow-up study containing directional hypotheses.

Control of Potentially Confounding Variables

There are several ways a researcher can control potentially confounding variables. These variables are sometimes referred to as competing explainers; in this text, we call them threats to internal and external validity. Some of these variables can be logically or theoretically eliminated. For example, the number of letters in a person's last name is logically unrelated to mental health. A re-

TABLE 10-9   Maria's design for a one-way ANOVA.

Group	Treatment	Observation
1	FES Level-1	EAT posttest
2	FES Level-2	EAT posttest
3	FES Level-3	EAT posttest

searcher's theory might identify some variables that are of no concern or by omission suggest that some variables are of no concern.

If a researcher is concerned about a potential competing explainer, there are several ways to proceed. First, the population of interest can be defined so as to eliminate certain groups. If gender is foreseen as a possible problem, then for the time being, the research can be undertaken on females only. If the researcher thinks both genders should be included, the genders should be samples proportionately. Therefore, if 60% of the population were female, 60% of the sample should be female.

Another approach is to include gender as another variable in the ANOVA design. Here, not only would one consider, for example, four treatment methods, but also gender. The design then is extended from the four treatment methods to two genders within each treatment method as depicted in Figure 10-6.

In this design, the results for a particular treatment cannot be unduly influenced by gender, because there is the same proportion of males and females in each group. The researcher may already know that gender is an important variable and may therefore not be interested in its effects. If gender is used this way, it is called a **blocking variable.** On the other hand, the researcher may be interested in the effects of gender as well as treatment. The two-way ANOVA allows for testing the **main effect,** or overall effect of both treatment and gender. The main effect research hypothesis for Treatment would be:

For the population, not all Treatment means (averaged over males and females) are the same. Symbolically:

$$\frac{(\mu_{MT1} + \mu_{FT1})}{2} \neq \frac{(\mu_{MT2} + \mu_{FT2})}{2} \neq \frac{(\mu_{MT3} + \mu_{FT3})}{2} \neq \frac{(\mu_{MT4} + \mu_{FT4})}{2}$$

Maria's RH #14a and RH #14b are examples of main effects hypotheses in a two-way ANOVA. Suppose that Maria wanted her sample to come from different FES levels. The best way to manage this is to assign half the women in the FES level-1 group randomly to the multifaceted treatment and the other half randomly to the educational treatment. Likewise, half the FES level-2 females should be randomly assigned to the multifaceted treatment and the other half randomly assigned to the educational treatment. Finally, half the level-3 FES women would be randomly assigned to the multifaceted treatment and half to the educational treatment.

		Treatment			
		1	2	3	4
Gender	Female	n = 30	n = 30	n = 45	n = 33
	Male	n = 20	n = 20	n = 30	n = 22

FIGURE 10-6   A two-factor design.

The research design would be diagrammed as in Table 10-10. Subjects in Groups 1 and 2 were assigned from FES level-1, subjects in Groups 3 and 4 were assigned from FES level-2, and subjects in Groups 5 and 6 were assigned from FES level-3. Maria's research hypothesis #14a is:

For the population of bulimic women, the three levels of FES do not have the same posttest BULIT means when averaged over the multifaceted and educational treatments. Symbolically:

$$\frac{(\mu_{MF\ FES1} + \mu_{E\ FES1})}{2} \neq \frac{(\mu_{MF\ FES2} + \mu_{E\ FES2})}{2} \neq \frac{(\mu_{MF\ FES3} + \mu_{E\ FES3})}{2}$$

The above hypothesis is referred to as the main effects for FES and is traditionally a nondirectional research hypothesis. Appendix C-13 contains the computer set-up and results. The F is 3.66, with a nondirectional probability of .0339. Since the probability is less than Maria's alpha of .05, Maria can accept the research hypothesis. Note that since this was a nondirectional hypothesis, Maria does not know which FES levels are different from which other ones. She can report the means for the purpose of subsequent research (from page 3 of Appendix C-13: FES level-1 mean = 101.4; FES level-2 mean = 96.8; FES level-3 mean = 98.3).

The design in Table 10-10 can also yield the main effect for treatment. Groups 1, 3, and 5 received the educational treatment, while groups 2, 4, and 6 received the multifaceted treatment. RH #14b states:

For the population of bulimic women, the multifaceted treatment is superior to the educational treatment in terms of posttest BULIT means averaged over the three FES levels. Symbolically:

$$\frac{(\mu_{MF\ FES1} + \mu_{MF\ FES2} + \mu_{MF\ FES3})}{3} < \frac{(\mu_{E\ FES1} + \mu_{E\ FES2} + \mu_{E\ FES3})}{3}$$

Appendix C-13 contains the computer set-up and the results for this main effect question. Notice that the SAS procedure statement yields the answer to RH #14a and RH #14b (also to RH #14c as we shall soon discover). The main effect for

TABLE 10-10 Maria's design for a 3 x 2 two-way ANOVA.

Group	FES Level	Assignment	Treatment	Observation
1	1	random	educational	BULIT
2	1	random	multifaceted	BULIT
3	2	random	educational	BULIT
4	2	random	multifaceted	BULIT
5	3	random	educational	BULIT
6	3	random	multifaceted	BULIT

treatment produces an F of 56.21 and an associated nondirectional probability of .0001. But since RH #14b was a directional research hypothesis (is superior to) the researcher needs to look at the means to verify that the means are in the direction hypothesized. The mean for the multifaceted treatment, averaged over the three FES levels is (from page 3 of Appendix C-13) 94.6, while the mean for the educational treatment, averaged over the three FES levels is 103.0. Since the means are in the hypothesized direction, the nondirectional probability must be divided by 2, yielding a probability value of .00005. Note that this directional interpretation can be made because the direction was hypothesized before the study was conducted; there was only one degree of freedom in the numerator of the F, resulting from two groups being compared; and the means were in the direction hypothesized. Such a directional hypothesis cannot be made when there are more than two groups.

In addition, the factorial ANOVA design allows for the testing of the **interaction** between independent variables. Interaction occurs when the difference in the effect of one variable is different across the levels of the other variable. In Maria's example, interaction would indicate that the difference between the multifaceted treatment and the educational treatment is different in at least two of the three FES levels. Some statisticians and researchers dislike obtaining interaction, because a significant interaction blurs the interpretation of the overall main effects. The present authors, on the other hand, feel that interaction can often provide meaningful insight. The data must be respected, that is, the researcher should attempt to understand what the data are, not what he or she thinks they should be.

An example of an interaction research hypothesis would be:

For the population, the difference between males and females is not the same in all treatment methods.
Symbolically:

$(\mu_{MT2} - \mu_{FT1}) \neq (\mu_{MT2} - \mu_{FT2}) \neq (\mu_{MT3} - \mu_{FT3}) \neq (\mu_{MT4} - \mu_{FT4})$ *for at least one pair*

Maria can ask an interaction question from the design in Table 10-10. Her interaction research hypothesis is RH #14c:

For the population of bulimic women, the difference on posttest BULIT means between the multifaceted and educational treatments is not the same across the three FES levels.
Symbolically:

$(\mu_{MF\ FES1} - \mu_{E\ FES1}) \neq (\mu_{MF\ FES2} - \mu_{E\ FES2}) \neq (\mu_{MF\ FES3} - \mu_{E\ FES3})$ *for at least one pair*

Appendix C-13 contains the computer set-up and the results for this interaction hypothesis. The F is 1.51 and its associated nondirectional probability is .2313. The means from Appendix C-13 are reproduced in Table 10-11. When there is significant interaction, a figure like Figure 10-7 is often provided. (Note that the differences in Figure 10-7 are not significantly different, since the nondirectional probability of .23 is not less than an alpha of .05.) The differences between the two treatments are easier to discern within the levels of FES in Figure 10-7 than in Table 10-11.

Often, the potentially confounding variable measured at pretest is a con-

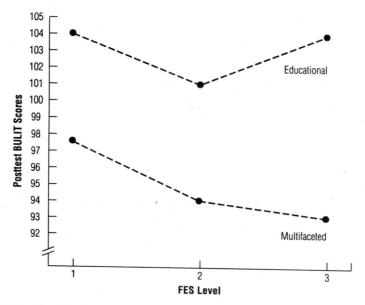

FIGURE 10-7   Graph of data from Table 10-11 resulting from RH #14c.

tinuous rather than a categorical variable. For instance, a researcher may feel that gender is not the important variable, rather that androgyny is the important variable (Bem, 1974). The particular operational measure of androgyny chosen is the BEM Sex-Role Inventory, which has a continuous score scale. Now the researcher could artificially categorize that continuum into two (or more) groups, but everyone in each group would be treated as similar. If the BEM is not very discriminating, the researcher would be justified in collapsing the data into two groups, but it is likely that the scores on the continuum do represent real differences on the androgyny continuum. Therefore, the researcher should control for the continuous variable. When such a continuous variable needs to

TABLE 10-11   Posttest BULIT means and standard deviations for FES levels within each treatment.

Group	FES Level	Treatment	M	SD
1	1	educational	104.0	4.47
2	1	multifaceted	97.6	2.37
3	2	educational	100.9	1.86
4	2	multifaceted	93.9	4.86
5	3	educational	103.6	3.81
6	3	multifaceted	93.0	3.02

be controlled, the statistical technique of **analysis of covariance (ANCOVA)** is employed. With this technique, androgyny is used to statistically adjust the posttest means, similar to the way bowling and golf scores are adjusted for a previous performance. Here, androgyny is referred to as a *covariate*. If more than one competing explainer is of concern, then a researcher should measure each and use each as a covariate. Maria's RH #15 uses the one covariate of psychological adjustment:

> For the population of bulimic women, the multifaceted treatment BULIT change is greater than the educational treatment change, over and above pretest Psychological Adjustment. Symbolically: $(\mu'_{MF} > \mu'_E)$ where μ' represents population mean decrease from pretest to posttest, adjusted for Psychological Adjustment

One of the assumptions in the analysis of covariance is that the regression lines (there are two in this case—one for each treatment) are parallel. If the lines are not parallel, then there is interaction, in the same sense discussed earlier in this chapter. Figure 10-8 presents several possible ways Treatment can interact with Psychological Adjustment. Unless the researcher specifically states one of the interacting situations, the analysis is nondirectional. Maria's RH #15 is an ex-

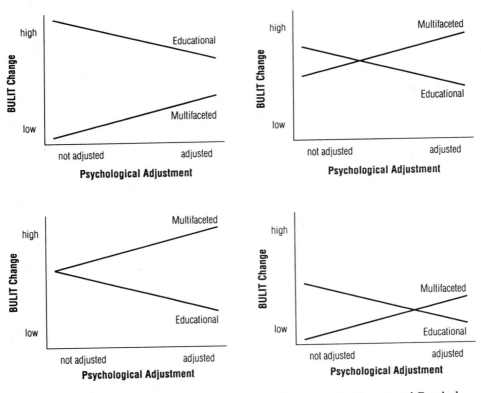

FIGURE 10-8   Four (of many) possible interactions between Treatment and Psychological Adjustment.

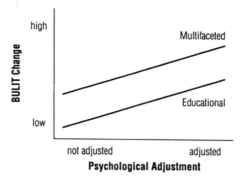

FIGURE 10-9a   Depiction of *no* interaction between continuous variable (Psychological Adjustment) and categorical variable (Treatment).

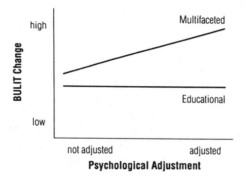

FIGURE 10-9b   Depiction of interaction between continuous variable (Psychological Adjustment) and categorical variable (Treatment).

ample of testing for interaction between a categorical variable and a continuous variable.

RH #15 is different from the interaction question in RH #14c, because in RH #15, the variable of Psychological Adjustment is being considered as a continuous variable. That is, in RH #14c six group means were calculated, whereas in RH #15 two lines of best fit were calculated. Appendix C-14 presents the computer set-up and results for Maria's analysis of covariance hypothesis. Page 4 of Appendix C-14 presents the test of the assumption of no interaction, referred to in the literature as homogeneity of regression slopes. The nondirectional probability is .1509, so Maria can assume that there is no interaction—if her alpha is .05 or .10. The F test of the adjusted means has a nondirectional probability of .0001, and since the parameter estimates for the two treatments are in the hypothesized direction, the nondirectional probability can be divided by 2, resulting in the directional probability of .00005. Thus, Maria can accept RH #15. The picture of her results would look like Figure 10-9a rather than like Figure 10-9b.

MULTIPLE DEPENDENT VARIABLES

Many researchers are interested in several dependent variables because most treatment programs have multiple and often diverse goals. Also, even if a researcher is interested in only one construct, rarely is there one best operational measure of that construct; there are usually several fairly good measures. If time and money allow, most researchers would choose to obtain those various approximations of the construct.

When there is only one dependent and one independent variable, the technique is called bivariate. The Pearson and Spearman correlational analyses, as well as the one-way ANOVA, are bivariate analyses. Those techniques incorporating multiple independent variables but only one dependent variable are referred to as *multivariable*. Multiple correlation and factorial ANOVA fall into this category. When multiple dependent variables are analyzed simultaneously, the statistical technique is referred to as a *multivariate technique*. We next discuss these multivariate analyses.

One Set of Variables

If many variables are obtained but all are either independent variables (predictors) or all are dependent variables (criteria), the researcher would use the technique of **factor analysis**. Factor analysis can determine (1) if the set of variables is measuring a one-dimensional construct or (2) if there are several dimensions (factors) underlying that construct. Instruments such as the 16PF and MMPI-2 provide subscores on factors. Since only one set of variables is obtained, the distinction between predictor variable and criterion variable is unnecessary and, indeed, fruitless.

Multiple Groups

If a researcher has not only multiple variables but also multiple groups, the technique of discriminant analysis may be used. The research hypothesis in this case would be:

> For the population, there is a difference between groups on the underlying factors of the set of variables.

Continuous Dependent Variables

We subdivide this section into the analysis of continuous predictor variables **(canonical analysis)** and categorical predictor variables **[multivariate analysis of variance (MANOVA)]**. While canonical analysis can be used in the latter case, most researchers have used the computationally simpler and conceptually generalizable technique of MANOVA.

PREDICTOR VARIABLES CATEGORICAL. When the ANOVA design is expanded by including multiple dependent variables, MANOVA is the statistic of choice. With this technique, the researcher can investigate multiple dependent variables simultaneously rather than one at a time. If two dependent variables are measuring exactly the same construct (Pearson correlation of 1.00), the MANOVA procedure will indicate this. What is essentially accomplished is a factor analysis of the dependent variables and then an ANOVA on those factors.

MULTIPLE CONTINUOUS PREDICTORS. Since ANOVA and MANOVA cannot deal with continuous predictor variables, we must turn to a technique that can. Canonical analysis is the technique of choice when both predictor and criterion sets of variables are continuous. What is accomplished here is a factor analysis of each set separately, and then the correlation between the factors is determined. The two sets of variables could be a set of pretest variables and a set of posttest variables; or the two sets could be a set of psychological variables and a set of behavioral variables.

While the present authors agree with the attempt to investigate multiple dependent variables simultaneously because the real world is complex, we feel that the level of sophistication necessary to design, execute, and interpret such a study is far beyond the scope of most researchers. The availability of computer programs alleviates some of the problem of calculating the statistics but not the difficulty of interpreting the results. Computerized packages entice researchers to attempt a multivariate study, even though the researcher may not have sufficiently conceived the rationale or the design and may not have any idea how to interpret the results correctly.

CONCLUDING COMMENTS

In the recent past, statisticians viewed all the above designs as falling within two camps—the correlational camp and the ANOVA camp. Indeed, many universities had courses so labeled. The computer has facilitated the resurgence of the **general linear model (GLM)**, which can be used in place of all the single dependent variable techniques, including both correlational analyses and ANOVA. Appendix C-15 provides the computer set-up as to how GLM can answer all Maria's hypotheses. McNeil et al. (1996) provide an extended discussion of these designs within the GLM framework.

Canonical analysis actually subsumes all techniques previously mentioned in this chapter. The only advantage of keeping the other techniques is that they appear in the literature, they are sometimes easier to comprehend, and they are often easier to display.

Figure 10-10 illustrates how all these techniques are related. Two points need emphasis. First, techniques that deal with categorical variables are subsets of those that deal with continuous variables. Second, techniques that deal with single variables are subsets of those that deal with multiple variables.

In the final chapter, we will present guidelines for writing theses and journal articles. This is the ultimate purpose of conducting research—disseminating information so that the knowledge base is shared and can be increased.

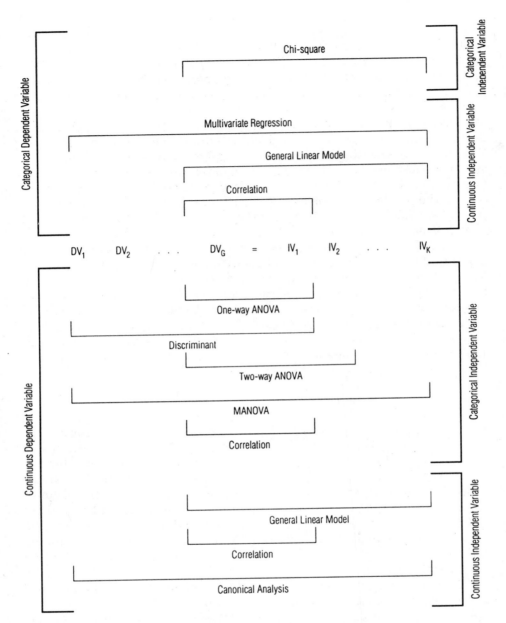

FIGURE 10-10   Relationship among all the statistical procedures.

EXERCISES

1. Why is information about interaction useful?
2. Briefly discuss the concept of skewness.
3. What is the difference between statistical significance and practical significance?
4. Discuss the purpose of hypothesis testing in the two articles in Appendix E.
5. For those planning on doing a thesis, what statistical tools would be used for the descriptive and inferential parts of the study?

11

SHARING RESEARCH RESULTS: PUBLICATION AND DISSEMINATION OF RESEARCH

MARIA HAS FINISHED COLLECTING and analyzing her data in accordance with the procedures outlined in the previous chapters. What does she do now? While Maria is satisfied with her contribution to research, the rest of the professional community is not aware of what she found. Maria in fact has an obligation to communicate her results to the professional community so others can evaluate her data. But how will she do that? Will she present the study at a conference? Will she use this study as her master's thesis? Will she submit an article for publication in a journal? Or will she try to disseminate pieces of the study in several places? Once this decision is made, she will then plan the writing of the publication. The dissemination outlet she selects will have a bearing on how she writes up the study.

The major focus of this chapter will be on what to include in journal articles and what to include in master's theses. Since both journal articles and theses report research, there will be many common elements; since the two have different purposes and different audiences, there will be some differences.

First, we discuss the purpose of disseminating research and the problem of finding a publishing outlet. Next, we discuss the nature of scientific writing style, the components of a journal article, the journal review process, components of a master's thesis, and conference papers and poster sessions. In a final visit with Maria, we discuss her journal article submission and how she revised it in order to get it published.

DISSEMINATING RESEARCH

The growth of knowledge in any field is based on consistent findings; these must be documented so that researchers and consumers can readily identify them. Also, the findings must have some generality, otherwise every individual and every event can only be viewed as an isolated case, which would not allow for predictability, generalizability, or understanding. The ultimate goal in any field is to raise our level of understanding.

The purposes of research literature are to (1) communicate the design and methodology of the research so that it could be replicated (the research must be internally valid); (2) communicate the results to show there is generalizability (external validity); and (3) fit the results into the current knowledge base.

Internal Validity

No part of the knowledge base in any field is constructed from a single study. Results must be replicated before being accepted by the professional community. As the careful reader realizes by now, there are many ways a research study can go awry and many decisions a researcher must make that will have an effect on the results—decisions that should have no biasing effect on those results. If a decision introduces additional error, significant results are less likely to be found. On the other hand, decisions that have a systematic effect on the results could lead to spuriously significant findings or to spurious nonsignificant findings, that is, findings that without the error might have been significant. Unfortunately, researchers are often unaware of such decisions. When they are aware of them, they cannot usually tell whether the decision led to random or systematic error. Therefore, the need to have other researchers replicate the study is imperative.

Strictly speaking, replication of a study requires repeating the original study methods exactly on another sample from the same population and assessing the dependent variable in exactly the same way. Replications are hindered when the authors of the original study do not report information adequately. Even when all the requisite information is presented, replications are difficult to implement since there are so many ways a research study can go awry. Sometimes the researcher must make fast decisions that can have far-reaching consequences. For instance, if half of the participants show up 20 minutes late, should the group counseling session still be conducted? If the female nurse providing shots becomes ill, should she be replaced with another, equally qualified male nurse? If a subject becomes ill during the posttest, should she be excused even though she says she is not that ill? A replication study that faithfully follows all the original procedures—difficult though that may be—provides support for the internal validity of a study; replications that deviate in some ways but still conclude with the same results provide external validity.

External Validity

Research is only valuable if it is, to some extent, generalizable. If we developed a new test and administer it to only one subject, how could we interpret that subject's test score of 42? Since no other data exist on that test, there is no basis for knowing why the one subject scored as she did, and there is no basis for making an inference about how that subject would score on any similar test. That test result would not be generalizable and would consequently not be publishable.

In a research report, all relevant information about the subjects and the procedure must be described well enough for a reader to make accurate generalizations and for a researcher to replicate the study as precisely as possible. For example, was the operational measure of the construct really a good measure of the construct? Was the measure conveniently available, requiring the researcher to make a big leap of faith in assuming that the available measure was a good measure of the construct? Was the sample one that really does not relate to the population the reader is interested in? A well-written report allows the reader to answer such questions.

With respect to Maria's study, would the multifaceted approach also be successful with other measures of bulimia, with other researchers, and with women who are not enrolled in a university? No reader cares about Maria's subjects, partly because they are anonymous and partly because they have already been helped by Maria. The reader cares about helping bulimics at the reader's university or the reader's clinic.

Knowledge Base

Assuming that the study is internally and externally valid, the journal article still needs to fit the results into the current knowledge base. This is done partly in the literature review and completed in the discussion and conclusion sections of the report. Each reader must make her or his decision about the impact of the study on the knowledge base, but the author is also obliged to make such a statement. Having conducted the literature review and the study, the author is in a good position to do so. Since this is the ultimate purpose of research, the author should try hard to weave the results convincingly into the knowledge base.

Maria's literature review identified the potential value of the multifaceted approach. By comparing this approach to the existing standard, she showed that the multifaceted approach was the best of the existing approaches. Her discussion of the various components identified what made up the multifaceted approach. Suppose that she interviewed her participants after the study and they suggested eliminating at least one component. She could not conclude that the component should be eliminated; she could only recommend that future research be undertaken to verify that the component could be omitted. Since the educational approach is the standard method for treating bulimics, Maria's study must be replicated before the multifaceted treatment can be added to the knowledge base. Note that the knowledge base is not set in mortar, as other, more successful, ways of treating bulimia might be developed in the future.

The Reason for Publishing

You may be wondering why you should publish at all. Perhaps you are happy because you learned a lot from doing a study. You should publish it in order to add to the knowledge base. If you do not, only you will know about the results of your study. Publishing is an important but often difficult step, because it requires describing the entire study on paper. Such a task is very time-consuming and reveals a great deal to your professional colleagues. We describe the crucial steps in Table 11-1.

Identifying the fundamental publication aspects of the study is difficult, because all the researcher's actions and decisions must be communicated: those that are unique to the field, those that had an impact on the results, and those that other researchers might have made differently need to be communicated. Aspects of the study that are well-known in the field, such as a particular counseling technique, a piece of equipment, or a computerized statistical procedure do not need to be discussed in detail.

All the information in the document will be available for scrutiny for many years to come, so you do not want to make a mistake that is professionally embarrassing. Many researchers find writing the most difficult aspect of doing research; they become immobilized for fear of saying the wrong thing. You are taking a big step by publishing, but having read this book, you will be well-prepared for the task.

DETERMINING THE PUBLISHING OUTLET

Most researchers have a good idea of where they will disseminate their study even before they begin the study. Someone working on a master's degree will probably have the thesis as the initial outlet. Many master's theses are important enough to also be disseminated at conferences or in journals. Generally speaking, it is easier to get an article accepted to a conference—particularly to a regional rather than a national or international conference—than in a journal. Some journals have a higher rejection rate than others. If you plan to publish in either a journal or at a conference, pick the one that best fits your research. Some journals only accept data-based articles, while others contain practitioner information or position papers. You might even consider sending your literature review to a journal that specializes in that sort of information. Time spent in reviewing the focus of a number of journals is time well-spent. Your adviser and other members of your committee should also be able to provide some good advice.

Whichever outlet you decide upon, make sure that you review the requirements and follow the preferred style manual and procedures. Due dates are particularly crucial for conferences, and these due dates are often 6 months in

TABLE 11-1 Publishing process for theses, journal articles, and conference papers.

Thesis	Journal	Conference
Get guidelines from graduate school	Decide which one	Decide which one
Check with adviser to make sure topic appropriate	Get guidelines from recent issue	Get guidelines from conference announcement
Obtain style manual	Review focus to make sure article appropriate	Review focus to make sure paper appropriate
Check due dates	Obtain style manual	Obtain style manual
Develop outline	Develop outline	Check due dates
Draft chapters	Draft article	Develop outline of abstract
Have chair and other committee members review	Let sit for awhile	Develop outline of paper
Check style manual	Revise	Draft paper
Give final copy to chair	Request review by colleague	Submit abstract
Revise per chair's comments	Check style manual	Make hotel and travel arrangements
Set oral exam	Finalize	Let sit for awhile
Distribute to commitee 2–3 weeks before oral	Submit, per journal instructions	Revise
Prepare 10–15 minute overview	Wait several months	Request review by colleague
Prepare visuals (optional)	Receive rejection notice	Finalize
Practice presentation	Let sit several months	Prepare 10–15 minute presentation
Do dry run with colleagues	Revise per rejection	Prepare visuals or handouts
Defend in oral exam	Resubmit, or submit to another journal	Do dry run in front of colleagues
Revise per chair's notes	Receive acceptance, do revisions	Take hard copies of paper, hand outs, and visuals to conference
Take copies to chair, committee (optional), department, and library	Revise	Present at conference
Keep data for 5 years	Respond to reprint requests, or direct to ERIC	Attempt to place in ERIC or similar database
	Keep data for 5 years	Keep data for 5 years

advance of the conference. Regional and state conferences usually have due dates closer to the conference time.

Researchers must identify the most appropriate journals for their articles. Suppose that a social work researcher is looking for an appropriate journal. Not all journals in the field would be appropriate, because some do not publish material in the special emphasis of the article. If the article is empirical in nature, those journals that only report nonempirical research should be avoided. Furthermore, some journals are oriented toward practitioners. If the article's focus is on the knowledge base and has little immediate value for practitioners, then practitioner-oriented journals should be avoided. Skimming the remaining journals helps determine which have published similar articles in the recent past; these should be read thoroughly to verify which journal is most appropriate. Researchers should read several journals on a regular basis.

You may have decided to publish your results at a convention. A convention paper is a good way to quickly disseminate your research, and you may very well meet other researchers who are interested in the same topic. While most convention papers are presented orally, a paper should be provided for the audience to take with them. Because all publication outlets require a written document, the style of that document is discussed in the next section.

SCIENTIFIC WRITING STYLE

Journal articles, convention papers, and master's theses do not read like newspapers or books of fiction. They are brief; they rely on specialized terms and symbols; they omit the personal prejudices of the researcher, and they rely on data and manipulations of data. It takes practice to understand and appreciate this style of writing. Understanding such writing also takes some knowledge of the research field, the design of the study, treatments used, dependent variables used, and statistical manipulation of the resulting data.

When researchers conduct a study, they are trying to provide some support for their assertions. Their literature review and theoretical orientation lead to the expectation that the results will be in a particular direction. Yet, if the results should turn out to be opposite to those expected—hypothesized—the researcher is obligated to report these opposite results, along with a cautionary word. Other researchers should be encouraged to try to replicate these discrepant results. In other words, all results must be reported, not just those that confirm the theory or fit into the existing research base.

Results that contradict the research base need to be mentioned and researched again as soon as possible. If the opposite direction results occur again, there is reason for questioning the existing research base.

Since the style of writing research differs substantially from most other writing, we include a few guidelines. While this section contains general statements that are likely to be true, you should review the guidelines at your institution or for the journal to which you plan to submit an article.

All journals and university departments require a particular writing style. Most of the readers of this text will likely be using the *Publication Manual of the American Psychological Association* (1994). This document provides direction in all areas of writing, from the use of punctuation and capitalization to the construction of tables and figures, to referencing published works. Other style manuals often used are *The Chicago Manual of Style, 14th edition* (1993) and *A Manual for Writers of Term Papers, Theses, and Dissertations* (Turabian, 1987).

Adhering to the guidelines in the required style manual is crucial for the acceptance of master's theses and articles submitted to journals. Editors will check the document once it is accepted for publication, but reviewers and committee members often downgrade documents when they do not follow style manual requirements. In the following section, we will discuss the two major style differences between literature in general and research literature—organization and language.

Organization

The necessity and value of a good outline cannot be overemphasized. The research report must be developed in a logical and even fashion with emphasis on the major topics. Paragraphs must be internally consistent as well as consistent with other paragraphs. The reader should be provided with summarizing sentences or paragraphs. Transitional sentences or paragraphs should lead the reader to the material that follows. When choices are reported (such as instruments and length of treatment), the basis for making those choices should have been discussed previously and the reader should concur that those choices are good ones. Table 11-2 contains tips for preparing the manuscript, most of which are related to organization.

Language

The language of research is formal and concise, but it also should be flowing and lively. All terms that are unusual or crucial should be defined, particularly in the master's thesis. Synonyms for these terms should not be used, because synonyms may lead the reader to believe that new constructs are being referred to. Although using the same term time and again may seem boring, each use of the term serves to further define it for the reader. Repetition emphasizes the

TABLE 11-2 Tips for preparing the manuscript.

1. Start with an outline.
2. Write regularly.
3. Write in the same place with dictionary and reference materials at hand.
4. Organize and prioritize your tasks.
5. Periodically set the draft aside and take a fresh look in several days.
6. Focus on communication; always keep the reader in mind.
7. Get someone to critique your draft.
8. Be willing to make thorough revisions.

key concepts and keeps readers from perceiving a shift in meaning when none is intended. The text is always written in the third person, not the first person, except when referring to other researchers. Finally, the past tense is used, unless (1) referring to tables and figures, (2) discussing well-established principles, (3) discussing the results and conclusions, or (4) discussing the possibilities for future research.

Writing Process

Any writing involves three stages: planning, writing, and revising; we have discussed the crucial need for planning. The more effort you expend in planning, the less effort you will need to make in the other two stages. The actual writing stage should take the least amount of time.

Revising drafts is the most difficult task. Revising involves comparing the draft with the outline (and revising the outline if necessary), checking for consistency in the paragraphs and summarizing sentences, making sure there are transitional sentences, checking for consistency of word use, and assessing the general flow of the document. Finally, revising is a recurring stage—recurring as a result of (1) the author's rereading, (2) colleagues' reviews, and (3) journal editors' and reviewers' comments.

COMPONENTS OF A JOURNAL ARTICLE

After identifying the appropriate journal for your article, you need to familiarize yourself with the publication guidelines of that particular journal; these are usually found in each issue. Be sure to follow those guidelines exactly, as most journal editors will return manuscripts that do not fit those guidelines.

Most readers of this text will be considering journals that follow the APA publication guidelines, but each journal usually has its own variations, if only on how the journal submission should be packaged. Table 11-3 contains the submission guidelines of several journals. Note that while they refer to the APA guidelines, each requires a slightly different submission packet. Not all journals require the same components, but most follow those presented in Table 11-4. Each of these four sections is discussed in detail.

Introduction

In the introduction section, the researcher states why the study was conducted. The beginning of the article identifies the purpose of the study, how it fits into the existing knowledge base, the general research question, and usually concludes with the specific hypotheses that will be tested. The introduction orients the reader to the knowledge base, the gap in the knowledge base, and how the current study will fill that gap. The purpose of the study is described. Some literature might be referenced in this description, but it should be written so

TABLE 11-3   Submission requirements of two journals. (Note: Information may not be current.)

CHILD AND ADOLESCENT SOCIAL WORK JOURNAL publishes original articles that illuminate clinical social work practice with children, adolescents and their families. Issues evolving from theory, research, social policy, special problems and special populations are used to inform clinical practice.

MANUSCRIPTS accompanied by an abstract of about 100 words should be submitted in triplicate to Florence Lieberman, D.S.W., Editor, *Child and Adolescent Social Work Journal*, 315 Wyndcliff Rd., Scarsdale, NY 10583. Include a self-addressed envelope with sufficient postage for the return of the manuscript.

The entire manuscript, including references, quotations, and tables, should be double-spaced. References should be arranged alphabetically at the end and referred to in the text by author and year of publication. Overall style should conform to that outlined in the PUBLICATION MANUAL OF THE AMERICAN PSYCHOLOGICAL ASSOCIATION, 3rd Edition. To facilitate anonymous review by one or more readers, only the title of the article should appear on the first page of the manuscript. An attached cover page should contain the title of the article, authorship and the author's professional titles, academic degrees, mailing addresses, and any statements of credit or research support.

Only original articles are accepted for publication. Submission of the manuscript represents certification on the part of the authors that neither the article submitted nor a version of it has been published, nor is being considered for publication elsewhere.

SUBSCRIPTION inquiries and subscription orders should be addressed to the publisher at Subscription Department, Human Sciences Press, Inc., 233 Spring Street, New York, N.Y. 10013-1578 or faxed to the Subscription Department at its number (212) 807-1047. Subscription rates:
   Volume 9, 1992 (6 issues) $185.00 (outside the U.S., $215.00). Price for individual subscribers certifying that the journal is for their personal use, $48.00 (outside the U.S., $57.00).

ADVERTISING inquiries should be addressed to the Advertising Sales Representative, Daniel S. Lipner, Weston Media Associates, P.O. Box 1110, Greens Farms, Connecticut 06436—telephone (203) 2612-2500 and fax (203) 261-0101.

INDEXED OR ABSTRACTED IN: *Current Journal Literature, Social Science Documentation Center,* Chicago Psychoanalytic Literature Index, APA-Psychological Abstracts, Sociological Abstracts, Current Contents, Social Work Research Abstracts, Family Abstracts, Abstracts of Research Papers, and International Bibliography of Periodical Literature.

PHOTOCOPYING: Authorization to photocopy items for internal or personal use, or the internal use of specific clients, is granted by Human Sciences Press for users registered with Copyright Clearance Center (CCC) Transactional Reporting Service, provided that the copier pay the flat fee of $6.50 per copy per article (no additional per-page fees) directly to CCC, 27 Congress St., Salem, MA 01970. For those organizations that have been granted a photocopy license by CCC, a separate system of payment has been arranged. The fee code of the Transactional Reporting Service is: ISSN 0738-0151/92 $6.50.

COPYRIGHT 1992 by Human Sciences Press, Inc. Published bimonthly in February, April, June, August, October, and December. Child and Adolescent Social Work Journal is a trademark of Human Sciences Press, Inc. Second-class postage paid at New York, N.Y., and at additional mailing offices. **Postmaster:** Send address change to the *Child and Adolescent Social Work Journal,* Human Sciences Press, Inc., 233 Spring Street, New York, N.Y. 10013-1578.
ISSN 0738-0151

CASWDD 9(1)1-96(1992)

Instructions to Authors

Purpose: NURSING SCIENCE QUARTERLY is devoted exclusively to the enhancement of nursing knowledge. The major purpose of the journal is to publish original manuscripts focusing on nursing theory development, nursing theory-based practice, and quantitative and qualitative research related to existing nursing frameworks.

Policies: Manuscripts are accepted for exclusive publication in NURSING SCIENCE QUARTERLY. The editor reserves the right to accept or reject all submitted manuscripts. Accepted manuscripts become the property of NURSING SCIENCE QUARTERLY and may be reproduced in other publications in whole or in part only with permission from the Editor and Publisher. Upon acceptance of a manuscript, it wil be necessary for the editorial office to receive in writing the assignment

of copyright from all authors of the manuscript. Manuscripts that are rejected will not be returned.

Peer Review and Acceptance Policies: All submitted manuscripts are subject to review by the Editor and are then forwarded to a minimum of two anonymous reviewers for blind review. The manuscript must be written clearly, presented logically, and must not have been published previously or concurrently in another journal, nor be under simultaneous consideration. NURSING SCIENCE QUARTERLY reserves the right to edit all manuscripts for clarity and conformation to its style and space requirements. Edited copy will be submitted to authors for approval. Authors are responsible for checking the accuracy of the copy as it appears in the edited version. Authors may be billed

TABLE 11-3 *(Continued)*

for extensive alterations in the page proofs. Accepted manuscripts must be submitted on a 3½" disk, in Microsoft Word for the Macintosh. Manuscripts executed in other programs or on DOS machines must be presented in ASCII Text Only format. We cannot access some high density formats, so please present disk in a low density format.

Preparation of the Manuscript: Authors should submit four *double-spaced* copies of the original manuscript on 8½ × 11 paper, with 1 inch margins. Type size (font) should be no smaller than 12 point. Include separate *double-spaced* pages for title page, tables, and legends for illustrations. Type page numbers consecutively in the top right-hand corner of each page, beginning with the abstract and text. We do not accept for review manuscripts that exceed 15 pages. On a separate page the author should sign a statement as follows: *The author guarantees that neither all nor part of this manuscript has been published elsewhere in its present form, in another publication or under a different title by either this author(s) or another author(s). It is also acknowledged that this manuscript is not currently under review by any other publication.*

Organization of Manuscript: All manuscripts should contain the following sections in the order listed.

1. Identification Page: Give the name, address, phone and FAX numbers (office and home) of the author to whom proofs should be sent.

2. Title Page: Include a brief informative title of no more than two lines and running title of three or four words. Include the first name, middle initial, and last name of each author with highest academic degree, position and title, institutional affiliation, and FAAN (if applicable). List three or four Keywords for indexing purposes. Acknowledgments should be limited to persons making a substantial contribution to the author's work and to institutions supplying grants.

3. Abstract: Include an abstract of no more than 100 words that includes the central theme of the paper. An abstract for a research paper should include the general purpose, methodology, results, and conclusions of the study. The abstract should not contain abbreviations, footnotes, or references.

4. Text: *Articles about nursing theory and theory development* should include a brief introduction followed by the body of the article. Subheadings should be used to divide areas of the article. *Articles on practice* should include assumptions, propositions, or concepts from a nursing perspective, with detailed examples of how theory is used in practice. Subheadings should be used to divide areas of the article. *Articles reporting findings of quantitative and qualitative nursing research* should include a brief introduction, the research question, frame of reference, brief review of literature, methodology, findings, and conclusions of the study as related to theory development, further research, and practice.

5. Tables and Figures: Tables and figures are used only when they express more clearly and briefly than can be done by words in the same amount of space. All tables and figures should be referred to in the text but should be largely self-explanatory and should not duplicate the text.

a. Tables: Type each table, double-spaced, on a separate sheet of 8½ × 11 paper. Number tables consecutively,

supply a brief descriptive title for each, and indicate the source of the data. Any inconsistencies in marginal totals or other figures should be explained in a table footnote. Charts and tables should be complete.

b. Figures: Figures should be professionally drawn and photographed; freehand or typewritten lettering is unacceptable. Send sharp, glossy black and white prints (unmounted) no larger than 8 × 10 inches. The name of the author(s) and figure number should be written *lightly* on a label on the back of each figure to avoid impressions onto the front which cannot be eliminated by the printer. Indicate "top" with an arrow on the back of each figure. On a separate page, type the legend for each figure.

c. Permission to Reprint: If the manuscript contains direct use of previously published material, signed permission of the author and publisher of such works must be submitted with the manuscript.

Style and Format: Authors should follow the *Publication Manual of the American Psychological Association.*

Abbreviations: Abbreviations should be spelled out the first time they are used, with the abbreviation placed in parentheses following the word. Greek letters or other special symbols should be identified the first time they are used. (This does not apply to the standard symbols used in statistical tests.) Addenda and appendices are not used.

Footnotes and References: Incidental comments and qualifications, other than reference sources, ordinarily are worked into the text. Personal communications should not be included in the references; list in parentheses in the text with the date and communicator's name. References should be limited to those directly pertinent to the paper and be listed at the end of the paper according to APA format. For example:

Journal article, two authors:
Spetch, M. L., & Wilkie, D. M. (1983). Subjective shortening: A model of pigeons' memory for event duration. *Journal of Experimental Psychology: Animal Behavior Processes, 9,* 14–30.

Chapter in a Book:
Hartley, J. T., Harker, J. O., & Walsh, D. A. (1980). Contemporary issues and new directions in adult development of learning and memory. In L. W. Poon (Ed.), *Aging in the 1980s: Psychological issues* (pp. 239–252). Washington, DC: American Psychological Association.

Complete Book:
Strunk, W., & White, E. B. (1972). *The elements of style.* New York: Macmillan.

Edited Book:
Bernstein, T. M. (Ed.). (1965). *The careful writer: A modern guide to English usage.* New York: Atheneum.

Correspondence Regarding Manuscript: Mail four copies of the manuscript, as well as any corespondence, to Rosemarie Rizzo Parse, Editor, NURSING SCIENCE QUARTERLY, 320 Fort Duquesne Boulevard, Suite 25J, Pittsburgh, PA 15222.

that most readers would say, Yes, that definitely is a problem, and I really think someone should solve it.

Any technical terms that are crucial to the study should be clearly defined. The author should not assume that only experts in the content area will be reading the article. Also, the author must convince the reader that there is a gap in the knowledge base and, more importantly, that the present study helps to fill that gap. Therefore, the review of literature should not be a listing of articles and findings but a well-integrated review that illuminates critical issues, particularly the gap that the current research is to fill.

The research hypotheses should clearly flow from the statement of the problem and the literature review. Conclusive answers to those hypotheses should help fill the gap in the knowledge base. Since the remainder of the article builds support for those hypotheses, they should be clearly stated. This means that all dependent variables, independent variables, subgroups, and expected relationships should be identified.

Method

In the method section, the researcher reports how the study was implemented. Many novice researchers jump right into the method section, describing the design and procedures of the study. The method, though, is driven by the

TABLE 11-4 Typical components of a journal article.

INTRODUCTION (why the researcher conducted the study)

    Purpose of the study
    Key terms
    Relationship to knowledge base
    Research question
    Research hypotheses

METHOD (how the researcher did the study)

    Subjects and population
    Design of the study
    Specification of treatments
    Measures used and their reliability and validity

RESULTS (what was found out by doing the study)

    Results reported by hypothesis

DISCUSSION (how the results fit into the knowledge base)

    Interpretation of results
    Limitations of the study
    Implications for future research

NOTE: Read articles in the journal to which you plan to submit. Style requirements vary between research fields and between journals within fields.

hypotheses; this section carefully lays out the plan of action for testing the hypotheses and for generating results that can be meaningfully interpreted. This plan of action should include (1) subjects and population, (2) design of the study, (3) specification of the treatments, and (4) measures used to assess the constructs.

The discussion of subjects should show how they were sampled and what target population they are presumed to represent. Descriptive information about them should also be given. The purpose of this information is to allow readers to determine how representative the subjects are of the target population as well as how applicable the results are to their own population of interest.

The design of the study should include a verbal or pictorial description of the treatments, or groups, and of testing periods. If a comparison group is included, that should be clearly specified here. If a pretest is used, that should be clear here. The X and O designation introduced in Chapter 3 is a useful way for authors to communicate the design of the study.

The number of treatments and the similarities and differences between treatments should be clearly specified. The length of treatment is particularly important, as the length of treatment needs to be long enough to have an effect. Many nonsignificant results occur from potentially effective treatments that were not implemented long enough to have an effect. If no treatments are used, the procedures that were used must be documented, such as the procedures for survey development and administration.

Finally, the method section contains the technical information about the measures used. The reliability and validity of the instruments for the researcher's target population need to be reported. In addition, the type of data, where they were collected, what instructions were used, who collected them, and when they were collected should be reported. For instance, a drug survey of elementary students administered by state officials during Drug-Free Week will likely provide different results than one administered by classroom teachers during a normal week.

The method used in a research study delimits the possible conclusions; if the method is flawed, conclusions cannot be made. Therefore, readers of research usually review all methods used carefully and look for flaws in those methods. A researcher should think of research methods as tools with which to solve a problem. If the wrong tools are used, either the problem will be inadequately solved or the problem cannot be solved at all.

Results

In the results section, the author tells what was discovered by conducting the study. The results section should be structured to follow the hypotheses and will often include tables and figures. Tables offer a way to report much information concisely, while figures provide graphical assistance in understanding the data. Both a table and a figure should not be used for the same data. While tables and figures should contain all the data and should essentially stand alone, the text may contain only the significant or important results. The text should never duplicate what is in a table or figure.

The results section should focus on the actual results, with no interpretation or tie-in with other studies. Such contextual links should be made in a clearly identified discussion section.

Discussion

In the discussion section, the author indicates (1) limitations of the study, (2) how the results fit into the knowledge base, and (3) what other related research ought to be undertaken. Some of the limitations will be known before the study is conducted, because they will result from the design of the study. Other limitations will become apparent as the research progresses. All research has limitations of one sort or another, and readers need to be informed so they can judge the seriousness of those limitations.

What the study results mean in terms of the knowledge base—how the results relate to studies mentioned in the literature review—should also be included in the discussion section. This tie-in with the knowledge base should have been the driving force for the research, and hence this section should be carefully planned, thoroughly covered, and professionally executed. Of all the sections of a journal article, this is the one that will be read most. Often, it is the only section read. A good strategy is to anticipate that sentences will be quoted, often with little surrounding context or with no context. Each sentence in this part of the discussion section should therefore reflect the results of your study accurately.

Poorly conceived studies can be identified here when authors indicate that future researchers should, for instance, (1) sample more subjects, (2) conduct the treatment for a longer period of time, or (3) use a more reliable or more valid measure of the construct. Recommendations such as these are really limitations of the study as planned, and usually appear when the researcher was unable to obtain the desired results. Obtaining a sufficient sample size, conducting the study for a sufficient period of time, and using a good operational measure of the dependent variable construct are all things the researcher should have done in the first place. The discussion section usually concludes with recommendations for future research, which should be more creative and expansive than the sections listed above. Here, the author suggests how other researchers might expand the knowledge base by using the findings of the current study.

THE JOURNAL REVIEW PROCESS

If the journal to which you submit has a review board, expect to wait several months before hearing about the outcome of that review. Acceptance rates vary from journal to journal; some run as low as 10%. You will likely not be accepted on your first submission. Read the reviewers' comments carefully and with professional respect. Do not be surprised if two reviewers focus on different aspects of your study or disagree on one aspect. There are so many ways to critique research that it is no wonder different reviewers find different weaknesses in the same manuscript. You should take advantage of those comments

TABLE 11-5   Example of a rejection letter for a conference presentation.

Dear Dr. McNeil:

The Division X Co-chairs have forwarded their recomendations to me for the paper proposals submitted to them for the 1992 XXXXX Annual Meeting. I regret to inform you that they do not recommend that your proposal, entitled "XXXXX XXXXXXXXXXXXXXXXXXXXXXXXXXXXXXXXXXXXXXXXXXX" be accepted for the Annual Meeting. I have also reviewed your proposal and reluctantly reached a similar conclusion.

The reviewers did not find information or knowledge presented beyond what can be found in a typical textbook.

In closing, I wish to express my sincere appreciation in your interest in XXXXX and look forward to your future participation in the organization.

Sincerely

XXXXXXXXXXXXXXXXXXXXXXXXXXXXXXXXX

Vice President & Program Chair

1992 Annual Meeting

Reviewer's comments:

Reviewer A: "I strongly agree with the author's position. However, what is being presented is what one would tend to find in a textbook."

Reviewer B: "A trivial study. I do not recommend its inclusion in the conference."

and revise your manuscript accordingly. If the journal editor has left the door open for resubmission, then do that. Otherwise, look for another journal that is a better fit for your research. We include in Table 11-5 one rejection letter that one of us received for a conference presentation. Table 11-6 contains a rejection letter for an article that one of us submitted.

COMPONENTS OF A MASTER'S THESIS

Master's theses contain the same components as those just described for journal articles, but the purpose of the thesis and the experience of the researcher both have an impact on the nature of the components. Table 11-7 summarizes the differences between a journal article and a master's thesis.

In general, master's theses are often conducted to demonstrate the ability of the student to develop a plan for doing research and then conducting that research. Master's theses are thus usually less rigorous and less likely to make an impact on the knowledge base. Because master's theses are not constrained by page limitations, they are usually longer than journal articles.

Introduction

Master's theses usually focus on a smaller gap in the knowledge base than do journal articles. Often the master's thesis is a replication of another researcher's study. Although replications are usually not accepted in journals (although we think they should be), they can provide valuable support for the knowledge base. Conducting a replication exactly like the original study can be a difficult task, because the researcher cannot deviate from the original study. The review of literature for that replication study would require little additional work, since only research published after the original research would need to be added to the original review.

The literature review is often longer in a master's thesis than in a journal article because there are no page limitations. Finally, the research hypotheses in a master's thesis are often simpler, requiring simple statistical procedures. This is based on the assumption that a master's researcher is less sophisticated in the knowledge base, research design, and statistical analysis.

Method

Because the research hypotheses are usually simpler in master's theses than in journal articles, the research designs are usually simpler also. There are usually fewer treatments, fewer constructs, fewer measures of those constructs, and a shorter duration of the study. For instance, seldom will a master's thesis inves-

TABLE 11-6   Example of reviewers' comments for a journal submission.

Reviewer #1

This paper reports the correlates of "epistemological styles." As such it is addressing a novel and interesting topic. The results are moderately interesting, but the paper suffers from a number of weaknesses which prevent it, in my opinion, from being accepted in its current form. Substantial revisions could remedy the problems. The most prominent weaknesses are:

(1) The manuscript is written sloppily . . .

(2) The manuscript is too long for what it says. The literature review could be shortened greatly, and the Method and Results section could be made more efficient. For example, there is no need to repeat statistics given in a table (alternatively, there is no need for the table).

(3) I don't see a great deal of self criticism in this paper. Two examples of this are (a) the causal model underlying the results (how do students become "relativists"? does their style determine their problem solving processes, or vice versa?), and (b) what the Ink Blot Test scores might represent (could they relate to stylistic characteristics, such as willingness to other interpretations, rather than "problem solving"). These issues will occur to readers, and should be addressed.

Reviewer #2

This manuscript addresses a theoretically interesting topic with potentially important ramifications for both student learning and instructional practice. The authors provide a good (if somewhat overlong) general description of previous research in this area, and present a theoretical framework for the questions they pose concerning the effects of epistemological orientation on cognitive processing The authors make an especially important point on p. 8 where they state the epistemological style needs to be related to specific cognitive recessing components underlying performance of complex skils. However, in the end, I believe this manuscript promises much more than it ultimately delivers. Although the overall framework is good, I have serious reservations concerning: (a) the tasks selected as dependent variables, (b) the failue to control for variables known to influence both performance and strategy selection on tasks similar to the ones employed in this study, (c) the author's interpretation of their results, and (d) instances of what appear to be contradictory statements in the manuscript.

(The reviewer then provides detail for each of the above points)

In sum, the topic of this manuscript is important, the analyses are appropriate, and it is generally well-written. However, even if the authors were to rewrite the Introduction, the problem of uncontrolled variables remains. The basic finding here is that epistemological styles seem to exert an influence on the processes used to answer ill-structured problems. I'm not convinced that that finding, in and of itself, makes a significant contribution. I strongly encourage the author(s) to collect additional data designed to resolve some of the ambiguities in this study which then could be submitted to XXXX.

TABLE 11-7   A master's thesis compared to a journal article.

Master's Thesis	Journal Article
IN GENERAL	
Displays ability of author to conduct research Often not rigorous Long because not constrained by page limitation	Fills gap in knowledge base Usually rigorous Constrained by space limitations
INTRODUCTION	
Focuses on small gap in knowledge base or replication Long and detailed literature review Simple hypotheses, design, and statistical analysis	Should fill gap in knowledge base Focused literature review Statistical analysis sometimes technical
METHOD	
Usually simple design Usually short duration of treatment Measures usually not thoroughly documented Subjects usually convenient sample	Often complicated design Can be long duration of treatment Measures should be referenced to other literature Subjects may be randomly selected but often convenient sample
RESEARCH	
Often overinterpreted or underinterpreted Often weak weaving results into knowledge base	Often overinterpreted Should weave results into knowledge base

tigate a treatment beyond one or two semesters. The reliability and validity of the measures used will often be described neither as extensively nor as well as in a journal article. Because of cost and time constraints on master's students, subjects often are a convenient sample rather than a representative or random sample.

Results

This section in a master's thesis is often the most different from journal articles, primarily because all previous sections affect the results. Simpler questions, simpler designs, weaker measurement instruments, and limited samples all lead to reduced effects. In addition, the presumed inexperience of a master's student often leads to either overinterpretation of results or to underinterpretation. Often, the weaving of results into the knowledge base is weak because enough time may not be allotted to this highly integrative, highly analytical and creative process. A secure comprehension of the knowledge base is often lacking, which clearly limits the quality and depth of the conclusions section.

We are neither condemning all master's theses research nor condoning all journal articles. Sometimes, some parts of master's theses are much better than journal articles; some master's theses have made genuine contributions to the knowledge base. Indeed, we are confident that many master's theses can make a contribution or else we would not have written this text. New researchers should realize that the research process is very complex, very detailed, and has many interrelated components. The answers to the research questions may be in error if any one of the components is not implemented well, but what we (and novice researchers) must acknowledge is that experienced researchers sometimes do not implement components well. All researchers should be critical, caring, and careful in conducting their research and in reviewing others' research.

CONFERENCE PAPERS AND POSTERS

The conference paper and poster are usually less formal than a journal article and are usually disseminated in a more timely fashion. These conference presentations are accepted on the basis of an abstract, and then the presentation is developed. The one other advantage of a conference presentation is that the presenter has the opportunity to interact with colleagues who have the same interest.

The conference paper is usually shorter than a journal article and less likely to be scrutinized for style. If the paper is to be included in convention proceedings, the author will want it to meet all style guidelines, but usually there is no editorial review. The author is responsible for how the paper looks.

Many conference paper presenters ignore the fact that the conference presentation requires different skills, preparation, and materials than does the production of the paper. A presentation must usually be made within a short period of time, obviating reading the paper in its entirety—a very dull approach anyway. The presenter must identify the highlights of the paper and make sure they are presented within the tight time frame. Most audiences are more interested in what you did and what you found than in a long description of your literature review. Also, most conference attendees want to ask questions, so be sure to allow time for those questions. Succinct and attractive handouts or visuals will draw and keep the attention of your audience. Table 11-8, adapted from Renfrow and Impara (1989), provides a valuable comparison of the oral presentation and the written presentation.

Poster sessions offer a presenter an alternative way of disseminating results. A visual display of the study (usually focused on the methodology and the results) is placed on a table. People who are interested in that one topic will look over the poster and will likely initiate a conversation. One disadvantage of the poster session is that while conversing with one person, another may ask a question. The presenter is soon in the middle of several conversations. Poster sessions are a relatively easy way to get involved with the dissemination process.

APA WRITING STYLE

Since readers of this text will most likely be reading APA documents or will need to conform to APA style, a few words regarding the *Publication Manual* (APA, 1994) are in order. The *Manual* contains both general rules about English use as well as guides for journal writing. The first two chapters should be read. The manuscript itself is discussed in the first chapter in detail. Since journal manuscripts

TABLE 11-8   Presentations versus papers.

Speech	Paper	Poster
1. Listeners	1. Readers	1. Small number of colleagues
2. Journalistic	2. Scholarly prose	2. Respond to questions
3. Words, pictures, delivery	3. Only words and pictures	3. Pictures, prose, and oral
4. Earn audience attention	4. Readers are committed	4. Need to attract audience
5. Audience interested—you'll know	5. No direct gauge of audience interest	5. Audience specifically interested
6. One chance to get message across	6. Multiple readings are possible	6. Opportunity for clarification
7. Interactive	7. Not interactive	7. Very interactive
8. You determine pace	8. Reader sets pace	8. Audience usually sets pace
9. Speaker organizes content	9. Reader can scan to prepare mindset	9. Content organized by poster
10. Audience feedback can be direct	10. Audience feedback is remote	10. Audience may provide overload feedback

are different from other literature, including term papers, researchers should become familiar with just how a journal manuscript is organized. Chapter 1 concludes with a list of general questions you can ask of your manuscript, such as (1) Is the topic appropriate for the journal to which the manuscript is submitted? (2) Are the citations appropriate and complete? and (3) Is the discussion thorough? (APA, 1994, p. 21)

The second chapter of the *Manual* discusses writing style, grammar, and guidelines to reduce bias in language. The section on writing style is more extensive than the ideas we presented earlier about scientific writing style.

The remaining chapters of the *Manual* present specific information on all aspects of a manuscript. The table of contents should be referred to for general topics. The index is particularly valuable if you know the nature of the problem. In addition, Appendix B of the *Manual* provides a checklist, including such specifics as (1) Are the margins 1 inch? (2) Do the text citations and reference list entries agree both in spelling and in date? (3) Are page numbers provided in text for all quotations? (4) Is the required number of copies of the manuscript, including the original, being sent?

A VIEW FROM THE OTHER SIDE

(This section was written by Lois Colbridge, one of our students, who saw the publication process from the inside. We think you will benefit from her experience and insights.)

I used to work as an editorial assistant for a psychotherapy journal; my job was to track articles as they moved through the system. As a result of this experience, I can tell you what happens, at least at one journal, during the stage of the publishing process in which you, the researcher, "wait several months."

You have gone through all the steps described in this book. You have put your heart and soul into this study and, with a mixture of pride and trepidation, you ship it off to the editor of the journal you have selected.

The editor is not sitting in his (it was a he in this case) office waiting with bated breath for submissions. The editor of the journal where I worked had a very busy practice and did numerous consultations and presentations, in addition to editing the journal. Your article arrives, along with somewhere between 5 and 20 other articles that week. And I wasn't working at one of the big journals! Your article gets logged in, then it sits in a pile on the editor's desk until he has a chance to look at it.

His review is cursory. He usually reads the title, occasionally the abstract. First, he decides whether he thinks your study has any merit at all. If so, how does it fit with other articles the journal has published? Is it appropriate for this journal? Have too many articles regarding the same topic been published in this journal and in comparable journals? What's already in the pipeline?

At this point, for one reason or another, your article may be returned to you with a "thanks, but no thanks." So in one sense, waiting several months is good, because at least you've passed the first hurdle!

If your article is still being considered, the editor will decide to whom it should now be sent. Which members of the editorial board have the most expertise in the area your study addresses? That decision made, your article once again arrives at the desk of the editorial assistant.

Now it is sent to one or more members of the editorial board for review. Meanwhile you wait. It's not that those people don't care. It is not that they are purposefully trying to torture you. It is just that they are, truly, very, very, busy. They are prominent clinicians, authors, academicians. You would readily recognize many of their names.

Sometimes the reviewer is "too busy at this time" to review your submission. Once again it crosses the desk of the assistant editor, on its way to a different reviewer. Eventually, your article comes back with comments. It is now set for one of three fates: either the reviewer really likes it (very rare), basically believes it to be bunk (unfortunately all too often), or has comments regarding revisions that need to be made (this is by far the most common response). Then you receive a reply from the editor.

Of course, acceptance is wonderful. Mission accomplished! But you should also feel encouraged if you have received suggestions for revisions. This means that the editor and the reviewers think that your study has the potential to be an important addition to the knowledge base. Let me stress again—these are the people who are prominent in their fields.

What would I suggest if you receive suggestions for revision? Lick your wounded ego. Give their suggestions serious consideration. Yes, they may be opinionated. Yes, they have their biases. (I know. I worked with them!) Still these people, who have earned positions of respect in their areas of expertise, have communicated to you that they believe that you have information to share with your colleagues that is potentially valuable.

And what if you receive a rejection letter? It may be a matter of submitting to the wrong journal at the wrong time. Or the reviewers may have problems with any of a number of components of your study. Give serious consideration to their comments. They did not get where they are for no reason. But keep your own counsel also. If you truly believe you are right, and if you truly want to prove that, firm up your position. Show them why and how your conclusions are correct. Be persistent, and some day you may be the expert in the field! Write on!

CONCLUDING COMMENTS

Acceptance of a master's thesis by your committee, an article by a journal, or a paper by a conference is a professionally exhilarating experience. It is an acknowledgment that your research does have an impact on the knowledge base. The development of the dissemination is a long and arduous task, as was indicated in Table 11-1. The careful reader will notice the similarities as well as the differences in the three outlets. Now you must make every effort to represent that research in the best way possible. Be proud of the research and be proud of the way you present it. Also be prepared to answer questions about it, not only in the immediate future but also in the years to come.

A FINAL VISIT WITH MARIA

MARIA DECIDED TO WRITE up her study both as a master's thesis and as a journal article. She felt that the effectiveness of the multifaceted approach needed to be shared with other researchers and practitioners. She decided to write the article because she rightfully feared that few would read her master's thesis.

The article that Maria developed and sent for review appears in Appendix D. We refer to the article as a way of summarizing and emphasizing crucial aspects of reporting results. Notice that line numbers appear in Appendix D, although they would not appear in an article submission. We use these numbers as a way of referencing the article.

Line 1. Title is brief, but could have been more specific with regard to the kind of treatment.

Line 4. Abstract is brief and summarizes the important aspects of the study.

Line 10. Note that the specific dependent variables were not mentioned, only the construct.

Line 15. Statement of research question is clear and at the beginning of the paper.

Line 21. Brief definition provided so that the casual reader will understand the construct.

Lines 24–39. Rationale given for why the behavior should be investigated. Severity, rising incidence, and consequences of not providing therapy are given.

Line 56. Three specific research hypotheses are given. The first two are directional in that the newly devised treatment is expected to be better than the current therapy of choice. The third research hypothesis is nondirectional, because the researcher really desired that there would be no difference in the effectiveness of the new treatment for the two ethnicities.

Line 66. Method of soliciting subjects identified—a convenient sample.

TABLE 11-9   Acceptance letter for Maria's journal article.

Maria Gonzalez   February 2, 1993
Counseling Center
Southwestern University
Southwestern, New Mexico

Dear Ms. Gonzalez:
    We are pleased to inform you that your article, "A new treatment for bulimic women" has been accepted for publication. The ratings of the three reviewers are included. In my opinion, the only comment that you need to attend to is to provide a rationale for why the research hypothesis concerning ethnicities was investigated. Please note that we are encouraged that you included Hispanic American women; we just want you to provide a rationale for the reader. If you can provide this to us within 2 weeks, we can include your article in the next issue of the journal.
    You will need to read and correct the page proofs, which should arrive about 1 month after receipt of your rationale.

                                        Cordially,

                        XXXXXXXXXXXXXXXXXXXXXXXXXXXXXXXXXX
_____

    Line 71. Random assignment of volunteers to one of two treatments.
    Line 73. Independent variable of treatment clearly delineated.
    Line 86. Test administration procedures followed those in the manual.
    Line 93. Reliability and validity information for the dependent variable.
    Line 98. Demographic information provided on Psychological Adjustment and Family Environmental Scale. These measures should have been discussed in the Method sections.
    Line 105. Results presented for each research hypothesis, along with test statistic and probability.
    Line 115. Sample means are represented by M.
    Line 117. Generalization to target population, along with rationale for generalizing results to an even larger population.
    Line 120. Author questions generalization of results to other populations (younger, older, not in college, African American).
    Line 131. Elimination of history as threat to internal validity (by design) and to external validity (because no major bulimic event).
    Line 135. Author questions ability to identify which of the multifaceted components caused the success of the multifaceted approach. Posttreatment inquiry identified one weak component—a candidate for future investigation.
    Line 141. Procedures for establishing that no demand characteristics operated are discussed.
    Line 147. Posttest sensitization identified as a possible threat to validity but argued that it should become part of the treatment.
    Line 150. Timing of posttest administration identified as a problem. A longer time delay is suggested.
    Line 153. Researcher bias discussed as a potential threat; precautions taken are elucidated.
    Line 167. Recommendations for future research.
    Line 173. References are in accord with APA style manual.
    Line 215. Acknowledgments indicate (1) where other versions of the research were reported, (2) source of funds, (3) persons who assisted with the study, and (4) how reprints can be obtained.
    Line 244. References are in accord with APA style manual.

Because Maria was extremely careful with every step of her research project (literature review, design of the study, selection of dependent variable, implementation, analysis of the data, and writing the study), her submission was accepted with only one editorial stipulation (see Table 11-9). That stipulation was to provide a rationale for why the research hypothesis concerning ethnicities was investigated. Maria at first felt that the rationale for investigating the performance of Hispanic American and Anglo-American women was obvious, but eventually came to the realization that the rationale was not as obvious to others less involved with the treatment of bulimia. She soon came to realize that she was one of the experts on the treatment of bulimia.

EXERCISES

1. Access the publication guidelines of three different journals in your field and compare their publication requirements.

2. Write up Maria's section on why she decided to analyze Anglo-American *and* Hispanic American women. Use fictitious references, and concentrate on the logical flow.

3. Why is it important to adopt a standardized format for reporting research?

4. Rate each of the articles in Appendix E in terms of fulfilling the objectives of each of the article's sections.

5. For those planning on doing a thesis, obtain a "call for papers" from some organization. Prepare the abstract as if you were submitting your thesis for the conference.

APPENDIX A

APA ETHICS REGARDING RESEARCH

ETHICAL PRINCIPLES OF PSYCHOLOGISTS AND CODE OF CONDUCT

CONTENTS

INTRODUCTION

The American Psychological Association's (APA's) Ethical Principles of Psychologists and Code of Conduct (hereinafter referred to as the Ethics Code) consists of an Introduction, a Preamble, six General Principles (A–F), and specific Ethical Standards. The Introduction discusses the intent, organization, procedural considerations, and scope of application of the Ethics Code. The Preamble and General Principles are *aspirational* goals to guide psychologists toward the highest ideals of psychology. Although the Preamble and General Principles are not themselves enforceable rules, they should be considered by psychologists in arriving at an ethical course of action and may be considered by ethics bodies in interpreting the Ethical Standards. The Ethical Standards set forth *enforceable* rules for conduct as psychologists. Most of the Ethical Standards are written broadly, in order to apply to psychologists in varied roles, although the application of an Ethical Standard may vary depending on the context. The Ethical Standards are not exhaustive. The fact that a given conduct is not specifically addressed by the Ethics Code does not mean that it is necessarily either ethical or unethical.

Membership in the APA commits members to adhere to the APA Ethics Code and to the rules and procedures used to implement it. Psychologists and students, whether or not they are APA members, should be aware that the Ethics Code may be applied to them by state psychology boards, courts, or other public bodies.

This Ethics Code applies only to psychologists' work-related activities, that is, activities that are part of the psychologists' scientific and professional functions or that are psychological in nature. It includes the clinical or counseling practice of psychology, research, teaching, supervision of trainees, development of assessment instruments, conducting assessments, educational counseling, organizational consulting, social intervention, administration, and other activities as well. These work-related activities can be distinguished from the purely private conduct of a psychologist, which ordinarily is not within the purview of the Ethics Code.

The Ethics Code is intended to provide standards of professional conduct that can be applied by the APA and by other bodies that choose to adopt them. Whether or not a psychologist has violated the Ethics Code does not by itself determine whether he or she is legally liable in a court action, whether a contract is enforceable, or whether other legal consequences occur. These results are based on legal rather than ethical rules. However, compliance with or violation of the Ethics Code may be admissible as evidence in some legal proceedings, depending on the circumstances.

In the process of making decisions regarding their professional behavior, psychologists must consider this Ethics Code, in addition to applicable laws and psychology board regulations. If the Ethics Code establishes a higher standard of conduct than is required by law, psychologists must meet the higher ethical standard. If the Ethics Code standard appears to conflict with the requirements of law, then psychologists make known their commitment to the Ethics Code and take steps to resolve the conflict in a responsible manner. If neither law nor the Ethics Code resolves an issue, psychologists should consider other professional materials[1] and the dictates of their own conscience, as well as seek consultation with others within the field when this is practical.

This version of the APA Ethics Code was adopted by the American Psychological Association's Council of Representatives during its meeting, August 13 and 16, 1992, and is effective beginning December 1, 1992. Inquiries concerning the substance or interpretation of the

APA Ethics Code should be addressed to the Director, Office of Ethics, American Psychological Association, 750 First Street, NE, Washington, DC 20002-4242.

This Code will be used to adjudicate complaints brought concerning alleged conduct occurring on or after the effective date. Complaints regarding conduct occurring prior to the effective date will be adjudicated on the basis of the version of the Code that was in effect at the time the conduct occurred, except that no provisions repealed in June 1989, will be enforced even if an earlier version contains the provision. The Ethics Code will undergo continuing review and study for future revisions; comments on the Code may be sent to the above address.

The APA has previously published its Ethical Standards as follows:

American Psychological Association. (1953). *Ethical standards of psychologists.* Washington, DC: Author.

American Psychological Association. (1958). Standards of ethical behavior for psychologists. *American Psychologist, 13,* 268–271.

American Psychological Association. (1963). Ethical standards of psychologists. *American Psychologist, 18,* 56–60.

American Psychological Association. (1968). Ethical standards of psychologists. *American Psychologist, 23,* 357–361.

American Psychological Association. (1977, March). Ethical standards of psychologists. *APA Monitor,* pp. 22–23.

American Psychological Association. (1979). *Ethical standards of psychologists.* Washington, DC: Author.

American Psychological Association. (1981). Ethical principles of psychologists. *American Psychologist, 36,* 633–638.

American Psychological Association. (1990). Ethical principles of psychologists (Amended June 2, 1989). *American Psychologist, 45,* 390–395.

Request copies of the APA's Ethical Principles of Psychologists and Code of Conduct from the APA Order Department, 750 First Street, NE, Washington, DC 20002-4242, or phone (202) 336-5510.

The procedures for filing, investigating, and resolving complaints of unethical conduct are described in the current Rules and Procedures of the APA Ethics Committee. The actions that APA may take for violations of the Ethics Code include actions such as reprimand, censure, termination of APA membership, and referral of the matter to other bodies. Complainants who seek remedies such as monetary damages in alleging ethical violations by a psychologist must resort to private negotiation, administrative bodies, or the courts. Actions that violate the Ethics Code may lead to the imposition of sanctions on a psychologist by bodies other than APA, including

---

[1] Professional materials that are most helpful in this regard are guidelines and standards that have been adopted or endorsed by professional psychological organizations. Such guidelines and standards, whether adopted by the American Psychological Association (APA) or its Divisions, are not enforceable as such by this Ethics Code, but are of educative value to psychologists, courts, and professional bodies. Such materials include, but are not limited to, the APA's *General Guidelines for Providers of Psychological Services* (1987), *Specialty Guidelines for the Delivery of Services by Clinical Psychologists, Counseling Psychologists, Industrial/Organizational Psychologists, and School Psychologists* (1981), *Guidelines for Computer Based Tests and Interpretations* (1987), *Standards for Educational and Psychological Testing* (1985), *Ethical Principles in the Conduct of Research With Human Participants* (1982), *Guidelines for Ethical Conduct in the Care and Use of Animals* (1986), *Guidelines for Providers of Psychological Services to Ethnic, Linguistic, and Culturally Diverse Populations* (1990), and *Publication Manual of the American Psychological Association* (3rd ed., 1983). Materials not adopted by APA as a whole include the APA Division 41 (Forensic Psychology)/American Psychology–Law Society's *Specialty Guidelines for Forensic Psychologists* (1991).

state psychological associations, other professional groups, psychology boards, other state or federal agencies, and payors for health services. In addition to actions for violation of the Ethics Code, the APA Bylaws provide that APA may take action against a member after his or her conviction of a felony, expulsion or suspension from an affiliated state psychological association, or suspension or loss of licensure.

PREAMBLE

Psychologists work to develop a valid and reliable body of scientific knowledge based on research. They may apply that knowledge to human behavior in a variety of contexts. In doing so, they perform many roles, such as researcher, educator, diagnostician, therapist, supervisor, consultant, administrator, social interventionist, and expert witness. Their goal is to broaden knowledge of behavior and, where appropriate, to apply it pragmatically to improve the condition of both the individual and society. Psychologists respect the central importance of freedom of inquiry and expression in research, teaching, and publication. They also strive to help the public in developing informed judgments and choices concerning human behavior. This Ethics Code provides a common set of values upon which psychologists build their professional and scientific work.

This Code is intended to provide both the general principles and the decision rules to cover most situations encountered by psychologists. It has as its primary goal the welfare and protection of the individuals and groups with whom psychologists work. It is the individual responsibility of each psychologist to aspire to the highest possible standards of conduct. Psychologists respect and protect human and civil rights, and do not knowingly participate in or condone unfair discriminatory practices.

The development of a dynamic set of ethical standards for a psychologist's work-related conduct requires a personal commitment to a lifelong effort to act ethically; to encourage ethical behavior by students, supervisees, employees, and colleagues, as appropriate; and to consult with others, as needed, concerning ethical problems. Each psychologist supplements, but does not violate, the Ethics Code's values and rules on the basis of guidance drawn from personal values, culture, and experience.

GENERAL PRINCIPLES

Principle A: Competence

Psychologists strive to maintain high standards of competence in their work. They recognize the boundaries of their particular competencies and the limitations of their expertise. They provide only those services and use only those techniques for which they are qualified by education, training, or experience. Psychologists are cognizant of the fact that the competencies required in serving, teaching, and/or studying groups of people vary with the distinctive characteristics of those groups. In those areas in which recognized professional standards do not yet exist, psychologists exercise careful judgment and take appropriate precautions to protect the welfare of those with whom they work. They maintain knowledge of relevant scientific and professional information related to the services they render, and they recognize the need for ongoing education. Psychologists make appropriate use of scientific, professional, technical, and administrative resources.

Principle B: Integrity

Psychologists seek to promote integrity in the science, teaching, and practice of psychology. In these activities psychologists are honest, fair, and respectful of others. In describing or reporting their qualifications, services, products, fees, research, or teaching, they do not make statements that are false, misleading, or deceptive. Psychologists strive to be aware of their own belief systems, values, needs, and limitations and the effect of these on their work. To the extent feasible, they attempt to clarify for relevant parties the roles they are performing and to function appropriately in accordance with those roles. Psychologists avoid improper and potentially harmful dual relationships.

Principle C: Professional and Scientific Responsibility

Psychologists uphold professional standards of conduct, clarify their professional roles and obligations, accept appropriate responsibility for their behavior, and adapt their methods to the needs of different populations. Psychologists consult with, refer to, or cooperate with other professionals and institutions to the extent needed to serve the best interests of their patients, clients, or other recipients of their services. Psychologists' moral standards and conduct are personal matters to the same degree as is true for any other person, except as psychologists' conduct may compromise their professional responsibilities or reduce the public's trust in psychology and psychologists. Psychologists are concerned about the ethical compliance of their colleagues' scientific and professional conduct. When appropriate, they consult with colleagues in order to prevent or avoid unethical conduct.

Principle D: Respect for People's Rights and Dignity

Psychologists accord appropriate respect to the fundamental rights, dignity, and worth of all people. They respect the rights of individuals to privacy, confidentiality, self-determination, and autonomy, mindful that legal and other obligations may lead to inconsistency and conflict with the exercise of these rights. Psychologists are aware of cultural, individual, and role differences, including those due to age, gender, race, ethnicity, national origin, religion, sexual orientation, disability, language, and so-

cioeconomic status. Psychologists try to eliminate the effect on their work of biases based on those factors, and they do not knowingly participate in or condone unfair discriminatory practices.

Principle E: Concern for Others' Welfare

Psychologists seek to contribute to the welfare of those with whom they interact professionally. In their professional actions, psychologists weigh the welfare and rights of their patients or clients, students, supervisees, human research participants, and other affected persons, and the welfare of animal subjects of research. When conflicts occur among psychologists' obligations or concerns, they attempt to resolve these conflicts and to perform their roles in a responsible fashion that avoids or minimizes harm. Psychologists are sensitive to real and ascribed differences in power between themselves and others, and they do not exploit or mislead other people during or after professional relationships.

Principle F: Social Responsibility

Psychologists are aware of their professional and scientific responsibilities to the community and the society in which they work and live. They apply and make public their knowledge of psychology in order to contribute to human welfare. Psychologists are concerned about and work to mitigate the causes of human suffering. When undertaking research, they strive to advance human welfare and the science of psychology. Psychologists try to avoid misuse of their work. Psychologists comply with the law and encourage the development of law and social policy that serve the interests of their patients and clients and the public. They are encouraged to contribute a portion of their professional time for little or no personal advantage.

6.06 Planning Research

(a) Psychologists design, conduct, and report research in accordance with recognized standards of scientific competence and ethical research.

(b) Psychologists plan their research so as to minimize the possibility that results will be misleading.

(c) In planning research, psychologists consider its ethical acceptability under the Ethics Code. If an ethical issue is unclear, psychologists seek to resolve the issue through consultation with institutional review boards, animal care and use committees, peer consultations, or other proper mechanisms.

(d) Psychologists take reasonable steps to implement appropriate protections for the rights and welfare of human participants, other persons affected by the research, and the welfare of animal subjects.

6.07 Responsibility

(a) Psychologists conduct research competently and with due concern for the dignity and welfare of the participants.

(b) Psychologists are responsible for the ethical conduct of research conducted by them or by others under their supervision or control.

(c) Researchers and assistants are permitted to perform only those tasks for which they are appropriately trained and prepared.

(d) As part of the process of development and implementation of research projects, psychologists consult those with expertise concerning any special population under investigation or most likely to be affected.

6.08 Compliance With Law and Standards

Psychologists plan and conduct research in a manner consistent with federal and state law and regulations, as well as professional standards governing the conduct of research, and particularly those standards governing research with human participants and animal subjects.

6.09 Institutional Approval

Psychologists obtain from host institutions or organizations appropriate approval prior to conducting research, and they provide accurate information about their research proposals. They conduct the research in accordance with the approved research protocol.

6.10 Research Responsibilities

Prior to conducting research (except research involving only anonymous surveys, naturalistic observations, or similar research), psychologists enter into an agreement with participants that clarifies the nature of the research and the responsibilities of each party.

6.11 Informed Consent to Research

(a) Psychologists use language that is reasonably understandable to research participants in obtaining their appropriate informed consent (except as provided in Standard 6.12, Dispensing With Informed Consent). Such informed consent is appropriately documented.

(b) Using language that is reasonably understandable to participants, psychologists inform participants of the nature of the research; they inform participants that they are free to participate or to decline to participate or to withdraw from the research; they explain the foreseeable consequences of declining or withdrawing; they inform participants of significant factors that may be expected to influence their willingness to participate (such as risks, discomfort, adverse effects, or limitations on confidentiality, except as provided in Standard 6.15, Deception in Research); and they explain other aspects about which the prospective participants inquire.

(c) When psychologists conduct research with individuals such as students or subordinates, psychologists take special care to protect the prospective participants from adverse consequences of declining or withdrawing from participation.

(d) When research participation is a course requirement or opportunity for extra credit, the prospective participant is given the choice of equitable alternative activities.

(e) For persons who are legally incapable of giving informed consent, psychologists nevertheless (1) provide an appropriate explanation, (2) obtain the participant's assent, and (3) obtain appropriate permission from a legally authorized person, if such substitute consent is permitted by law.

6.12 Dispensing With Informed Consent

Before determining that planned research (such as research involving only anonymous questionnaires, naturalistic observations, or certain kinds of archival research) does not require the informed consent of research participants, psychologists consider applicable regulations and institutional review board requirements, and they consult with colleagues as appropriate.

6.13 Informed Consent in Research Filming or Recording

Psychologists obtain informed consent from research participants prior to filming or recording them in any form, unless the research involves simply naturalistic observations in public places and it is not anticipated that the recording will be used in a manner that could cause personal identification or harm.

6.14 Offering Inducements for Research Participants

(a) In offering professional services as an inducement to obtain research participants, psychologists make clear the nature of the services, as well as the risks, obligations, and limitations. (See also Standard 1.18, Barter [With Patients or Clients].)

(b) Psychologists do not offer excessive or inappropriate financial or other inducements to obtain research participants, particularly when it might tend to coerce participation.

6.15 Deception in Research

(a) Psychologists do not conduct a study involving deception unless they have determined that the use of deceptive techniques is justified by the study's prospective scientific, educational, or applied value and that equally effective alternative procedures that do not use deception are not feasible.

(b) Psychologists never deceive research participants about significant aspects that would affect their willingness to participate, such as physical risks, discomfort, or unpleasant emotional experiences.

(c) Any other deception that is an integral feature of the design and conduct of an experiment must be explained to participants as early as is feasible, preferably at the conclusion of their participation, but no later than at the conclusion of the research. (See also Standard 6.18, Providing Participants With Information About the Study.)

6.16 Sharing and Utilizing Data

Psychologists inform research participants of their anticipated sharing or further use of personally identifiable research data and of the possibility of unanticipated future uses.

6.17 Minimizing Invasiveness

In conducting research, psychologists interfere with the participants or milieu from which data are collected only in a manner that is warranted by an appropriate research design and that is consistent with psychologists' roles as scientific investigators.

6.18 Providing Participants With Information About the Study

(a) Psychologists provide a prompt opportunity for participants to obtain appropriate information about the nature, results, and conclusions of the research, and psychologists attempt to correct any misconceptions that participants may have.

(b) If scientific or humane values justify delaying or withholding this information, psychologists take reasonable measures to reduce the risk of harm.

6.19 Honoring Commitments

Psychologists take reasonable measures to honor all commitments they have made to research participants.

6.20 Care and Use of Animals in Research

(a) Psychologists who conduct research involving animals treat them humanely.

(b) Psychologists acquire, care for, use, and dispose of animals in compliance with current federal, state, and local laws and regulations, and with professional standards.

(c) Psychologists trained in research methods and experienced in the care of laboratory animals supervise all procedures involving animals and are responsible for ensuring appropriate consideration of their comfort, health, and humane treatment.

(d) Psychologists ensure that all individuals using animals under their supervision have received instruction in research methods and in the care, maintenance, and handling of the species being used, to the extent appropriate to their role.

(e) Responsibilities and activities of individuals assisting in a research project are consistent with their respective competencies.

(f) Psychologists make reasonable efforts to minimize the discomfort, infection, illness, and pain of animal subjects.

(g) A procedure subjecting animals to pain, stress, or privation is used only when an alternative procedure is unavailable and the goal is justified by its prospective scientific, educational, or applied value.

(h) Surgical procedures are performed under appropriate anesthesia; techniques to avoid infection and minimize pain are followed during and after surgery.

(i) When it is appropriate that the animal's life be terminated, it is done rapidly, with an effort to minimize pain, and in accordance with accepted procedures.

6.21 Reporting of Results

(a) Psychologists do not fabricate data or falsify results in their publications.

(b) If psychologists discover significant errors in their published data, they take reasonable steps to correct such errors in a correction, retraction, erratum, or other appropriate publication means.

6.22 Plagiarism

Psychologists do not present substantial portions or elements of another's work or data as their own, even if the other work or data source is cited occasionally.

6.23 Publication Credit

(a) Psychologists take responsibility and credit, including authorship credit, only for work they have actually performed or to which they have contributed.

(b) Principal authorship and other publication credits accurately reflect the relative scientific or professional contributions of the individuals involved, regardless of their relative status. Mere possession of an institutional position, such as Department Chair, does not justify authorship credit. Minor contributions to the research or to the writing for publications are appropriately acknowledged, such as in footnotes or in an introductory statement.

(c) A student is usually listed as principal author on any multiple-authored article that is substantially based on the student's dissertation or thesis.

6.24 Duplicate Publication of Data

Psychologists do not publish, as original data, data that have been previously published. This does not preclude republishing data when they are accompanied by proper acknowledgment.

6.25 Sharing Data

After research results are published, psychologists do not withhold the data on which their conclusions are based from other competent professionals who seek to verify the substantive claims through reanalysis and who intend to use such data only for that purpose, provided that the confidentiality of the participants can be protected and unless legal rights concerning proprietary data preclude their release.

6.26 Professional Reviewers

Psychologists who review material submitted for publication, grant, or other research proposal review respect the confidentiality of and the proprietary rights in such information of those who submitted it.

APPENDIX B

MARIA'S DATA

18:03 Monday, May 8, 1995

OBS	ID	PREBULIT	POSBULIT	PSYCHADJ	FES	TREAT	EAT
1	1	110	100	1	2	1	52
2	2	112	104	1	3	1	51
3	3	108	98	2	3	1	53
4	4	112	107	2	1	1	58
5	5	106	103	1	1	1	61
6	6	109	102	1	2	1	54
7	7	114	106	3	3	1	57
8	8	115	108	1	1	1	59
9	9	107	100	1	1	1	58
10	10	106	98	2	1	1	53
11	11	118	109	2	3	1	60
12	12	110	102	2	2	1	47
13	13	106	99	3	3	1	42
14	14	108	99	2	2	1	48
15	15	112	108	2	1	1	59
16	16	110	100	3	2	1	41
17	17	111	104	2	2	1	61
18	18	109	103	2	1	1	50
19	19	117	111	2	1	1	60
20	20	116	107	2	3	1	55
21	21	113	104	2	3	1	58
22	22	105	98	2	1	1	54
23	23	109	102	3	3	1	53
24	24	106	104	3	1	1	53
25	25	107	99	3	2	1	47
26	26	110	97	1	1	2	52
27	27	112	102	2	1	2	55
28	28	108	91	2	3	2	38
29	29	112	96	3	1	2	41
30	30	106	90	3	3	2	45
31	31	109	87	1	2	2	43
32	32	114	99	3	1	2	52

33	33	115	99	2	3	2	44
34	34	107	92	3	2	2	42
35	35	106	90	3	2	2	41
36	36	118	103	3	2	2	47
37	37	106	92	3	2	2	42
38	38	108	92	1	3	2	42
39	39	112	95	3	2	2	42
40	40	110	93	2	3	2	40
41	41	111	96	1	1	2	43
42	42	109	91	3	2	2	36
43	43	117	100	2	2	2	48
44	44	116	97	2	2	2	49
45	45	113	96	1	3	2	47
46	46	105	91	3	3	2	43
47	47	109	92	1	3	2	37
48	48	106	95	1	1	2	40
49	49	107	98	2	1	2	46
50	50	109	92	1	2	2	50

APPENDIX B-2
SELECTED DESCRIPTIVE STATISTICS

TREAT=EDUCATIONAL

Variable	N	Mean	Std Dev	Minimum	Maximum
PSYCHADJ	25	2.0000000	0.7071068	1.0000000	3.0000000
PREBULIT	25	110.2400000	3.7000000	105.0000000	118.0000000
POSBULIT	25	103.0000000	3.8078866	98.0000000	111.0000000
EAT	25	53.7600000	5.6145644	41.0000000	61.0000000

TREAT=MULTIFACETED

Variable	N	Mean	Std Dev	Minimum	Maximum
PSYCHADJ	25	2.0800000	0.8621678	1.0000000	3.0000000
PREBULIT	25	110.2000000	3.7080992	105.0000000	118.0000000
POSBULIT	25	94.6400000	4.0710359	87.0000000	103.0000000
EAT	25	44.2000000	4.8562674	36.0000000	55.0000000

PREBULIT	Frequency	Percent	Cumulative Frequency	Cumulative Percent
105	2	4.0	2	4.0
106	8	16.0	10	20.0
107	4	8.0	14	28.0
108	4	8.0	18	36.0
109	7	14.0	25	50.0
110	5	10.0	30	60.0
111	2	4.0	32	64.0
112	6	12.0	38	76.0
113	2	4.0	40	80.0
114	2	4.0	42	84.0
115	2	4.0	44	88.0
116	2	4.0	46	92.0
117	2	4.0	48	96.0
118	2	4.0	50	100.0

POSBULIT	Frequency	Percent	Cumulative Frequency	Cumulative Percent
87	1	2.0	1	2.0
90	2	4.0	3	6.0
91	3	6.0	6	12.0
92	5	10.0	11	22.0
93	1	2.0	12	24.0
95	2	4.0	14	28.0
96	3	6.0	17	34.0
97	2	4.0	19	38.0
98	4	8.0	23	46.0
99	5	10.0	28	56.0
100	4	8.0	32	64.0
102	4	8.0	36	72.0
103	3	6.0	39	78.0
104	4	8.0	43	86.0
106	1	2.0	44	88.0
107	2	4.0	46	92.0
108	2	4.0	48	96.0
109	1	2.0	49	98.0
111	1	2.0	50	100.0

MARIA'S DATA

TABLE OF TREAT BY FES

TREAT   FES

Frequency
Percent
Row Pct
Col Pct

	1	1	1	TOTAL
EDUCATIONAL	10 20.00 40.00 58.82	7 14.00 28.00 41.18	8 16.00 32.00 50.00	25 50.00
MULTIFACETED	7 14.00 28.00 41.18	10 20.00 40.00 58.82	8 16.00 32.00 50.00	25 50.00
Total	17 34.00	17 34.00	50.00 100.00	50 100.00

STATISTICS FOR TABLE OF TREAT BY FES

Statistic	DF	Value	Prob
Chi-Square	2	1.059	0.589
Likelihood Ratio Chi-Square	2	1.064	0.587
Mantel-Haenszel Chi-Square	1	0.267	0.605
Phi Coefficient		0.146	
Contingency Coefficient		0.144	
Cramer's V		0.146	

Sample Size = 50

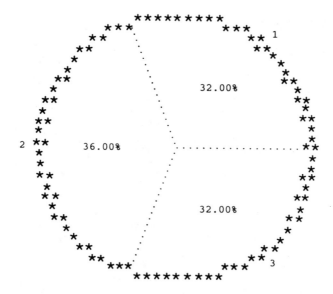

Percentage of TREAT by FES

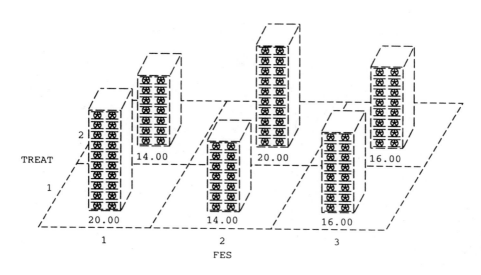

Percentage of FES grouped by TREAT

Frequency

```
17 +    MMMMM      MMMMM
   |    MMMMM      MMMMM      MMMMM
16 +    MMMMM      MMMMM      MMMMM
   |    MMMMM      MMMMM      MMMMM
15 +    MMMMM      MMMMM      MMMMM
   |    MMMMM      MMMMM      MMMMM
14 +    MMMMM      MMMMM      MMMMM
   |    MMMMM      MMMMM      MMMMM
13 +    MMMMM      MMMMM      MMMMM
   |    MMMMM      MMMMM      MMMMM
12 +    MMMMM      MMMMM      MMMMM
   |    MMMMM      MMMMM      MMMMM
11 +    MMMMM      MMMMM      MMMMM
   |    MMMMM      MMMMM      MMMMM
10 +    EEEEE      MMMMM      MMMMM
   |    EEEEE      MMMMM      MMMMM
 9 +    EEEEE      MMMMM      MMMMM
   |    EEEEE      MMMMM      MMMMM
 8 +    EEEEE      MMMMM      EEEEE
   |    EEEEE      MMMMM      EEEEE
 7 +    EEEEE      EEEEE      EEEEE
   |    EEEEE      EEEEE      EEEEE
 6 +    EEEEE      EEEEE      EEEEE
   |    EEEEE      EEEEE      EEEEE
 5 +    EEEEE      EEEEE      EEEEE
   |    EEEEE      EEEEE      EEEEE
 4 +    EEEEE      EEEEE      EEEEE
   |    EEEEE      EEEEE      EEEEE
 3 +    EEEEE      EEEEE      EEEEE
   |    EEEEE      EEEEE      EEEEE
 2 +    EEEEE      EEEEE      EEEEE
   |    EEEEE      EEEEE      EEEEE
 1 +    EEEEE      EEEEE      EEEEE
   |    EEEEE      EEEEE      EEEEE
_____

        1          2          3
                  FES
  Symbol TREAT        Symbol TREAT
    E EDUCATIONAL        M MULTIFACETED
```

```
OPTIONS LINESIZE = 74 PAGESIZE = 52;
TITLE1 "            APPENDIX B-1               ";
TITLE2 "            MARIA'S RAW DATA           ";
PROC FORMAT; VALUE TREATF 1 = 'EDUCATIONAL' 2 = 'MULTI-
FACETED'; CMSFILEDEF NEW DISK MARIA DATA A1;
DATA ALL;
INFILE NEW;
INPUT ID 1-2 PREBULIT 4-6 POSBULIT 8-10 PSYCHADJ 12
FES   14 TREAT 16 EAT 18-19;
PROC PRINT;
PROC PRINT DATA = ALL;
PROC MEANS; VAR PSYCHADJ PREBULIT POSBULIT EAT;
  BY TREAT; FORMAT TREAT TREATF.;
PROC FREQ; TABLE PREBULIT POSBULIT;
PROC FREQ; TABLE TREAT * FES / CHISQ;
  FORMAT TREAT TREATF.;
PROC CHART; VBAR FES / DISCRETE SUBGROUP = TREAT;
  FORMAT TREAT TREATF.;
PROC CHART; PIE FES / DISCRETE TYPE = PERCENT FREQ =
  TREAT; FORMAT TREAT TREATF.;
PROC CHART; BLOCK FES/TYPE = PERCENT GROUP = TREAT
  DISCRETE SYMBOL='XOA';
FORMAT TREAT TREATF.;
```

APPENDIX C

COMPUTER ANALYSIS OF MARIA'S RESEARCH HYPOTHESES

```
APPENDIX C-1                                              1
                    13:03 Saturday, July 30, 1994
RH #3 POSITIVE CORRELATION BETWEEN BULIT CHANGE SCORES
              AND PSYCHOLOGICAL ADJUSTMENT
NOTE THAT THE PEARSON CORRELATION IS THE TOP NUMBER
     IN THE RIGHT-HAND CELL R = .02803 AND THE
NONDIRECTIONAL PROBABILITY IS BELOW IT P = .8468


                  Correlation Analysis

       2 'VAR' Variables: DECREASE  PSYCHADJ

                  Simple Statistics
```

Variable	N	Mean	Std Dev	Sum	Minimum	Maximum
DECREASE	50	11.4000	4.8445	570.0000	2.0000	22.0000
PSYCHADJ	50	2.0400	0.7814	102.0000	1.0000	3.0000

```
Pearson Correlation Coefficients / Prob > |R| under
Ho: Rho=0 / N = 50

                        DECREASE        PSYCHADJ
          DECREASE      1.00000         0.02803
                        0.0             0.8468

          PSYCHADJ      0.02803         1.00000
                        0.8468          0.0
OPTIONS LINESIZE = 74 PAGESIZE = 52;
CMS FILEDEF NEW DISK MARIA DATA A1;
DATA ALL;
INFILE NEW;
```

```
INPUT PREBULIT 4-6 POSBULIT 8-10 PSYCHADJ 12;
DECREASE = PREBULIT - POSBULIT;
PROC CORR; VAR DECREASE PSYCHADJ;
TITLE1 " APPENDIX C-1 ";
TITLE2 "                    ";
TITLE3 " RH #3 POSITIVE CORRELATION BETWEEN BULIT
         CHANGE SCORES ";
TITLE4 " AND PSYCHOLOGICAL ADJUSTMENT ";
TITLE5 " NOTE THAT THE PEARSON CORRELATION IS THE TOP
         NUMBER ";
TITLE6 " IN THE RIGHT-HAND CELL R = .02803 AND THE ";
TITLE7 " NONDIRECTIONAL PROBABILITY IS BELOW IT P =
         .8468 ";
```

11:52 Saturday, July 30, 1994

RH #4 POSITIVE CORRELATION GREATER THAN .60 BETWEEN
POSTTEST BULIT AND EAT.
NEED TO PLUG THE RESULTING CORRELATION INTO THE
FISCHER Z FORMULA IN ORDER TO TEST FOR SIGNIFICANCE
FROM A VALUE OTHER THAN ZERO. SEE HINKLE ET AL., P222
Z = (ZR - ZP)/ SQUARE ROOT OF (1 / N-3):
R=.80, ZR = 1.099 AND RHO=.60 Z60 = .693 THUS Z=2.78
AND HAS AN ASSOCIATED P OF .0027.

Correlation Analysis

2 'VAR' Variables: POSBULIT EAT

Simple Statistics

Variable	N	Mean	Std Dev	Sum	Minimum	Maximum
POSBULIT	50	98.8200	5.7488	4941	87.0000	111.0000
EAT	50	48.9800	7.0927	2449	36.0000	61.0000

Pearson Correlation Coefficients / Prob > |R| under
Ho: Rho=0 / N = 50

	POSBULIT	EAT
POSBULIT	1.00000	0.80724
	0.0	0.0001
EAT	0.80724	1.00000
	0.0001	0.0


```
OPTIONS LINESIZE = 74 PAGESIZE = 52;
CMS FILEDEF NEW DISK MARIA DATA A1;
DATA ALL;
INFILE NEW;
INPUT POSBULIT 8-10 EAT 18-19;
PROC CORR; VAR POSBULIT EAT;
TITLE1 " APPENDIX C-2 ";
TITLE2 "              ";
TITLE3 " RH #4 POSITIVE CORRELATION GREATER THAN .60
        BETWEEN ";
TITLE4 " POSTTEST BULIT AND EAT. ";
TITLE5 " NEED TO PLUG THE RESULTING CORRELATION INTO
        THE ";
```

```
TITLE6  " FISCHER Z FORMULA IN ORDER TO TEST FOR
          SIGNIFICANCE ";
TITLE7  " FROM A VALUE OTHER THAN ZERO. SEE HINKLE ET
          AL., P222 ";
TITLE8  " Z = (ZR - ZP)/ SQUARE ROOT OF (1 / N-3): ";
TITLE9  " R=.80, ZR = 1.099 AND RHO=.60 Z60 = .693 THUS
          Z=2.78 ";
TITLE10" AND HAS AN ASSOCIATED P OF .0027.";
```

12:44 Sunday, July 31, 1994

RH #5 POSITIVE CORRELATION GREATER THAN .70 BETWEEN
THE TWO ADMINISTRATIONS OF THE BULIT WITHIN EACH GROUP.
NOTE THAT TWO CORRELATIONS ARE CALLED FOR, ONE WITHIN
THE MULTIFACETED GROUP AND ONE WITHIN THE EDUCATIONAL
TREATMENT—THIS RH SHOULD BE TWO SEPARATE HYPOTHESES!!
NEED TO PLUG THE RESULTING CORRELATION INTO THE
FISCHER Z FORMULA IN ORDER TO TEST FOR SIGNIFICANCE
FROM A VALUE OTHER THAN ZERO. SEE HINKLE ET AL., P222
Z = (ZR - ZP)/ SQUARE ROOT OF (1 / N-3), FOR EDUCATIONAL:
R=.84, ZR = 1.221 AND RHO=.70 Z70 = .867 THUS Z=2.42, P=.0078

TREAT=1

Correlation Analysis

2 'VAR' Variables: PREBULIT POSBULIT

Simple Statistics

Variable	N	Mean	Std Dev	Sum	Minimum	Maximum
PREBULIT	25	110.2400	3.7000	2756	105.0000	118.0000
POSBULIT	25	103.0000	3.8079	2575	98.0000	111.0000

Pearson Correlation Coefficients / Prob > |R| under
Ho: Rho=0 / N = 25

	PREBULIT	POSBULIT
PREBULIT	1.00000	0.84876
	0.0	0.0001
POSBULIT	0.84876	1.00000
	0.00001	0.0

RH #5 POSITIVE CORRELATION GREATER THAN .70 BETWEEN
THE TWO ADMINISTRATIONS OF THE BULIT WITHIN EACH GROUP.
NOTE THAT TWO CORRELATIONS ARE CALLED FOR, ONE WITHIN
THE MULTIFACETED GROUP AND ONE WITHIN THE EDUCATIONAL
TREATMENT—THIS RH SHOULD BE TWO SEPARATE HYPOTHESES!!
NEED TO PLUG THE RESULTING CORRELATION INTO THE
FISCHER Z FORMULA IN ORDER TO TEST FOR SIGNIFICANCE
FROM A VALUE OTHER THAN ZERO. SEE HINKLE ET AL., P222
Z = (ZR - ZP)/ SQUARE ROOT OF (1 / N-3),
FOR EDUCATIONAL: R=.84, ZR = 1.221 AND RHO=.70
Z70 = .867 THUS Z=2.42, P=.0078

TREAT=2

Correlation Analysis

2 'VAR' Variables: PREBULIT POSBULIT

Simple Statistics

Variable	N	Mean	Std Dev	Sum	Minimum	Maximum
PREBULIT	25	110.2000	3.7081	2755	105.0000	118.0000
POSBULIT	25	94.6400	4.0710	2366	87.0000	103.0000

Pearson Correlation Coefficients / Prob > |R| under
Ho: Rho=0 / N = 25

	PREBULIT	POSBULIT
PREBULIT	1.00000	0.75297
	0.0	0.0001
POSBULIT	0.75297	1.00000
	0.0001	0.0

```
OPTIONS LINESIZE = 74 PAGESIZE = 52;
TITLE " APPENDIX C-3";
CMS FILEDEF NEW DISK MARIA DATA A1;
DATA ALL;
INFILE NEW;
INPUT PREBULIT 4-6 POSBULIT 8-10 TREAT 16;
PROC CORR; VAR PREBULIT POSBULIT; BY TREAT;
TITLE1 " APPENDIX C-3 ";
TITLE2 "             ";
TITLE3 " RH #5 POSITIVE CORRELATION GREATER THAN .70
        BETWEEN ";
TITLE4 " THE TWO ADMINISTRATIONS OF THE BULIT WITHIN
        EACH GROUP. ";
TITLE5 " NOTE THAT TWO CORRELATIONS ARE CALLED FOR,
        ONE WITHIN ";
TITLE6 " THE MULTIFACETED GROUP AND ONE WITHIN THE
        EDUCATIONAL ";
TITLE7 " TREATMENT—THIS RH SHOULD BE TWO SEPARATE
        HYPOTHESES!! ";
TITLE8 " NEED TO PLUG THE RESULTING CORRELATION INTO
        THE ";
```

```
TITLE9  " FISCHER Z FORMULA IN ORDER TO TEST FOR
          SIGNIFICANCE ";
TITLE10 "FROM A VALUE OTHER THAN ZERO. SEE HINKLE ET
          AL., P222 ";
TITLE11 "Z = (ZR - ZP)/ SQUARE ROOT OF (1 / N-3), FOR
          EDUCATIONAL: ";
TITLE12 "R=.84, ZR = 1.221 AND RHO=.70 Z70 = .867 THUS
          Z=2.42, P=.0078";
```

RH #6 POSITIVE RANK CORRELATION > THAN .70 BETWEEN
THE TWO ADMINISTRATIONS OF THE BULIT WITHIN EACH GROUP.
THE SPEARMAN OPTION YIELDS THE RANK CORRELATION.
NEED TO PLUG THE RESULTING CORRELATION INTO THE
FISCHER Z FORMULA IN ORDER TO TEST FOR SIGNIFICANCE
FROM A VALUE OTHER THAN ZERO. SEE HINKLE ET AL., P222
Z = (ZR - ZP)/ SQUARE ROOT OF (1 / N-3), FOR EDUCATIONAL:
R=.81, ZR = 1.142 AND RHO=.70 Z70 = .867 THUS Z=1.88, P =.0301

TREAT=EDUCATIONAL

Correlation Analysis

2 'VAR' Variables: PREBULIT POSBULIT

Simple Statistics

Variable	N	Mean	Std Dev	Median	Minimum	Maximum
PREBULIT	25	110.2400	3.7000	110.0000	105.0000	118.0000
POSBULIT	25	103.0000	3.8079	103.0000	98.0000	111.0000

Spearman Correlation Coefficients / Prob > |R| under
Ho: Rho=0 / N = 25

	PREBULIT	POSBULIT
PREBULIT	1.00000	0.81562
	0.0	0.0001
POSBULIT	0.81562	1.00000
	0.0001	0.0

RH #6 POSITIVE RANK CORRELATION > THAN .70 BETWEEN
THE TWO ADMINISTRATIONS OF THE BULIT WITHIN EACH GROUP.
THE SPEARMAN OPTION YIELDS THE RANK CORRELATION.
NEED TO PLUG THE RESULTING CORRELATION INTO THE
FISCHER Z FORMULA IN ORDER TO TEST FOR SIGNIFICANCE
FROM A VALUE OTHER THAN ZERO. SEE HINKLE ET AL., P222
Z = (ZR - ZP)/ SQUARE ROOT OF (1 / N-3), FOR EDUCATIONAL:
R=.81, ZR = 1.142 AND RHO=.70 Z70 = .867 THUS Z=1.88, P =.0301

TREAT=MULTIFACETED

Correlation Analysis

2 'VAR' Variables: PREBULIT POSBULIT

Simple Statistics

Variable	N	Mean	Std Dev	Median	Minimum	Maximum
PREBULIT	25	110.2000	3.7081	109.0000	105.0000	118.0000
POSBULIT	25	94.6400	4.0710	95.0000	87.0000	103.0000

Spearman Correlation Coefficients / Prob > |R| under
Ho: Rho=0 / N = 25

	PREBULIT	POSBULIT
PREBULIT	1.00000 0.0	0.75316 0.0001
POSBULIT	0.75316 0.0001	1.00000 0.0

```
OPTIONS LINESIZE = 74 PAGESIZE = 52;
PROC FORMAT; VALUE TREATF 1 = "EDUCATIONAL" 2 =
        "MULTIFACETED";
CMS FILEDEF NEW DISK MARIA DATA A1;
DATA ALL;
INFILE NEW;
INPUT PREBULIT 4-6 POSBULIT 8-10 TREAT 16;
PROC CORR SPEARMAN ;VAR PREBULIT POSBULIT; BY TREAT;
        FORMAT TREAT TREATF.;
TITLE1 " APPENDIX C-4 ";
TITLE2 "              ";
```

```
TITLE3  " RH #6 POSITIVE RANK CORRELATION > THAN .70
          BETWEEN ";
TITLE4  " THE TWO ADMINISTRATIONS OF THE BULIT WITHIN
          EACH GROUP. ";
TITLE5  " THE SPEARMAN OPTION YIELDS THE RANK
          CORRELATION. ";
TITLE6  " NEED TO PLUG THE RESULTING CORRELATION INTO
          THE ";
TITLE7  " FISCHER Z FORMULA IN ORDER TO TEST FOR
          SIGNIFICANCE ";
TITLE8  " FROM A VALUE OTHER THAN ZERO. SEE HINKLE ET
          AL., P222 ";
TITLE9  " Z = (ZR - ZP)/ SQUARE ROOT OF (1 / N-3), FOR
          EDUCATIONAL: ";
TITLE10 "R=.81, ZR = 1.142 AND RHO=.70 Z70 = .867 THUS
          Z=1.88, P =.0301";
```

13:06 Saturday, July 30, 1994
RH #7 PSYCHOLOGICAL ADJUSTMENT AND FES
ARE PREDICTIVE OF CHANGE IN BULIT.
PROBABILITY IS AT TOP RIGHT OF PRINTOUT
F = 2.892 AND ASSOCIATED PROB = .0654

Model: MODEL1
Dependent Variable: DECREASE

Analysis of Variance

Source	DF	Sum of Squares	Mean Square	F Value	Prob>F
Model	2	125.99951	62.99975	2.892	0.0654
Error	47	1024.00049	21.78724		
C Total	49	1150.00000			

Root MSE	4.66768	R-square	0.1096	
Dep Mean	11.40000	Adj R-sq	0.0717	
C.V.	40.94457			

Parameter Estimates

Variable	DF	Parameter Estimate	Standard Error	T for HO: Parameter=0	Prob > |T|
INTERCEP	1	7.697910	2.32762744	3.307	0.0018
PSYCHADJ	1	-0.091381	0.86048268	-0.106	0.9159
FES	1	1.963893	0.81959180	2.396	0.0206

Correlation Analysis

2 'VAR' Variables: FES   DECREASE

Simple Statistics

Variable	N	Mean	Std Dev	Sum	Minimum	Maximum
FES	50	1.9800	0.8204	99.0000	1.0000	3.0000
DECREASE	50	11.4000	4.8445	570.0000	2.0000	22.0000

Pearson Correlation Coefficients / Prob > |R| under
Ho: Rho=0 / N = 50

	FES	DECREASE
FES	1.00000	0.33068
	0.0	0.0190
DECREASE	0.33068	1.00000
	0.0190	0.0

```
OPTIONS LINESIZE = 74 PAGESIZE = 52;
CMS FILEDEF NEW DISK MARIA DATA A1;
DATA ALL;
INFILE NEW;
INPUT ID 1-2 PREBULIT 4-6 POSBULIT 8-10 PSYCHADJ 12
        FES 14;
DECREASE = PREBULIT - POSBULIT;
PROC REG; MODEL DECREASE = PSYCHADJ FES;
TITLE1 " APPENDIX C-5 ";
TITLE2 "                    ";
TITLE3 " RH #7 PSYCHOLOGICAL ADJUSTMENT AND FES ";
TITLE4 " ARE PREDICTIVE OF CHANGE IN BULIT. ";
TITLE5 " PROBABILITY IS AT TOP RIGHT OF PRINTOUT ";
TITLE6 " F = 2.892 AND ASSOCIATED PROB = .0654 ";
PROC CORR; VAR FES DECREASE;
TITLE1 " ADDITIONAL INFORMATION FOR RH #7";
```

12:48 Sunday, July 31, 1994
RH #8 MEAN PRETEST BULIT IS GREATER THAN 104.
NOTE THAT THE VARIABLE PREADJ IS CALCULATED ABOVE AND
IS THE PRETEST BULIT MINUS THE HYPOTHESIZED VALUE OF 104
MEAN ABOVE 104 IS 6.22
T:MEAN=0 IS THE TEST STATISTIC T= 11.9969
NONDIRECTIONAL PROBABILITY IS .0001.

Univariate Procedure

Variable=PREADJ

Moments

N	50	Sum Wgts	50
Mean	6.22	Sum	311
Std Dev	3.666116	Variance	13.44041
Skewness	0.552151	Kurtosis	-0.641
USS	2593	CSS	658.58
CV	58.94078	Std Mean	0.518467
T:Mean=0	11.9969	Pr>|T|	0.0001
Num ¬= 0	50	Num > 0	50
M(Sign)	25	Pr>=|M|	0.0001
Sgn Rank	637.5	Pr>=|S|	0.0001

Quantiles(Def=5)

100%	Max	14	99%	14
75%	Q3	8	95%	13
50%	Med	5.5	90%	12
25%	Q1	3	10%	2
0%	Min	1	5%	2
			1%	1
Range		13		
Q3-Q1		5		
Mode		2		

Extremes

Lowest	Obs	Highest	Obs
1(	46)	12(	44)
1(	22)	13(	19)
2(	48)	13(	43)
2(	37)	14(	11)
2(	35)	14(	36)

OPTIONS LINESIZE = 74 PAGESIZE = 52;

```
CMS FILEDEF NEW DISK MARIA DATA A1;
DATA ALL;
INFILE NEW;
INPUT PREBULIT 4-6;
PREADJ = PREBULIT - 104;
PROC UNIVARIATE; VAR PREADJ;
TITLE1 " APPENDIX C-6 ";
TITLE2 "                    ";
TITLE3 " RH #8 MEAN PRETEST BULIT IS GREATER THAN 104. ";
TITLE4 " NOTE THAT THE VARIABLE PREADJ IS CALCULATED
         ABOVE AND ";
TITLE5 " IS THE PRETEST BULIT MINUS THE HYPOTHESIZED
         VALUE OF 104 ";
TITLE6 " MEAN ABOVE 104 IS 6.22 ";
TITLE7 " T:MEAN=0 IS THE TEST STATISTIC T= 11.9969 ";
TITLE8 " NONDIRECTIONAL PROBABILITY IS .0001. ";
```

RH #9 MEAN DECREASE FROM PRETEST BULIT TO POSTTEST BULIT
IS MORE THAN 0. DECREASE WAS CALCULATED ABOVE.
MEAN DECREASE WAS 11.4 T:MEAN=0 IS 16.6395
WITH AN ASSOCIATED PROBABILITY OF .0001/2 OR .00005.

Univariate Procedure

Variable=DECREASE

Moments

N	50	Sum Wgts	50
Mean	11.4	Sum	570
Std Dev	4.844521	Variance	23.46939
Skewness	0.108594	Kurtosis	-1.08262
USS	7648	CSS	1150
CV	42.4958	Std Mean	0.685119
T:Mean=0	16.63945	Pr>|T|	0.0001
Num ¬= 0	50	Num > 0	50
M(Sign)	25	Pr>=|M|	0.0001
Sgn Rank	637.5	Pr>=|S|	0.0001

Quantiles(Def=5)

100%	Max	22	99%	22
75%	Q3	16	95%	18
50%	Med	10	90%	17
25%	Q1	7	10%	6
0%	Min	2	5%	4
			1%	2
Range		20		
Q3-Q1		9		
Mode		7		

Extremes

Lowest	Obs	Highest	Obs
2(	24)	17(	47)
3(	5)	17(	50)
4(	15)	18(	42)
5(	4)	19(	44)
6(	19)	22(	31)

RH #10 MEAN DECREASE FROM PRETEST BULIT TO POSTTEST BULIT
IS MORE THAN 8.
MEAN FOR DECREAS8 WAS 3.4 T:MEAN=0 IS 4.96264
WITH AN ASSOCIATED PROBABILITY OF .0001/2 OR .00005.

Univariate Procedure

Variable=DECREAS8

Moments

N	50	Sum Wgts	50
Mean	3.4	Sum	170
Std Dev	4.844521	Variance	23.46939
Skewness	0.108594	Kurtosis	-1.08262
USS	1728	CSS	1150
CV	142.4859	Std Mean	0.685119
T:Mean=0	4.962643	Pr>|T|	0.0001
Num ¬= 0	45	Num > 0	32
M(Sign)	9.5	Pr>=|M|	0.0066
Sgn Rank	353	Pr>=|S|	0.0001

Quantiles(Def=5)

100%	Max	14	99%	14
75%	Q3	8	95%	10
50%	Med	2	90%	9
25%	Q1	-1	10%	-2
0%	Min	-6	5%	-4
			1%	-6

Range	20
Q3-Q1	9
Mode	-1

Extremes

Lowest	Obs	Highest	Obs
-6(	24)	9(	47)
-5(	5)	9(	50)
-4(	15)	10(	42)
-3(	4)	11(	44)
-2(	19)	14(	31)

12:41 Sunday, July 31, 1994
RH #10 MEAN DECREASE FROM PRETEST BULIT TO POSTTEST BULIT
IS MORE THAN 8.
MEAN FOR DECREAS8 WAS 3.4 T:MEAN=0 IS 4.96264
WITH AN ASSOCIATED PROBABILITY OF .0001/2 OR .00005.

Univariate Procedure

Variable=DECREAS8

Frequency Table

Value	Count	Percents Cell	Cum	Value	Count	Percents Cell	Cum
-6	1	2.0	2.0	3	1	2.0	56.0
-5	1	2.0	4.0	5	1	2.0	58.0
-4	1	2.0	6.0	6	2	4.0	62.0
-3	1	2.0	8.0	7	4	8.0	70.0
-2	2	4.0	12.0	8	5	10.0	80.0
-1	7	14.0	26.0	9	7	14.0	94.0
0	5	10.0	36.0	10	1	2.0	96.0
1	5	10.0	46.0	11	1	2.0	98.0
2	4	8.0	54.0	14	1	2.0	100.0

```
OPTIONS LINESIZE = 74 PAGESIZE = 52;
CMS FILEDEF NEW DISK MARIA DATA A1;
DATA ALL;
INFILE NEW;
INPUT PREBULIT 4-6 POSBULIT 8-10;
DECREASE = PREBULIT - POSBULIT;
DECREAS8 = PREBULIT - POSBULIT - 8;
PROC UNIVARIATE; VAR DECREASE;
TITLE1 " APPENDIX C-7 ";
TITLE2 "          ";
TITLE3 " RH #9 MEAN DECREASE FROM PRETEST BULIT TO POSTTEST
        BULIT ";
TITLE4 " IS MORE THAN 0. DECREASE WAS CALCULATED ABOVE. ";
TITLE5 " MEAN DECREASE WAS 11.4 T:MEAN=0 IS 16.6395 ";
TITLE6 " WITH AN ASSOCIATED PROBABILITY OF .0001/2 OR .00005. ";
PROC UNIVARIATE FREQ; VAR DECREAS8;
TITLE1 " APPENDIX C-7 ";
TITLE2 "          ";
TITLE3 " RH #10 MEAN DECREASE FROM PRETEST BULIT TO
        POSTTEST BULIT ";
TITLE4 " IS MORE THAN 8. ";
TITLE5 " MEAN FOR DECREAS8 WAS 3.4 T:MEAN=0 IS 4.96264 ";
TITLE6 " WITH AN ASSOCIATED PROBABILITY OF .0001/2 OR .00005. ";
```

                    12:37 Sunday, July 31, 1994
RH #1 MULTIFACETED MORE EFFECTIVE THAN EDUCATIONAL IN
      DECREASING BULIMIA FROM PRETEST TO POSTTEST
TEST OF EQUAL POPULATION VARIANCE RESULTS IN A PROBABILITY
OF .1666, WHICH IS NOT LESS THAN, SAY, AN ALPHA OF .10.
THEREFORE REFER TO THE 'EQUAL' OR SECOND LINE T AND P VALUES
  T IS 12.07 AND REPORTED P IS .0000, BUT THAT IS ONLY THE
    LIMIT OF THE NUMBER OF SIGNIFICANT DIGITS REPORTED.
  THE DIRECTIONAL IS .0001 AND THE NONDIRECTIONAL P IS
                    .0001/2 = .00005.

                      TTEST PROCEDURE

Variable: DECREASE

TREAT	N	Mean	Std Dev	Std Error
EDUCATIONAL	25	7.24000000	2.06720423	0.41344085
MULTIFACETED	25	15.56000000	2.75499546	0.55099909

Variances	T	DF	Prob>|T|
Unequal	-12.0779	44.5	0.0001
Equal	-12.0779	48.0	0.0000

For HO: Variances are equal, F' = 1.78 DF = (24,24)
          Prob>F' = 0.1666


```
OPTIONS LINESIZE = 74 PAGESIZE = 52;
PROC FORMAT; VALUE TREATF 1= 'EDUCATIONAL' 2 =
        'MULTIFACETED';
CMS FILEDEF NEW DISK MARIA DATA A1;
DATA ALL;
INFILE NEW;
INPUT ID 1-2 PREBULIT 4-6 POSBULIT 8-10 TREAT 16;
DECREASE = PREBULIT - POSBULIT;
PROC TTEST; CLASS TREAT; VAR DECREASE;
        FORMAT TREAT TREATF.;
TITLE1 " APPENDIX C-8 ";
TITLE2 "                   ";
TITLE3 " RH #1 MULTIFACETED MORE EFFECTIVE THAN
        EDUCATIONAL IN ";
TITLE4 " DECREASING BULIMIA FROM PRETEST TO POSTTEST ";
TITLE5 " TEST OF EQUAL POPULATION VARIANCE RESULTS IN
        A PROBABILITY ";
TITLE6 " OF .1666, WHICH IS NOT LESS THAN, SAY, AN
        ALPHA OF .10. ";
```

```
TITLE7   " THEREFORE REFER TO THE 'EQUAL' OR SECOND LINE
           T AND P VALUES ";
TITLE8   " T IS 12.07 AND REPORTED P IS .0000, BUT THAT
           IS ONLY THE ";
TITLE9   " LIMIT OF THE NUMBER OF SIGNIFICANT DIGITS
           REPORTED. ";
TITLE10  " THE DIRECTIONAL P IS .0001 AND THE
           NONDIRECTIONAL P IS .0001/2 = .0005 ";
```

RH #11 MULTIFACETED TREATMENT WILL RESULT IN A
POSTTEST MEAN THAT IS MORE THAN 6 UNITS LOWER
THAN THE EDUCATIONAL

TTEST PROCEDURE

Variable: POSTM6

TREAT	N	Mean	Std Dev	Std Error
EDUCATIONAL	25	103.00000000	3.80788655	0.76157731
MULTIFACETED	25	100.64000000	4.07103590	0.81420718

Variances	T	DF	Prob>|T|
Unequal	2.1168	47.8	0.0395
Equal	2.1168	48.0	0.0395

For HO: Variances are equal, F' = 1.14 DF = (24,24)
Prob>F' = 0.7460

```
OPTIONS LINESIZE = 74 PAGESIZE = 52;
PROC FORMAT; VALUE TREATF 1 = 'EDUCATIONAL' 2 =
        'MULTIFACETED';
CMS FILEDEF NEW DISK MARIA DATA A1;
DATA ALL;
INFILE NEW;
INPUT POSBULIT 8-10 TREAT 16;
MULTI = TREAT - 1;
POSTM6 = POSBULIT + 6 * MULTI;
PROC TTEST; CLASS TREAT; VAR POSTM6;
    FORMAT TREAT TREATF.;
TITLE1 " APPENDIX C-9 ";
TITLE2 "               ";
TITLE3 " RH #11 MULTIFACETED TREATMENT WILL RESULT IN
        A ";
TITLE4 " POSTTEST MEAN THAT IS MORE THAN 6 UNITS LOWER
        ";
TITLE5 " THAN THE EDUCATIONAL ";
```

RH #2 MULTIFACETED MORE EFFECTIVE THAN EDUCATIONAL
ON POSBULIT
TTEST PROCEDURE

Variable: POSBULIT

TREAT	N	Mean	Std Dev	Std Error
EDUCATIONAL	25	103.00000000	3.80788655	0.76157731
MULTIFACETED	25	94.64000000	4.07103590	0.81420718

Variances	T	DF	Prob>|T|
Unequal	7.4986	47.8	0.0001
Equal	7.4986	48.0	0.0000

For HO: Variances are equal, F' = 1.14 DF = (24,24)
Prob>F' = 0.7460

```
OPTIONS LINESIZE = 74 PAGESIZE = 52;
PROC FORMAT; VALUE TREATF 1 = 'EDUCATIONAL' 2 =
        'MULTIFACETED';
CMS FILEDEF NEW DISK MARIA DATA A1;
DATA ALL;
INFILE NEW;
INPUT POSBULIT 8-10 TREAT 16;
PROC TTEST; CLASS TREAT; VAR POSBULIT;
    FORMAT TREAT TREATF.;
TITLE1 " APPENDIX C-10 ";
TITLE2 "                    ";
TITLE3 " RH #2 MULTIFACETED MORE EFFECTIVE THAN
        EDUCATIONAL";
TITLE4 "ON POSBULIT";
```

12:49 Sunday, July 31, 1994
RH #12 THE EAT MEANS WILL NOT BE THE SAME
FOR THE THREE FES GROUPS.
LAST PART OF THIS APPENDIX HAS THE TUKEY AND NEWMAN-KEULS
POST HOC RESULTS

General Linear Models Procedure
Class Level Information

Class	Levels	Values
FES	3	LEVEL 1 LEVEL 2 LEVEL 3

Number of observations in data set = 50

12:49 Sunday, July 31, 1994
RH #12 THE EAT MEANS WILL NOT BE THE SAME
FOR THE THREE FES GROUPS.
LAST PART OF THIS APPENDIX HAS THE TUKEY AND NEWMAN-KEULS
POST HOC RESULTS

General Linear Models Procedure

Dependent Variable: EAT

Source	DF	Sum of Squares	Mean Square	F Value	Pr > F
Model	2	350.18956	175.09478	3.89	0.0273
Error	47	2114.79044	44.99554		
Corrected Total	49	2464.98000			

R-Square	C.V.	Root MSE	EAT Mean
0.142066	13.69512	6.7079	48.980

Source	DF	Type I SS	Mean Square	F Value	Pr > F
FES	2	350.18956	175.09478	3.89	0.0273

Source	DF	Type III SS	Mean Square	F Value	Pr > F
FES	2	350.18956	175.09478	3.89	0.0273

APPENDIX C-11   3
                    12:49 Sunday, July 31, 1994
     RH #12 THE EAT MEANS WILL NOT BE THE SAME
          FOR THE THREE FES GROUPS.
LAST PART OF THIS APPENDIX HAS THE TUKEY AND NEWMAN-KEULS
              POST HOC RESULTS

          General Linear Models Procedure

     Student-Newman-Keuls test for variable: EAT

NOTE: This test controls the type I experimentwise
error rate under the complete null hypothesis but not
under partial null hypotheses.

          Alpha= 0.05 df= 47 MSE= 44.99554
          WARNING: Cell sizes are not equal.
          Harmonic Mean of cell sizes= 16.65306

     Number of Means   2   3
     Critical Range   4.6766254   5.6258779

Means with the same letter are not significantly
different.

     SNK Grouping   Mean   N   FES

          A   52.588   17   LEVEL 1
          B   47.813   16   LEVEL 3
          B
          B   46.471   17   LEVEL 2

370   APPENDIX C

RH #12 THE EAT MEANS WILL NOT BE THE SAME
FOR THE THREE FES GROUPS.
LAST PART OF THIS APPENDIX HAS THE TUKEY AND NEWMAN-KEULS
POST HOC RESULTS

General Linear Models Procedure

Tukey's Studentized Range (HSD) Test for variable: EAT

NOTE: This test controls the type I experimentwise
error rate, but generally has a higher type II
error rate than REGWQ.

Alpha= 0.05 df= 47 MSE= 44.99554
Critical Value of Studentized Range= 3.423
Minimum Significant Difference= 5.6259
WARNING: Cell sizes are not equal.
Harmonic Mean of cell sizes= 16.65306

Means with the same letter are not significantly
different.

Tukey Grouping		Mean	N	FES
	A	52.588	17	LEVEL 1
	A			
B	A	47.813	16	LEVEL 3
B				
B		46.471	17	LEVEL 2

```
OPTIONS LINESIZE = 74 PAGESIZE = 52;
PROC FORMAT; VALUE FESF 1 = 'LEVEL 1' 2 = 'LEVEL 2' 3
    = 'LEVEL 3';
CMS FILEDEF NEW DISK MARIA DATA A1;
DATA ALL;
INFILE NEW;
INPUT FES 14 EAT 18-19;
PROC SORT; BY FES;
PROC GLM; CLASSES FES; MODEL EAT = FES;
 FORMAT FES FESF.;
TITLE1 " APPENDIX C-11 ";
TITLE2 "                    ";
TITLE3 " RH #12 THE EAT MEANS WILL NOT BE THE SAME ";
TITLE4 " FOR THE THREE FES GROUPS. ";
TITLE5 " LAST PART OF THIS APPENDIX HAS THE TUKEY AND
        NEWMAN-KEULS";
TITLE6 " POST HOC RESULTS ";
MEANS FES/TUKEY SNK;
```

12:49 Sunday, July 31, 1994

RH #13 TESTING WHETHER BULIT PRETEST IS DIFFERENT FOR THOSE
WOMEN WHO LEAVE BEFORE THE POSTTEST THAN FOR THOSE WHO FINISH.

TTEST PROCEDURE

Variable: PREBULIT

MISS	N	Mean	Std Dev	Std Error
STAYERS	15	110.46666667	4.06846174	1.05047230
LEAVERS	10	109.90000000	3.24722103	1.02686145

Variances	T	DF	Prob>|T|
Unequal	0.3858	22.1	0.7034
Equal	0.3683	23.0	0.7160

For HO: Variances are equal, $F' = 1.57$ DF = (14,9)
Prob>F' = 0.5020

```
OPTIONS LINESIZE = 74 PAGESIZE = 52;
CMS FILEDEF NEW DISK MARIA DATA A1;
PROC FORMAT; VALUE MISSF 1 = 'LEAVERS' 0 = 'STAYERS';
DATA NEW;
INFILE NEW;
INPUT ID 1-2 PREBULIT 4-6 TREAT 16;
* SELECTS ONLY EDUCATIONAL TREATMENT SUBJECTS;
IF TREAT = 1;
* CREATES NEW VARIABLE — 1 IF SUBJECT ID FROM 1 TO 10
        — LEAVERS;
IF ID < 11 THEN MISS = 1;
* ADDS TO THE NEW VARIABLE — 0 IF SUBJECT ID GREATER
        THAN 10—STAYERS;
IF ID > 10 THEN MISS = 0;
PROC TTEST; CLASS MISS; VAR PREBULIT;
 FORMAT MISS MISSF.;
TITLE1 " APPENDIX  C-12";
TITLE2 "              ";
TITLE3 " RH #13 TESTING WHETHER BULIT PRETEST IS
        DIFFERENT FOR THOSE ";
TITLE4 " WOMEN WHO LEAVE BEFORE THE POSTTEST THAN FOR
        THOSE WHO FINISH. ";
```

RH #14A FES MAIN EFFECT F = 3.66 PROBABILITY = .0339
RH #14B TREATMENT MAIN EFFECT F = 56.21 PROBABILITY = .0001
RH 14C INTERACTION BETWEEN FES AND TREATMENT F = 1.51 P = .2313
                          13:22 Saturday, July 30, 1994

                  General Linear Models Procedure
                     Class Level Information

        Class   Levels   Values

        FES   3   1 2 3

        TREAT   2   EDUCATIONAL MULTIFACETED

          Number of observations in data set = 50

RH #14A FES MAIN EFFECT F = 3.66 PROBABILITY = .0339
RH #14B TREATMENT MAIN EFFECT F = 56.21 PROBABILITY = .0001
RH14C INTERACTION BETWEEN FES AND TREATMENT F = 1.51 P = .2313

General Linear Models Procedure

Dependent Variable: POSBULIT

Source	DF	Sum of Squares	Mean Square	F Value	Pr > f
Model	5	1006.0336	201.2067	14.43	0.0001
Error	44	613.3464	13.9397		
Corrected Total	49	1619.3800			

R-Square	C.V.	Root MSE	POSBULIT Mean
0.621246	3.778172	3.7336	98.820

Source	DF	Type I SS	Mean Square	F Value	Pr > F
FES	2	185.00132	92.50066	6.64	0.0030
TREAT	1	778.82926	778.82926	55.87	0.0001
FES*TREAT	2	42.20299	21.10150	1.51	0.2313

Source	DF	Type III SS	Mean Square	F Value	Pr > F
FES	2	101.97958	50.98979	3.66	0.0339
TREAT	1	783.61181	783.61181	56.21	0.0001
FES*TREAT	2	42.20299	21.10150	1.51	0.2313

13:22 Saturday, July 30, 1994
RH #14A FES MAIN EFFECT F = 3.66 PROBABILITY = .0339
RH #14B TREATMENT MAIN EFFECT F = 56.21 PROBABILITY = .0001
RH14C INTERACTION BETWEEN FES AND TREATMENT F = 1.51 P = .2313

General Linear Models Procedure

Level of FES	N	POSBULIT Mean	SD
1	17	101.352941	4.89822897
2	17	96.764706	5.20251636
3	16	98.312500	6.41580081

Level of TREAT	N	POSBULIT Mean	SD
EDUCATIONAL	25	103.000000	3.80788655
MULTIFACETED	25	94.640000	4.07103590

Level of TREAT	Level of TREAT	N	POSBULIT Mean	SD
1	EDUCATIONAL	10	104.000000	4.47213595
1	MULTIFACETED	7	97.571429	2.37045304
2	EDUCATIONAL	7	100.857143	1.86445447
2	MULTIFACETED	10	93.900000	4.86369772
3	EDUCATIONAL	8	103.625000	3.81491434
3	MULTIFACETED	8	93.000000	3.02371578

```
OPTIONS LINESIZE = 74 PAGESIZE = 52;
PROC FORMAT; VALUE TREATF 1 = 'EDUCATIONAL' 2 =
        'MULTIFACETED';
CMS FILEDEF NEW DISK MARIA DATA A1;
DATA ALL;
INFILE NEW;
INPUT POSBULIT 8-10 FES 14 TREAT 16;
* NOTE THAT A PROC SORT NEEDS TO BE INCLUDED FOR EACH
        CLASS VARIABLE.
PROC SORT; BY FES;
PROC SORT; BY TREAT;
* NOTE THAT THE INTERACTION TERM IS GENERATED BY
        MULTIPLICATION, THE '*';
PROC GLM; CLASS FES TREAT; MODEL POSBULIT = FES TREAT
        FES*TREAT;
  FORMAT TREAT TREATF.;
    MEANS FES TREAT FES * TREAT;
```

```
TITLE1  "  APPENDIX  C-13  ";
TITLE2  "                    ";
TITLE3  "  RH  #14A  FES  MAIN  EFFECT  F  =  3.66  PROBABILITY
           =  .0339  ";
TITLE4  RH  #14B  TREATMENT  MAIN  EFFECT  F  =  56.21
           PROBABILITY  =  .0001  ";
TITLE5  "  RH14C  INTERACTION  BETWEEN  FES  AND  TREATMENT  F
           =  1.51  P  =  .2313";
```

17:22 Monday, May 8, 1995

RH #15 (ANCOVA TEST) MULTIFACETED DECREASE GREATER THAN FOR
EDUCATIONAL, OVER AND ABOVE PSYCHADJ F = 25.7459, P = .0001.
AND SINCE MF HAS A GREATER DECREASE THAN EDUCATIONAL, THE
DIRECTIONAL P IS .0001/2 = .00005. THE CONCLUSION IS:
MF DECREASES MORE THAN EDUCATIONAL, OVER AND ABOVE PSYCHADJ.

Model: MODEL1
NOTE: No intercept in model. R-square is redefined.
Dependent Variable: DECREASE

Analysis of Variance

Source	DF	Sum of Squares	Mean Square	F Value	Prob>F
Model	3	192752.81802	64250.93934	43.329	0.0001
Error	47	69695.18198	1482.87621		
U Total	50	262448.00000			

Root MSE	38.50813	R-square	0.7344	
Dep Mean	55.40000	Adj R-sq	0.7175	
C.V.	69.50926			

Parameter Estimates

Variable	DF	Parameter Estimate	Standard Error	T for HO: Parameter=0	Prob > |T|
EDUCA	1	91.760107	16.06524263	5.712	0.0001
MULTI	1	36.420912	16.56237367	2.199	0.0328
PSYCHADJ	1	-4.260054	7.04941438	-0.604	0.5485

Variable	DF	Variable Label
EDUCA	1	EDUCATIONAL
MULTI	1	MULTIFACETED
PSYCHADJ	1	

Dependent Variable: DECREASE
Test: ANCOVA   Numerator: 38177.9784 DF: 1 F value: 25.7459
              Denominator: 1482.876 DF: 47 Prob> F: 0.0001

Model: MODEL1
NOTE: No intercept in model. R-square is redefined.
Dependent Variable: DECREASE

Analysis of Variance

Source	DF	Sum of Squares	Mean Square	F Value	Prob>F
Model	4	195842.34284	48960.58571	33.814	0.0001
Error	46	66605.65716	1447.94907		
U Total	50	262448.00000			

Root MSE	38.05193	R-square	0.7462	
Dep Mean	55.40000	Adj R-sq	0.7241	
C.V.	68.68579			

Parameter Estimates

Variable	DF	Parameter Estimate	Standard Error	T for H0: Parameter=0	Prob > |T|
EDUCA	1	116.573333	23.25011080	5.014	0.0001
MULTI	1	19.062780	20.22527737	0.943	0.3508
SLED	1	-16.666667	10.98464485	-1.517	0.1360
SLMF	1	4.085202	9.00905458	0.453	0.6524

Variable	DF	Variable Label
EDUCA	1	EDUCATIONAL
MULTI	1	MULTIFACETED
SLED	1	SLOPE FOR EDUCATIONAL
SLMF	1	SLOPE FOR MULTIFACETED

Dependent Variable: DECREASE
Test: INTERACT Numerator: 3089.5248 DF: 1 F value: 2.1337
Denominator: 1447.949 DF: 46 Prob>F: 0.1509

```
OPTIONS LINESIZE = 74 PAGESIZE = 52;
CMS FILEDEF NEW DISK MARIA DATA A1;
DATA ALL;
INFILE NEW;
INPUT PREBULIT 4-6 POSBULIT 9-10 PSYCHADJ 12 TREAT 16;
LABEL EDUCA = 'EDUCATIONAL';
LABEL MULTI = 'MULTIFACETED';
LABEL SLED = 'SLOPE FOR EDUCATIONAL';
LABEL SLMF = 'SLOPE FOR MULTIFACETED'
MULTI = TREAT - 1;
EDUCA = 1 - MULTI;
SLED = EDUCA * PSYCHADJ;
SLMF = MULTI * PSYCHADJ;
DECREASE = PREBULIT - POSBULIT;
PROC REG; MODEL DECREASE = EDUCA MULTI PSYCHADJ / NOINT;
         ANCOVA: TEST EDUCA = MULTI ;
TITLE1 " APPENDIX C-14 ";
TITLE2 "                     ";
TITLE3 " RH #15 (ANCOVA TEST) MULTIFACETED DECREASE
         GREATER THAN FOR";
TITLE4 " EDUCATIONAL, OVER AND ABOVE PSYCHADJ F =
         25.7459, P = .0001.";
TITLE5 " AND SINCE MF HAS A GREATER DECREASE THAN
         EDUCATIONAL, THE ";
TITLE6 " DIRECTIONAL P IS .0001/2 = .00005. THE
         CONCLUSION IS:";
TITLE7 " MF DECREASES MORE THAN EDUCATIONAL, OVER AND
         ABOVE PSYCHADJ.";
PROC REG; MODEL DECREASE = EDUCA MULTI SLED SLMF /
         NOINT ; INTERACT: TEST SLED = SLMF;
TITLE3 " ANCOVA TEST OF ASSUMPTION OF        ";
TITLE4 " HOMOGENEITY OF REGRESSION SLOPES—ALSO KNOWN
             AS     ";
TITLE5 " INTERACTION BETWEEN CONTINUOUS AND
         CATEGORICAL.              ";
TITLE6 " F = 2.1337, P = .1509, THEREFORE THERE IS NO
         INTERACTION";
TITLE7 " THE TWO REGRESSION LINES ARE HOMOGENEOUS AND
         THE ANCOVA";
TITLE8 " CONCLUSION ABOVE IS APPROPRIATE.";
```

```
OPTIONS LINESIZE = 74 PAGESIZE = 52;
TITLE " MARIA'S VARIOUS RESEARCH HYPOTHESES";
DATA NEW;
INPUT ID 1-2 PREBULIT 4-6 TREAT 9;
U = 1;
X1 = RANNOR (16);
FES = 2;
IF X1 > .44 THEN FES = 1;
IF X1 < -.44 THEN FES = 3;
FES1 = 0; FES2 = 0; FES3 = 0;
IF FES = 1 THEN FES1 = 1;
IF FES = 2 THEN FES2 = 1;
IF FES = 3 THEN FES3 = 1;
X2 = RANNOR (170);
PSYCHADJ = 2;
IF X2 > .44 THEN PSYCHADJ = 1;
IF X2 < -.44 THEN PSYCHADJ = 3;
MULTI = TREAT - 1;
EDUCA = 1 - MULTI;
SLED = EDUCA * PSYCHADJ;
SLMF = MULTI * PSYCHADJ;
POSBULIT = INT (PREBULIT - 8 * TREAT + RANNOR (13) *
          2);
IF X1 > .44 THEN POSBULIT = POSBULIT + 3;
DECREASE=PREBULIT - POSBULIT;
ADJUST = INT (DECREASE + 20 + 10 * RANNOR (14));
DECREAS8= PREBULIT - POSBULIT + 8;
EAT = INT (POSBULIT -50 + 4 * RANNOR (15));
IF FES = 1 THEN EAT = EAT + 2;
PREADJ = PREBULIT - 104;
PREADJ8 = PREBULIT - 110.24;
DECRE9 = PREBULIT - POSBULIT - 11.4;
DECRE10 = PREBULIT - POSBULIT - 8;
POSTM6 = POSBULIT + 6 * MULTI;
FES1T1 = FES1 * MULTI;
FES2T1 = FES2 * MULTI;
FES3T1 = FES3 * MULTI;
FES1T2 = FES1 * EDUCA;
FES2T2 = FES2 * EDUCA;
FES3T2 = FES3 * EDUCA;
CARDS;
01 110 1
02 112 1
03 108 1
04 112 1
```

```
05  106  1
06  109  1
07  114  1
08  115  1
09  107  1
10  106  1
11  118  1
12  110  1
13  106  1
14  108  1
15  112  1
16  110  1
17  111  1
18  109  1
19  117  1
20  116  1
21  113  1
22  105  1
23  109  1
24  106  1
25  107  1
26  110  2
27  112  2
28  108  2
29  112  2
30  106  2
31  109  2
32  114  2
33  115  2
34  107  2
35  106  2
36  118  2
37  106  2
38  108  2
39  112  2
40  110  2
41  111  2
42  109  2
43  117  2
44  116  2
45  113  2
46  105  2
47  109  2
48  106  2
49  107  2
50  109  2
```

```
PROC REG; MODEL DECREASE = TREAT;
TITLE1 " RH #1 MULTIFACETED MORE EFFECTIVE THAN
         EDUCATIONAL IN ";
TITLE2 " DECREASING BULIMIA FROM PRETEST TO POSTTEST ";
PROC FORMAT; VALUE TREAT 1 = 'EDUCATIONAL' 2 =
         'MULTIFACETED';
PROC REG ; MODEL POSBULIT = TREAT;
TITLE1 " RH #2 MULTIFACETED MORE EFFECTIVE THAN
         EDUCATIONAL ON POSBULIT ";
PROC REG ; MODEL DECREASE=PSYCHADJ;
TITLE1 " RH #3 POSITIVE CORRELATION BETWEEN BULIT
         CHANGE SCORES ";
TITLE2 " AND PSYCHOLOGICAL ADJUSTMENT ";
TITLE3 " NOTE THAT THE PEARSON CORRELATION IS THE
         SQUARE ROOT";
TITLE4 " OF THE R SQUARED VALUE R = .0008 THEREFORE R
         = .028";
TITLE5 " NON-DIRECTIONAL PROBABILITY IS ABOVE IT P =
         .8468";
PROC REG ; MODEL POSBULIT = EAT;
TITLE1 " RH #4 POSITIVE CORRELATION GREATER THAN .60
         BETWEEN ";
TITLE2 " POST BULIT AND EAT. ";
TITLE3 " ACTUAL R SQUARE IS .65, AND THE SQUARE ROOT
         OF THAT ";
TITLE4 " VALUE IS .81. PLUGGING THE R SQUARE VALUES OF
         .65";
TITLE5 " AND .36 INTO THE GENERAL F FORMULA YIELDS AN
         F OF 39.8,";
TITLE6 " WHICH IS SIGNIFICANT AT THE .01 LEVEL.";
PROC REG ; MODEL PREBULIT = POSBULIT; BY TREAT;
TITLE1 " RH #5 POSITIVE CORRELATION GREATER THAN .70
         BETWEEN ";
TITLE2 " THE TWO ADMINISTRATIONS OF THE BULIT WITHIN
         EACH GROUP. ";
TITLE3 " NOTE THAT TWO CORRELATIONS ARE CALLED FOR,
         ONE WITHIN ";
TITLE4 " THE MULTIFACETED GROUP AND ONE WITHIN THE
         EDUCATIONAL ";
TITLE5 " NEED TO PLUG THE RESULTING R SQUARE INTO THE
         GENERAL ";
TITLE6 " F FORMULA R SQUARE FULL IS .7204 WHILE .70
         SQUARED IS .49,";
TITLE7 " WHICH IS THE R SQUARE RESTRICTED ";
TITLE8 " THE RESULTING F IS ABOUT 36 WHICH WITH 1 AND
         48 DF IS ";
TITLE9 " SIGNIFICANT AT ALPHA = .01.";
```

```
PROC CORR SPEARMAN; VAR PREBULIT POSBULIT; BY TREAT;
TITLE1 " RH #6 POSITIVE RANK CORRELATION > THAN .70
          BETWEEN ";
TITLE2 " THE TWO ADMINISTRATIONS OF THE BULIT WITHIN
          EACH GROUP. ";
TITLE3 " THE SPEARMAN OPTION YIELDS THE RANK
          CORRELATION ";
TITLE4 " NEED TO PLUG THE RESULTING R SQUARE INTO THE
          GENERAL ";
TITLE5 " F FORMULA R SQUARE FULL IS .7204 WHILE .70
          SQUARED IS .49,";
TITLE6 " WHICH IS THE R SQUARE RESTRICTED ";
TITLE7 " THE RESULTING F IS ABOUT 36 WHICH WITH 1 AND
          48 DF IS ";
TITLE8 " SIGNIFICANT AT ALPHA = .01.";
PROC REG; MODEL DECREASE = PSYCHADJ FES;
    TEST PSYCHADJ = 0, FES = 0
TITLE1 " RH #7 PSYCHOLOGICAL ADJUSTMENT AND FES ";
TITLE2 " ARE PREDICTIVE OF CHANGE IN BULIT. ";
TITLE3 " PROBABILITY IS AT TOP RIGHT OF PRINTOUT ";
TITLE4 " F = 2.892 AND ASSOCIATED PROB = .0654 ";
PROC REG ; MODEL DECREASE = FES;
TITLE1 " INFORMATION FOR RH #7";
PROC MEANS USS; VAR PREADJ8 DECREASE;
TITLE1 " RH #8 MEAN PRETEST BULIT IS GREATER THAN 104. ";
TITLE2 " NOTE THAT THE VARIABLE PREADJ8 IS CALCULATED
          ABOVE AND ";
TITLE3 " IS THE PRETEST BULIT MINUS THE HYPOTHESIZED
          VALUE OF 110.24 ";
TITLE4 " MEAN ABOVE 104 IS 6.22 ";
TITLE5 " T:MEAN=0 IS THE TEST STATISTIC T= 11.9967 ";
TITLE6 " NON-DIRECTIONAL PROBABILITY IS .0001. ";
TITLE7 " ESS FORMULA IS (ESSR - ESSF)/ ESSF/(N-1) ";
TITLE8 " ESSR = 1934.2 ESSF = 658.60 N = 50 F = 143,
          WHICH IS THE";
TITLE9 " OF THE T VALUE OF 11.9969";
PROC MEANS USS; VAR DECRE9 DECREASE;
TITLE1 " RH #9 MEAN DECREASE FROM PRETEST BULIT TO
          POSTTEST BULIT ";
TITLE2 " IS MORE THAN 0. DECREASE WAS CALCULATED ABOVE
          AS 'DECREASE'";
TITLE3 " MEAN DECREASE WAS 11.4 T WAS 16.6395 ";
TITLE4 " ESS FORMULA IS (ESSR - ESSF)/ ESSF/(N-1) ";
TITLE5 " ESSR = 7648 ESSF = 1150 N = 50 F = 282,
          WHICH IS THE SQUARE";
TITLE6 " OF THE T VALUE OF 16.6395";
```

```
PROC MEANS USS; VAR DECRE10 DECREAS8 DECREASE;
TITLE1 " RH #10 MEAN DECREASE FROM PRETEST BULIT TO
          POSTTEST BULIT ";
TITLE2 " IS MORE THAN 8. DECREASE WAS CALCULATED ABOVE
          AS 'DECREAS8' ";
TITLE3 "              ";
TITLE4 " WITH AN ASSOCIATED PROBABILITY OF P = .00005 ";
TITLE5 " ESS FORMULA IS (ESSR - ESSF)/ ESSF/(N-1) ";
TITLE6 " ESSR = 1728 ESSF = 1150 N = 50 F = 24, WHICH
          IS THE SQUARE";
TITLE7 " OF THE T VALUE OF 4.96264";
PROC REG ; MODEL POSTM6 = TREAT;
   TEST TREAT = 0;
TITLE1 " RH #11 MULTIFACETED TREATMENT WILL RESULT IN
          A ";
TITLE2 " POSTTEST MEAN THAT IS MORE THAN 6 UNITS LOWER ";
TITLE3 " THAN THE EDUCATIONAL ";
PROC REG; MODEL EAT = FES1 FES2;
   TEST FES1 = 0, FES2 = 0;
TITLE1 " RH #12 THE EAT MEANS WILL NOT BE THE SAME ";
TITLE2 " FOR THE THREE FES GROUPS. ";
TITLE3 " MEAN FOR THE FES1 GROUP IS THE PARAMETER
          ESTIMATE";
TITLE4 " FOR FES1 PLUS THE INTERCEP (48.81 + 4.77 =
          52.58).";
TITLE5 " MEAN FOR THE FES2 GROUP IS THE PARAMETER
          ESTIMATE FOR FES2";
TITLE6 " PLUS THE INTERCEP (47.81 - 1.34 = 46.47)";
TITLE7 " MEAN FOR FES3 IS THE PARAMETER ESTIMATE FOR
          INTERCEP (47.81).";
TITLE8 " F FOR THE HYPOTHESIS IS AT THE END, 3.891
          WITH ASSOCIATED";
TITLE9 " PROBABILITY OF .0273";
PROC REG;MODEL POSBULIT=FES1T1 FES1T2 FES2T1 FES2T2
          FES3T1 FES3T2 /NOINT;
TITLE1 " RH #14A FES MAIN EFFECT F = 3.66 PROBABILITY
          = .0339 ";
INTERACT: TEST FES2T1-FES2T2 + FES1T2 - FES1T1 = 0,
          FES3T1-FES3T2 + FES2T2 - FES2T1 = 0;
TREAT: TEST FES1T1 + FES2T1 + FES3T1 - FES1T2 - FES2T2
          - FES3T2 = 0
FES: TEST   FES2T1 + FES2T2 - FES1T2 - FES1T1 = 0,
            FES3T1 + FES3T2 - FES2T2 - FES2T1 = 0;
TITLE2 " RH #14B TREATMENT MAIN EFFECT F = 56.21
          PROBABILITY = .0001 ";
TITLE3 " RH #14c INTERACTION BETWEEN FES AND TREATMENT
          F = 1.51 P = .2313";
```

```
PROC REG;  MODEL DECREASE=EDUCA PSYCHADJ  ;
   ANCOVA:  TEST EDUCA = 0;
TITLE1  "RH #15 (ANCOVA TEST) DIFFERENCE BETWEEN
           TREATMENTS,  OVER AND";
TITLE2  "ABOVE PSYCHADJ. T = 11.95,  T SQUARED = 142.90
           WHICH IS THE F;";
TITLE3  "BOTH YIELD THE SAME PROBABILITY OF .0001.
           THEREFORE THERE ARE";
TITLE4  "DIFFERENCES BETWEEN TREATMENTS,  OVER AND ABOVE
           PSYCHADJ.";
PROC REG;  MODEL DECREASE=EDUCA SLED SLMF  ;
   INTERACT:  TEST SLED = SLMF;
TITLE1  "THE SECOND F IS THE ANCOVA INTERACTION TEST OF
           ASSUMPTION OF";
TITLE2  " HOMOGENEITY OF REGRESSION SLOPES—ALSO KNOWN AS ";
TITLE3  " INTERACTION BETWEEN CONTINUOUS AND
           CATEGORICAL.          ";
TITLE4  " F = .0355, P = .8513.  THEREFORE MARIA CAN
           CONCLUDE THAT";
TITLE5  " THERE IS NO INTERACTION BETWEEN PSYCHADJ AND
           TREATMENT.";
TITLE6  " THE TWO REGRESSION LINES ARE HOMOGENEOUS,  AND
           THE ANCOVA";
TITLE7  " CONCLUSION IS APPROPRIATE.";
```

MARIA'S RESEARCH
JOURNAL SUBMISSION

1   A New Treatment for Bulimic Women
2   Maria Gonzalez
3   Southwestern University

4 **ABSTRACT**

5   Young female adults who responded to an ad for a new approach
6 for treating bulimia were administered a pretest self-report instrument
7 to determine if they had bulimia. Those who met the criteria were
8 randomly assigned to one of two treatment groups—multifaceted or
9 educational. After 3 months of treatment, the multifaceted treatment
10 was found to be more effective at posttest and to have caused more
11 reduction in the bulimic behavior of the women from pretest to posttest.
12 The effectiveness of the multifaceted approach was observed for both
13 Hispanic American and Anglo-American women.

14 **Introduction**

15   This study focuses on the research question, What are the effects of
16 treatment on bulimia? Specifically, a new treatment, referred to as *mul-*
17 *tifaceted* was constructed from evidence in the literature that led the
18 researcher to believe that it would be more effective than the current
19 practice called *educational*.

20 **Literature Review**

21   Bulimia is characterized by binging and purging. Women in their
22 20s are the primary population that is afflicted with this disease. The
23 incidence of bulimia has increased drastically over the last 10 years
24 (Ordma & Kirschenbaum, 1985; Mitchell & Eckert, 1987). If the disease
25 is not diagnosed early in its development, it can lead to major health
26 problems, some of which are not reversible, and ultimately to death.
27 One of the problems associated with this disease is that women who
28 are bulimic appear outwardly as normal-weight women, whereas with
29 anorexia there is extreme weight loss and with compulsive overeating
30 there is extreme weight gain. Those who enter therapy for whatever

31 reason are often reluctant to admit to the binging and purging. As such,
32 most of these women adopt pathological behavior or pathological ex-
33 planations for their behavior.
34   There are many different theories as to why women develop bu-
35 limia, including sociocultural expectations (Boskind-Lodal & White,
36 1978), intrapsychic expectations (Bruch, 1973), and family of origin issues
37 (Minuchin, Roman, & Baker, 1978). The purpose of this study is not to
38 resolve the etiology of bulimia but to evaluate the effectiveness of a new
39 treatment with respect to the current practice.
40   There have been a number of studies conducted with the MMPI,
41 investigating the profile of bulimic women as contrasted with women
42 who eat normally, women who are anorexic, and women with other
43 eating disorders (Ross, 1983; Scott & Baroffio, 1985). The value of the
44 MMPI is in the comparisons to other clinical groups. A limitation to
45 the MMPI is that the items were not developed specifically for bulimia,
46 consequently several specific measures have been developed. Garner
47 and Garfinkel (1979) developed the Eating Attitudes Test. Garner, Olm-
48 stead, and Polivy (1983) developed the Eating Disorders Inventory.
49 Both of these tests were based on the DSM-III definition of bulimia.
50 That definition was revised by the American Psychiatric Association in
51 1987, and consequently those two tests do not measure the current
52 definition of bulimia. The BULIT (Smith & Thelen, 1984) had been
53 widely used by various researchers and was revised to be in line with
54 the new APA definition (Thelen, Farmer, Wonderlich, & Smith, 1990).
55 **Research Hypotheses**
56   Three research hypotheses were tested. Research hypothesis #1
57 was, The multifaceted approach will result in lower BULIT-R scores after
58 treatment than will the educational approach. Research hypothesis #2
59 was, The multifaceted approach will result in a greater decrease in
60 BULIT-R scores than will the educational approach. Research hypothe-
61 sis #3 was concerned with the effect of the treatment on the two eth-
62 nicities in the population: The multifaceted approach will have a differ-
63 ent effect from pretest to posttest for Hispanic American women than
64 it will for Anglo-American women.
65 **Method**
66   Subjects were recruited from two places. One place was the Uni-
67 versity Counseling Center, where students came for assistance with
68 their bulimic problem. Since not enough subjects were available from
69 this pool, advertisements were placed throughout the community. Sub-
70 jects were administered the BULIT-R to see if they met the minimum
71 score of 104. If they did, they were randomly assigned to one of the two
72 treatment groups.
73   The educational approach is the current treatment approach of
74 choice and is well-documented in Current (1990). The multifaceted ap-
75 proach was constructed by the present author and is based on the work
76 of Decker (1989) and Black (1988). The entire 3 months of treatment was
77 scripted for each treatment, copies of which are available from the

78 author. Each group met at the same time period for 1 hour each week.
79 Subjects were not told that they were being compared to another treat-
80 ment but were informed that after 3 months of treatment, their bulimic
81 behavior would be assessed.
82   The BULIT-R was administered before treatment to determine if
83 subjects were bulimic and then at the end of the 3-month treatment.
84 Research hypothesis #1 used the posttest BULIT-R as the dependent
85 measure, and research hypotheses #2 and #3 used the change in BU-
86 LIT-R (from pretest to posttest) as the dependent measure. The BULIT-R
87 was administered by a trained examiner, following the test administra-
88 tion instructions.
89   The BULIT-R is a five-point, Likert scale in which severity of re-
90 sponse is indicated with a score of 5 indicating the most severe response.
91 Total scores range from a low of 28 to a high of 140. Previous researchers
92 have used scores of 104 and above to indicate bulimia, and that was the
93 criterion used in this study. Thelen et al. (1990) report a test-retest reliability
94 correlation of .87, with predictive validity results ranging from .64 to .89.
95 **Results**
96   Subjects in the two treatments were very similar on both the pretest
97 BULIT-R (both having a mean of 110.2) as well as the pretest measure
98 of psychological adjustment (multifaceted mean of 2.0 and educational
99 mean of 2.1). The FES categories were not equally distributed in the
100 two treatments (10 FES level-1, 7 FES level-2, and 8 FES level-3 in
101 multifaceted; 7 FES level-1, 10 FES level-2, and 8 FES level-3 in educa-
102 tional), but the two distributions were not significantly different (χ^2 =
103 1.06, p = .58). Therefore, random assignment appeared to be effective
104 for the pretest BULIT-R, psychological adjustment, and FES.
105   The means for each group are presented in Table 1. Research hy-
106 pothesis #1 was accepted (t (48) = 7.49, p = .0001). The multifaceted
107 approach was more effective than the educational in getting the bulimic
108 women to a low posttest BULIT (multifaceted mean of 94.6 compared
109 to the educational mean of 103.0). Research hypothesis #2 was also
110 accepted (t (48) = 12.07, p = .0001). The multifaceted approach reduced
111 the BULIT-R score 15.6 from pretest to posttest, while the educational
112 approach only reduced the BULIT-R score 7.2 from pretest to posttest.
113 Research hypothesis #3 was not accepted (t (23) = .18, p = .85). There

TABLE 1   Descriptive information from Maria's study.

Variable	Educational Treatment		Multifaceted Treatment	
	M	**SD**	**M**	**SD**
PREBULIT	110.2	3.7	110.2	3.7
POSBULIT	103.0	3.8	94.6	4.1
CHANGE	−7.2	2.1	−15.6	2.7
PSYCHADJ	2.0	.71	2.1	.86
EAT	53.8	5.6	44.2	4.9

114   was not a difference in the decrease from pretest to posttest for Hispanic
115   American ($M = 15.7$) and Anglo-American ($M = 15.5$).

116   **Discussion**

117   The results of this study can readily be generalized to university
118   women who seek counseling for their bulimia. The sample in this study,
119   while a convenient sample, would not appear to be any different than
120   a volunteer sample from any other university. That the results can be
121   generalized to women who are younger, or older than college age, or
122   who have not gone to college is less defensible. It may be that the
123   multifaceted approach is particularly appealing to college-age women.
124   Since this study, as well as most of the studies on bulimia, focus on
125   Anglo-American women, generalization to minority women is question-
126   able. Since about half of the subjects were Hispanic American, and there
127   was no difference in the effectiveness of the multifaceted approach for
128   the Hispanic American and Anglo-American women, the results can be
129   generalized to those ethnic groups, but generalizations to other groups,
130   such as African Americans, is unwarranted.

131   The treatment groups were conducted simultaneously, so history
132   is not a threat to the internal validity of the study. Also, there were no
133   major historical events related to bulimia during the 3 months of the
134   treatment, so these results should be generalizable to the future.

135   While the researcher concludes that the multifaceted approach is
136   better, the components of that approach that actually resulted in the
137   improved performance cannot be isolated. Follow-up interviews of the
138   participants in the multifaceted approach indicated that they felt that
139   the weakest component was the video during week 4. Perhaps further
140   research can test the effects of omitting this component.

141   Participants were asked in the follow-up interviews if they were
142   aware of any other treatments being offered bulimic women. None of
143   the women in either group indicated that they were aware of the other
144   group. Consequently, the researcher feels that neither the Hawthorne
145   effect, nor resentful demoralization, nor experimental diffusion oc-
146   curred.

147   The subjects were aware that they were to complete a posttest at
148   the end of 3 months. This expectation may well have kept them on-task,
149   and that is viewed as being part of the treatment (both groups were
150   given the same expectation). Because the goal of any therapy is long-
151   term improvement, further research should look into a posttest that is
152   administered several months after the end of treatment.

153   The results may have been influenced by the fact that the researcher
154   was also the therapist in each of the two groups. The expected supe-
155   riority of the multifaceted approach may have been transmitted to the
156   subjects. Several precautions were taken to minimize the possibility of
157   this happening. First, the multifaceted group was never told that they
158   were getting what the researcher thought was the best possible treat-
159   ment, nor was the educational group told that they were being given
160   what the researcher thought was an inferior treatment. Second, as

a counselor, the therapist had the ethical responsibility to provide quality therapy to all women. Third, during the follow-up interviews, none of the women indicated that they knew of any other treatment. Finally, during these same interviews, none of the women indicated that they had ever talked with another woman in the last 3 months about some alternative therapy for bulimia.

The recommendations for future research include (1) investigating the multifaceted approach on African American and Asian American women, (2) including nonuniversity women in future studies, (3) testing directly for the effectiveness of the multifaceted approach with the different family types, (4) using outcome measures other than self-report, and (e) checking for long-term effects of the treatment.

REFERENCES

Adam, M. (1990). The best bulimic treatment yet: Refinements and extensions of Black and Decker's multifaceted approach. *Journal of Insights, 3*(1), 1–11.

American Psychiatric Association (1980). *Diagnostic and statistical manual of mental disorders* (3rd ed.). Washington, DC: American Psychiatric Association.

American Psychiatric Association (1987). *Diagnostic and statistical manual of mental disorders* (3rd ed. rev.). Washington, DC: American Psychiatric Association.

Black, C. (1988). A new treatment for bulimia. *Journal of Insights, 1*(1), 1–11.

Boskind-Lodahl, M., & White, W. C. (1978). The definition and treatment of bulimarexia in college women: A pilot study. *Journal of the American College Health Association, 27*, 84–87.

Bruch, H. (1973). *Eating disorders.* New York: Basic Books.

Current, N. (1990). The best treatment around for bulimia. *Journal of Stagnant Truth, 101*(6), 1–99.

Decker, A. (1989). Refinements on Black's new treatment for bulimia. *Journal of Insights, 2*(1), 1–11.

Garner, D. M., & Garfinkel, P. E. (1979). The Eating Attitude Test: An index of the symptoms of anorexia nervosa. *Psychological Medicine, 9*, 273–279.

Garner, D. M., Olmstead, M. P., & Polivy, J. (1983). Development and validation of a multidimensional eating disorder inventory for anorexia nervosa and bulimia. *International Journal of Eating Disorders, 2*, 15–34.

Minuchin, S., Roman, B., & Baker, L. (1978). *Psychosomatic families: Anorexia nervosa in context.* Cambridge, MA: Harvard University Press.

Mitchell, J. E., & Eckert, E. D. (1987). Scope and significance of eating disorders. *Journal of Consulting and Clinical Psychology, 55*, 628–634.

Ordma, A. M., & Kirschenbaum, D. S. (1985). Cognitive-behavior therapy for bulimia: An initial outcome study. *Journal of Consulting and Clinical Psychology, 53*, 305–313.

Ross, S. M. (1983). *Evidence for an anorexic/bulimic MMPI profile.* Paper

219   presented at The Rocky Mountain Psychological Association, Snowbird,
220   Utah.
221   Scott, R. L., & Baroffio, J. R. (1968). An MMPI analysis of similarities
222   and differences in three classifications of eating disorders: Anorexia
223   nervosa, bulimia, and morbid obesity. *Journal of Clinical Psychology, 42*(5),
224   708–713.
225   Smith, M. C., & Thelen, M. H. (1984). Development and validation
226   of a test for bulimia. *Journal of Consulting and Clinical Psychology, 52,*
227   863–872.
228   Thelen, M. H., Farmer, J., Wonderlich, S., & Smith, M. (1990). *The*
229   *BULIT-R: A revision of the Bulimia Test.* Poster session presented at the
230   annual meeting of the American Psychological Association, Boston, MA.

This article is an abbreviated form of the author's master's thesis of the same title. The thesis was conducted at Southwestern University under the direction of Dr. Correct. The project was supported by the National Institute of Mental Health Grant MH99999, which was awarded to Dr. Correct. Partial support was also provided by the Counseling Center at Southwestern University.

Opinions expressed in this article are those of the author and in no way reflect those of NIMH or Southwestern University.

The author would like to thank Dr. Director, the Director of the Southwestern University Counseling Center for the use of the facilities, and Dr. Crunchit for assistance in the analysis and interpretation of the statistics.

Requests for reprints should not be made, because this is a totally fictitious paper.

JOURNAL ARTICLES

A Multidimensional Analysis of the Mental Health of Graduate Counselors in Training

PAUL E. WHITE
JANET B. FRANZONI

The mental health of graduate counselor trainees was examined. Trainees demonstrated more psychopathy than did the normal population on 6 of the 10 scales used.

The mental health of helping professionals has been a topic of discussion for decades. It has been asserted by psychotherapists from numerous theoretical orientations that the therapist's mental and emotional well-being is foundational to the therapeutic process (Freud, 1937/1964; Rogers, 1957; Strupp, 1982; Whitfield, 1980). But, interestingly, this has not been supported empirically (Ju, 1982; Rowe, Murphy, & de Csipkes, 1975).

A prevalent belief is that many mental health professionals are emotionally damaged and have chosen their vocation to solve their own problems. This belief seems to be held by the populace in general (Maeder, 1989a, 1989b) as well as within the helping profession community (Holt & Luborsky, 1958; Miller, 1981; Warkentin, 1963).

The level of mental health has been investigated for psychiatrists (Bermak, 1977; Ford, 1963; Looney, Harding, Blotcky & Barnhart, 1980), psychologists (Mausner & Steppacher, 1973; Thoreson, Budd, & Krauskopf, 1986) and psychotherapists in general (Deutsch, 1985; Henry, Sims, & Spray, 1971, 1973; Maeder, 1989a). These groups of helping professionals were consistently found to have

Paul E. White is a doctoral student in counseling psychology in the Department of Counseling and Psychological Services and Janet B. Franzoni is an associate professor in the Department of Counseling and Psychological Services, both at Georgia State University, Atlanta.

significantly higher rates of depression, intense anxiety, and more relationship problems than did the general populace.

But virtually no research has examined the mental health level of master's level counselors or counseling trainees. This is noteworthy, given the large number of counselor training programs and master's level practitioners currently in the mental health field.

The purpose of this study was to examine the level of mental health of graduate counselor trainees from a multidimensional mental health perspective. Mental health has been defined as "a state of mind characterized by emotional well-being, relative freedom from anxiety and disabling symptoms, and a capacity to establish constructive relationships and cope with the ordinary demands and stress of life" (Goldenson, 1984, p. 451).

Psychopathy is generally perceived as the converse of mental health. In this research, four diverse approaches to assessing mental health (or psychopathy) were used.

METHODOLOGY

Participants

The participants were 180 beginning graduate counselors in training at a major university located in the southeastern United States. The graduate training program from which the students were drawn is a 75 quarter-hour Council for Accreditation of Counseling and Related Educational Programs (CACREP) accredited program located in a major urban university, to which all students commute. The training department has 17 full-time faculty members, and the program is known to be the largest graduate counselor training program in the United States.

Participants were volunteer students from an introductory counseling course, which all 1st-year students in the master's level counselor education department must take. Of the 256 students enrolled in the class sections for one academic year, 191 chose to participate in the study. Eleven individuals, however, did not complete all of the instruments used in the study. This left 180 participants for the study who completed all of the personality measures (a 71% participation rate).

The mean age of the participants was 31.7 years, with 155 women (86.1%) and 25 men (13.9%). Of the participants, 156 were Caucasian (86.6%), 16 were African American (8.9%), 4 were Hispanic (2.2%), 3 were Asian (1.7%), and 1 was from American Indian descent (0.6%).

Given the anonymous conditions of the study, it is not possible to determine why the remaining students did not participate. Potential reasons may have been schedule problems, time limitations, no need or desire for the extra credit given, or paranoia about the research project and use of the results.

Instruments

MINNESOTA MULTIPHASIC PERSONALITY INVENTORY (MMPI). The MMPI is the most widely used objective personality inventory in psychology today and has been utilized in over 8,000 studies (Anastasi, 1988). The MMPI was designed to measure factors associated with psychological and social maladjustment (Dahlstrom, Welsh, & Dahlstrom, 1972).

The MMPI has been criticized with regard to two psychometric issues. Anastasi (1988) has reported that the MMPI has poor test-retest reliability (ranging between .49 and .69 for individual scales over a 2-week period). Second, she has stated that the size and representativeness of the original normative sample is inadequate for the purpose of the test. Despite these criticisms, Dahlstrom (1969) has argued that the large volume of validity research on the MMPI compensates for these weaknesses.

Seven of the 10 clinical scales were used in this research. These scales were the Hypochondriasis scale (Hs), the Depression scale (D), the Hysteria scale (Hy), the Psychopathic Deviate scale (Pd), the Paranoia scale (Pa), the Psychasthenia scale (Pt), and the Schizophrenia scale (Sc). The remaining standard MMPI clinical scales were not included because of their limited applicability to the stated problem.

As suggested by Butcher and Tellegen (1978), non-K-corrected scores were used because they provide a more accurate picture of the level of psychopathy for research participants. Additionally, because this study combined the data from both sexes, T scores (rather than raw scores) were used. These T scores are standard scores with a mean of 50 and a standard deviation of 10.

ADULT NOWICKI-STRICKLAND INTERNAL-EXTERNAL CONTROL SCALE (ANSIE). The ANSIE is a written measure developed by Nowicki and Duke (1974) consisting of 40 yes-or-no questions to which the participants respond. The higher the scale score, the more the individual is characterized by an external locus of control. External locus of control has been associated with depression (Abramowitz, 1969), schizophrenia (Harrow & Ferrante, 1969), neuroticism (Nowicki, 1972), and debilitating anxiety (Kendall, Finch, & Mahoney, 1976).

The ANSIE has been highly acclaimed for its psychometric properties (Lefcourt, 1983); Nowicki and Duke (1974) reported test-retest reliability of .83 for college students over 6 weeks. Also, ANSIE scores have been shown to be relatively free of social desirability (Duke & Nowicki, 1974) and it has been documented that there are no consistent sex differences in ANSIE scores (Dixon, McKee, & McRae, 1976; Nowicki & Duke, 1974, 1983). The construct validity of ANSIE has been studied in more than 400 research investigations (Nowicki, 1981).

LIFE STYLE PERSONALITY INVENTORY (LSPI). The LSPI is a standardized objective personality inventory based on Adlerian personality theory developed by Wheeler, Kern, and Curlette (1982), which assesses the level of an individual's social interest. Social interest has been defined as "the willingness to cooperate with others for the common good and the awareness of the universal interrelatedness of all human beings" (Dinkmeyer, Pew, & Dinkmeyer, 1979, p. 8). Adler proposed that social interest is the cornerstone of mental health (Ansbacher & Ansbacher, 1956).

The LSPI has 164 items that begin with the phrase. "When I was a child, I..." These items are rated by the respondents on a 5-point Likert scale, ranging from *strongly disagree* to *strongly agree:* a higher score on the Social Interest Index (SII) indicates a higher level of social interest.

The LSPI has been in development for more than a decade. Three factor analytic studies (Mullis, Kern, & Curlette, 1987; Wheeler, 1980; Wheeler, Kern, & Curlette, 1986) found the SII to account for more variance than any of the eight personality factors the LSPI assesses. The internal consistency of the SII is high, with a coefficent alpha of .926 (Curlette, Wheeler, Kern, & Mullis, 1987). The SII has been found to correlate negatively with measures of depression (Earles, 1982; Highlander, 1984), numerous indexes of psychopathy (Johnston, 1988), and behavioral symptom checklists (Boynton, 1988).

COPING RESOURCES INVENTORY FOR STRESS (CRIS). The CRIS is a self-report instrument developed by Matheny, Curlette, Aycock, Pugh, and Taylor (1987) to assess a person's resources for coping with stress. Stress has been shown to be an important factor related to psychological problems (Billings, Cronkite, & Moos, 1983; Dohrenwend, 1979; Paykel, Prusoff, & Myers, 1975; Spielberger, 1975); and the ability of coping resources and behaviors to mediate the consequences of stress has been repeatedly documented (Greenberg, 1983). Coping behaviors and resources have also been found to impact individuals' mental health (Andrews, Tennant, Hewson, & Vaillant, 1978; Brown, 1980, 1983; Felton & Revenson, 1984).

The content of the CRIS is based on a taxonomy of coping behaviors and resources developed from a meta-analysis of 54 studies done by Matheny, Aycock, Pugh, Curlette, and Cannella (1986). The CRIS provides a global score called the Coping Resource Effectiveness scale (CRE) that is based on 260 true-false items. The CRE scale has an extremely high degree of internal consistency, demonstrated by a coefficient alpha of .973. Similarly, the test-retest reliability with a 4-week interval was also found to be high, $r = .949$ (Curlette, Aycock, Matheny, Pugh, & Taylor, 1988). The CRE has been shown to correlate negatively with depression (Gulesserian, 1984), bulimia (Linton, 1985), and physical illness (Cupp, 1986) and to correlate positively with life satisfaction (Wedl, 1987).

Procedure

The tests were administered by the primary author and one assistant, using standardized instructions. The total time required to take all the tests was $3\frac{1}{2}$ to 4 hours; the tests were given in two 2-hour segments, 1 week apart. To prevent order effects, the order of the tests was systematically counterbalanced. To ensure anonymity and confidentiality with regard to the test results, students chose a 5-letter identification code that they used as their "name" on each instrument.

Hypotheses

It was hypothesized that for counselors in training, (a) the elevation of their MMPI clinical scales would not be significantly higher than would be the MMPI scales of the general population, (b) they would not be characterized by more external locus of control than would be the general population, (c) their level of social interest would not be lower than would be the level found in the general population, and (d) their coping resources would not be less than are those available to the general population.

RESULTS

The general hypothesis that counselors in training do not have greater levels of psychopathy or lower levels of mental health than does the general population was not supported by the results of this study. The results of the Hotelling $T2(T2 = 883.24, df = 10, p < .0001)$ indicate that, on at least one variable, counselor trainees as a group had a lower level of mental health than did the general population.

To determine on which variables the counselors in training differed from the general population, t tests were calculated on each variable. The means and standard deviations for both groups and the results of the t tests are reported in Table 1.

TABLE 1   Means, standard deviations, and T-test results for all variables.

Variable	Counselors in training[a]		Standardization sample		T-tests		
	M	SD	M	SD	t	df	p level
Hypochondriasis (MMPI)	48.18	8.41	50.00	10.00	−2.90[b]	179	.0042
Depression (MMPI)	54.09	11.84	50.00	10.00	4.64	179	.0001
Hysteria (MMPI)	57.68	7.95	50.00	10.00	12.97	179	.0001
Psychopathic Deviate (MMPI)	57.74	11.00	50.00	10.00	9.45	179	.0001
Paranoia (MMPI)	66.83	10.06	50.00	10.00	22.43	179	.0001
Psychasthenia (MMPI)	53.29	7.72	50.00	10.00	5.72	179	.0001
Schizophrenia (MMPI)	56.82	9.64	50.00	10.00	9.48	179	.0001
Social Interest Index (LSPI)	3.67	.6956	3.68	.6107	0.02	179	.9829
Locus of Control (ANSIE)	8.21	3.86	9.23	3.73	−3.56[b]	179	.0005
Coping Resource Effectiveness (CRIS)	69.67	15.20	65.99	15.85	−3.25[b]	179	.0014

NOTE: MMPI = Minnesota Multiphasic Personality Inventory; LSPI = Life Style Personality Inventory; ANSIE = Adult Nowicki-Strickland Internal-External Control Scale; CRIS = Coping Resources Inventory for Stress.
[a] The means for the remaining MMPI scales were: L, 47.36; F, 53.38; K, 59.07; Ma, 55.78; Si, 55.98.
[b] Supports the alternative hypothesis; null hypothesis is not rejected.

Counselors in training were found to have significantly higher levels of psychopathy than did the general population on six of the seven MMPI scales. Only on the Hypochondriasis scale was the null not rejected. The null was not rejected for the hypotheses regarding the level of social interest, external locus of control, and coping resources.

DISCUSSION

The results indicate, for at least the graduate counseling students of the university investigated, that master's level counseling students have higher levels of psychological disturbance than does the general populace. The results support previous research that has found that other mental health professionals have higher levels of psychological disturbance than was found in the general population (Deutsch, 1985; Looney et al., 1980; Mausner & Steppacher, 1973).

Various questions arise in response to this study's findings. First, can one conclude that counselors in training are in fact characterized by more pathology than is the general adult population? That is, are the differences found practically significant, or are the group means just shifted a few points higher? A population with more than 5% of its individuals obtaining T scores of 70 or above would have more individuals considered to be pathological than exists in the general population. When one examines the frequency distribution obtained for this sample (see Table 2), it can be observed that on six of the seven MMPI scales examined, the percentage of individuals who obtained T scores of 70 or higher was higher than was the expected 5% on five of the scales. Therefore, the differences do appear to be practically significant.

Second, if counselor trainees have higher levels of *psychopathy* than does the general population, would not their levels of *mental health* be lower than that of the general population? This did not seem to be the case. As can be seen in Table

TABLE 2   Frequencies and percentages of individuals obtaining T scores of 70 or above on MMPI scales.

Scale	N[a]	Percentage of total population
Hypochondriasis	4	2.4
Depression[b]	12	6.7
Hysteria[b]	13	7.2
Psychopathic Deviate[b]	23	12.8
Paranoia[b]	76	42.2
Psychasthenia[b]	4	2.4
Schizophrenia[b]	16	8.8

[a]Total $N = 180$.
[b]Scales whose means were significantly different between counselors in training and the standardization sample.

TABLE 3   Means and standard deviations of the ANSIE, LSPI, and CRIS scales.

Participants	ANSIE (Locus of control)		LSPI (Social interest)		CRIS (CRE)	
	M	SD	M	SD	M	SD
Total N (N = 180)	8.21	3.86	3.67	.6956	69.67	15.20
T scores ≥ 70 (N = 92)	8.83	4.46	3.50	.7444	64.61	16.44
Two or more T scores ≥ 70 (N = 29)	10.76	5.00	3.24	.6759	54.47	14.59

3, however, as the groups examined become more pathological (as assessed by the MMPI), they are characterized by a more external locus of control, less social interest, and less resources for coping with stress, as one would expect. One may conclude that as the level of psychopathy increases to extreme levels, the inverse relation between psychopathy and mental health becomes more evident.

The most critical question raised by these results is "What are the implications for graduate counselor training programs and the counseling field in general?" One response to the findings of this study may be for professionals in counselor training programs to begin to identify those students with psychological problems and then offer counseling services to these students. A related issue is that of screening those who apply to graduate counseling programs.

A clear relationship, however, has not been established between counselor effectiveness and the mental health level of the counselor (Ju, 1982; Rowe, Murphy, & de Csipkes, 1975; Whiteley, 1969).

The ability to generalize the results of this study is limited. It would be inappropriate to attempt to generalize these findings to all graduate counseling students or to postgraduate master's level counselors. Clearly, more research needs to be done in this area.

First, it will be important to replicate this study across a more representative population of graduate counselors in training. It also would be helpful to investigate the mental health level of master's level counselors who have already completed their training. Another area of research would be to compare the mental health levels of counselors with pathological populations. A fourth area of research would be to examine more closely the proposed inverse relation between psychopathy and mental health. Finally, the question arises: Is it appropriate to expect counselors to be free of psychological or emotional disturbance?

REFERENCES

Abramowitz, S. I. (1969). Locus of control and self-reported depression among college students. *Psychological Reports, 25,* 149–150.

Anastasi, A. (1988). *Psychological testing* (6th ed.). New York: Macmillan.

Andrews, G., Tennant, C., Hewson, D., & Vaillant, G. E. (1978). Life event stress, social support, coping style, and risk of psychological impairment. Journal of Nervous and *Mental Disorder, 166,* 307–316.

Ansbacher, H. L., & Ansbacher, R. R. (Eds.). (1956). *The individual psychology of Alfred Adler: A systematic presentation in selections from his writings.* New York: Basic Books.

Bermak, G. E. (1977). Do psychiatrists have special emotional problems? *American Journal of Psychoanalysis, 37,* 141–146.

Billings, A. G., Cronkite, R. C., & Moos, R. H. (1983). Social-environmental factors in unipolar depression: Comparisons of depressed patients and nondepressed controls. *Journal of Abnormal Psychology, 92,* 119–133.

Boynton, R. D. (1988). *Drug addiction, life style personality factors and psychopathology.* Unpublished doctoral dissertation. Georgia State University, Atlanta.

Brown, S. D. (1980). Coping skills training: An evaluation of a psychoeducational program in a community mental health setting. *Journal of Counseling Psychology, 27,* 340–345.

Brown, S. D. (1983). Coping skills training: Attitude toward mental illness, depression, and quality of life 1 year later. *Journal of Counseling Psychology, 30,* 117–120.

Butcher, J. N., & Tellegen, A. (1978). Common methodological problems in MMPI research. *Journal of Consulting and Clinical Psychology, 46,* 620–628.

Cupp, P. K. (1986). Prediction of illness based on life and coping resources: A study of sex differences (Doctoral dissertation, Georgia State University). *Dissertation Abstracts International, 46,* 2563A.

Curlette, W. L., Aycock, D. W., Matheny, K. B., Pugh, J. L., & Taylor, H. F. (1988). *Coping Resources Inventory for Stress manual.* Atlanta: Health Prisms, Inc.

Curlette, W. L., Wheeler, M. S., Kern, R. M., & Mullis, F. Y. (1987). *Test manual for the Life Style Personality Inventory.* Unpublished manual.

Dahlstrom, W. G. (1969). Recurrent issues in the development of the MMPI. In J. N. Butcher (Ed.), *MMPI: Research developments and clinical applications.* New York: McGraw-Hill.

Dahlstrom, W. G., Welsh, G. S., & Dahlstrom, L. E. (1972). *An MMPI handbook: Clinical interpretations* (Vol. 1). Minneapolis: University of Minnesota Press.

Deutsch, C. J. (1985). A survey of therapists' personal problems and treatment. *Professional Psychology: Research & Practice, 16,* 305–315.

Dinkmeyer, D. C., Pew, W. L., & Dinkmeyer, D. C., Jr. (1979). *Adlerian counseling and psychotherapy.* Monterey, CA: Brooks/Cole.

Dixon, D. N., McKee, C. S., & McRae, M. (1976). Dimensionality of three adult objective locus of control scales. *Journal of Personality Assessment, 40,* 310–319.

Dohrenwend, B. P. (1979). Stressful life events and psychopathology: Some issues of theory and method. In J. E. Barrett, R. M. Rose, & G. L. Klerman (Eds.), *Stress and mental disorder.* New York: Raven Press.

Duke, M. P., & Nowicki, S., Jr. (1974). Locus of control and achievement: Confirmation of a theoretical perspective. *Journal of Psychology, 87,* 262–267.

Earles, T. D. (1982). Adlerian life style and clinical depression in mothers of disturbed children (Doctoral dissertation, Georgia State University). *Dissertation Abstracts International, 43,* 2614–2615A.

Felton, B. J., & Revenson, T. A. (1984). Coping with chronic illness: A study of illness controllability and the influence of coping strategies on psychological adjustment *Journal of Consulting and Clinical Psychology, 52,* 343–353.

Ford, E. S. C. (1963). Being and becoming a psychotherapist: The search for identity. *American Journal of Psychotherapy, 17*, 472–482.

Freud, S. (1964). Analysis terminable and interminable. In J. Strachey (Ed. and Trans.), *The standard edition of the complete psychological works of Sigmund Freud* (Vol. 23, pp. 226–255). London: Hogarth Press. (Original work published 1937).

Goldenson, R. M. (1984). *Longman dictionary of psychology and psychiatry.* New York: Longman.

Greenberg, J. S. (1983). *Comprehensive stress management.* Dubuque, IA: Brown.

Gulesserian, B. (1984). *The relationship between coping resources of depressed psychiatric inpatients and their degree of depression.* Unpublished master's thesis, Georgia State University, Atlanta.

Harrow, M., & Ferrante, A. (1969). Locus of control in psychiatric patients. *Journal of Consulting and Clinical Psychology, 33*, 382–589.

Henry, W. E., Sims, J. H., & Spray, S. L. (1971). *The fifth profession.* San Francisco: Jossey-Bass.

Henry, W. E., Sims, J. H., & Spray, S. L. (1973). *Public and private lives of psychotherapists.* San Francisco: Jossey-Bass.

Highlander, D. H., Jr. (1984). Adlerian life style, social interest and depression in parents (Doctoral dissertation, Georgia State University). *Dissertation Abstracts International, 45*, 12516A.

Holt, R. R., & Luborsky, L. (1958). *Personality patterns of psychiatrists: A study of methods for selecting residents* (Minninger Clinic Monograph Series No. 13). New York: Basic Books.

Johnston, T. (1988). Validation of the life style personality inventory and the prediction of success in treating pain (Doctoral dissertation, Georgia State University). *Dissertation Abstracts International, 49*, 2046B.

Ju, J. J. (1982). Counselor variables and rehabilitation outcomes: A literature overview. *Journal of Applied Rehabilitation Counseling, 13*, 28–31, 43.

Kendall, P. C., Finch, A. J., & Mahoney, J. (1976). Factor-specific differences in locus of control for emotionally disturbed and normal children. *Journal of Personality Assessment, 40*, 42–45.

Lefcourt, H. M. (1983). *Research with the locus of control construct* (Vol. 2). New York: Academic Press.

Linton, S. C. (1985). *Self-imposed delay and cognitive restructuring as a treatment for bulimia.* Unpublished doctoral dissertation, Georgia State University, Atlanta.

Looney, J. G., Harding, R. K., Blotcky, M. J., & Barnhart, F. D. (1980). Psychiatrists' transition from training to career: Stress and mastery. *American Journal of Psychiatry, 137*, 32–35.

Maeder, T. (1989a). *Children of psychiatrists and other psychotherapists.* New York: Harper & Row.

Maeder, T. (1989b. January). Wounded healers. *The Atlantic Monthly*, pp. 37–47.

Matheny, K. B., Aycock, D. W., Pugh, J. L., Curlette, W. L., Cannella, K. A. S. (1986). Stress coping: A qualitative and quantitative synthesis with implications for treatment. *The Counseling Psychologist, 14*, 499–549.

Matheny, K. B., Curlette, W. L., Aycock, D. W., Pugh, J. L., & Taylor, H. F. (1987). *Coping Resources Inventory for Stress (CRIS).* Atlanta: Health Prisms, Inc.

Mausner, J., & Steppacher, R. (1973). Suicide in professionals: A study of male and female psychologists. *American Journal of Epidemiology, 98*, 436–445.

Miller, A. (1981). *The drama of the gifted child.* New York: Basic Books.

Mullis, F. Y., Kern, R. M., & Curlette, W. L. (1987). Life-style themes and social interest: A further factor analytic study. *Individual Psychology, 43,* 339–352.

Nowicki, S., Jr. (1972). *Expectancies of clients applying for service at a college counseling center.* Paper presented at the Southeastern Psychological Association annual meeting, Atlanta.

Nowicki, S., Jr. (1981). *A manual for the Nowicki-Strickland scales.* Atlanta: Emory University Department of Psychology.

Nowicki, S., Jr., & Duke, M. P. (1974). A locus of control scale for college as well as noncollege adults. *Journal of Personality Assessment, 38,* 136–137.

Nowicki, S., Jr., & Duke, M. P. (1983). The Nowicki-Strickland life-span locus of control scales: Construct validation. In H. M. Lefcourt (Ed.). *Research with the locus of control construct* (Vol. 2). Orlando, FL: Academic Press.

Paykel, E. S., Prusoff, B. A., & Myers, J. K. (1975). Suicide attempts and recent life events. *Archives of General Psychiatry, 32,* 327–333.

Rogers, C. (1957). The necessary and sufficient conditions of therapeutic personality change. *Journal of Consulting Psychology, 21,* 95–103.

Rowe, W., Murphy, H. B., & de Csipkes, R. A. (1975). The relationship of counselor characteristics and counseling effectiveness. *Review of Educational Research, 45,* 231–246.

Spielberger, C. D. (1975). Anxiety: State-trait-process. In C. D. Spielberger & I. G. Sarason (Eds.), *Stress and anxiety* (Vol. 1). Washington, DC: Hemisphere Publishers.

Strupp, H. H. (1982). Some critical comments on the future of psychoanalytic theory. In M. R. Goldfried (Ed.), *Converging themes in psychotherapy: Trends in psychodynamic, humanistic, and behavioral practice.* New York: Springer Publisher Co.

Thoreson, R. W., Budd, F. C., & Krauskopf, C. J. (1986). Perceptions of alcohol misuse and work behavior among professionals: Identification and intervention. *Professional Psychology: Research & Practice, 17,* 210–216.

Warkentin, J. (1963). The therapist's significant other. *Annals of Psychotherapy, 4,* 54–59.

Wedl, L. C. (1987). Stress coping resources and their relationship to life satisfaction among older persons (Doctoral dissertation, Ohio University, 1986). *Dissertation Abstracts International, 47,* 3847A.

Wheeler, M. S. (1980). Factor analysis of an instrument developed to measure Adlerian life styles (Doctoral dissertation, Georgia State University). *Dissertation Abstracts International, 40,* 5032B.

Wheeler, M. S., Kern, R. M., & Curlette, W. L. (1982). *Life Style Personality Inventory.* Atlanta: Georgia State University.

Wheeler, M. S., Kern, R. M., & Curlette, W. L. (1986). Factor analytic scales designed to measure Adlerian life style themes. *Individual Psychology, 42,* 1–6.

Whiteley, J. M. (1969). Counselor education. *Review of Educational Research, 39,* 173–189.

Treatment Effectiveness of Anxiety Management Training in Small and Large Group Formats

PAUL C. DALEY, LARRY J. BLOOM,
JERRY L. DEFFENBACHER, AND ROB STEWART
Colorado State University

The relative efficiency of anxiety management training (AMT) in a large group was compared to AMT in small groups and to a wait-list control. Immediately after treatment, small-group AMT participants reported significantly less general anxiety than controls. Seven-week follow-up revealed maintenance of this reduction of general anxiety and a further significant difference on a measure of anxiety and neuroticism. In all comparisons, large-group AMT was not significantly different from either small group AMT or controls. No other significant differences among groups were found for personality variables, nontargeted anxieties, or grades.

Anxiety and stress are significant, pervasive problems on college campuses. Recently, numerous stress management workshops have been developed to teach students how to manage stress (Case, 1978; Deffenbacher & McKinley, in press; Romano, 1978) and at the same time reach large numbers of students. Some efforts have gone as far as presenting the workshop over the radio (Lowenstein, 1978; Lowenstein & Robyak, 1979). This demand for efficient programming is likely to increase as fiscal tightening further reduces resources at a time when student stress is likely to increase.

These workshops typically incorporate principles and procedures that are effective with individuals or small groups. It is assumed that the effectiveness of these procedures extends to the larger group delivery. Rarely, however, is this assumption checked empirically; either no program evaluation is done at all, or it is of the pre-post single-group variety. Yet, the effectiveness may be lost with the increased efficiency of the workshop. Quality evaluation, which includes both traditional (individual or small group) delivery and untreated controls, is needed to see if effectiveness is carried over to the more efficient delivery models.

The present study addressed this issue by evaluating the efficacy of anxiety management training (AMT; Suinn, 1977) for a large group of generally anxious students. Large-group AMT was compared to traditional small-group AMT and to a wait-list control. AMT was chosen because prior research has shown it to be effective in reducing both specific (e.g., Deffenbacher & Shelton, 1978) and

Requests for reprints and an extended report should be sent to Larry J. Bloom, Department of Psychology, Colorado State University, Fort Collins, Colorado 80523.

general anxieties (Hutchings, Denney, Basgall, & Houston, 1980; Jannoun, Oppenheimer, & Gelder, 1982) in groups of 5–10 clients.

METHOD

Subjects

Intially, 86 subjects (28 males and 58 females) were drawn from a pool of 1,200 introductory psychology students, if they (a) scored in the upper 15% of the 1,200 students (scores > 44) on the Trait Anxiety Inventory (Spielberger, Gorsuch, & Lushene, 1970); (b) volunteered for treatment of general anxiety; and (c) completed pretreatment assessment. Subjects were within the constraints of scheduling randomly assigned for conditions. Subsequently, 8 control, 5 large-group AMT, and 6 small-group AMT subjects were dropped from analyses because they received other psychological services during the course of the study. The AMT subjects did, however, complete treatment. Final numbers of subjects were 22 for large-group AMT, 25 for small-group AMT, and 20 for control. Subjects completed a 2-hour research requirement by participants.

Instruments

General anxiety was measured by the Trait Anxiety Inventory, a 20-item, Likert-type self-report measure of trait anxiety. Specific nontargeted anxieties were measured by the Fear Inventory (Wolpe, 1969), a Likert-type self-report instrument tapping 87 specific fears. Personality adjustment was assessed by the Psychological Screening Inventory (Lanyon, 1973), which yields the following subscales of adjustment: alienation, social nonconformity, discomfort, expression, and defensiveness. Semester grade point averages were obtained from the registrar's office. A 12-item Likert-type questionnaire assessing subject evaluations of counselor interest, communication ability, expectations for success, group size, and so on was given to AMT subjects.

Procedure

Students in six introductory psychology classes completed the Trait Anxiety Inventory and indicated interest in treatment for general anxiety. Two weeks later highly anxious volunteers completed the Fear Inventory and Psychological Screening Inventory at a pretreatment assessment session. At posttesting 1 week after treatment and at 7-week follow-up, subjects again completed the three instruments. AMT subjects also completed the questionnaire regarding perceptions of treatment. Assessment was done by the fourth author, who was experimentally blind to treatment conditions.

AMT consisted of seven weekly 60-minute sessions administered by the first author, an advanced doctoral student with prior supervised experience with

AMT. Groups met in a small classroom and used the padded straight-backed chairs available.

SMALL-GROUP AMT.   Procedure followed Suinn's (1977) manual with minor adaptations for groups. Treatment rationale emphasized AMT as a means of learning relaxation as an active coping skill. Relaxation training emphasized awareness of tension and included training in three applied relaxation coping skills: (a) cuing relaxation with deep breathing; (b) focusing on and relaxing away tension without tensing muscles; and (c) relaxing through visualization of a personally relaxing image. Subjects developed two highly stressful scenes from their past experience. Explanation of rationale, scene construction, and relaxation training were done in the first three sessions. Remaining sessions focused upon training the self-control of the relaxation coping skills. In the third session the counselor had subjects imagine the anxiety-arousing scenes for increasing intervals up to a minute. He then terminated the scene and instructed subjects in specific ways to relax away felt tension, for example, through employment of the relaxing image. The fourth session paralleled the third, except that subjects initiated their own relaxation procedures following scene termination. In the fifth session, subjects terminated the scene when they were ready and initiated the relaxation coping skills that worked best for them. In Sessions 6 and 7, subjects actively relaxed away tension while continuing the anxiety-arousing scene in imagination. Throughout sessions employing anxiety imagery, subjects were instructed to pay attention to the internal cues of anxiety arousal and use these as "early warning cues" for the self-application of relaxation. Homework stressed real-life application of coping skills starting with the third session; first in situations without stress, then with mild to moderate stress, and finally with all stress levels. Small group AMT was administered in groups of 10 or 11.

LARGE-GROUP AMT.   This paralleled small group AMT, except that all 27 subjects were treated in a single group.

WAIT-LIST CONTROL.   Wait-list control subjects were informed, as part of the informed consent procedures, that some individuals would at random have their treatment delayed until the beginning of the next semester. Following pretreatment assessment, they were informed that they were in this group. Small-group AMT was offered the next semester.

RESULTS

A chi-square analysis revealed no differential dropout rates caused by eliminating subjects who had sought other treatment during the study, $\chi^2(2) = 1.02$. Analyses of variance on premeasures (Table 1) revealed no significant between-group differences. Change on repeated measures was analyzed by analyses of covariance (Cronbach & Furby, 1970), with pretreatment scores covaried against

TABLE 1   Means, Standard Deviations, and F Values for Small Group AMT, Large Group AMT, and Controls.

Measure	Control group		Large-group AMT		Small-group AMT		F
	M	SD	M	SD	M	SD	
Trait Anxiety Inventory							
Pre	51.35	5.82	48.27	3.68	50.60	7.15	1.65
Post	46.69	9.13	43.65	7.25	39.17	5.61	7.10**
Follow-up	45.13	10.85	42.29	7.05	38.91	7.66	3.94*
Fear Inventory							
Pre	224.15	48.74	201.05	52.13	205.60	50.02	1.23
Post	194.89	52.95	198.14	48.64	189.25	42.57	.69
Follow-up	190.32	57.23	182.02	41.22	178.43	44.07	1.02
Psychological Screening Inventory: Alienation							
Pre	53.75	9.01	52.48	7.38	52.28	11.57	.15
Post	53.10	11.39	51.03	9.30	52.55	11.61	.33
Follow-up	52.70	9.70	48.43	8.53	52.28	10.02	2.16
Social Nonconformity							
Pre	50.15	7.18	48.90	9.49	50.16	10.36	.13
Post	51.20	8.38	50.85	11.19	50.82	10.48	.03
Follow-up	50.10	7.71	50.27	10.77	49.45	9.08	.12
Discomfort							
Pre	58.50	10.52	57.38	6.95	57.48	10.56	.09
Post	58.20	11.81	55.20	10.53	52.79	10.57	1.75
Follow-up	56.77	11.43	52.89	9.08	49.04	9.80	4.48*
Expression							
Pre	49.50	11.29	48.29	9.56	48.32	8.09	.11
Post	50.05	13.57	48.48	11.24	51.09	9.44	.79
Follow-up	49.51	10.12	49.26	11.08	52.32	8.84	2.69
Defensiveness							
Pre	43.00	9.75	44.71	6.81	46.72	7.69	1.18
Post	42.81	7.83	44.54	6.14	44.50	7.01	.58
Follow-up	45.16	8.96	45.00	7.03	48.03	8.23	1.50
Grade point average							
Follow-up	2.73	.43	2.62	.59	2.56	.82	.38

NOTE:. Analyses of variance were performed on the pre scores. Analyses of covariance were performed on the post and follow-up scores with respective pre scores serving as the covariate. AMT = Anxiety Management Training.
*p < .05. **p < .01.

posttreatment and follow-up scores (Table 1). Post hoc comparisons on adjusted means were made by Newman-Keuls analyses.

Significant posttreatment and follow-up differences were found on the Trait Anxiety Inventory with small-group AMT reporting significantly less general anxiety than controls ($ps < .05$). Large-group AMT did not differ significantly from either small-group AMT or controls. At follow-up, the discomfort scale of the Psychological Screening Inventory also showed a significant between-groups difference. Again, small-group AMT was significantly improved relative to controls ($p < .05$), and large-group AMT was not significantly different from other groups. No significant differences were found on other measures.

Attendance and reactions to treatment were compared for AMT subjects. Large-group AMT subjects missed more sessions ($M = 1.00$) than did small-group AMT subjects ($M = .44$), $F(1, 45) = 6.82$, $p < .05$. No significant differences between AMT groups were found at post or follow-up assessments on 10 of the 12 questions dealing with perceptions of treatment. However, at the posttreatment assessment, large-group subjects responded less positively to two questions regarding the size of their group, $Fs(1, 45) = 5.43$ and 4.50, respectively, $ps < .05$.

DISCUSSION

Small-group AMT effectively reduced general anxiety, and these gains were maintained at 7-week follow-up. Additionally, a personality factor that loads heavily with generalized anxiety showed significant reduction for small-group AMT at follow-up, representing posttreatment consolidation found by others for self-control interventions (e.g., Deffenbacher & Shelton, 1978). Thus, the present study adds to the small literature (Hutchings et al., 1980; Jannoun et al., 1982) that has found small-group AMT effective in reducing general anxiety.

The attempt at increasing the efficiency of AMT by increasing group size was, however, a failure. Large-group AMT evidenced no significant anxiety reduction and was never significantly different from the control group. The size of the group appeared to alter the way subjects reacted to otherwise identical treatments. For example, it may have been easier to remain anonymous and uninvolved in the larger group (Baron, Byrne, & Griffitt, 1974). Consistent with this possibility was the finding that large-group AMT subjects missed more sessions and felt more negatively about group size at the posttreatment assessment. Future efforts at increasing group size must attend to factors that would personalize the group and maximize commitment. For example, sessions might be extended from an hour to an hour and a half with added time devoted to group rapport-building activities. Although efforts should be directed to increasing the efficiency through larger groups, the effectiveness of such efforts cannot be assumed from prior work. It must be evaluated carefully, as the present study suggests something was lost with increased group size.

A caution about overgeneralization of the present findings, is needed, however. Large-group AMT employed a single leader. Although this is consistent with AMT procedures, many workshops employ co-leaders. This could improve the effectiveness of the large-group medium, because group identity and involvement may increase as the ratio of members to leaders decreases. This too, however, needs careful empirical documentation.

REFERENCES

Baron, R. A., Byrne, D., & Griffitt, W. *Social psychology: Understanding human interaction.* Boston: Allyn & Bacon, 1974.

Case, J. S. A test-anxiety workshop. *Journal of College Student Personnel,* 1978, *19,* 473.

Cronbach, L. J., & Furby, L. How we should measure change—Or should we? *Psychological Bulletin,* 1970, *74,* 68–80.

Deffenbacher, J. L., & McKinley, D. L. Stress management: Issues in intervention design. In E. M. Altmaier (Ed.), *New directions for student services: Stress management.* San Francisco: Jossey-Bass, in press.

Deffenbacher, J. L., & Shelton, J. L. Comparison of anxiety management training and desensitization in reducing test and other anxieties. *Journal of Counseling Psychology,* 1978, *25,* 277–282.

Hutchings, D. F., Denney, D. R., Basgall, J., & Houston, B. K. Anxiety management and applied relaxation in reducing general anxiety. *Behaviour Research and Therapy,* 1980, *18,* 181–190.

Jannoun, L., Oppenheimer, C., & Gelder, M. A self-help treatment program for anxiety state patients. *Behavior Therapy,* 1982, *13,* 103–111.

Lanyon, R. I. *PSI: Psychological Screening Inventory Manual.* New York: Research Psychologists Press, 1973.

Lowenstein, T. J. Biofeedback relaxation training via radio. *Journal of College Student Personnel,* 1978, *19,* 372–373.

Lowenstein, T. J., & Robyak, J. E. Study skills and stress reduction: The radio as a medium for community programming. *Personnel and Guidance Journal,* 1979, *57,* 553–554.

Romano, J. L. A stress reduction workshop. *Journal of College Student Personnel,* 1978, *19,* 374.

Spielberger, C. D., Gorsuch, R. L., & Lushene, R. E. *Manual for the state-trait anxiety inventory (self-evaluation questionnaire).* Palo Alto, Calif.: Consulting Psychologists Press, 1970.

Suinn, R. M. *Manual: Anxiety management training (AMT).* Fort Collins, Colorado: Rocky Mountain Behavioral Science Institute, Inc., 1977.

Wolpe, J. *The practice of behavior therapy.* New York: Pergamon Press, 1969.

Received May 25, 1982
Revision received July 22, 1982

RESEARCH EVALUATION FORM AND GUIDELINES FOR COMPLETION

RESEARCH EVALUATION FORM

CITATION:

RESEARCH QUESTIONS:

RESEARCH HYPOTHESES:

REVIEW OF LITERATURE. RELATIONSHIP OF RESEARCH QUESTION AND RESEARCH HYPOTHESES TO PREVIOUS RESEARCH CLEAR:

METHODS
    SAMPLE: TOTAL SIZE ___ SIZE PER CELL ___
    SAMPLING PROCEDURE: CONVENIENT ___ RANDOM ___
    STRATIFIED ___
    ASSIGNMENT PROCEDURE: RANDOM ___ INTACT ___ OTHER ___

POPULATION:

PROCEDURES
    DATA COLLECTION PROCESS CLEAR:

INDEPENDENT VARIABLE(S) CLEARLY DEFINED:

DEPENDENT VARIABLE(S) CLEARLY DEFINED:

HOW MEASURED:
  VALIDITY INFORMATION:

  RELIABILITY INFORMATION:

DESIGN (X AND O):

DATA ANALYSIS
  STATISTICAL TECHNIQUES USED:

  TABLES AND FIGURES CLEAR AND COMMUNICATIVE:

THREATS TO INTERNAL VALIDITY
  SELECTION BIAS:

  SUBJECT BIAS:

  RESEARCHER BIAS:

  HISTORY:

  MATURATION:

  TESTING:

  MORTALITY:

  INSTRUMENTATION:

REGRESSION:

THREATS TO EXTERNAL VALIDITY
    POPULATION:

    METHODS:

    SETTINGS:

SUMMARY AND CONCLUSIONS
    CONCLUSIONS SUBSTANTIATED FROM THE RESULTS:

    CONCLUSIONS PRACTICALLY SIGNIFICANT:

GUIDELINES FOR RESEARCH EVALUATION FORM

CITATION: [Use APA style.]

RESEARCH QUESTIONS: [Need a short sentence.]

RESEARCH HYPOTHESES: [May need more space to identify all.]

REVIEW OF LITERATURE. RELATIONSHIP OF RESEARCH QUESTION AND RESEARCH HYPOTHESES TO PREVIOUS RESEARCH CLEAR: [Number of references, variety of references, currency of references, and spread of references.]

METHODS [Fill in both blanks for sample, but check only one for procedure.]

SAMPLE: TOTAL SIZE ____ SIZE PER CELL ____

SAMPLING PROCEDURE: CONVENIENT ____ RANDOM ____
STRATIFIED ____

ASSIGNMENT PROCEDURE: RANDOM ____ INTACT ____
OTHER ____
POPULATION: [Identify all defining characteristics.]

PROCEDURES
DATA COLLECTION PROCESS CLEAR: [If not Yes, briefly state why.]

INDEPENDENT VARIABLE(S) CLEARLY DEFINED: [If not Yes, briefly state why.]

DEPENDENT VARIABLE(S) CLEARLY DEFINED: [If not Yes, briefly state why.]

HOW MEASURED:
VALIDITY INFORMATION: [None presented, seems adequate, or not adequate.]

RELIABILITY INFORMATION: [None presented, seems adequate, or not adequate.]

DESIGN (X AND O): [Use chapter 8 and 9 notation.]

DATA ANALYSIS
STATISTICAL TECHNIQUES USED: [e.g., t, F, chi square]

TABLES AND FIGURES CLEAR AND COMMUNICATIVE: [Yes or No]

THREATS TO INTERNAL VALIDITY
SELECTION BIAS: [If yes, describe.]

SUBJECT BIAS: [Are the subjects attempting to 'help' the researcher in some way?]

RESEARCHER BIAS: [Could biases of the researcher have influenced the results?]

HISTORY: [Were there any historical events that could account for the results?]

MATURATION: [Could changes from pre to post be due to maturation?]

TESTING: [Could subjects have done better on the post-test because they took the pretest?]

MORTALITY: [Was dropout or non-response rate the same for all groups?]

INSTRUMENTATION: [Did measuring instrument stay stable during pretest?]

REGRESSION: [Were Ss selected because they were high (or low) on the pretest?]

THREATS TO EXTERNAL VALIDITY
POPULATION: [Is the population too restrictive to be of interest?]

METHODS: [Are the methods replicable, and of sufficient interest for someone to replicate them?]

SETTINGS: [Is the setting restrictive in any way?]

SUMMARY AND CONCLUSIONS
CONCLUSIONS SUBSTANTIATED FROM THE RESULTS: [Need a short sentence.]

CONCLUSIONS PRACTICALLY SIGNIFICANT: [Go beyond statistics and author's conclusion to indicate significance to the field.]

GLOSSARY

Accessible population One that the researcher has access to; it is usually biased in some ways (see convenience sample).

Accountability Refers to evidence that a helping professional is practicing competently.

Achievement tests Tests that provide a measure of the subject's general educational development and amount of school learning.

Alpha Proportion of times that the researcher is willing to make a mistake by rejecting a true statistical hypothesis.

Alternate forms reliability Obtained from the correlation between two forms of the same test successively administered.

Alternate hypothesis Traditional term for the hypothesis of interest to the researcher (see research hypothesis).

Analogue research Research that is conducted in settings that are as similar as possible to real life.

Analysis of covariance (ANCOVA) Statistical analysis used when a variable needs to be controlled and cannot be controlled for experimentally.

Analysis of variance (ANOVA) Statistical analysis used when more than two groups are being investigated; this technique is employed to ascertain significant differences between groups.

Anecdotal A way of knowing that is unscientific; includes observations made without controlled, systematic methods.

Applied research Research without emphasis on theory, explanation, or prediction but rather on the application and development of research-based knowledge.

Aptitude tests Tests that measure specific skills; useful in helping a person make educational or occupational decisions about the future.

Average A score that represents a middle point; mean, median, and mode are examples. (An arithmetic average is obtained by summing the scores in a distribution and dividing by the number of scores to yield a mean.)

Basic research Investigators focus on theory as the primary context for developing an empirical research study; studies are not designed to be applied immediately to practice.

Behavioral checklists A record of observations that systematize and quantify a subject's behavior.

Behavioral observations Recordings of behavior made by an observer.

Between-subject design A research design in which subjects are placed in one and only one design cell, that is, they represent only one level of the experimental condition.

Bimodal distribution   This occurs when two scores separated on the score scale are equally most frequent.

Blocking   A strategy in which the researcher builds an extraneous variable into a study so that its effects on the dependent variable can be assessed (see also blocking variable and stratified random sampling).

Blocking variable   A variable that the researcher may already know is important; its effects may not be of interest, but the researcher may want to reduce the variability within each group (see also blocking and stratified random sampling).

Budget   An enumeration of the cost of all research expenses.

Canonical analysis   The statistical technique used when both predictor and criterion sets of variables are continuous.

Career interest inventories   Tests to measure people's likes and dislikes of various occupations.

Case study   An in-depth study of an individual or a situation, usually using qualitative research methods.

Cause and effect   A relationship determined in research studies in which independent variables are manipulated and these can be inferred to cause change in the dependent variable measure.

Cells   The particular combination of the levels of independent variable(s) the subject receives, or the number of boxes in an experimental or quasi-experimental design.

Central sources   Databases that store thousands of references and brief abstracts to journal articles, books, dissertations, and other manuscripts.

Cognitive tests   Tests to measure the knowledge, learning, and skill level of a subject.

Comparison group   The group whose dependent variable score is used as a baseline or expectation (see also control group).

Compensatory equalization of treatments   When subjects in one group perceive that subjects in the other group are receiving more beneficial experiences and thus demand that their group receive similar treatment or some additional attention (or the researcher makes these adjustments).

Compensatory rivalry   When subjects in an untreated comparison group learn that subjects in the treatment group are expected to perform better, and this knowledge results in the comparison subjects working extra hard to see that the expected effect does not occur.

Complex experiments   These are also known as **factorial designs**; an investigator examines the effects of at least two independent variables on one or more dependent variables.

Concealment   When subjects are not informed of key features of a study, such as particular methodological manipulations.

Concurrent validity   The extent to which a test correlates with another test administered at about the same time.

Conditions of participation   The specific inclusion and exclusion requirements for subjects being in a study.

Confidentiality   Refers to subjects' right to privacy and includes subject anonymity and disclosure of information. Assurance is given that none other than the persons working on the study will have access to the data without subjects' permission.

Confounding   When some of the differences on the dependent variable may be due to another variable or set of variables; especially problematic with ex post facto designs.

Constant   A characteristic that does not vary in a particular group (opposite of a variable).

Construct   A hypothetical term designed to classify and give meaning to behavior. A construct cannot be observed but must be operationally defined by either an independent variable or a dependent variable.

Construct validity   An indication of how well a test measures the construct it purports to measure.

Content validity   The extent to which the behaviors being measured are judged to represent the construct; can be determined by comparing test items with a table of specifications that guided the development of the test.

Continuous variable   A variable that at least ranks people.

Control group   Group in which participants agree to have treatment withheld to compare the effects of newly developed interventions with no-intervention baseline. Withholding of treatment is often not ethical, hence the group is usually given some sort of treatment (we prefer the term, *comparison group*).

Convenience (or convenient) sample   is the sample nearest at hand, or those subjects who happen to be most available for re-search participation (see *accessible population*).

Correlation   Indicates the relationship between two variables, that is how the scores on one variable are related to scores on another variable. The index of correlation is *r* and ranges from high positive *r* of 1.00 to high negative *r* of −1.00. Lack of correlation is an *r* of .00.

Correlational research   Research that determines whether two or more events occur together.

Counterbalancing   A strategy researchers use to combat order effects; the order of one independent variable is taken into consideration by randomly assigning subjects to different orders. Order of treatment then becomes another between-subject variable, and the effects of ordering are eliminated.

Criterion variable   The outcome measure synonymous with *dependent variable*.

Cronbach alpha   A procedure for estimating internal consistency reliability, based on parts of a test.

Cross-sectional design   When data from different age-groups, or cohorts, is obtained at a single time.

Cross-sequential design   When different age groups are measured repeatedly, usually over long periods of time—months or years.

Data   Results obtained from research; interpretations and conclusions are drawn from data. (The singular is *datum*.)

Data collector-blind method   When those who collect the data in a research study are unaware of the research hypotheses; an attempt to keep those who interact with participants free of bias.

Debriefing   The concluding information provided to subjects following a research study. Typically, when subjects are debriefed, misconceptions and vagaries that may have developed during participation are clarified.

Deception   When subjects are purposefully misled about the study.

Decompose   To separate and study the individual parts of a treatment.

Decomposition   (see Decompose)

Deduction   A type of reasoning that operates downward from theory to prediction.

Demand characteristics   Cues in the research context that participants use to figure out the true purpose of the investigation.

Dependent variable   The variable presumably affected by an independent variable. The measures of a dependent variable are collected after the effects of an independent variable are exerted.

Descriptive statistics   Statistics used to describe the sample the researcher investigated; they communicate the nature of the sample to the reader. Descriptive statistics typically used are means, medians, modes, and frequencies.

Developmental research Research focusing on those aspects of human behavior that change over time.

Deviation score The score that indicates how many raw score units a person deviates from the mean.

DIALOG Information Retrieval Service An information company that contains about 300 major databases, including all five of the central sources noted in Chapter 2.

Dichotomizing the independent variable Designing the independent variable so that its levels differ as much as possible.

Dichotomous choice questions These divide the universe of possible answers into two categories, usually true-false or yes-no.

Differential attrition Occurs when more subjects drop out of one group than do subjects in other groups. If dropping out is due to treatment, the researcher has a problem with the study.

Directional hypothesis A statement in which the researcher predicts the direction of the outcome. For example, either Group A will be *higher* than Group B, or Group B will be *higher* than Group A, or there is a *positive* correlation or a *negative* correlation.

Discriminant analysis The statistical technique used when a researcher has multiple dependent variables and an independent variable with multiple groups.

Dissertation Abstracts International (DAI) The best source for dissertation information, since it is published monthly by University Microfilms International (UMI) and contains the abstracts of dissertations submitted by almost 500 universities in the United States and Canada.

Double-blind method When both subjects and data collectors are unaware of the purpose of the study.

Ecological external validity The settings in which a replication obtains the same results as in the original study.

Educational Resources Information Center (ERIC) A national information system that collects and stores research information about education.

Effect size The difference between the treatment and comparison group means, divided by the standard deviation. This scale-free index indicates the effectiveness of the treatment.

Empirical approach This way of knowing occurs when experiences are structured so that they are based on carefully controlled, systematic, and objective observation.

Empirical research Refers to data-based investigations in which researchers systematically study some aspect of human behavior.

Error Refers to any event, characteristic, or situation that is unsystematic and randomly fluctuates.

Ethics Moral principles, which, in the context of research, pertain to treating subjects fairly and responsibly throughout the research process.

Ethnographic observation Observation of phenomena in naturally occurring situations over an extended period of time.

Ex post facto After-the-fact research; subjects already possess the level of the independent variable of interest before the research study begins.

Experiment A type of research in which an independent variable is manipulated to see its effect on a dependent variable.

Experimental design Research in which the independent variable is manipulated to investigate the cause and effect relationship between the independent variable and the dependent variable.

Existing records Sources of information that are already available.

Expert opinion Opinions of those who are experts in their fields.

External funding   Financial support given the researcher by outside (the university) funding agencies.

External validity   A measure of the degree to which research results are generalizable to other populations, operations, or settings.

External validity of operations   The extent to which other researchers could obtain the same results, using similar operational definitions of the independent variable and dependent variables.

Extraneous variable   When some factor produces error that becomes systematic and directional in nature.

Face validity   When a test *appears* to the test administrator as well as to the subject as a reasonable way to measure the construct.

Factor analysis   A statistical technique applied to a single set of variables that can determine (1) the number of constructs underlying the set of variables and (2) the nature of those constructs.

Field experiment   A research study with all the qualities of experimental research but is conducted outside the laboratory, in more natural settings.

Factorial design   See complex experiments.

Forced-choice response   Test items that force a respondent to choose between two options.

General Linear Model   A statistical analysis which encompasses all the single dependent variable techniques, including ANOVA and correlation.

Grants   The external money (funds coming from outside the university) used to conduct research.

Hawthorne effect   occurs when subjects, simply as a function of knowing they are in an experiment, perform better.

Helping professional   Any individual with special skills and knowledge related to improving the human condition.

History   When an event (other than the independent variable) affects subjects during their research participation and that event explains some of the changes in the dependent variable.

Homogeneous samples   Samples of subjects that are very similar on certain characteristics; used on the assumption that similar subjects will not differ systematically on any extraneous variable.

Hypothesis   A declarative statement about problem solution and predicted outcomes.

Hypothesis testing   Determining the likelihood of the observed value differing from the hypothesized value through chance alone.

Idiographic methods   Research that focuses on single cases and the documentation of interventions on a case-by-case basis.

Independent variables   Any characteristics, events, or situations that are presumed to cause change in another variable.

Independent variable levels   Experimental conditions not classified as separate variables per se but instead make up the categories defining the variables.

Individual differences   The differences that exist between human beings. This source of variability can be controlled for in repeated measures designs (see also within-subject design).

Inductive   A type of theory in which data are analyzed and a theory built (upward) that links and ultimately explains the data on which it was constructed.

Inferential statistics   The process whereby statements are made about a population of interest, either the population sampled, or one to which an inference might be made in the future.

Informed consent   An explicit agreement between subject and researcher that specifies the responsibilities of each.

Instrumentation   The subtle nuances in the procedural process that may systematically bias the results of the study.

Intact groups   Groups of subjects who enter a study already possessing a particular level of the independent variable, such as age or gender.

Intelligence test   A test that measures the ability to acquire knowledge for solving problems and adapting to the world.

Interaction   When the difference in the effect on the dependent variable of one independent variable is *not* the same across the levels of another independent variable.

Interlibrary loan   An arrangement between participating institutions, usually defined by geographic location, to help patrons in different libraries retrieve the information they need by pooling resources.

Internal funding   The financial support given the researcher by the researcher's employing agency.

Internal consistency reliability   The extent to which parts of a test are consistent.

Internal validity   A measure of the degree to which the variables under investigation, and only those variables, explain research results.

Interquartile range   A measure of variability used in conjunction with the median; the distance on the score scale from the 25th percentile to the 75th percentile.

Interrater reliability   It is the extent of agreement of several raters and is required when a measure is not scored objectively but subjectively.

Interviews   When conducted by the researcher or trained observer can provide in-depth information from different information providers.

Intuition   A way of knowing; sometimes referred to as common sense.

Latin square design   A research design that systematically orders the levels of the independent variable so that no level appears twice on the same row or column for each group.

Likert scale   A type of scale on which subjects express degrees of agreement or disagreement with a statement.

Linear correlation   The extent to which there is a straight-line relationship between two variables; usually represented by the Pearson product-moment correlation.

Longitudinal design   When the same subject group is repeatedly studied over time.

Main effect   In ANOVA, the overall effect attributed to the levels of one independent variable averaged over all levels of the other independent variables.

Manipulated variable   The operational definition of the independent variable; the researcher exposes subjects to different levels of this variable and observes their effects on the dependent measure.

Matching   Identifying equivalent scores on a confound variable across all groups of interest.

Maturation   The processes that systematically change subjects over the period of the research study but are unrelated to the variables under study.

MAXMINCON principle   Internal validity is increased when researchers (1) maximize the effects of the independent variable on the dependent variable, (2) minimize error factors, and (3) control extraneous variables.

Mean   The most widely used measure of central tendency; calculated by adding all of the scores and then dividing by the number of scores.

Measurement   Defines how numbers are assigned to subjects.

Measurement error   The error inherent in instruments used to obtain subjects' scores.

Measures of central tendency   A single point on the score scale at which scores tend to bunch upidentifying the typical score. There are three commonly used measures of central tendency mode, mean, and median.

Measures of variability The degree of spread of the scores, or a distance on the score scale. There are three commonly used measures of variabilityrange, interquartile range, and standard deviation.

Median That point on the score scale at which half of the scores fall below and half fall above.

Medline A comprehensive central source for biomedical research.

Meta-analysis A computational way to combine the results of many similar studies.

Mode The most frequently occurring score in a distribution.

Mortality Loss, which in research is the loss (not necessarily death) of subjects.

Multiple correlation or multiple regression A statistical technique that allows the simultaneous investigation of the effects of multiple independent variables on one dependent variable.

Multiple-baseline design Several baselines are obtained and generally consist of different subjects; for one subject, different situations or behaviors are observed. The researcher then systematically applies the treatment to one baseline at a time.

Multivariate analysis of variance (MANOVA) The statistic to use when a researcher has multiple dependent variables and one or more categorical independent variables.

Negatively skewed distribution Scores are piled up at the top end of the distribution. An example of a negatively skewed distribution would be scores on an extremely easy test.

Nested When subjects pass through two cells within each treatment.

Neurological measure Tests that identify brain-behavior relationships.

Nomothetic Research that concentrates on the aggregate unit the average of the group rather than on any one person.

Noncognitive tests Tests that measure attributes other than knowledge, like preferences, beliefs, and attitudes.

Nondirectional hypothesis A statement that experimental groups will differ or that a correlation exists. How the groups will differ or whether the correlation is positive or negative is not specified.

Nonempirical study When the researcher does not gather new data but reads previous studies for the purpose of developing an innovative position, such as integrating different theories or summarizing previous research to distill logical or methodological issues in need of further study.

Nonequivalent comparison group design When subjects have not been randomly assigned to the comparison and treatment groups.

Nonmanipulated variable When the independent variable cannot be manipulated or has not been manipulated; the research is labeled nonexperimental.

Nonstandardized measures Measures that do not meet one of the three criteria for standardized tests. That is, measures that are not (1) administered in a standardized way, (2) scored in a standardized way, and (3) interpreted with reference to a known reference group the norm group.

Norm group Sample used as the basis for interpreting test scores.

Normal distribution When the distribution of scores looks like the bell-shaped curve, with most of the scores near the middle and a few deviating either above or below the mean.

Novelty and disruption effects These can occur when a treatment is different from one that subjects usually receive.

Null hypothesis A hypothesis stating that there is no relationship between variables or no difference between groups and that whatever differences are observed are so small as to be due to chance (also referred to as *statistical hypothesis*).

One-group, pretest-posttest design
One group is pretested on the dependent variable (O_1), receives some sort of treatment (X), and then is posttested on the same dependent variable as at pretest (O_2).

Open-ended questions Questions that allow respondents to answer in the detail they choose.

Operational definitions The specific methods used to quantify constructs; operational definitions turn a construct into either an independent variable or a dependent variable.

Order effects When treatment effects are due to the order in which treatment was received but not to the treatment per se.

Outlier An extremely high or low score, or a score that is markedly different from the others in a distribution.

Pearson product-moment correlation A statistical index ranging from -1.0 to 1.0, indicating the strength of the linear relationship between two variables.

Percent correct The number of correct answers divided by the total number of items.

Percentile Indicates how a person performs relative to others the proportion of people in the norm group scoring below that subject.

Pilot research Testing research procedures before a study begins in order to increase the consistency of procedures used to administer the variables.

Placebo-control When subjects are getting some treatment that they believe is genuine but in fact has no merit.

Population Usually a large group from which the sample is taken and to which the results will be generalized.

Population external validity The population of subjects that one can generalize to.

Population validity The degree to which results generalize to (1) the researcher's population of interest or (2) the consumer's population of interest.

Positively skewed distribution Scores are piled up at the bottom end of the distribution. An example would be scores on a difficult test; only a few students would obtain high scores, and most would obtain very low scores.

Post hoc techniques Statistical techniques researchers can use to isolate where the differences between groups are. Post hoc techniques control for the potential increase in making a Type I error when performing multiple tests on the same data.

Postinvestigative inquiry Obtaining information from participants after their research involvement concludes.

Posttest-only, comparison group design An experimental design in which subjects are randomly assigned to experimental and comparison groups, treated, and then measured to determine the effect.

Posttest sensitization When subjects are influenced by the particular dependent variable used.

Predictive validity A measure of the extent to which a test correlates with some future behavior.

Pretest Assessment of performance given before treatment.

Pretest sensitization When the pretest alerts the subjects as to what the study is about.

Principal investigator The person who conceives of, designs, and plans the research study.

Procedural error The random, unpredictable fluctuations occurring during the administration of the independent variable.

Projective tests Test such as the Rorschach that elicit inner feelings that are different for each examinee. Projective tests provide an ambiguous stimulus to the examinee.

PsycBOOKS An annual index that includes a cumulative author and subject index and four separate subject volumes: (1) Experimental Psychology: Basic and Applied, (2) Developmental, Personality, and Applied, (3) Professional Psychology: Disorders and Treatment, and (4) Educational and Health Psychology.

Psychological Abstracts (PA) A publication that provides brief descriptions of journal articles taken from roughly 1300 journals in psychology and education.

Purposive sampling A technique used to make sure that particular types of people are included in the research. Examples would be (1) selecting only typical people, (2) selecting from across the entire range of some variable, and (3) selecting only the extremes on some variable.

Qualitative research Data are reported in narrative form.

Quantitative research Data are reported numerically.

Quasi-experiments All research in which (1) the researcher manipulates at least one or more independent variables, (2) the researcher exerts control in the form of standardized data collection and perhaps, a comparison group, and (3) random assignment of subjects to groups is *not* possible because of practical or ethical constraints.

Questionnaire or survey Used when the information needed to answer the research question can be obtained from subjects without the researcher being in their presence.

Random assignment Not a sampling procedure per se but a method for assigning each member of a selected sample to a certain group or treatment.

Range One of the measures of variability; found by subtracting the lowest score from the highest and adding 1.

Raw score The originally collected score.

Reasoning The use of logic, which defines one way to knowledge.

Regression A statistical artifact—individuals who score at the extreme on one occasion (either high or low) tend to produce scores closer to the mean on the second occasion.

Relationship How two or more variables correspond to each other.

Reliability The degree of consistency of scores over repeated testing.

Repeated measures design When there is more than one testing period, such as in a pretest-posttest design.

Replication A study that repeats all aspects of an original study on another sample from the same target population.

Research The process of investigation, or the activity of getting more information.

Research assistant The individual who assists the principal investigator with such activities as subject recruitment, data collection, and data analysis.

Researcher bias When researchers give subjects subtle feedback about their expected behavior.

Research design The procedures the research employs to address the research employs to address the research question and associated hypotheses.

Research hypothesis A declarative statement about problem solution and predicted outcomes. It modifies the general research question by making it clear what solution will be used to answer the question, as well as the expected outcomes of the solution.

Research plan The blueprint that guides the researcher in answering the question posed.

Research question Shows the overall focus of a research study by revealing the general topic under investigation.

Research supervisor Typically, an experienced researcher or academic trainer who advises students or employees in independent research.

Research topic   The unique domain of knowledge that the researcher wants to investigate.

Resentful demoralization   A reaction that can occur in subjects when untreated comparison subjects learn that another group is receiving more beneficial treatment. However, instead of compensating, subjects in the comparison group become angry, disillusioned, and less motivated, adopting attitudes that adversely effect their status on the dependent variable.

Review journal   A journal that contains extensive literature reviews. Typically, the authors of review papers summarize past fundings, attempting to shed light on theoretical issues or methodological weaknesses and to provide recommendations for future research.

Sample   A subset of people or objects selected from a population. A sample is a segment of the population but not the entire population.

Sample selection procedures   How samples are selected from populations.

Scaled-choice   Likert-scaled items that contain more than two points; usually five points are used (see *Likert scale*).

Scatterdiagram   Depicts each subject's placement on each of the two variables on a graph rather than in a table.

Scientific method   A way of pursuing knowledge that presumes a logical, observational, and cautious approach.

Scientist-practitioner model   Provides a feedback loop between theory, research, and practice.

Selection bias   A phenomenon that occurs when comparing intact groups. It is possible for the groups to differ on a variable known to influence the dependent variable.

Semistructured interview   A combination of the structured and unstructured interview that capitalizes on the unique benefits of each.

Simple experiment   When the researcher studies the effects of one independent variable (with two or more levels) on one or more dependent variables.

Simple random sample   Requires that (1) every member of the population has an equal chance of being selected to the sample and (2) the selection of any member of the population does not preclude the selection of any other population member.

Single-subject researchers   Researchers who study only one subject at a time by (1) manipulating the independent variable, (2) gathering data in a systematic, controlled manner, and (3) *not* randomly assigning subjects to groups.

Skewness   Indicates how far the shape of the distribution is from being normal.

Socially desirable responses   Responses subjects think they should be giving.

Sociological Abstracts **(SA)**   A publication that centers on a variety of social topics such as group interaction, the family and social welfare, studies in violence and power, women's studies, and social development.

Sociometric methods   these obtain information on the interaction or lack of interaction in social relationships.

Spearman rank correlation   A statistical technique used when the scores on the variables have been ranked.

Specialized abilities tests   Tests that measure any one of a number of psychomotor abilities.

Standard deviation   A measure of variability that is calculated from all the scores and hence is influenced by all those scores; indicates the standard amount that scores deviate from the mean.

Standard error of measurement   A measure of the reliability or consistency of measurement; the standard deviation of error scorespermitting a probability statement of where the subject's true score is. (If the score is 16 plus or minus 3, and 3 is the standard error of measurement, the resulting probability would be .67 that the true score is between 13 and 19.)

Standard score   The deviation of the raw score from its mean, divided by the standard deviation. These scores are thus converted from the original score scale but have consistent means and standard deviations (examples are z, Z, T, CEEB).

Standardized test   A test that has been administered and scored in a standard way. Most standardized tests are also normed, that is, they are administered to a large group of specially selected people (the norming sample) who are representative of some population.

Statistical control of extraneous variables   This requires the researcher to pretest subjects, then use various statistical techniques to adjust between-group differences on the posttest measure.

Statistical hypothesis   The antithesis of the research hypothesis in that only one population value is specified; often referred to in the literature as the *null hypothesis*.

Statistical significance   A term used in research to indicate that results are probably not due to chance.

Stratified random sampling   A procedure requiring the researcher to reduce the population into levels of a variable of interest, then use simple random sampling to select subjects from within those levels.

Structured tests   Tests that provide the same stimulus to each subject, the same set of possible responses, and are scored by some set procedure for each subject.

Subject bias   Refers to participants' attitudes that systematically slant investigative results in a particular direction.

Subject-blind method   Occurs when subjects are uninformed about critical aspects of the research like the hypotheses or what level of the independent variable they are in.

Subject error   Results in unpredictable changes in subjects' physical or mental states during research participation.

Survey research   Research aimed at describing some variable by indicating its frequency in a particular population (see questionnaire).

T score   A type of standard score with a mean of 50 and a standard deviation of 10 (see standard score, z score, and Z score).

Target population   The population defined by the researcherthe population the researcher would like to generalize to.

Test usability   Includes administration, interpretation, and reporting of test scores and the costs associated with each.

Test-retest reliability   The correlation between two successive administrations of the same test; should be used when the construct being measured can be assumed to be stable over that time period.

Testing effects   The initial measurement of subjects, which may alter the quality being measured; subsequent measurements may not be due to the independent variable but to the effects of the first test.

Theory   A coherent set of propositions that explain and predict.

Threats to internal validity   Factors other than the variables studied that may also explain study outcomes.

Time line   Graphically displays the expected dates by which the various research stages will be completed.

Tradition   A way of knowing that accepts prior practices as knowledge.

Treatment fidelity   Evidence that the treatment was administered as it was intended to be administered.

Triangulation   The use of multiple sources; term is borrowed from surveying more than one point is needed to determine a fixation point.

Truncation Obtaining a limited range of scores on any of the measured variables.

Two-group experimental design Random assignment (R) of subjects to treatment groups (X) and the comparison group (C), followed by a posttest (O).

Unimodal distribution When one score is most frequent.

Unobtrusive measures When subjects do not know they are being observed or measurement has occurred prior to research participation.

Unstructured measures Measures that allow both subject and observer to make changes during the process.

Usability The practical considerations in using the test, such as time, cost, and the availability of qualified test administrators for a particular application.

Validity A measure of a test's usefulness; validity subsumes the concept of reliability and is the more important criteria of a test.

Variability A measure of the dispersion of the scores; range, interquartile range, and standard deviation are examples (see measures of variability).

Variable Any phenomenon that can exist in at least two different states.

Voluntary When subjects are informed that they have the freedom to participate or withdraw their participation at any time and without penalty.

Wait-list control group Participants who do not receive treatment during the course of the study but will have immediate access to treatment once the study is over and the results are known.

Within-subject design Each subject passes through at least two cells. In other words, the same group of subjects is always measured at least twice, hence the term *repeated measures* (see between-subject design).

z score Standard deviation unit scores are referred to as standard scores in general; when based on a mean of 0 and a standard deviation of 1.0 are called z scores.

Z score A type of standard score with a mean of 500 and a standard deviation of 100 (see standard score and z score).

REFERENCES

Adler, A. (1927). *Understanding human nature.* Garden City, NY: Garden City Publishers.

Amaro, H., & Russo, N. F. (1987). Hispanic women and mental health: An overview of contemporary issues in research and practice. *Psychology of Women Quarterly, 11,* 303–407.

American Psychiatric Association (1980). *Diagnostic and Statistical Manual of Mental Disorders* (3rd ed.). Washington, DC: Author.

American Psychiatric Association (1987). *Diagnostic and Statistical Manual of Mental Disorders* (3rd ed. rev.). Washington, DC: Author.

American Psychiatric Association (1994). *Diagnostic and Statistical Manual of Mental Disorders* (4th ed.). Washington, DC: Author.

American Psychological Association (1982). *Ethical principles in the conduct of research with human participants.* Washington, DC: Author.

American Psychological Association (1992). Ethical principles of psychologists and code of conduct. *American Psychologist, 47*(12), 1597–1611.

Anastasi, A. (1988). *Psychological testing* (5th ed.). New York: Macmillan.

Andrade, S. J. (1982). Social science stereotypes of the Mexican American woman: Policy implications for research. *Hispanic Journal of Behavioral Sciences, 4*(2), 223–224.

Antonuccio, D. O., Lewinsohn, P. M., & Steinmetz, J. L. (1982). Identification of therapist differences in a group treatment for depression. *Journal of Consulting and Clinical Psychology, 50*(3), 433–435.

Atkinson, D. R., Morten, G., & Sue, D. W. (1983). *Counseling American minorities: A cross-cultural perspective.* Dubuque, IA: Brown.

Atkinson, J. (1987). Gender roles in marriage and the family: A critique and some proposals. *Journal of Family Issues, 8*(1), 5–41.

Attneave, C. (1982). American Indians and Alaska Native families: Emigrants in their own homeland. In M. McGoldrick, J. K. Pearce, & J. Giordano (Eds.), *Ethnicity and family therapy* (pp. 55–83). New York: Guilford Press.

Axelson, J. A. (1985). *Counseling and development in a multicultural society.* Belmont, CA.: Wadsworth Inc.

Barlow, D. H., Hayes, S. C., & Nelson, R. O. (1984). *The scientist practitioner.* New York, NY: Pergamon.

Barton, W. H., & Butts, J. A. (1990). Viable options: Intensive supervision programs for juvenile delinquents. *Crime & Delinquency, 36*(2), 238–256.

Beery, K. E. (1982). *Revised administration, scoring, and teaching manual for the Developmental Tests of Visual-Motor Integration.* Cleveland, OH: Modern Curriculum Press.

Bem, S. L. (1974). The measure of psychological androgyny. *Journal of Counseling and Clinical Psychology, 42,* 155–163.

Bennett, M. J. (1986). A developmental approach to training for intercultural sensitivity. *International Journal of Intercultural Relations, 10,* 179–196.

Berdie, D. R., & Anderson, J. F. (1974). *Questionnaires: Design and use.* Metuchen, NJ: Scarecrow Press.

Best, J. W., & Kahn, J. C. (1989). *Research in education.* Englewood-Cliffs, NJ: Prentice-Hall.

Borg, W. R., & Gall, M. D. (1989). *Educational research.* New York: Long man.

Bowman, J. T., & Reeves, T. G. (1987). Moral development and empathy in counseling. *Counselor Education and Supervision, 6,* 293–298.

Bowman, P. J. (1993). The impact of economic marginality among African American husbands and fathers. In H. P. McAdoo (Ed.), *Family ethnicity: Strength in diversity* (pp. 120–140). Newbury Park, CA: Sage.

Bracht, G. H., & Glass, G. V. (1968). The external validity of experiments. *American Educational Research Journal, 5,* 437–444.

Burbach, D. J., Kashani, J. H., & Rosenberg, T. K. (1989). Parental bonding and depressive disorders in adolescents. *Journal of Child Psychology and Psychiatry, 30*(3), 417–429.

Butcher, J. N., Dahlstrom, W. G., Graham, J. R., Tellegen, A., & Kaemmer, B. (1989). *Manual for the restandardized Minnesota Multiphasic Personality Inventory: MMPI-2. An administrative and interpretive guide.* Minneapolis, MN: University of Minnesota Press.

Campbell, D. P. (1965). A cross-sectional and longitudinal study of scholastic abilities over twenty-five years. *Journal of Counseling Psychology, 12,* 55–61.

Campbell, D. T., & Stanley, J. C. (1966). *Experimental and quasi-experimental designs for research.* Chicago: Rand McNally.

Capaldi, N. (1969). *Human knowledge: A philosophical analysis of its meaning and scope.* New York: Pegasus.

Cattell, R. B. (1949). *Manual for forms A and B: Sixteen personality factors questionnaire.* Champaign, IL: Institute for Personality and Ability Testing.

Cattell, R. B., Eber, H. W., & Tatsuoka, M. M. (1970). *Handbook for the sixteen personality factor questionnaire (16PF).* Champaign, IL: Institute for Personality and Ability Testing.

Chicago manual of style (14th ed.) (1993). Chicago: The University of Chicago Press.

Christopher, F. S., & Roosa, M. W. (1990). An evaluation of an adolescent pregnancy prevention program: Is "just say no" enough? *Family Relations, 39,* 68–72.

Chun, K. T., Cobb, S., & French, J. R. P., Jr. (1974). *Measures for psychological assessment: A guide to 3000 original sources and their application.* Ann Arbor, MI: Institute for Social Research, University of Michigan.

Combs, A. W., Avila, D. L., & Purkey, W. W. (1978). *Helping relationships: Basic concepts for the helping professions.* Boston: Allyn & Bacon.

Committee to Develop Standards for Educational and Psychological Testing (1985). *Standards for educational and psychological testing.* Washington, DC: American Psychological Association.

Conners, C. K. (1985). *The Conners rating scales: Instruments for the assessment* of childhood psychopathology. Unpublished manuscript, Children's Hospital National Medical Center, Washington, DC.

Conoley, J. C., & Kramer, J. J. (1989). *The tenth mental measurements yearbook.* The Buros Institute of Mental Measurement, The University of Nebraska-Lincoln: University of Nebraska Press.

Cowdery, G. E., Iwata, B. A., & Pace, G. M. (1990). Effects and side effects of DRO as a treatment for self-injurious behavior. *Journal of Applied Behavior Analysis, 23*(4), 497–506.

Cromwell, R. E., & Ruiz, R. A. (1979). The myth of macho dominance in decision making within Mexican and Chicano families. *Hispanic Journal of Behavioral Sciences, 1*(4), 355–373.

Cronbach, L. J. (1984). *Essentials of educational testing* (4th ed.). New York: Harper & Row.

Daley, P. C., Bloom, L. J., Deffenbacher, J. L., & Stewart, R. (1983). Treatment effectiveness of anxiety management training in small and large group formats. *Journal of Counseling Psychology, 30*(1), 104–107.

Daniels, L. K. (1977). Treatment of migraine headache by hypnosis and behavioral therapy: A case study. *The American Journal of Clinical Hypnosis, 19*(4), 241–244.

Davison, G. C., & Stuart, C. B. (1975). Behavioral therapy and civil liberties. *American Psychologist, 30*, 750–763.

Diaz, J. O. P. (1988). Assessment of Puerto Rican children in bilingual education programs in the United States: A critique of Lloyd M. Dunn's monograph. *Hispanic Journal of Behavioral Sciences, 10*, 237–252.

Exner, J. E. (1974). *The Rorschach: A comprehensive system.* New York: Wiley.

Exner, J. E., & Weiner, I. B. (1981). *The Rorschach: A comprehensive system. III: Assessment of children and adolescents.* New York: Wiley.

Federal Register (1978, May 4).

Washington, DC: Government Printing Office.

Fouad, N. A., & Bracken, B. A. (1986). Cross-cultural translation and validation of two U.S. psychoeducational assessment instruments. *School Psychology International, 7*, 167–172.

Fouad, N. A., Cudeck, R., & Hansen, J. C. (1984). Convergent validity of the Spanish and English forms of the Strong-Campbell Interest Inventory for bilingual Hispanic high school students. *Journal of Counseling Psychology, 31*, 339–348.

Fraenkel, J. R., & Wallen, N. E. (1990). *How to design and evaluate research.* New York: McGraw-Hill.

Freud, S. (1920). *A general introduction to psychoanalysis.* New York: Boni and Liveright.

Freud, S. (1961). The ego and the id. In J. Strachen (Ed. and Trans.), *The standard edition of the complete psychological works of Sigmund Freud* (Vol. 3). London: Hogarth Press. (Original work published 1909).

Freud, S. (1963). *Three case studies.* New York: Collier Books.

Garner, D. M., & Garfinkel, P. E. (1979). The Eating Attitude Test: An index of the symptoms of anorexia nervosa. *Psychological Medicine, 9*, 273–279.

Garner, D. M., Olmstead, M. P., & Polivy, J. (1983). Development and validation of a multidimensional eating disorder inventory for anorexia nervosa and bulimia. *International Journal of Eating Disorders, 2*, 15–34.

Gay, L. R. (1987). *Educational research competencies for analysis and application.* Columbus, OH: Merrill.

Gibbons, J. L., Stiles, D. A., Schnellmann, J. G., & Morales-Hidalgo, I. (1990). Images of work, gender, and social commitment among Guatemalan adolescents. *Journal of Early Adolescence, 10*(1), 89–103.

Gibbons, J. L., Stiles, D. A., & Shkodriani, G. M. (1991). Adolescents' attitudes toward family and gender roles: An international comparison. *Sex Roles, 25*(11/12), 625–643.

Gift, A. G., Moore, T., & Soeken, K. (1992). Relaxation to reduce dyspnea and anxiety in COPD patients. *Nursing Research, 41*(4), 242–247.

Glass, G. V., McGaw, B., & Smith, M. L. (1981). *Meta-analysis in social research.* Beverly Hills, CA: Sage.

Goldberg, L. R. (1977). Psychology in action. *American Psychologist, 32,* 663–668.

Golden, C. J. (1987). *Luria-Nebraska neuropsychological battery: Children's revision.* Los Angeles: Western Psychological Services.

Goldfried, M. R., Stricker, G., & Weiner, I. R. (1971). *Rorschach Handbook of Clinical and Research Applications.* Englewood Cliffs, NJ: Prentice-Hall.

Goldman, B. A., & Osbourne, W. (1985). *Unpublished mental measurements* (Vol. 4). New York: Human Sciences Press.

Gough, H. G. (1957). *California Psychological Inventory manual.* Palo Alto, CA: Consulting Psychologists Press.

Grimm, L. G. (1993). *Statistical applications for the behavioral sciences.* New York: John Wiley.

Gross, L. J., & Scott, J. W. (1989). Translating a health professional certification test to another language. *Evaluations and the Health Professions, 12,* 61–72.

Hall, E. T. (1976). *Beyond culture.* Garden City, N.Y.: Doubleday.

Hallinan, M., & Sorensen, A. (1983). The formation and stability of instructional groups. *American Sociological Review, 48*(6), 838–851.

Hansen, J. C. (1987). Cross-cultural research on vocational interests. *Measurement and Evaluation in Counseling and Development, 19,* 163–176.

Harmon, L. W., Hansen, J. C., Borgen, F. H., & Hammer, A. L. (1994). *Strong Interest Inventory: Applications and technical guide.* Stanford, CA: Stanford University Press.

Harrington, T. F. (1989). *Adapting instruments for use in other cultures* (ERIC Document Reproduction Service No. ED 317 613).

Hathaway, S. R., & McKinley, J. C. (1943). A multiphasic personality schedule (Minnesota): 1. Construction of the schedule. *Journal of Psychology, 10,* 249–254.

Hayes-Bautista, D. E., & Chapa, J. (1987). Latino terminology: Conceptual bases for standardized terminology. *American Journal of Public Health, 77,* 61–68.

Helms, J. E. (1984). Toward a theoretical model of the effects of race on counseling: A black and white model. *The Counseling Psychologist, 12,* 153–165.

Henderson, D. J., Sampselle, C., Mayes, F., & Oakley, D. (1992). Toward culturally sensitive research in a multicultural society. *Health Care for Women International, 13,* 339–350.

Herrera, R. S., DelCampo, R. L., & Ames, M. (1993). A serial approach for translating family science instrumentation. *Family Relations, 42,* 357–360.

Hinkle, D. E., Wiersma, W., & Jurs, S. G. (1994). Applied statistics for the behavioral sciences (3rd ed.). Boston: Houghton Mifflin.

Holtzman, W. H., Thorpe, J. S., Swartz, J. D., & Herron, E. W. (1961). *Inkblot perception and personality.* Austin: University of Texas Press.

Hull, C. (1943). *Principles of behavior.* New York: Appleton.

Inter-university Consortium for Political and Social Research (1991). *Guide to resources and services 1991–1992.* Ann Arbor: Author.

Kazdin, A. E. (1982). *Single-case re-*

search designs: Methods for clinical and applied settings. New York: Oxford University Press.

Kedas, A., Lux, W., & Amodeo, S. (1989). A critical review of aging and sleep research. *Western Journal of Nursing Research, 11*(2), 196–206.

Kelly, F. J., Newman, I., & McNeil, K. A. (1973). Suggested inferential statistical models for research in behavior modification. *The Journal of Experimental Education, 41*(4), 54–63.

Kerlinger, F. (1986). *Foundations of behavioral research.* New York: Holt, Rinehart & Winston.

Keyser, D. J., & Sweetland, R. C. (Eds.). (1985). *Test critiques* (Vol. 1). Kansas City, MO: Test Corporation of America.

Kuder, G. F. (1979). *Manual, Kuder Occupational Interest Survey, 1979 revision.* Chicago: Science Research Associates.

Kuder, G. F., & Richardson, M. W. (1937). The theory of the estimation of test reliability. *Psychometrika, 2,* 151–160.

Kumabe, K. T., Nishida, C., & Hepworth, D. H. (1985). *Bridging ethnocultural diversity in social work and health.* Honolulu: University of Hawaii, School of Social Work.

Kupfer, D. J., & Reynolds, C. F. (1983). A critical review of sleep and its disorders from a developmental perspective. *Psychiatric Development, 1,* 367–386.

Lee, C. C., & Richardson, B. L. (1991). *Multicultural issues in counseling: New approaches to diversity.* Alexandria, VA: American Association for Counseling and Development.

Lefrancois, G. R. (1987). *Of children: An introduction to child development.* Belmont, CA: Wadsworth.

Light, R. J., & Pillemer, D. B. (1984). *Summing up: The science of reviewing research.* Cambridge, MA: Harvard University Press.

Lloyd, A. P. (1987). Multicultural counseling: Does it belong in a counselor education program? *Counselor Education and Supervision, 26,* 164–167.

Marin, G. (1984). Stereotyping Hispanics: The differential effect of research method, label and degree of contact. *International Journal of Intercultural Relations, 8,* 17–27.

Marin, G., & Marin, B. V. (1991). *Research with Hispanic populations.* Newbury Park, CA: Sage Publications.

Mason, E. J., & Bramble, W. J. (1989). *Understanding and conducting research: Applications in education and the social sciences.* New York: McGraw-Hill.

Mayberry, P. W. (1984). *Analysis of cross-cultural attitudinal scale translation using maximum likelihood factor analysis.* (ERIC Document Reproduction Service No. ED 243 947).

McAdoo, H. P. (1993) (Ed.). *Family ethnicity: Strength in diversity.* Newbury Park, CA: Sage.

McGoldrick, M., Pearce, J. K., & Giordano, J. (Eds.). (1982). *Ethnicity and family therapy.* New York: Guilford Press.

McNeil, K. A. (1994). Testing directional research hypotheses. *Multiple Linear Regression Viewpoints, 21*(1), 23–31.

McNeil, K. A., Newman, I., & Kelly, F. J. (1996). *Testing research hypotheses with the General Linear Model.* Carbondale, IL: Southern Illinois University Press.

Mitchell, D. C., & Frederickson, W. A. (1975). Preferences for physically dis-abled counselors in hypothetical counseling situations. *Journal of Counseling Psychology, 22*(6), 477–482.

Mitchell, J. V. (1983). *Tests in print III: An index to tests, test reviews, and the literature on specific tests.* The Buros Institute of Mental Measurement, The University of Nebraska-Lincoln: University of Nebraska Press.

Murray, H. A. (1943). *Thematic Apperception Test Manual.* Cambridge, MA: Harvard University Press.

Neale, J. M., & Liebert, R. M. (1986).

Science and behavior: An introduction to methods of research. Englewood Cliffs, NJ: Prentice-Hall.

Pedersen, P. (1987). Ten frequent assumptions of cultural bias in counseling. *Journal of Multicultural Counseling and Development, 15*, 16–24.

Pedersen, P. (1988). *A handbook for developing multicultural awareness.* Alexandria, VA.: American Association for Counseling and Development.

Pedersen, P. (1991). Multiculturalism as a generic approach to counseling. *Journal of Counseling and Development, 70*, 6–12.

Perez-Stable, E. J. (1987). Issues in Latino health care. *Western Journal of Medicine, 146*, 213–218.

Perls, F. (1971). Gestalt therapy verbatim. New York: Bantam Books.

Peterson, K. J. (1991). Social workers' knowledge about AIDS: A national survey. *Social Work, 36*(1), 31–37.

Piaget, J. (1952). *The origins of intelligence in children.* New York: International Universities Press.

Ponterotto, J. G. (1988). Racial/ethnic minority research in the *Journal of Counseling Psychology:* A content analysis and methodological critique. *Journal of Counseling Psychology, 35*(4), 410–418.

Post-Kammer, P. (1987). Intrinsic and extrinsic work values and career maturity of 9th and 11th grade boys and girls. *Journal of Counseling and Development, 65*, 420–423.

Purdy, J. E., Reinher, R. C., & Schwartz, J. D. (1989). Graduate admissions criteria of leading psychology departments. *American Psychologist, 44*, 960–961.

Renfrow, D., & Impara, J. C. (1989). Making academic presentations—effectively! *Educational Researcher, 18*(2), 20–21.

Research and Education Association (1981). *Handbook of psychiatric rating scales.* New York: Research and Education Association.

Robinson, J. P., Shaver, P. R., & Wrightsman, L. S. (1991). *Measures of personality and social psychological attitudes.* New York: Academic Press.

Rorschach, H. (1921). *Psychodiagnostik.* Bern: Bircher.

Rosenthal, R. (1976). *Experimenter effects in behavioral research* (Enlarged ed.). New York: Irvington.

Rosenthal, R. (1984). *Meta-analytic procedures for social research.* Beverly Hills, CA: Sage.

Rotter, J. B., & Rafferty, J. E. (1950). *Manual: The Rotter Incomplete Sentences Blank.* San Antonio, TX: Psychological Corporation.

Sabnani, H. B., Ponterotto, J. G., & Borodovsky, L. G. (1991). White racial identity development and cross-cultural counselor training: A stage model. *The Counseling Psychologist, 19*(1), 76–102.

Sarason, I. G., Levine, H. M., Bashhnan, R. B., & Sarason, B. R. (1983). Assessing social support: The social support questionnaire. *Journal of Personality and Social Psychology, 44*, 127–139.

SAS Institute (1985). *SAS user's guide: Basics,* version 5 edition. Cary, NC: Author.

Schaie, K. W., & Gribbon, K. (1975). Adult development and aging. *Annual Review of Psychology, 26*, 65–96.

Scheuneman, J. (1979). A method of assessing bias in test items. *Journal of Educational Measurement, 16*, 143–152.

Schulman, J. L., Stevens, T. M., Suran, B. G., Kupst, M. J., & Naughton, M. J. (1978). Modification of activity level through biofeedback and operant conditioning. *Journal of Applied Behavior Analysis, 11*(1), 145–152.

Semeomoff, B. (1976). *Projective techniques.* New York: Wiley.

Sharkin, B. S. (1989). How counselor trainees respond to client anger. *Journal of Counseling and Development, 67*, 561–564.

Shepard, L. (1993, April). *Evaluating test validity*. Invited address at the meeting of the American Educational Research Association, Atlanta, GA.

Shon, S. P., & Ja, D. Y. (1982). Asian families. In M. McGoldrick, J. K. Pearce, & J. Giordano (Eds.), Ethnicity and family therapy (pp. 55–83). New York: Guilford Press.

Skeen, P., Paguio, L. P., Robinson, B. E., & Deal, J. E. (1988). Mothers working outside of the home: Attitudes of fathers and mothers in three cultures. *Journal of Social Behavior and Personality, 3*(4), 389–398.

Smith, M. C., & Thelen, M. H. (1984). Development and validation of a test for bulimia. *Journal of Consulting and Clinical Psychology, 52,* 863–872.

Smith, M. L., & Glass, G. V. (1987). *Research and evaluation in education and the social sicences.* Engelwood Cliffs, NJ: Prentice-Hall.

Spiegel, J. (1982). An ecological model of ethnic families. In M. McGoldrick, J. K. Pearce, & J. Giordano (Eds.), *Ethnicity and family therapy* (pp. 55–83). New York: Guilford Press.

Stagner, R. (1988). *A history of psychological theories.* New York: Macmillan.

Stiles, D. A., Gibbons, J. L., & Schnellmann, J. D. L. A. (1990). Opposite sex ideal in the U.S.A. and Mexico as perceived by young adolescents. *Journal of Cross-Cultural Psychology, 21*(2), 180–199.

Straus, M. A. (1978). *Family measurement techniques: Abstracts of published instruments, 1935–1974.* Minneapolis, MN: University of Minnesota Press.

Suarez, Z. E. (1993). Cuban Americans: From golden exiles to social undesirables. In H. P. McAdoo (Ed.), *Family ethnicity: Strength in diversity* (pp. 164–176). Newbury Park, CA: Sage.

Sue, D. W., Arredondo, P., & McDavis, R. J. (1992). Multicultural counseling competencies and standards: A call to the profession. *Journal of Counseling and Development, 70,* 477–483.

Survey Research Center (1976). *Interviewer's manual.* Ann Arbor, MI: Institute for Social Research, University of Michigan.

Sweetland, R. C., & Keyser, D. J. (Eds.). (1983). *Tests: A comprehensive reference for assessment in psychology, education, and business.* Kansas City, MO: Test Corporation of America.

Thelen, M. H., Farmer, J. Wonderlich, S., & Smith, M. (1990). *The BULIT-R: A revision of the Bulimia Test.* Poster presented at the meeting of the American Psychological Association. Boston, MA.

Trenerry, M. R., Crosson, B., De Boe, J., & Leber, W. R. (1989). *STROOP neuropsychological screening test manual.* Psychological Assessment Resources, Inc.

Turabian, K. L. (1987). *A manual for writers of term papers, theses, and dissertations* (5th ed.). Chicago: The University of Chicago Press.

Valencia, R. R., & Rankin, R. J. (1985). Evidence of content bias on the McCarthy Scales with Mexican American children: Implications for test translation and nonbiased assessment. *Journal of Educational Psychology, 77,* 197–207.

Vega, W. A., Patterson, T., Sallis, J., Nader, P., Atkins, C., & Abramson, I. (1986). Cohesion and adaptability in Mexican-American and Anglo families. *Journal of Marriage and the Family, 48,* 857–867.

Watkins, C. E., Campbell, V. L., & McGregor, P. (1989). APA-affiliated master's-level counselors. *The Counseling Psychologist, 17*(2), 289–300.

Watkins, C. E., Lopez, F. G., Campbell, V. L., & Himmell, C. D. (1986). Contemporary counseling psychology: Results of a national survey. *Journal of Counseling Psychology, 33,* 301–309.

Wechsler, D. (1949). *Wechsler Intelligence Scale for Children, manual.* New York: The Psychological Corporation.

Wechsler, D. (1991). *Wechsler Intelligence Scale for Children* (3rd ed.). San Antonio: Harcourt Brace Jovanovich.

White, M. A., Williams, P. D., Alexander, D. J., Powell-Cope, G. M., & Conlon, M. (1990). Sleep onset latency and distress in hospitalized children. *Nursing Research, 39*(3), 134–139.

Wilkinson, W. K., & Migotsky, C. P. (1994). A factor analytic study of epistemological style inventories. *Journal of Psychology, 128,* 499–516.

Winfrey, J. K. (1984). Research as an area of renewal for counselor educators and supervisors. *Measurement and Evaluation in Counseling and Development, 17*(3) 139–141.

Wrenn, C. G. (1962). The culturally-encapsulated counselor. *Harvard Educational Review, 32,* 444–449.

Yin, R. T. (1984). *Case study research: Design and methods.* Beverly Hills, CA: Sage.

INDEX

NOTE: Bold pages indicate that the term is defined on that page.

Continuous variable, 176, 299, 301
Control group, **69**, 210, 233–234, 245, 257
Convenience sample, 65, **167**, 169, 251
Correlation, 222, **278–279**, 286
Correlational research, 79, 209, 220–221, 224–226
Counterbalancing, **148**, 256
Criterion, 221–222, 283, 302–303
Cronbach alpha, 110
Cross-sectional design, 228–229, 231
Cross-sequential design, 231
Culture-fair, 94

Debriefing, 68, **72**, 74
Deception, **70–72**, 91
Decompose, **267**
Deduction, **8**
Demand characteristics, **134–135**, 147, 149, 262, 327
Dependent variable, 17, **77**, 79, 107, 118, 126–127, 129, 134, 145, 149, 156, 172–173, 246, 250, 327
Descriptive research, 209–211, 238–239
Descriptive statistics, **273–274**
Design, 45, 62–63, 79, 132, 142, 149, 155, 176, 178, 239, 246–250, 253–256, 259–261, 263–264, 266–267, 269–270, 290–291, 293, 296–298, 317–319
Developmental researchers, 227–232
Deviation score, **279–280**
DIALOG, 33
dichotomous choice, **115**
Differential attrition, **139**, 150, 262–263
Directional hypothesis, **59**, 287–288, 295, 297, 312
Discriminant analysis, **302**
Discussion section, 319
Dissertation Abstracts International, 30, **32**
Double-blind, **147**

Ecological external validity, **156**, 169
Educational Resources Information Center (ERIC), **30–35**, 37, 41
Effect size, **179**, 253
Empirical approach to knowing, **14**
Empirical research, 3–4, 6, 8–9, 11–13, 21–23, 47, 50
Error, 108–110, 125, **126–131**, 137, 151, 161, 242, 248, 258, 299, 308
Error of measurement, 140, 149, 226
Ethics, **16**, 67–69

Ex post facto, 134, 209, 232–240
Existing records, **90**
Experience, **14**
Experimenter bias, 241–245, **271**
Expert opinion, **13–14**, 21
External funding, 80–**81**
External validity, 63, 153, **154–178**, 180–185, 295, 308–309, 327
External validity of operations, **156**, 172–175
Extraneous variable, **126**, 131–152, 259

Face validity, **112**
Factor analysis, 223, **302–303**
Factorial design, 145, **248–257**
Field experiment, 245
Forced-choice, **116–117**

General linear model, **303**
Grants, **22**

Hawthorne Effect, **134**, 147, 177
Helping professional, **2**, 19–23, 96
History, **136**, 141–143, 172, 230–231, 259, 262–264, 269–270, 327
Homogeneous samples, **142**
Hypothesis, **58–62**, 288–298
Hypothesis testing, 59, 273, 282–286

Idiographic methods, **18**
Independent variable, 17, **77–79**, 125–129, 132, 134, 142, 145, 151, 174, 228, 232, 235–237, 242–264, 285, 327
Independent variable levels, **77**
Individual differences, **17**
Inductive use of theory, **8**
Inferential statistics, **273**, 282–301
Informed consent, 68, **70–74**
Instrumentation, **139**, 143, 149, 202, 245, 269–271
Instrumentation effects, 127, 148–150, 244
Intact groups, **141–142**, 257–263, 290
Intelligence, 88–90, **93**–94, 122, 134–135, 221, 225, 232, 235–236
Interrater reliability, **110**, 131, 148, 202, 214, 226, 264–265
Interaction, 171, 178, 235, 248, 255, 261–263, **298**, 300–301
Interlibrary loan, **38–39**
Internal consistency, **110**

Internal funding, **80**
Internal validity, 63, 125–152, 154–158, 167,
    170–173, 178–179, 185, 195, 197,
    230–231, 237, 242, 248, 308, 327
Interquartile range, **277**
Interviews, 88–89, 104–**105**, 115, 122, 201,
    216
Intuition, **14–15**

Knowledge base, 4, 157, 180, 182–184, 273,
    303, 308–310, 312, 314, 317, 319–322,
    325–326

Latin-square design, **256**
Level, 134, 142, 256
Library card catalogue, **39**
Linear correlation, **278**
Literature review, 30–32, 40–42, 47–51, 219,
    309–310, 317, 319, 321, 323
Longitudinal design, 228–232

Main effect, **296–297**
Manipulated, 16, **77**, 79, 129, 157, 228, 232,
    238, 241–242, 252, 264, 271
MANOVA, **302**–303
Matching, **144**–145, 238
Maturation, 129, **136**–137, 141–143, 148,
    230, 261, 269–270, 292
Maxmincon principle, **126**–127, 258
Mean, 140, 192, 227, 234, **275**–280, 283,
    290–293, 297–298, 300, 327
Measurement, 49, **75**–76, 79, 87, 104, 113,
    172, 174, 197, 322
Measurement error, **129**–131, 149
Measures of central tendency, 273, **275–276**
Measures of variability, 273, **276**
Median, **275**–278
Medline, 30–**31**, 32
Meta-analysis, **179**
Method section, 12, 317–318
Mode, **275**–277
Mortality, **138**–139, 141–143, 149, 243–245
Multiple correlation, 223, 286, **289**–290, 302
Multiple dependent variables, 178, 303
Multiple regression, 223, 286, **289**
Multiple treatment interference, 175
Multiple-baseline design, **267**
Multivariate analysis of variance, **302**

Narrower term, **35**
Negatively skewed distribution, **277**

Nested, **250**
Neurological measures, **94**
Nomothetic, **17–18**
Noncognitive measures, **97–98**
Noncognitive tests, **89**, 92, 97
Nondirectional hypothesis, **59**, 297
Nonempirical studies, **3**
Nonequivalent comparison group de-
    sign, **142**, 259–264
Nonequivalent groups, 236, 260–263
Nonexperimental, 77, 126–127, 209–240
Nonstandardized measures, **88**, 104–107
Normal distribution, 274, **277**
Norms, 88, 102, 104
Novelty and disruption effects, **171**
Null hypothesis, **59**, 139, 283, 285

Open-ended questions, **115**
Operational definitions, 76–79, 87, 156,
    162, 172–180
OR connector, **36**
Order effects, **254**–256
Outlier, **276**–278, 289

Pearson, 222–227, **278**–279, 286, 289,
    302–303
Percent correct, **280**
Percentiles, 275, **280**
Pilot research, **129**–131, 148–150
Placebo-control, **146**, 245
Population, 63–67, 88, 102, 153–169,
    175–176, 178, 199–201, 227, 237,
    269, 273, 277, 282–283, 308, 318,
    327
Population external validity, **156**,
    158–159, 163
Population validity, **63**
Positively skewed distribution, **277**
Post hoc techniques, **294**
Postinvestigative inquiry, **147**
Posttest only comparison group design,
    246
Posttest sensitization, **173**, 327
Predictive validity, 96, **112**–113, 121, 287
Pretest, 79, 138, 141–142, 146, 173, 250,
    259–263, 289–294, 300
Pretest sensitization, **173**
Principal investigator, **68**, 72
Procedural error, 127, **129**–130, 149, 220
PsycBOOKS, **39**–40
Psychlit, 31, 33

Psychological Abstracts, 9, 30–31
Purposive sampling, **176**

Questionnaire, **104**, 116, 121, 195–196, 215–219

Random assignment, 17, **65**–66, 79, 142, 144, 157, 167, 236, 241–242, 246, 253, 256–258, 260–261, 263, 293, 327
Random sample, 64–65, 158, 162, 166, 322
Range, **276**
Raw scores, **279**–280
Reasoning, **14**–15
References, 29–31, 42–43, 327
Regression, **140**–143
Related term, **35**
Relationship, 210–211, 221–227, 235, 240, **275**, 278–279
Reliability, **107**–113, 121, 143, 288, 318, 322, 327
Repeated measure design, **249**, 291
Replication, 4, 161, 176, **178**, 215, 308, 312, 320–321
Representative sample, 88
Research, **3**
Research assistant, **68**
Research design, **62**–63, 67, 75, 79, 82, 228–232, 264, 321
Research hypothesis, 61, 86, 91, 121, 135, 206, **283**, 285, 287–298, 302, 326–328
Research plan, 11–12, 23, 44–45, 55–**56**, 57, 60, 67, 82, 126, 241
Research problem, **44**
Research question, 28, 47, 55, **56**–62, 85–88, 118, 126, 149, 209, 212, 227–229, 238–239, 326
Research supervisor, **68**, 72
Research topics, **9**, 26–29, 41, 45
Researcher bias, 135, 142–143, 148–149, 170, 214, 269–270, 327
Researcher blind method, 147
Resentful demoralization, **243**–244
Response bias, 97–98, 220
Results section, 318
Review journal, **40**

Sample, **64**, 164
Sample selection procedures, **164**
SAS, 285, 297
Scaled choice, **116**
Scatterdiagram, 222

Science, **3**
Scientific method, **3**–4, 21, 23
Scientist-practitioner model, **20**–22
Selection bias, **132**, 134, 141–142, 144, 146, 258–263
Semistructured interview, **106**
Significance, 58, 128, 226, 285, 287–288, 292, 294
Simple experiment, **246**–257
Simple random sample, **64**
Single-subject, 176, 259, 264–271
Skewness, **274**, 277
Socially desirable responses, **116**–118
Sociological Abstracts, 30–31
Sociometric methods, **105**
Spearman Rank Correlation, 286, 288–**289**
Specialized abilities tests, **94**
Standard deviation, 179, 276–**277**, 280
Standard error of measurement, 108, 129
Standard score, 280–281
Standardized test, **87**–89, 92–103, 113
Statistic, 285–290, 294, 302, 327
Statistical control, **146**
Statistical hypothesis, 59, **283**–285, 287–288, 291–294
Statistical significance, **226**
Stratified random sampling, **64**, 166
Structured tests, **88**, 98
Subject bias, **134**–135, 146–149, 243
Subject error, **128**–129, 137
Subject-blind method, **147**
Survey research, **104**, 209, 211, 215–220

t test, 285, 294
Target population, 88, 105, 154, 157–163, 165–169, 176–178, 215, 217–220, 282, 318, 327
Test usability, 113
Test-retest reliability, **109**, 121, 226, 288
Testing effects, **138**, 230, 241, 263
Theory, 7–**8**, 9, 20–21, 48, 212, 229, 231
Threats to internal validity, **126**
Time line, 56, 58, **80**
Tradition, **14**–15
Treatment effect, 137–138, 140, 170, 174, 177–179
Treatment variable, 138
Triangulation, **86**–87, 90
True experiment, 79
True score, 108

TO THE OWNER OF THIS BOOK:

We hope that you have enjoyed *Research for the Helping Professions* as much as we have enjoyed writing it. We'd like to know as much about your experiences with the book as you care to offer. Only through your comments and the comments of others can we learn how to make *Research for the Helping Professions* a better book for future readers.

School: _____

Your instructor's name: _____

1. For what course was this book assigned? _____

2. What did you like most about the book? _____

_____

_____

3. What did you like least about the book? _____

_____

_____

_____

4. Were all of the chapters of the book assigned for you to read?

   If not, which ones weren't?_____

_____

5. If you used the glossary, how helpful was it as an aid in understanding psychological concepts and terms? _____

_____

6. In the space below, or on a separate sheet of paper, please write specific suggestions for improving this book and anything else you'd care to share about your experience in using the book.

_____

_____

_____

_____

_____

ptional:

Your name: _____ Date: _____

May Brooks/Cole quote you, either in promotion for *Research for The Helping Professions* or in future publishing ventures?

Yes: _____ No: _____

Sincerely,

William K. Wilkinson
Keith McNeil

FOLD HERE

- -

- -

FOLD HERE

Brooks/Cole is dedicated to publishing quality publications for education in the human services fields. If you are interested in learning more about our publications, please fill in your name and address and request our latest catalogue, using ths prepaid mailer.

Name: _____

Street Address: _____

City, State, and Zip: _____